Readings in

D0461925

Volume 1: The Great Traditions

Readings in World Civilizations

Volume 1: The Great Traditions

KEVIN REILLY

St. Martin's Press • New York

For my friends in the World History Association

Library of Congress Catalog Card Number: 87-060524
Copyright © 1988 by St. Martin's Press, Inc.
All rights reserved
210
fe

For information, write St. Martin's Press, Inc.
175 Fifth Avenue, New York, NY 10010

cover design: Darby Downey
Cover photo: Courtesy Rare Book Room, The New York Public Library

ISBN: 0-312-003064

CONTENTS

PREFACE   ix

    A Note About the Cover   xi

INTRODUCTION   1

I.   THE ANCIENT WORLD: TO 1000 B.C.   3

1.   Hunter-Gatherers and the Agricultural Revolution   5

    Hunters and Gatherers: Pygmies / COLIN TURNBULL   5

    Hunter Religion: An Eskimo Shaman / MIRCEA ELIADE   11

    Origins of Agriculture / CHARLES B. HEISER, JR.   13

    Women and the Agricultural Revolution /
    ELISE BOULDING   21

    The Origin of Corn Legend / NATCHEZ INDIANS OF NORTH
    AMERICA   25

2.   The Urban Revolution in the Near East and North Africa   27

    City and Civilization / KEVIN REILLY   27

    The Epic of Gilgamesh   31

    Hammurabi's Code   40

    The Story of Si-nuhe   43

3.   The Ancient Civilizations of Asia   52

    Indus Civilization and the Aryan Invasion /
    FRANCIS WATSON   52

    The Vedas: 1. The Rig-Veda—Sacrifice as Creation   57

             2. The Upanishads—Brahman and
               Atman   58

             3. The Upanishads—Karma   59

    Shang China / DUN J. LI   60

II.   THE CLASSICAL WORLD: 1000 B.C. TO A.D. 500   65

4.   Greek Civilization   67

The Definition of Greek Civilization to 500 B.C. /
WILLIAM H. MCNEILL   67

The Funeral Oration of Pericles / THUCYDIDES   69

The Republic / PLATO   75

5.   Roman Civilization   86

War, Slaves, and Land Reform: Tiberius Gracchus /
APPIAN OF ALEXANDRIA   86

Women and Roman Religion / SARAH B. POMEROY   92

The Roman Empire in the Year One / M. I. FINLEY   99

6.   Judeo-Christian Tradition   111

The Bible   111

Paul and His Opponents / S. G. BRANDON   ·122

The Significance of Christmas / ERNEST JONES   131

7.   Indian Civilization   139

The Bhagavad-Gita   139

Buddhism: 1. Gotama's Discovery   145

2. The Buddha's First Sermon   150

3. The Story of Isidāsī, a Buddhist Nun   151

Indian Cave Sanctuaries / RICHARD LANNOY   156

8.   Chinese Civilization   161

The *Analects* of Confucius   161

Confucianism: The *Mencius* / MENCIUS   167

Taoism: The *Tao Te Ching* / LAO TZU   168

Ko Hung's Autobiography   172

III.   THE TRADITIONAL WORLD: 500 TO 1500   **183**

9.   Hindu-Buddhist Civilization   **185**

Buddhism in China / PAUL THOMAS WELTY   185

Hinduism and Buddhism in Southeast Asia /
JOHN F. CADY   189

The Introduction of Buddhism into Japan: *The Chronicles
of Japan* (*Nihongi*)   196

10.   East Asian Civilizations   **199**

Chinese Ancestral Rites / SSU-MA KUANG   199

Neo-Confucianism: 1. The Western Inscription /
CHANG TSAI   205

2. The Great Learning   206

The Chinese Civil Service Exam System /
ICHISADA MIYAZAKI   207

Japan: *The Tale of Genji* / LADY MURASAKI SHIKIBU   215

11.   Islamic Civilization   **223**

The Koran: 1. Scripture and Literature /
JAMES KRITZECK   223

2. Selections   232

Sufism: 1. Rabi'a   235

2. Al-Hallaj   236

12.   Byzantine Civilization   **239**

Byzantium and Its Sphere / J. M. ROBERTS   239

Monasticism / THEODORE OF STUDIUS   245

The Alexiad / ANNA COMNENA   248

13.   Western European Civilization   **253**

Charlemagne / JOSEPH STRAYER   253

Erik the Red and the Vikings   259

Albelard and Héloïse   264

Magna Carta   270

14. **Mongol Eurasia** 275

The Impact of Turkish and Mongol Conquests, 1000–1500 / WILLIAM H. MCNEILL 275

A Chinese Taoist Travels to Genghis Khan 283

Marco Polo Travels to Kubilai Khan 287

15. **Mature Islamic Civilization** 294

The Civilization of Medieval Islam / J. J. SAUNDERS 294

The Great Islamic Empires / C. E. BOSWORTH 303

The Gulistan / SA'DI 309

Poems of Kabir and Nanak 311

16. **African Civilizations** 314

Mali in the Fourteenth Century / AL OMARI 314

Travels in Mali / IBN BATTUTA 317

African Law / PAUL BOHANNAN AND PHILIP CURTIN 324

African Art / PAUL BOHANNAN AND PHILIP CURTIN 328

17. **American Civilizations** 333

The Secrets of the Maya Decoded / ERIK ECKHOLM 333

The Aztec Civilization of Mexico / BERNAL DIAZ 337

The Inca Empire / WILLIAM H. PRESCOTT 346

PREFACE

When I began my teaching career at Rutgers University in the 1960s, there was no course in world history. We taught a course called "Western Civilization" that had developed in American universities between World War I and World War II. It was a course that identified America's fate with that of Europe; the idea of "Europe" or "the West" made more sense to Americans swept up in European wars than it did to many Europeans (who taught their national histories). A course in Western civilization also seemed the appropriate way for an American population largely descended from Europeans to find their roots.

There were problems with this idea from the beginning. One was that it ignored the heritage of Americans whose ancestors came from Africa and other parts of the world. Another was that the world was becoming a much smaller place. Transoceanic journeys that formerly took a week or more had been reduced by jet planes to a few hours. Since the 1960s, the importance of the non-European world for Americans has increased even more. Trade with Japan has become larger than that with European countries. More new American immigrants have come from Asia and Latin America than from Europe. The daily newspaper carries more stories concerning the Middle East, Asia, Africa, and Latin America than Europe. The interests of the United States are more global than ever. For these good reasons, increasingly colleges and universities (including Rutgers) are now offering world history or "World Civilizations."

Compiling an anthology for use in such introductory world history classes is a task that requires many decisions and that benefits from many friends. The instructor who considers using the result should be apprised of both.

First the decisions. These two volumes are intended for introductory courses. For me, that consideration prescribes a survey format that encompasses all of world history. (The two volumes of this work divide roughly at the year 1500.) It also mandates that the readings be understandable, at least in their essentials, by typical first-year college students.

In nearly every chapter I have included both primary and secondary sources. Primary sources were selected partly to represent "great works" and cultural legacies and partly to provide students with an authentic glimpse of a particular historical time and place. Some readings do both. The Epic of Gilgamesh in volume 1, for example, is a "great work" that also opens a window on Sumer. From it students can learn about Sumerian religion, gender roles, and ideas of kingship and also acquire a basis for making important historical comparisons—the Biblical account of the flood is often compared with the flood in Gilgamesh. The selection in volume 2 from *Aké*, the autobiography of Nobel Prize winner Wole Soyinka, illuminates the process of westernization in a Nigerian village in the 1940s.

Secondary sources were chosen for their capacity to challenge students with information and points of view probably not found in their survey texts, as well, of course, for their interest and accessibility. Some readings will introduce students to the work of leading modern historians—such as William H. McNeill, Philip Curtin, Natalie Davis, Fernand Braudel, and L. S. Stavrianos—and perhaps even induce them to read further in the writings of these great scholars. In some cases the selections may lead students to look at additional primary sources beyond what I have been able to include here. In volume 1, for example, S. G. Brandon's "Paul and His Opponents" should encourage students to examine the New Testament letters of Paul with a keener eye. In volume 2, the secondary readings on "Dependence and Independence" in Africa and Latin America (chapters 15 and 16) will enable students to get more out of their daily newspapers.

I wanted each reading to be able to stand on its own. (I do expect, however, that most students will also be assigned a survey text.) I know how frustrating it can be to find that a favorite selection or passage has been so condensed as to become almost worthless. Although space considerations have dictated that some abridging be done, I have tried very hard to be as sensitive as possible to this concern.

I also wanted students *to read the readings*. Therefore the readings are not preceded by lengthy introductions that, in students' minds, may make the readings seem superfluous. For each reading I have provided an introduction that establishes a context but that principally directs students with a series of questions. These questions ask: What is said? What is the evidence? What conclusion or judgment can be drawn? They are intended to aid students in developing critical thinking skills—recall, analysis and evaluation, and self-expression.

The historical understanding that, I am hopeful, will develop from the study of these volumes is qualitative. Different students will remember different specifics. All, however, should gain an increased understanding of past civilizations and ways of life and a greater awareness of the connections and contrasts between past and present. My ultimate goal for these two volumes is that they help students to live in a broader world, both temporally and spatially.

Now for the friends. A work like this would not have been possible without many historian friends and colleagues. As president of the World History Association, I have been fortunate in having many people who are both. Many members of the association—too many to name— offered suggestions, read drafts, sent me favorite selections, and in general helped me improve this work. But I am especially indebted to Lynda Shaffer of Tufts University, Steve Gosch of the University of Wisconsin–Eau Claire, Marc Gilbert of North Georgia College, Marty

Yanuck and Margery Ganz of Spelman College, Robert Roeder of the University of Denver, and Jerry Bentley of the University of Hawaii. Their criticisms and also, of course, the work of an earlier generation of world historians, especially William H. McNeill, Philip Curtin, and Leftan Stavrianos, have been invaluable.

My own institution, Somerset County College (with the assistance of New Jersey Department of Higher Education grants), gave me the opportunity to discuss with colleagues from different disciplines the selection and classroom use of readings for the introductory humanities course.

I have also been extremely fortunate in that a preliminary draft of these volumes was class-tested at Iona College. In 1986, when Iona decided to institute world civilization as a core course for all first-year students, the history faculty chose to use this work as "the core of the core." Thus, thanks to the support of Iona's president and administration and the active participation of the members of the history department, particularly Ernst Menze, Mary Evelyn Tucker, Zehra Arat, and the late Michael Zaremski, I was able to revise this book for publication with the benefit of extensive classroom use and student response.

I also want to thank Michael Weber, whose idea this work was, Andrea Guidoboni, and Emily Berleth of St. Martin's Press. Without their suggestions, encouragement, and hard work, and the superb copy-editing of Denise Quirk, this would be a far lesser work. Additionally, many thanks go to Joe C. Dixon of the Air Force Academy, Joe Gowaskie of Rider College, Charles F. Gruber of Marshall University, D. Brendan Nagle of the University of Southern California, Richard A. Overfield of the University of Nebraska at Omaha, and Ken Wolf of Murray State University for their constructive comments.

And I thank Pearl for her presence and her love.

A NOTE ABOUT THE COVER

St. Martin's Press and I have chosen for the covers of these volumes maps that are both historically valuable and, we hope, attractive. On volume 1, courtesy of the Rare Book Room, New York Public Library, we have reproduced a rare map of the world, the *Ptolemaeus Cosmographia*, printed in the German city of Ulm in 1482. The Ulm map is a copy of one originally drawn by the Greco-Egyptian mathematician, astronomer, and geographer Ptolemy, who worked in the second century A.D. For volume 2 we have adapted from *The New State of the World Atlas* by Michael Kidron and Ronald Segal (New York: Simon & Schuster, 1988) a "cartogram" in which each country's size is drawn so as to indicate its share of the world's trade in the 1980s. Thus Brazil and the Soviet Union, for example, despite their large actual size, appear quite small on the map, while Japan appears relatively large.

KEVIN REILLY

Readings in World Civilizations

Volume 1: The Great Traditions

INTRODUCTION

This is a collection of readings from and about the human past. Those that are from the past are usually called *primary sources*. They can be anything from an old parking ticket to a famous ancient poem. Those that are about the past are what we call *secondary sources*, interpretations, or just plain "histories." They can be written immediately after the events they describe or centuries later, by professional historians or by average people.

We read primary sources and histories for the same reason: to find out what happened in the past. Different people have different motivations for finding out about the past. Some people are curious about everything. Some people are interested in knowing what it was like to live in a particular time or be a particular kind of person. Some people are interested in how things change, or how the world got to where it is. Some people wonder about human variety, trying to figure out how different or similar people have been throughout history. My hope is that this book will answer all of these questions.

The reading selections are what is important in this book. Each reading is preceded by an introduction that poses some questions. These questions are designed to guide your reading and to suggest approaches to the reading. There are no particular ideas or pieces of information that everyone should get from a particular reading. What you learn from a reading depends very much on who you are, what you already know, and how much attention you give it. My hope is that you get as much from each reading as you can. Each reading should affect you in some way. Some you will like more than others, but each should open a world previously closed.

Treat these readings, especially the primary sources, as openings to a lost world. Keep your eyes and ears open. Notice everything you can. But don't worry if you miss a sign, a name, or even the meaning people attach to some things. This is your discovery. In some cases, I have added explanatory notes, but I have tried to keep these to a bare minimum. Ultimately there are never enough explanations. But more importantly, I do not want my explanations to become the information that is read, remembered, and studied for an exam. The readings should bring you your own insights, discoveries, and questions. Like a good travel guide they should tell you where to go, not what you saw.

I. THE ANCIENT WORLD: TO 1000 B.C.

An Egyptian tomb painting of musicians.
(Photograph by Egyptian Expedition, The Metropolitan Museum of Art.)

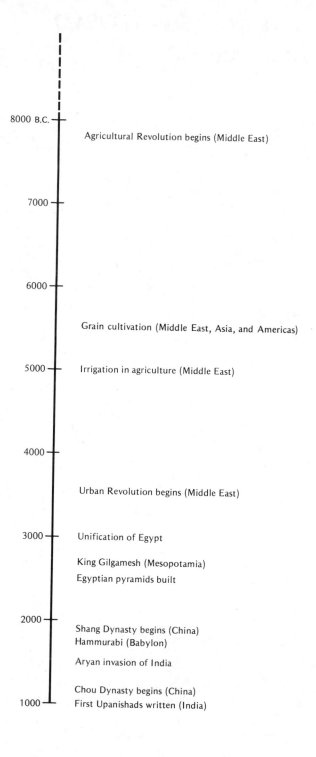

8000 B.C. ── Agricultural Revolution begins (Middle East)

7000 ──

6000 ──

Grain cultivation (Middle East, Asia, and Americas)

5000 ── Irrigation in agriculture (Middle East)

4000 ──

Urban Revolution begins (Middle East)

3000 ── Unification of Egypt

King Gilgamesh (Mesopotamia)
Egyptian pyramids built

2000 ──
Shang Dynasty begins (China)
Hammurabi (Babylon)

Aryan invasion of India

Chou Dynasty begins (China)
1000 ── First Upanishads written (India)

1. Hunter-Gatherers and the Agricultural Revolution

HUNTERS AND GATHERERS: PYGMIES

COLIN TURNBULL

The members of the earliest human societies were hunters and gatherers. Before the discovery of agriculture, about ten thousand years ago, all humans secured their food by hunting and gathering. Today there are only a few small hunting-gathering societies in remote areas of central Australia, the Arctic, the Amazon basin, and the tropical rain forest of central Africa. This selection is about a group of central African forest dwellers. They are the BaMbuti Pygmies of Zaire. They are described by the anthropologist Colin Turnbull, who lived among them in the 1950s.

What do you think the "molimo" is? Is life hard for the Pygmies? What is the work that men and women do? What do they do for enjoyment? How do they cope with "antisocial" or uncooperative behavior? Is this hunting-gathering society more "natural" or "ecological" than our own modern society?

The molimo was often referred to as "the animal of the forest," and the women were supposed to believe that it really was an animal, and that to see it would bring death. That of course is why they were all bundled off to bed with the children before the trumpet was ever brought into camp. And even when it *was* brought in it was often shielded by a number of youths so that if any woman should happen to look, she would see nothing. The animal sounds it produced were certainly realistic, but I wondered what the women thought when it sang. What kind of animal was it that one moment could make such threatening sounds, and the next instant sing more beautifully than anything else in the whole forest?

I remembered again Ausu's saying that the only important thing about the trumpet was the fact that it had a good voice and could sing well. I was reminded of the Pygmy legend of the Bird with the Most Beautiful Song. This bird was found by a young boy who heard such a Beautiful Song that he had to go and see who was singing. When he found the Bird he brought it back to the camp to feed it. His father was annoyed at having to give food to the Bird, but the son pleaded and the Bird was fed. The next day the Bird sang again; it sang the Most Beautiful Song in the Forest, and again the boy went to it and brought it back to feed it. This time the Father was even more angered, but once again he gave in and fed the Bird. The third day (most Pygmy stories repeat themselves at least three times) the same thing happened. But this time the father took the Bird from his son and told his son to go away. When his son had left, the father killed the Bird, the Bird with the Most Beautiful Song in the Forest, and with the Bird he killed the Song, and with the Song he killed himself and he dropped dead, completely dead, dead forever.

· · ·

Every night the men gathered to sing the songs of the molimo, and every morning the youths awakened the camp with their shouts and yells. This went on week after week, yet the daily life of the hunting group continued as though nothing particularly unusual was happening. The men were more sleepy in the mornings, and sometimes tempers were short, but never for long. The necessities of hunting and gathering for a living did not allow it.

As soon as the camp was light and there was no further danger of the molimo's making an appearance, the women emerged from their huts and went down to the river to bathe and to collect water to cook the morning meal. Back in the camp they sat outside their huts, legs straight out in front of them in what seemed the most uncomfortable position possible. From there they prepared the family repast, placing green plantains in the hot ashes to roast, or concocting a stew of mushrooms and chopped leaves with whatever meat was left over from the day before, covering the pot with large leaves to trap the steam and to keep out ashes and dirt. Any little chores that had to be done were done by their daughters, who scurried around collecting dry twigs to heat the fire up more quickly, or sat over the fire with their baby brothers, carefully guarding the pot and making sure it did not upset when the burning wood subsided. The younger women, freed in this way, relaxed and set to work making themselves beautiful. They sat in full view of the camp, unashamedly painting their bodies with black paste, calling their friends over to help with the more inaccessible regions. The buttocks in particular they found difficult to paint themselves, and rather than waste such an expansive area they would either bend over in front of a friend, or lie across her lap.

The men combined business with pleasure too, usually meeting at the kumamolimo* to drink from a steaming bowl of liko. The young bachelors mostly cooked their own simple breakfast here, and together they all discussed the day ahead of them—where they should go to hunt, what they might expect to find. Cephu never came over from his little camp at such times. He merely waited until all the others set off for the hunt, then he joined them.

The men also had to prepare their nets. Helping one another, they uncoiled long lengths of knotted twine, sometimes stretching for three hundred feet, inspecting every section with care. Then, standing upright, the assistant holding the net off the ground, each man coiled his net again so that it hung from one shoulder to within a few inches of his ankle. With a loose length of twine he deftly bound the coils together, gave the net a final shake and hung it from some convenient branch or tree stump. Sometimes, when hunting, nets have to be set up rapidly, and anyone whose net has become tangled through poor preparation and coiling can spoil the chances of all the others.

The women have little to do by way of preparation for the hunt, other than making sure of the strength of the bark tumpline by which they carry their baskets. They put some food in these in case the day's hunt is a long one, and they wrap a glowing ember from the family fire in large, damp leaves, and sit down and wait for the men to set off.

In normal times there is often a dance before everyone departs for the hunt. Men and women circle the camp, singing a hunting song, looking from right to left, clapping their hands and leaping extravagantly in imitation of the animals they hope to catch. But this was rare during the days of the molimo as all felt the lack of rest.

Another form of hunting magic, if you can call it that, was a paste made from various parts of an antelope, particularly the heart and the eye. The charred flesh is mixed with spittle and ground to a paste, then put in an inverted antelope horn and stuck in the ground near the family fire. Just before going on a hunt, members of the family smear one another with some of the paste, using a twig to dig it out of the horn. It is difficult to say whether this form of magic is of Pygmy or Negro origin. I rather think the latter, because only a few families practiced it, and they were highly criticized by the others as being antisocial. They were trying to get success for themselves at the expense of the others. On one such occasion a family had a long run of good luck, the animals always falling into their net, while others had no luck at all. It was decided that this must have been due to *anjo*, as the medicine was called, so everyone, including the offenders, agreed that the only thing to do was to destroy the horns that held the medicine. Everyone who had such a magic horn gave it to old Moke and promised not to make any more

---

* Literally, the heart of the molimo. This was the central meeting place of the men's religious organization.—Ed.

selfish magic. Moke threw the horns in a fire and no more was said. It so happened that the family in question continued to have good luck for some time.

Hunting, for a Pygmy group, is a co-operative affair—net-hunting particularly. The use of private magic is frowned on, though there is no law against it. The sacred hunting fire is all that they consider right and necessary, and this is found throughout the forest. It is thought to secure the blessing of the forest which provides the game, and to bring good luck to the entire group. Even those groups that hunt mainly with bow and arrow, hunt not as individuals, but for the group as a whole. For the net hunters it is impossible to hunt alone. Men, women and children all have to co-operate if the hunt is to be successful.

The "Fire of the Hunt" simply involves the lighting of a fire at the base of a tree a short distance from the camp. In other Pygmy groups I have seen a variation in which the fire is lighted within the camp, special sticks around it pointing in the direction the hunt is going to take. In this case the fire is surrounded by a long and heavy vine laid in a circle on the ground, and when the game is brought home it is placed within this circle before being divided. But this particular group, and others in the area, were less formal.

I remember one morning in particular when we went to kindle the Fire of the Hunt outside the camp, because it was the day that old Cephu committed one of the greatest sins possible in the forest.

I doubt if any of us had managed to snatch more than two hours' sleep, and we were all quiet while preparing for the hunt. In a Pygmy camp this is the surest danger signal of all, for usually everyone is talking and laughing and shouting rude remarks from one end of the camp to the other. It was not only that we were tired, but of late Cephu had refused to contribute to the molimo basket, and that morning he had been heard to call out, in his loudest voice, that he was fed up with the molimo of "that camp over there." Even though he always made his camp a short distance off it was close enough to be thought of as the same camp, and whether or not we appreciated his presence we thought of his camp and ours as being the same. Even his unwillingness to take part in the molimo was accepted, to maintain some semblance of unity; but this sudden statement made it impossible to ignore Cephu's feeling of rivalry any longer. Rather than cause an open breach, everyone in the main camp kept his thoughts to himself and was silent.

About an hour after dawn, four or five youths with their nets and spears went off to light the hunting fire. I went with them, and only when we had crossed the Lelo and were on the other side did they speak. Then it was about trivialities, and soon they were chatting and laughing as though nothing were wrong. Shortly afterward we were joined by half a dozen of the younger married men, the most active hunters, and we lit the fire at the top of the hill. Leaves and twigs were piled around the base of a young tree, and an ember brought from the camp set them ablaze. More leaves were thrown on so that dense clouds of smoke went billowing up to the invisible sky, until finally the flames burst through with a great roar of victory. There was no great ritual or ceremonial, but somehow this act put the hunters in harmony with the forest and secured its blessing and assistance for the day's hunt. The Pygmies regard fire as the most precious gift of the forest, and by offering it back to the forest they are acknowledging their debt and their dependence.

As we sat around waiting for the others, one or two couples passed by. They were going ahead so they would have extra time for gathering mushrooms on the way. They paused to chat and then walked on, lightly, swiftly, and gaily. Before long the main body of hunters arrived and asked where Cephu was. We had not seen him. It seemed that he had left the camp shortly after us but instead of passing by the hunting fire had followed a different path. Someone suggested that he was building a fire of his own. This brought cries of protest that not even Cephu would do such a thing. There was much shaking of heads, and when Ekianga arrived and was told what had happened he stood still for a moment, then turned around, looking in all directions to see if there was any sign of smoke for another fire. He said just one word, "Cephu," and spat on the ground.

By the time we got to the place where we were to make our first cast of the nets everyone was more silent and miserable than ever. It did not make matters any better to find Cephu there already, contentedly sitting over a fire eating roast plantains. He looked up and greeted us in a friendly way, and when asked why he had followed his own path he opened his eyes wide and softly said that he had misunderstood and taken the wrong trail. There were angry remarks, but Cephu ignored them all and went on munching at his plantain, smiling at everyone in his kind, gentle way.

Ekianga and a few others made a brief reconnaissance, and when they came back they gave instructions as to the best direction for setting up the nets. The womenfolk, who had been foraging around for mushrooms and nuts, picked up their baskets and went ahead with the small children. They trod lightly and made no noise beyond an occasional crunch of a rotten branch, buried deep beneath the carpet of leaves. We all spread out in a long semicircle, each man knowing exactly who should be to his right and who is to his left. I went with Maipe, who had been sent by Njobo with his net. We soon lost sight and sound of the others, but Maipe knew just where he would be expected to set up his net, and he took a short cut. I lost all sense of direction and could not even tell on which side of us the women were waiting for the signal to beat in toward our nets. We followed a little stream and paused by an enormous outcrop of huge stone boulders, almost perfectly square in shape, some of them eight feet across each face. Maipe looked around, then sat down to wait. After a few minutes Moke's nephew appeared to our left, stringing his net out through the undergrowth as he came.

The end of the net stopped a few feet short of the boulders, and Maipe deftly joined it to his net; then, slipping each coil off his shoulder in turn, he hung his own net, fastening it to low branches and saplings. It stretched for about three hundred feet, so that one end was completely out of sight from the other. It stood about four feet high, and Maipe walked the length of it, silently adjusting it so that it touched the ground all the way along and was securely fastened above. If he found the net drooping where there was no support, he cut a sapling, stuck it in the ground and hung the net on it, bending the top sharply back, twisting it around and through the mesh so that the net could not slip. When this was done he took up his spear and casually sharpened it with a stone picked off the ground.

It was about another five minutes before he suddenly stood up and beckoned me to do the same. He stood absolutely motionless, his head slightly on one side, listening; his spear was raised just a few inches from the ground. I listened too, but could hear nothing. The forest had become silent; even the crickets had stopped their almost incessant chirping. Maipe raised his spear higher, and then at some signal that I did not even notice there was a burst of shouting, yelling, hooting and clapping, as the women and children started the beat. They must have been about half a mile away, and as they came closer the noise was deafening. We saw one antelope, a large red sondu, ears back, leaping toward the boulders as though it were heading straight for our net, but at the last moment it saw us and veered away to the left. Maipe could probably have killed it with his spear, but he said, "That is not for us. It will probably fall into Ekianga's net." Just then there was a lot of yelling from Moke's nephew. Maipe vaulted over the net and ran swiftly, leaping and bounding like the sondu to avoid obstacles. I followed as best I could, but was passed by several youngsters from farther down the line before I reached the others. The sondu had gone into Ekianga's net, just as Maipe had said, but while all the attention was in that direction a water chevrotain, the *sindula*, had tried to fight its way through Moke's net.

The sindula is one of the most prized animals; it is not much larger than a small dog but is dangerous and vicious. Moke's nephew had been left all by himself to deal with it, as the others in that area were helping Ekianga with the sondu. The youngster, probably not much more than thirteen years old, had speared it with his first thrust, pinning the animal to the ground through the fleshy part of the stomach. But the animal was still very much alive, fighting for freedom. It had already bitten its way through the net, and now it was doubled up, gashing the spear shaft with its sharp teeth. Maipe put another spear into its neck, but it still writhed and fought. Not until a third spear pierced its heart did it give up the struggle.

It was at times like this that I found myself furthest removed from the Pygmies. They stood around in an excited group, pointing at the dying animal and laughing. One boy, about nine years old, threw himself on the ground and curled up in a grotesque heap and imitated the sindula's last convulsions. The men pulled their spears out and joked with one another about being afraid of a little animal like that, and to emphasize his point one of them kicked the torn and bleeding body. Then Maipe's mother came and swept the blood-streaked animal up by its hind legs and threw it over her shoulder into the basket on her back.

At other times I have seen Pygmies singeing feathers off birds that were still alive, explaining that the meat is more tender if death comes slowly. And the hunting dogs, valuable as they are, get kicked around mercilessly from the day they are born to the day they die. I have never seen any attempt at the domestication of any animal or bird apart from the hunting dog. When I talked to the Pygmies about their treatment of animals, they laughed at me and said, "The forest has given us animals for food—should we refuse this gift and starve?" I thought of turkey farms and Thanksgiving, and of the millions of animals reared by our own society with the sole intention of slaughtering them for food.

HUNTER RELIGION: AN ESKIMO SHAMAN

MIRCEA ELIADE

No one can say what the earliest human religion was, but the first religious specialists may have been the priests or medicine men of hunting-gathering societies. This reading is a description of the work of one such specialist, an Eskimo shaman. Shamans are the healers and spiritual leaders of Arctic hunters throughout Siberia, northeast Asia, and North America.

This selection is an anthropologist's account from 1930, summarized by Mircea Eliade, perhaps the leading twentieth-century student of the history of the world's religions.

From Mircea Eliade, *Shamanism: Archaic Techniques of Ecstasy*, translated by Willard R. Trask, Bollingen Series LXXVI. Copyright © 1964 by Princeton University Press. Reprinted by permission of Princeton University Press.

Why is the shaman called? What does he do? What role does his audience play? How is this event similar to rituals in other societies? Certainly the hunting world of the Eskimo was very different from that of the Pygmies, but are there similarities in religion?

Descent to the abode of Takánakapsâluk, the Mother of the Sea Beasts, is undertaken at an individual's request, sometimes because of illness, sometimes because of bad luck in hunting; only in the latter case is the shaman paid. But it sometimes happens that no game at all is to be found and the village is threatened with famine; then all the villagers gather in the house where the séance is held, and the shaman's ecstatic journey is made in the name of the whole community. Those present must unfasten their belts and laces, and remain silent, their eyes closed. For a time the shaman breathes deeply, in silence, before summoning his helping spirits. When they come the shaman begins to murmur, "The way is made ready for me; the way opens before me!" and the audience answer in chorus: "Let it be so." And now the earth opens, and the shaman struggles for a long time with unknown forces before he finally cries: "Now the way is open." And the audience exclaim in chorus: "Let the way be open before him; let there be way for him." Now, first under the bed, then farther away, under the passage, is heard the cry, "Halala-he-he-he, Halala-he-he-he"; this is the sign that the shaman has set off. The cry grows more and more distant until it is no longer heard.

During this time the audience sing in chorus, their eyes closed, and sometimes the shaman's clothes—which he had taken off before the séance—come to life and start flying about the house, over the heads of the audience. The signs and deep breathing of people long dead are also heard; they are dead shamans come to help their colleague on his dangerous journey. And their signs and their breathing seem to come from very far under water, as if they were sea beasts.

Reaching the bottom of the ocean, the shaman finds himself facing three great stones in constant motion barring his road; he must pass between them at the risk of being crushed. (This is another image of the "strait gate" that forbids access to the plane of higher being to anyone but an "initiate," that is, one who can act like a "spirit.") Successfully passing this obstacle, the shaman follows a path and comes to a sort of bay; on a hill stands Takánakapsâluk's house, made of stone and with a narrow entrance. The shaman hears sea beasts blowing and panting, but does not see them. A dog with bared teeth defends the entrance; the dog is dangerous to anyone who is afraid of it, but the shaman passes over it, and it understands that he is a very powerful magician. (All these obstacles oppose the ordinary shaman, but the really powerful shamans reach the bottom of the sea and the presence of Takánakapsâluk directly, by diving beneath their tent or snow hut, as if slipping through a tube.)

If the goddess is angry with men, a great wall rises before her house. And the shaman has to knock it down with his shoulder. Others say that Takánakapsâluk's house has no roof, so that the goddess can better see men's acts from her place by the fire. All kinds of marine animals are gathered in a pool to the right of the fire, and their cries and breathings are heard. The goddess's hair hangs down over her face and she is dirty and slovenly; this is the effect of men's sins, which have almost made her ill. The shaman must approach her, take her by the shoulder, and comb her hair (for the goddess has no fingers with which to comb herself). Before he can do this, there is another obstacle to be overcome; Takánakapsâluk's father, taking him for a dead man on the way to the land of shades, tries to seize him, but the shaman cries, "I am flesh and blood!" and succeeds in passing.

As he combs Takánakapsâluk's hair, the shaman tells her that men have no more seal. And the goddess answers in the spirit language: "The secret miscarriages of the women and breaches of taboo in eating boiled meat bar the way for the animals." The shaman now has to summon all his powers to appease her anger; finally she opens the pool and sets the animals free. The audience hears their movements at the bottom of the sea, and soon afterward the shaman's gasping breathing, as if he were emerging from the surface of the water. A long silence follows. Finally the shaman speaks: "I have something to say." All answer. "Let us hear, let us hear." And the shaman, in the spirit language, demands the confession of sins. One after another, all confess their miscarriages or their breaches of taboos and repent.

ORIGINS OF AGRICULTURE

CHARLES B. HEISER, JR.

The agricultural revolution occurred not just once, nor in only one region, but at least twice and probably many times, Charles B. Heiser, Jr., a modern archaeologist, argues. What are the two different areas the author refers to? How was the development of agriculture different in

From *Seed to Civilization*, second edition, by Charles B. Heiser, Jr. Copyright © 1981 W. H. Freeman and Company. Reprinted by permission.

these two areas? How have different parts of the world contributed different crops to the human diet?

In the sweat of thy face thou shalt eat bread.
Genesis 3:19

People have been on earth for some two million years. Except for a minute fraction of that time, they have been hunters of animals and gatherers of plants, strictly dependent upon nature for their food. They must, at many times during their long history as hunter-gatherers, have enjoyed full stomachs, when vegetable foods were abundant or ample game was available. Early humans certainly must have experimented with nearly all of the plant resources, thus becoming experts on which ones were good to eat. They became excellent hunters and fishermen. Contrary to earlier opinion, recent studies suggest that they didn't always have to search continually just to find enough to eat and, at times, must have had considerable leisure.

There undoubtedly were times and places, however, in which people did have to spend most of their waking hours searching for food, and hunger probably was common throughout much of the preagricultural period. Certainly there could never have been much of an opportunity for large populations to have built up, even among the successful hunter-gatherers. People probably lived in small groups, for with few exceptions a given area would provide enough food for only a few. Disease and malnutrition probably contributed to keeping populations small, and it is likely that there were also some sorts of intentional population control, such as infanticide.

Then, about 10,000 years ago, food-producing habits began to change, and in the course of time our ancestors became food producers rather than hunter-gatherers. At first they had to supplement the food they produced with food they obtained by hunting and gathering, but gradually they became less dependent on wild food sources as their domesticated plants and animals were increased in number and improved. The cultivation of plants and the keeping of animals probably required no less effort than did hunting and gathering, but in time they gave a more dependable source of food. Having a dependable food source made it possible for larger numbers of people to live together. More mouths to feed were no longer disastrous, but rather were advantageous, for with more bodies to till and reap, food could be produced more efficiently. Although some urban centers may have developed before agriculture, food production was probably the chief stimulus for the growth of villages and eventually of cities, and with the latter came civilization.

When food production became more efficient, there was time to develop the arts and sciences. Some hunter-gatherers, as was already pointed out, must have had considerable leisure, but they never made any notable advances toward civilization. An important difference between hunter-gatherers and farmers is that the former are usually nomadic whereas the latter are sedentary. But even those preagricultural people, such as certain fisherman, who had fairly stationary living sites did not develop in civilizing ways comparable to those of farmers. Agriculture probably required a far greater discipline than did any form of food collecting. Seeds had to be planted at certain seasons, some protection had to be given to the growing plants and animals, harvests had to be reaped, stored, and divided. Thus, we might argue that it was neither leisure time nor a sedentary existence but the more rigorous demands associated with an agricultural way of life that led to great cultural changes. It has been suggested, for example, that writing may have come into existence because records were needed by agricultural administrators. Plants and animals were being changed to suit needs; living in a new relation with plants and animals was, in turn, changing the way of life.

In recent years archaeological work has greatly increased our knowledge of the beginnings of agriculture, and without doubt future archaeological work will add a great deal more information. In contrast to previous generations of archaeologists who were mostly concerned with spectacular finds—tombs, and temples, the contents of which would make showy museum exhibits—recent archaeologists have taken a greater interest in how people lived, what they ate, and how they managed their environment. A few charred seeds or broken bones may appear rather insignificant in a museum, but they can reveal a great deal about early human activities. As a result of recent work in archaeology, done in cooperation with scientists from many other fields, we are beginning to understand the ecology of prehistoric people in many different parts of the world.

Our knowledge of what humans ate and did thousands of years ago comes from the remains of plants and animals recovered from archaeological excavations. Unlike many tools, which were made of stone and are indestructible, foods are perishable and are preserved only where conditions are ideal. The best sites are in dry regions, often in caves, and from such sites we obtain remains to use in the reconstruction of our ancestors' diet. Other human artifacts, such as flint sickles and stone querns, or grinding wheels, may also provide clues about diet, but they leave us to speculate about what plants were being harvested and prepared, and whether these were wild or cultivated. Obviously, the record of what prehistoric people ate is very incomplete, and for many areas of the earth, significant remains have yet to be found.

Drawings of animals, particularly from the later prehistoric periods, have come down to us and sometimes (but not always, by any means) can be fairly readily identified, but it is animal bones, or even fragments of them, that provide the best clues about the animals that were closely connected with people. An expert zoologist can identify species from bones, but it is not always possible to say whether remains are from domestic or wild animals.

Plant remains comprise a variety of forms. Most are seeds or fruits, but other parts, such as flower bracts, stalks, and leaves are sometimes found. A few remarkably well-preserved seeds are recovered, looking as if they had been harvested only a year before, but most seeds are charred and broken. A skilled botanist can identify such plant remains, and it can often be determined if they are from domesticated or wild plants.

Another source of information about the ancient diet is coprolites—fossil feces. By suitable preparation they can be restored to an almost fresh condition (sometimes, it is said, including the odor). Whole seeds have been found in coprolites, but most of the food material is highly fragmented and requires lengthy, painstaking analysis for identification. Such analysis is highly significant because it tells us what was actually eaten, in what combinations, and whether it was cooked or raw.

Unfortunately, material collected at an archaeological dig is sometimes not accurately identified, as has been shown for some of the early archaeological reports from Peru. Fortunately, however, the material recovered from archaeological sites is usually preserved in museums, and future investigators can examine the material to verify or correct identifications.

With the development of radiocarbon methods of dating it became possible to date, fairly accurately, the beginnings of plant civilization. Sometimes radiocarbon dates, for one reason or another, may be open to suspicion, but when different materials from the same site are analyzed and several dates agree, we have fair assurance that they are correct within a few hundred years.

The evidence that has accumulated over the past several years indicates that agriculture probably has its origins in the Near East[1]—although not necessarily, as earlier supposed, in the fertile river valleys of Mesopotamia (which were to be important centers of early civilization), but more likely in the semiarid mountainous areas nearby. Dates determined for flint sickles and grinding stones discovered in these areas indicate that before 8000 B.C. humans had likely become collectors of wild grain, and there is evidence that a thousand or so years later they were actually cultivating grains and keeping domesticated animals. Several sites are now known in the Near East that give evidence of early agriculture. One of the first sites to give such evidence was at Jarmo, in

---

1. The *Near East* is the term used by archaeologists to refer to the countries of southwest Asia. The term *Middle East*, widely used in the news today, includes the Near East.

Iraq, where investigations were conducted under the direction of R. J. Braidwood. In deposits dated at 6750 B.C., seeds of wheat and barley and bones of goats were found. Other evidence of cultivation, dating from approximately the same time, has been found at several other sites in the Near East. Since the plants in these sites apparently represented cultivated species, we must suppose that there was an earlier period of their incipient domestication, which may have lasted for a few hundred years or more. How long it takes a plant to become fully domesticated cannot be answered precisely and it probably varies considerably from species to species. In deposits accumulated after 6500 B.C. we find evidence of other plants being cultivated in the Near East and Greece, and bones of various domesticated animals become more abundant.

Other centers of agriculture developed in the Old World. Whether these developments are stimulated by knowledge of agriculture in the Near East or whether they were independent developments is not certain, but the fact that some of them were based on completely different plants from those of the Near East might support the latter view. For a long time southeastern Asia had been considered an ancient center for domesticated plants, but until recently there was no archaeological support for this view; this is not wholly unexpected, since the climate for the most part in that area of the world is hardly conducive to preservation of food remains. In 1969, however, a report was published of an assemblage of plants from Thailand, including possibly a pea and a bean, dated at 7000 B.C. As it is not definitely clear whether the plants recovered represented wild or cultivated species, we cannot yet say that agriculture was practiced as early here as it was in the Near East. We do not yet know when rice, which was to become the basic food plant of southeastern Asia, was first brought under cultivation, but it was probably considerably later than the cereals of the Near East.

In the New World, agriculture began a few thousand years later than in the Near East and had its origins in Mexico and Peru. Through a series of excavations directed by R. S. MacNeish, we now have a remarkable sequence of plants giving evidence of the period of incipient domestication in Mexico. Some indication of the earliest cultivated plants is found in the mesquite-desert regions of southwestern Tamaulipas, with gourds, squashes, beans, and chili peppers being found at levels dated at between 7000 and 5500 B.C.

Following investigations at Tamaulipas, MacNeish made deliberate efforts to search for evidence of the domestication of maize [corn], which eventually became the most important plant in the Americas. A group of caves in the arid highlands near Tehuacan in south central Mexico showed promise, and a series of excavations was begun in 1961. The results give us the best picture yet of the transitional stages leading to full-scale agriculture. Humans were probably in the Tehuacan area

10,000 B.C. and for several millennia they depended on wild food sources, both plant and animal. Gradually more and more plants were cultivated, some perhaps having been domesticated at this site, others introduced from other regions. The first suggestion of cultivated plants occurs in material dated about 5000 B.C., with maize, squash, chili pepper, avocado, and amaranth being found. These plants were definitely cultivated during the next period (4900–3500 B.C.), together with various fruits and beans toward the end of the period. During the next thousand years other plants were added, including cotton and two new kinds of beans. The dog, which is known from historic records to have been an important food item in Mexico, is first associated with humans in the archaeological record at this time. At about the beginning of the Christian era, the inhabitants of Tehuacan had also acquired the turkey. From remains of the same period there are reports of some other plants: guava, pineapple, and peanut. The presence of these plants would be of particular interest, for the peanut is definitely South American in origin and the pineapple and guava perhaps are also, which would suggest that the peoples of this area had contact with South America at this time. None of these plants has been found in any other archaeological sites in Mexico to date. A study of historical records of both peanuts and pineapple would suggest that they arrived in Mexico recently, perhaps after the coming of the Spanish.

Another early development of agriculture in the Americas occurred in Peru, perhaps even earlier than in Mexico. Two kinds of cultivated beans and a chili pepper, dated at around 6000 B.C. or earlier, have been recovered in a highland valley at Callejon de Huaylas in north central Peru. Previous to this discovery, archaeological plant material had been found in dry coastal sites, such as Huaca Prieta in northern Peru. Gourds, squashes, cotton, lima beans, and chili peppers are among the first plants cultivated on the coast; present evidence indicates that agriculture developed here about 2000 years later than in the highlands.

At present it is difficult to say whether agriculture in the Americas appeared first in Peru or Mexico. The fact that many of the same plants were cultivated in the two areas might suggest that agriculture spread from one of the areas to the other, but the chile peppers and the squashes of the two regions belong to different species, and it seems possible that the common bean was domesticated independently in Mexico and Peru. Thus, although the possibility remains that agriculture, or at least the idea of growing plants, diffused from one area to the other, it is just as likely that agriculture arose independently in Mexico and Peru. That there was diffusion between the two areas at a later time is clear because maize, which almost certainly had its origin in Mexico, appears in Peru by 2500–3000 B.C. and, as already mentioned, certain South American plants may have appeared in Mexico in pre-Columbian times.

From the foregoing account it can be seen that agriculture arose in widely separated parts of the earth, probably quite independently from place to place. But agriculture began in the Old World more than a thousand years earlier than it did in the New—could the idea of agriculture have come to the New World from the Old? The New World was peopled by immigration across the Bering Strait long before agriculture was known, and if there were subsequent crossings at this place, it was by hunters rather than agriculturists. Thus, we would have to postulate a long ocean voyage at a very early date to account for agricultural knowledge being brought to the New World. Some anthropologists have postulated that there were such voyages in prehistoric times, but much later than the time at which agriculture was established in Mexico. Therefore, it seems highly unlikely that agriculture had but a single origin. It is, in fact, likely that it had several origins in both the Old and the New World, although some people still believe that it was invented only once.

An examination of the list of food plants from all the early sites in both the New and the Old World reveals that all of the plants were propagated by seed. A large number of present-day food plants, including such important ones as the white and sweet potato, manioc [a tropical plant grown for its edible fleshy root], yams, bananas, and sugar cane are propagated vegetatively—by stem cuttings, tubers, or roots—rather than from seed. Some people, notably the geographer Carl Sauer, have reasoned that cultivation of plants probably began with vegetative propagation, arguing that such cultivation is much simpler than seed planting. There is also some evidence from Old World mythology suggesting that vegetative cultivation is older than seed planting. The archaeological record, unfortunately, has not been able to provide us with clearcut answers, for many of the vegetatively cultivated plants are crops of the wet tropics, areas where the preservation of prehistoric food materials is rather unlikely. Moreover, even in dry areas, tubers and other fleshy plant parts are far less likely to be preserved than are relatively dry materials, such as seeds. While we cannot, perhaps, entirely rule out the possibility that agriculture based on vegetative propagation was earlier than seed-propagation agriculture, it seems fairly clear that it was seed planting that led to the most profound changes in our way of life. All the early high civilizations whose diets are known to us were based on seed-reproducing plants—wheat, maize, or rice—with or without accompanying animal husbandry.

Following the domestication of plants and animals, the next great advance in agriculture came with the control of water. Irrigation arose in the Near East around 5000 B.C. and in Mexico shortly after 1000 B.C. With irrigation, considerably more food could be produced in many areas; as a result, a few people could produce enough food to feed a large population, permitting others to spend time in pursuit of the arts and crafts and of religion. Elaborate temples, many of them standing today, were constructed by early societies that had perfected methods of irrigating their crops and testify to the amount of human labor that was made available for other pursuits.

Another important development in Old World agriculture was the use of animals to prepare the fields for planting, which was never done in the New World in prehistoric times. Along with this difference there was a basic difference in planting techniques. In the Old World the cereals (wheat, for example) were planted by broadcasting handfuls of grain, whereas in the New World the grains of maize were planted individually.

With the domestication of plants and animals there should have been a dependable food supply and, so it might be thought, hunger should have disappeared from the earth. As any intelligent person is acutely aware, however, hunger is still very much with us today. Harmony with nature has yet to be established. With the advent of agriculture, humans began changing their environment drastically. Irrigation, which initially led to greater food production, eventually destroyed some of the most fertile areas. Without adequate drainage, irrigation leads to an accumulation of salts in the soil that few plants can tolerate. That this happened in prehistoric times in the Near East is evident from archaeological findings; for barley, which is more salt tolerant than wheat, replaced the latter plant in some regions after irrigation was developed. The use of animals to till the soil led to increased areas being planted, which in time must have been accompanied by increased soil erosion. Then, along with the plants and animals that people brought under their control came others that they did not want and could not control. Rusts, smuts, and weeds soon found cultivated plants and fields a fertile territory for their development, and insects, rodents, and birds moved in to appropriate the new foods for themselves. Competition for the more fertile agricultural land led to warfare on an escalating scale, for which the powers of some of the domesticated animals were used. Hunger has always accompanied war.

Deserts now occupy many of the areas where high civilizations once flourished. Natural climatic change may in part be responsible for some of these deserts, but humankind most likely contributed through misuse of soil and water. Alteration of the environment, which began in a modest way 10,000 years ago, continues in the present on a scale never known before.

WOMEN AND THE AGRICULTURAL REVOLUTION

ELISE BOULDING

In hunting-gathering society men were usually the hunters and women were the gatherers. As gatherers (or foragers), women were the likely discoverers of plant reproduction. Elise Boulding, a sociologist, shows how the planting of wild einkorn, a grain of the Middle Eastern Fertile Crescent, transformed the lives of women and men.

In what ways was the early discovery of planting "women's work"? To what extent did it increase women's power or prestige? How were the lives of women and children changed by planting?

There is some disagreement about whether the domestication of animals or plants came first. In fact, both were probably happening at the same time. There is evidence from campfire remains as long ago as 20,000 B.C. that women had discovered the food value of einkorn, a kind of wild wheat that grows all through the fertile crescent. An enterprising Oklahoma agronomist, Professor Jack Harlan of the University of Oklahoma, noticed several years ago, on an expedition to eastern Turkey, how thick these stands of wild einkorn grew. He tried harvesting some, and once he had resorted to a nine-thousand-year-old flint sickle blade set in a new wooden handle (he tried to use his bare hands first, with disastrous results), he was able to come away with an excellent harvest. After weighing what he had reaped, he estimated that a single good stand of einkorn would feed a family for a whole year. He also found that the grains had 50 percent more protein than the wheat we use now in North America for bread flour. Einkorn grains are found everywhere on the ancient home-base sites of the fertile crescent, either as roasted hulls in cooking hearths, or as imprints in the mud-and-straw walls of the earliest preagriculture huts.

It would be inevitable that grains from sheaves of einkorn carried in from a distant field would drop in well-trodden soil just outside the home base, or perhaps in a nearby pile of refuse. When the band returned the following year to this campsite—perhaps a favorite one, since not all campsites were revisited—there would be a fine stand of einkorn waiting for them right at their doorstep. We might say that the plants taught the women how to cultivate them. Planting, however, was quite a step beyond just leaving some stalks at the site where they were picked, to seed themselves for the next year. There was less reason for deliberate planting as long as bands were primarily nomadic and there was plenty of game to follow. But in time there was a premium on campsites that would have abundant grain and fruit and nuts nearby, and then there was point in scattering extra grain on the ground near the campsite for the next year. Because of the construction of the seed, einkorn easily plants itself, so it was a good plant for initiating humans into agriculture.

Gradually, bands lengthened their stays at their more productive home bases, harvesting what had been "planted" more or less intentionally, and letting the few sheep they had raised from infancy graze on nearby hills. One year there would be such a fine stand of wheat at their favorite home base, and so many sheep ambling about, that a band would decide just to stay for a while, not to move on that year.

If any one band of nomads could have anticipated what lay in store for humankind as a result of that fateful decision (made separately by thousands of little bands over the next ten thousand years), would they after all have moved on? While it may have been a relief not to be on the move, they in fact exchanged a life of relative ease, with enough to eat and few possessions, for a life of hard work, enough to eat, and economic surplus. As Childe says, "a mild acquisitiveness could now take its place among human desires."

Successful nomads have a much easier life than do farmers. Among the Kung bushmen today, the men hunt about four days a week and the women only need to work two-and-a-half days at gathering to feed their families amply for a week. (At that, meat is a luxury item, and most of the nourishment comes from nuts and roots.) The rest of their time is leisure, to be enjoyed in visiting, creating and carrying out rituals, and just "being."

THE FIRST SETTLEMENTS

For better or worse, the women and the men settled down. They settled in the caves of Belt and Hotu to a prosperous life of farming and herding on the Caspian. They settled in Eynan, Jericho, Jarmo, Beidha, Catal Huyuk, Hacilar, Arpachiyah, and Kherokitia in Cyprus, and in uncounted villages that no archaeologist's shovel has touched. These places were home-base sites first, some going back thousands of years. By 10,000 B.C. Eynan had fifty houses, small stone domes, seven meters in diameter, around a central area with storage pits. This was probably preagricultural, still a hunting and gathering band, but a settled one. The village covered two thousand square meters. Each hut had a hearth, and child and infant burials were found under some of the floors. Three successive layers of fifty stone houses have been found at the same site, so it must have been a remarkably stable site for a settlement.

What was life like, once bands settled down? This was almost from the start a woman's world. She would mark out the fields for planting, because she knew where the grain grew best, and would probably work in the fields together with the other women of the band. There would not be separate fields at first, but as the former nomads shifted from each sleeping in individual huts to building houses for family groups of mother, father, and children, a separate family feeling must have developed and women may have divided the fields by family groups.

Their fire-hardened pointed digging sticks, formerly used in gathering, now became a multipurpose implement for planting and cultivating the soil. At harvest time everyone, including the children, would help bring in the grain. The women also continued to gather fruit and nuts, again with the help of the children. The children watched the sheep and goats, but the women did the milking and cheese making. Ethnologists who have studied both foraging and agricultural societies comment on the change in the way of life for children that comes with agriculture. Whereas in foraging societies they have no responsibilities beyond feeding themselves and learning the hunting and foraging skills they will need, and therefore they have much leisure, it is very common in agricultural societies to put children to work at the age of three, chasing birds from the food plots. Older children watch the animals, and keep them out of the planted areas.

The agriculture practiced by these first women farmers and their children, producing enough food for subsistence only, must be distinguished from that agriculture which developed out of subsistence farming and which produced surpluses and fed nonfarming populations in towns. The first type is commonly called horticulture and is carried out with hand tools only. The second is agriculture proper, and involves intensive cultivation with the use of plow and (where necessary) irrigation. In areas like the hilly flanks of the fertile crescent in the Middle East, horticulture moved fairly rapidly into agriculture as it spread to the fertile plains. As we shall see, trading centers grew into towns and cities needing food from the countryside. Women and children could not unaided produce the necessary surpluses, and by the time the digging stick had turned into an animal-drawn plow, they were no longer the primary workers of the fields.

The simpler form of farming continued in areas where the soil was less fertile, and particularly in the tropical forest areas of Africa. Here soils were quickly exhausted, and each year the village women would enlist the men in helping to clear new fields which were then burned over in the slash-and-burn pattern which helped reconstitute the soils for planting again. The slash-and-burn pattern of horticulture has continued into this century, since it is a highly adaptive technique for meager tropical soils. Where the simple horticultural methods continued to be used, women continued as the primary farmers, always with their children as helpers. In a few of these societies women continued also in the positions of power; these are usually the tribes labeled by ethnologists as matrilocal. Not many tribes have survived into the twentieth century with a matrilocal pattern, however, though traces of matrilineal descent reckoning are not infrequent.

The first women farmers in the Zagreb foothills were very busy. Not only did they tend the fields and do the other chores mentioned above, they also probably built the round stone or mud-brick houses in the first villages. The frequency with which women construct shelters in foraging societies has already been cited.

Women also began to spend more time on making tools and containers. No longer needing to hold the family possessions down to what they could carry, women could luxuriate in being able to choose larger and heavier grinding stones that crushed grain more efficiently. They could make containers to hold food stores that would never have to go on the road. They ground fine stone bowls, made rough baskets, and in the process of lining their baskets with mud accidentally discovered that a mudlined basket placed in the hearth would come out hardened—the first pottery. Sonja Cole suggests that pottery was invented in Khartoum in Africa about 8000 B.C., spreading northwest to the Mediterranean, but the same process probably happened over and over again as people became more sedentary.

The evidence from food remains in these early villages, 10,000 to 6000 B.C., indicates that men were still hunting, to supplement the agriculture and modest domestic herds. This means that they were not around very much. When they were, they probably shared in some of the home-base tasks.

Evidence from some of the earliest village layouts suggests that adults lived in individual huts, women keeping the children with them. Marriage agreements apparently did not at first entail shared living quarters. As the agricultural productivity of the women increased, and the shift was made to dwellings for family units, husband-wife interaction probably became more frequent and family living patterns more complex.

With the accumulation of property, decisions about how it was to be allocated had to be made. The nature of these agreements is hardly to be found in the archaeological record, so we must extrapolate from what we know of the "purest" matrilineal tribes of the recent past.

The senior woman of a family and her daughters and sons formed the property-holding unit for the family. The senior woman's *brother* would be the administrator of the properties. His power, whether over property or in political decision making, would be derivative from his status as brother (usually but not always the oldest) to the senior woman in a family. This role of the brother, so important in present-day matrilineal societies, may not have been very important in the period we are now considering, between 12,000 and 8000 B.C.

THE ORIGIN OF CORN LEGEND

NATCHEZ INDIANS OF NORTH AMERICA

This is a legend told by the Natchez native Americans. What does the legend seek to explain? Think of the legend as telling the truths of a dream; what truths does this dream reveal?

This is the third selection that deals with the origins of agriculture. In what ways does this legend reinforce any or all of the other selections? Drawing on all of these readings, you might try to develop your own theory about how agriculture was "invented" or discovered.

Corn-woman lived at a certain place in company with twin girls. When the corn was all gone she went into the corn house, taking two baskets, and came out with the baskets full. They lived on the hominy which she made from this.

One time the girls looked into this corn house and saw nothing there. They said to each other, "Where does she get it? Next time she goes in there we will creep up and watch her."

When the corn was all gone she started to go in and they saw her. So they crept after her and when she entered and closed the door they peeped through a crack. They saw her set down the basket, stand astride of it and rub and shake herself, and there was a noise, tságak, as if something fell off. In this way she filled one basket with corn. Then she stood over the other, rubbed herself and shook, the noise tságak, was heard and that basket was full of beans. After that the girls ran away.

"Let us not eat it," they said. "She defecates and then feeds us with the excrement." So when the hominy was cooked they did not eat it, and from that she knew they had seen her. "Since you think it is filthy, you

By permission of Smithsonian Institution Press from *Myths and Tales of the Southeastern Indians* by John R. Swanton. Bureau of American Ethnology Bulletin 88. Smithsonian Institution, Washington, D.C., 1929.

will have to help yourselves from now on. Kill me and burn my body. When summer comes things will spring up on the place where it was burned and you must cultivate them, and when they are matured they will be your food."

They killed Corn-woman and burned her body and when summer came corn, beans, and pumpkins sprang up. They kept cultivating these and every day, when they stopped, stuck their hoes up in the ground and went away. But on their return more ground would be hoed and the hoes would be sticking up in different places.

They said, "Let us creep up and find out who is hoeing for us," and they did so. When they looked they saw that the hoes were doing it of themselves and they laughed. Immediately the hoes fell down and did not work for them any more. They did not know that it was just those two hoes which were helping them and they themselves spoiled it.

2. The Urban Revolution in the Near East and North Africa

CITY AND CIVILIZATION

KEVIN REILLY

This reading is excerpted from a recent history of civilization.

The urban revolution that brought the first cities five thousand years ago also brought the beginnings of civilization. Why do we associate cities with civilization? What were some of the general media of communication that cities created? What does it mean to say that civilization created the "eye" and "I"? How could the city make life impersonal and personal at the same time? What was the importance of class divisions in the first cities? Does modern city life still have the features of the first cities?

The most obvious achievements of the first civilizations are the monuments—the pyramids, temples, palaces, statues, and treasures—that were created for the new ruling class of kings, nobles, priests, and their officials. But civilized life is much more than the capacity to create monuments.

Civilized life is secure life. At the most basic level this means security from the sudden destruction that village communities might suffer. Civilized life gives the feeling of permanence. It offers regularity, stability, order, even routine. Plans can be made. Expectations can be realized. People can be expected to act predictably, according to the rules.

The first cities were able to attain stability with walls that shielded the inhabitants from nomads and armies, with the first codes of law that defined human relationships, with police and officials that enforced the laws, and with institutions that functioned beyond the lives of their particular members. City life offered considerably more permanence and security than village life.

Civilization involves more than security, however. A city that provided

From *The West and the World: A Topical History of Civilization* by Kevin Reilly. New York: Harper & Row, 1980. Copyright © 1980 by Kevin Reilly. Reprinted by permission of Kevin Reilly.

only order would be more like a prison than a civilization. The first cities provided something that the best-ordered villages lacked. They provided far greater variety: more races and ethnic groups were speaking more languages, engaged in more occupations, and living a greater variety of life-styles. The abundance of choice, the opportunities for new sensations, new experiences, knowledge—these have always been the appeals of city life. The opportunities for growth and enrichment were far greater than the possibilities of plow and pasture life.

Security plus variety equals creativity. At least the possibility of a more creative, expressive life was available in the protected, semipermanent city enclosures which drew, like magnets, foreign traders and diplomats, new ideas about gods and nature, strange foods and customs, and the magicians, ministers, and mercenaries of the king's court. Civilization is the enriched life which this dynamic urban setting permitted and the human creativity and opportunity which it encouraged. At the very least, cities made even the most common slave think and feel a greater range of things than the tightly knit, clanish agricultural village allowed. That was (and still is) the root of innovation and creativity—of civilization itself.

The variety of people and the complexity of city life required new and more general means of communication. The villager knew everyone personally. Cities brought together people who often did not even speak the same language. Not only law codes but written language itself became a way to bridge the many gaps of human variety. Cities invented writing so that strangers could communicate, and so that those communications could become permanent—remembered publically, officially recorded. Emerson was right when he said that the city lives by memory, but it was the official memory which enabled the city to carry on its business or religion beyond the lifetime of the village elders. Written symbols that everyone could recognize became the basis of laws, invention, education, taxes, accounting, contracts, and obligations. In short, writing and records made it possible for each generation to begin on the shoulders of the ancestors. Village life and knowledge often seemed to start from scratch. Thus, cities cultivated not only memory and the past, but hope and the future as well. City civilizations invented not only history and record keeping but also prophecy and social planning.

Writing was one city invention that made more general communication possible. Money was another. Money made it possible to deal with anyone just as an agreed-upon public language did. Unnecessary in the village climate of mutual obligations, money was essential in the city society of strangers. Such general media of communication as writing and money vastly increased the number of things that could be said and thought, bought and sold. As a consequence, city life was more impersonal than village life, but also more dynamic and more exciting.

THE "EYE" AND "I"

Marshall McLuhan has written that "civilization gave the barbarian an eye for an ear." We might add that civilization also gave an "I" for an "us." City life made the "eye" and the "I" more important than they had been in the village. The invention of writing made knowledge more visual. The eye had to be trained to recognize the minute differences in letters and words. Eyes took in a greater abundance of detail: laws, prices, the strange cloak of the foreigner, the odd type of shoes made by the new craftsman from who-knows-where, the colors of the fruit and vegetable market, elaborate painting in the temple, as well as the written word. In the village one learned by listening. In the city seeing was believing. In the new city courts of law an "eyewitness account" was believed to be more reliable than "hearsay evidence." In some villages even today, the heard and the spoken are thought more reliable than the written and the seen. In the city, even spoken language took on the uniformity and absence of emotion that is unavoidable in the written word. Perhaps emotions themselves became less violent. "Civilized" is always used to mean emotional restraint, control of the more violent passions, and a greater understanding, even tolerance, of the different and foreign.

Perhaps empathy (the capacity to put yourself in someone else's shoes) increased in cities—so full of so many different others that had to be understood. When a Turkish villager was recently asked, "What would you do if you were president of your country?" he stammered: "My God! How can you ask such a thing? How can I . . . I cannot . . . president of Turkey . . . master of the whole world?" He was completely unable to imagine himself as president. It was as removed from his experience as if he were master of the world. Similarly, a Lebanese villager who was asked what he would do if he were editor of a newspaper accused the interviewer of ridiculing him, and frantically waved the interviewer on to another question. Such a life was beyond his comprehension. It was too foreign to imagine. The very variety of city life must have increased the capacity of the lowest commoner to imagine, empathize, sympathize, and criticize.

The oral culture of the village reinforced the accepted by saying and singing it almost monotonously. The elders, the storytellers, and the minstrels must have had a prodigious memory. But their stories changed only gradually and slightly. The spoken word was sacred. To say it differently was to change the truth. The written culture of cities taught "point of *view*." An urban individual did not have to remember everything. That was done permanently on paper. Knowledge became a recognition of different interpretations and the capacity to look up things. The awareness of variety meant the possibility of criticism, analysis, and an ever-newer synthesis. It is no wonder that the technical and scientific knowledge of cities increased at a geometric rate compared to the knowledge of villages. The multiplication of knowledge was implicit in the city's demand to recognize difference and variety. Civilization has come to mean that ever-expanding body of knowledge and skill. Its finest achievements have been that knowledge, its writing, and its visual art. The city and civilization (like the child) are to be seen and not heard.

It may seem strange to say that the impersonal life of cities contributed greatly to the development of personality—the "I" as well as the "eye." Village life was in a sense much more personal. Everything was taken personally. Villagers deal with each other not as "the blacksmith," "the baker," "that guy who owes me a goat," or "that no-good bum." They do not even "deal" with each other. They know each other by name and family. They love, hate, support, and murder each other because of who they are, because of personal feelings, because of personal and family responsibility. They have full, varied relationships with each member of the village. They do not merely buy salt from this person, talk about the weather with this other person, and discuss personal matters with only this other person. They share too much with each other to divide up their relationships in that way.

City life is a life of separated, partial relationships. In a city you do not know about the butcher's life, wife, kids, and problems. You do not care. You are in a hurry. You have too many other things to do. You might discuss the weather—but while he's cutting. You came to buy meat. Many urban relationships are like that. There are many business, trading, or "dealing" relationships because there are simply too many people to know them all as relatives.

The impersonality of city life is a shame in a way. (It makes it easier to get mugged by someone who does not even hate you.) But the luxurious variety of impersonal relationships (at least some of the time) provide the freedom for the individual personality to emerge. Maybe that is why people have often dreamed of leaving family and friends (usually for a city) in the hope of "finding themselves." Certainly, the camaraderie and community of village life had a darker side of surveillance and conformity. When everything was known about everyone, it was difficult for the individual to find his or her individuality. Family ties and village custom were often obstacles to asserting self-identity. The city offered its inhabitants a huge variety of possible relationships and personal identities. The urban inhabitant was freer than his village cousin to choose friends, lovers, associates, occupation, housing, and life-style. The city was full of choices that the village could not afford or condone. The village probably provided more security in being like everyone else and doing what was expected. But the city provided the variety of possibilities that could allow the individual to follow the "inner self" and cultivate inner gardens.

The class divisions of city society made it difficult for commoners to achieve an effective or creative individuality. But the wealthy and powerful—especially the king—were able to develop models of individuality and personality that were revolutionary. No one before had ever achieved such a sense of the self, and the model of the king's power and freedom became a goal for the rest of the society. The luxury, leisure, and opportunity of the king was a revolutionary force. Unlike a village elder, the king could do whatever he wanted. Recognizing that, more and more city inhabitants asked, "Why can't we?" City revolutions have continually extended class privilege and opportunities ever since.

Once a society has achieved a level of abundance, once it can offer the technological means, the educational opportunities, the creative outlets necessary for everyone to lead meaningful, happy, healthy lives, then classes may be a hindrance. Class divisions were, however, a definite stimulus to productivity and creativity in the early city civilizations. The democratic villagers preferred stability to improvement. As a result, their horizons were severely limited. They died early, lived precipitously, and suffered without much hope. The rulers of the first cities discovered the possibilities of leisure, creation, and the good life. They invented heaven and utopia—first for themselves. Only very gradually has the invention of civilization, of human potential, sifted down to those beneath the ruling class. In many cases, luxury, leisure, freedom, and opportunity are still the monopolies of the elite. But once the powerful have exploited the poor enough to establish their own paradise on earth and their own immortality after death, the poor also have broader horizons and plans.

THE EPIC OF GILGAMESH

Around 2700 B.C. the Mesopotamian city of Uruk was ruled by a king named Gilgamesh. This epic, however, was written much later—around 2000 B.C. Thus, the epic adds many layers of meaning to what might have originally been a straight historical account. In some ways those extra layers of meaning suggest more about the origins of cities and civilization than a straight history of an early king would.

Notice, for instance, how the king was thought of as part god. The ancient cities gave us our first kings, many of whom must have ruled like gods. Notice also how the conflict between Gilgamesh and Enkidu symbolizes the conflict between the city and the pasture. Ancient cities were continually threatened by the rough nomads of the pasture. The "barbarians" had to be "civilized."

What does the epic tell you about how early city people viewed themselves, their leaders, and the threatening herdsmen? How did they view women? What clues about ancient city life does the epic reveal?

PROLOGUE: GILGAMESH KING IN URUK

I will proclaim to the world the deeds of Gilgamesh. This was the man to whom all things were known; this was the king who knew the countries of the world. He was wise, he saw mysteries and knew secret things, he brought us a tale of the days before the flood. He went on a long journey, was weary, worn-out with labour, returning he rested, he engraved on a stone the whole story.

When the gods created Gilgamesh they gave him a perfect body. Shamash the glorious sun endowed him with beauty, Adad the god of the storm endowed him with courage, the great gods made his beauty perfect, surpassing all others, terrifying like a great wild bull. Two thirds they made him god and one third man.

In Uruk he built walls, a great rampart, and the temple of blessed Eanna for the god of the firmament Anu, and for Ishtar the goddess of love. Look at it still today: the outer wall where the cornice runs, it shines with the brilliance of copper; and the inner wall, it has no equal. Touch the threshold, it is ancient. Approach Eanna the dwelling of Ishtar, our lady of love and war, the like of which no latter-day king, no man alive can equal. Climb upon the wall of Uruk; walk along it, I say; regard the foundation terrace and examine the masonry: is it not burnt brick and good? The seven sages laid the foundations.

THE COMING OF ENKIDU

Gilgamesh went abroad in the world, but he met with none who could withstand his arms till he came to Uruk. But the men of Uruk muttered in their houses, "Gilgamesh sounds the tocsin for his amusement, his arrogance has no bounds by day or night. No son is left with his father, for Gilgamesh takes from all, even the children; yet the king should be a shepherd to his people. His lust leaves no virgin to her lover, neither the warrior's daughter nor the wife of the noble; yet this is the shepherd of the city, wise, comely, and resolute."

The gods heard their lament, the gods of heaven cried to the Lord of Uruk, to Anu the god of Uruk: "A goddess made him, strong as a savage bull, none can withstand his arms. No son is left with his father, for Gilgamesh takes them all; and is this the king, the shepherd of his people? His lust leaves no virgin to her lover, neither the warrior's daughter nor the wife of the noble." When Anu had heard their lamentation the gods cried to Aruru, the goddess of creation, "You made him, O Aruru, now create his equal; let it be as like him as his own reflection, his second self, stormy head for stormy heart. Let them contend together and leave Uruk in quiet."

So the goddess conceived an image in her mind, and it was of the stuff of Anu of the firmament. She dipped her hands in water and pinched off clay, she let it fall in the wilderness, and noble Enkidu was created. There was virtue in him of the god of war, of Ninurta himself. His body was rough, he had long hair like a woman's; it waved like the hair of Nisaba, the goddess of corn. His body was covered with matted hair like Samuqan's, the god of cattle. He was innocent of mankind; he knew nothing of cultivated land.

Enkidu ate grass in the hills with the gazelle and lurked with wild beasts at the water-holes; he had joy of the water with the herds of wild game. But there was a trapper who met him one day face to face at the drinking-hole, for the wild game had entered his territory. On three days he met him face to face, and the trapper was frozen with fear. He went back to his house with the game that he had caught, and he was dumb, benumbed with terror. His face was altered like that of one who has made a long journey. With awe in his heart he spoke to his father: "Father, there is a man, unlike any other, who comes down from the hills. He is the strongest in the world, he is like an immortal from heaven. He ranges over the hills with wild beasts and eats grass; he ranges through your land and comes down to the wells. I am afraid and dare not go near him. He fills in the pits which I dig and tears up my traps set for the game; he helps the beasts to escape and now they slip through my fingers."

His father opened his mouth and said to the trapper, "My son, in Uruk lives Gilgamesh; no one has ever prevailed against him, he is strong as a star from heaven. Go to Uruk, find Gilgamesh, extol the strength of this wild man. Ask him to give you a harlot, a wanton from the temple of love; return with her, and let her woman's power overpower this man. When next he comes down to drink at the wells she will be there, stripped naked; and when he sees her beckoning he will embrace her, and then the wild beasts will reject him."

So the trapper set out on his journey to Uruk and addressed himself to Gilgamesh saying, "A man unlike any other is roaming now in the pastures; he is as strong as a star from heaven and I am afraid to approach him. He helps the wild game to escape; he fills in my pits and pulls up my traps." Gilgamesh said, "Trapper, go back, take with you a harlot, a child of pleasure. At the drinking-hole she will strip, and when he sees her beckoning he will embrace her and the game of the wilderness will surely reject him."

Now the trapper returned, taking the harlot with him. After a three days' journey they came to the drinking-hole, and there they sat down; the harlot and the trapper sat facing one another and waited for the game to come. For the first day and for the second day the two sat waiting, but on the third day the herds came; they came down to drink and Enkidu was with them. The small wild creatures of the plains were glad of the water, and Enkidu with them, who ate grass with the gazelle and was born in the hills; and she saw him, the savage man, come from far-off in the hills. The trapper spoke to her: "There he is. Now, woman, make your breasts bare, have no shame, do not delay but welcome his love. Let him see you naked, let him possess your body. When he comes near uncover yourself and lie with him; teach him, the savage man, your woman's art, for when he murmurs love to you the wild beasts that shared his life in the hills will reject him."

She was not ashamed to take him, she made herself naked and welcomed his eagerness; as he lay on her murmuring love she taught him the woman's art. For six days and seven nights they lay together, for Enkidu had forgotten his home in the hills; but when he was satisfied he went back to the wild beasts. Then, when the gazelle saw him, they bolted away; when the wild creatures saw him they fled. Enkidu would have followed, but his body was bound as though with a cord, his knees gave way when he started to run, his swiftness was gone. And now the wild creatures had all fled away; Enkidu was grown weak, for wisdom was in him, and the thoughts of a man were in his heart. So he returned and sat down at the woman's feet, and listened intently to what she said. "You are wise, Enkidu, and now you have become like a god. Why do you want to run wild with the beasts in the hills? Come with me. I will take you to strong-walled Uruk, to the blessed temple of Ishtar and of Anu, of love and of heaven: there Gilgamesh lives, who is very strong, and like a wild bull he lords it over men."

When she had spoken Enkidu was pleased; he longed for a comrade, for one who would understand his heart. "Come, woman, and take me to that holy temple, to the house of Anu and of Ishtar, and to the place where Gilgamesh lords it over people. I will challenge him boldly, I will cry out aloud in Uruk, "I am the strongest here, I have come to change the old order, I am he who was born in the hills, I am he who is strongest of all.' "

She said, "Let us go, and let him see your face. I know very well where Gilgamesh is in great Uruk. O Enkidu, there all the people are dressed in their gorgeous robes, every day is holiday, the young men and the girls are wonderful to see. How sweet they smell! All the great ones are roused from their beds. O Enkidu, you who love life, I will show you Gilgamesh, a man of many moods; you shall look at him well in his radiant manhood. His body is perfect in strength and maturity; he never rests by night or day. He is stronger than you, so leave your boasting. Shamash the glorious sun has given favours to Gilgamesh, and Anu of the heavens, and Enlil, and Ea the wise has given him deep understanding. I tell you, even before you have left the wilderness, Gilgamesh will know in his dreams that you are coming."

Now Gilgamesh got up to tell his dream to his mother, Ninsun, one of the wise gods. "Mother, last night I had a dream. I was full of joy, the young heroes were round me and I walked through the night under the stars of the firmament, and one, a meteor of the stuff of Anu, fell down from heaven. I tried to lift it but it proved too heavy. All the people of Uruk came round to see it, the common people jostled and the nobles thronged to kiss its feet; and to me its attraction was like the love of woman. They helped me, I braced my forehead and I raised it with thongs and brought it to you, and you yourself pronounced it my brother."

Then Ninsun, who is well-beloved and wise, said to Gilgamesh, "This star of heaven which descended like a meteor from the sky; which you tried to lift, but found too heavy, when you tried to move it it would not budge, and so you brought it to my feet; I made it for you, a goad and spur, and you were drawn as though to a woman. This is the strong comrade, the one who brings help to his friend in his need. He is the strongest of wild creatures, the stuff of Anu; born in the grass-lands and the wild hills reared him; when you see him you will be glad; you will love him as a woman and he will never forsake you. This is the meaning of the dream."

Gilgamesh said, "Mother, I dreamed a second dream. In the streets of strong-walled Uruk there lay an axe; the shape of it was strange and the people thronged round. I saw it and was glad. I bent down, deeply drawn towards it; I loved it like a woman and wore it at my side." Ninsun answered, "That axe, which you saw, which drew you so powerfully like love of a woman, that is the comrade whom I give you, and he will come in his strength like one of the host of heaven. He is the brave companion who rescues his friend in necessity." Gilgamesh said to his mother, "A friend, a counsellor has come to me from Enlil, and now I shall befriend and counsel him." So Gilgamesh told his dreams; and the harlot retold them to Enkidu.

And now she said to Enkidu, "When I look at you you have become like a god. Why do you yearn to run wild again with the beasts in the hills? Get up from the ground, the bed of a shepherd." He listened to her words with care. It was good advice that she gave. She divided her clothing in two and with the one half she clothed him and with the other herself; and holding his hand she led him like a child to the sheepfolds, into the shepherds' tents. There all the shepherds crowded round to see him, they put down bread in front of him, but Enkidu could only suck the milk of wild animals. He fumbled and gaped, at a loss what to do or how he should eat the bread and drink the strong wine. Then the woman said, "Enkidu, eat bread, it is the staff of life; drink the wine, it is the custom of the land." So he ate till he was full and drank strong wine, seven goblets. He became merry, his heart exulted and his face shone. He rubbed down the matted hair of his body and anointed himself with oil. Enkidu had become a man; but when he had put on man's clothing he appeared like a bridegroom. He took arms to hunt the lion so that the shepherds could rest at night. He caught wolves and lions and the herdsmen lay down in peace; for Enkidu was their watchman, that strong man who had no rival.

He was merry living with the shepherds, till one day lifting his eyes he saw a man approaching. He said to the harlot, "Woman, fetch that man here. Why has he come? I wish to know his name." She went and called the man saying, "Sir, where are you going on this weary journey?" The man answered, saying to Enkidu, "Gilgamesh has gone into the marriage-house and shut out the people. He does strange things in Uruk, the city of great streets. At the roll of the drum work begins for the men, and work for the women. Gilgamesh the king is about to celebrate marriage with the Queen of Love, and he still demands to be first with the bride, the king to be first and the husband to follow, for that was ordained by the gods from his birth, from the time the umbilical cord was cut. But now the drums roll for the choice of the bride and the city groans." At these words Enkidu turned white in the face. "I will go to the place where Gilgamesh lords it over the people, I will challenge him boldly, and I will cry aloud in Uruk, 'I have come to change the old order, for I am the strongest here.'"

Now Enkidu strode in front and the woman followed behind. He entered Uruk, that great market, and all the folk thronged round him where he stood in the street in strong-walled Uruk. The people jostled; speaking of him they said, "He is the spit of Gilgamesh." "He is shorter." "He is bigger of bone." "This is the one who was reared on the milk of wild beasts. His is the greatest strength." The men rejoiced: "Now Gilgamesh has met his match. This great one, this hero whose beauty is like a god, he is a match even for Gilgamesh."

In Uruk the bridal bed was made, fit for the goddess of love. The bride waited for the bridegroom, but in the night Gilgamesh got up and came to the house. Then Enkidu stepped out, he stood in the street and blocked the way. Mighty Gilgamesh came on and Enkidu met him at the gate. He put out his foot and prevented Gilgamesh from entering the house, so they grappled, holding each other like bulls. They broke the doorposts and the walls shook, they snorted like bulls locked together. They shattered the doorposts and the walls shook. Gilgamesh bent his knee with his foot planted on the ground and with a turn Enkidu was thrown. Then immediately his fury died. When Enkidu was thrown he said to Gilgamesh, "There is not another like you in the world. Ninsun, who is as strong as a wild ox in the byre, she was the mother who bore you, and now you are raised above all men, and Enlil has given you the kingship, for your strength surpasses the strength of men." So Enkidu and Gilgamesh embraced and their friendship was sealed.

There are many stories in the Epic of Gilgamesh. *The following story of the flood is one of the most interesting because of its similarity to the later biblical story of the flood in the book of Genesis.*

The speaker is Utnapishtim, who has a story for Gilgamesh. What is the story? What does this story suggest about Sumerian religion? How is the story similar to the biblical one? What accounts for such similarity?

THE STORY OF THE FLOOD

"You know the city Shurrupak, it stands on the banks of Euphrates? That city grew old and the gods that were in it were old. There was Anu, lord of the firmament, their father, and warrior Enlil their counsellor, Ninurta the helper, and Ennugi watcher over canals; and with them also was Ea. In those days the world teemed, the people multiplied, the world bellowed like a wild bull, and the great god was aroused by the clamour. Enlil heard the clamour and he said to the gods in council, 'The uproar of mankind is intolerable and sleep is no longer possible by reason of the babel.' So the gods agreed to exterminate mankind. Enlil did this, but Ea because of his oath warned me in a dream. He whispered their words to my house of reeds, 'Reed-house, reed-house! Wall, O wall, hearken reed-house, wall reflect; O man of Shurrupak, son of Ubara-Tutu; tear down your house and build a boat, abandon possessions and look for life, despise worldly goods and save your soul alive. Tear down your house, I say, and build a boat. These are the measurements of the barque as you shall build her: let her beam equal her length, let her deck be roofed like the vault that covers the abyss; then take up into the boat the seed of all living creatures.'

"When I had understood I said to my lord, 'Behold, what you have commanded I will honour and perform, but how shall I answer the people, the city, the elders?' The Ea opened his mouth and said to me, his servant, 'Tell them this: I have learnt that Enlil is wrathful against me, I dare no longer walk in his land nor live in his city; I will go down to the Gulf to dwell with Ea my lord. But on you he will rain down abundance, rare fish and shy wild-fowl, a rich harvest-tide. In the evening the rider of the storm will bring you wheat in torrents.'

"In the first light of dawn all my household gathered round me, the children brought pitch and the men whatever was necessary. On the fifth day I laid the keel and the ribs, then I made fast the planking. The ground-space was one acre, each side of the deck measured one hundred and twenty cubits, making a square. I built six decks below, seven in all, I divided them into nine sections with bulkheads between. I drove in wedges where needed, I saw to the punt-poles, and laid in supplies. The carriers brought oil in baskets, I poured pitch into the furnace and asphalt and oil; more oil was consumed in caulking, and more again the master of the boat took into his stores. I slaughtered bullocks for the people and every day I killed sheep. I gave the shipwrights wine to drink as though it were river water, raw wine and red wine and oil and white wine. There was feasting then as there is at the time of the New Year's festival; I myself anointed my head. On the seventh day the boat was complete.

"Then was the launching full of difficulty; there was shifting of ballast above and below till two thirds was submerged. I loaded into her all that I had of gold and of living things, my family, my kin, the beast of the field both wild and tame, and all the craftsmen. I sent them on board, for the time that Shamash had ordained was already fulfilled when he said 'In the evening, when the rider of the storm sends down the destroying rain, enter the boat and batten her down.' The time was fulfilled, the evening came, the rider of the storm sent down the rain. I looked out at the weather and it was terrible, so I too boarded the boat and battened her down. All was now complete, the battening and the caulking; so I handed the tiller to Puzur-Amurri the steersman, with the navigation and the care of the whole boat.

"With the first light of dawn a black cloud came from the horizon; it thundered within where Adad, lord of the storm was riding. In front over hill and plain Shullat and Hanish, heralds of the storm, led on. Then the gods of the abyss rose up; Nergal pulled out the dams of the nether waters, Ninurta the war-lord threw down the dykes, and the seven judges of hell, the Annunaki, raised their torches, lighting the land with their livid flame. A stupor of despair went up to heaven when the god of the storm turned daylight to darkness, when he smashed the land like a cup. One whole day the tempest raged, gathering fury as it went, it poured over the people like the tides of battle; a man could not see his brother nor the people be seen from heaven. Even the gods were terrified at the flood, they fled to the highest heaven, the firmament of Anu; they crouched against the walls, cowering like curs. Then Ishtar the sweet-voiced Queen of Heaven cried out like a woman in travail: 'Alas the days of old are turned to dust because I commanded evil; why did I command this evil in the council of all the gods? I commanded wars to destroy the people, but are they not my people, for I brought them forth? Now like the spawn of fish they float in the ocean.' The great gods of heaven and of hell wept, they covered their mouths.

"For six days and six nights the winds blew, torrent and tempest and flood overwhelmed the world, tempest and flood raged together like warring hosts. When the seventh day dawned the storm from the south subsided, the sea grew calm, the flood was stilled; I looked at the face of the world and there was silence, all mankind was turned to clay. The surface of the sea stretched as flat as a roof-top; I opened a hatch and the light fell on my face. Then I bowed low, I sat down and I wept, the tears streamed down my face, for on every side was the waste of water. I looked for land in vain, but fourteen leagues distant there appeared a mountain, and there the boat grounded; on the mountain of Nisir the boat held fast, she held fast and did not budge. One day she held, and a second day on the mountain of Nisir she held fast and did not budge. A third day, and a fourth day she held fast on the mountain and did not budge; a fifth day and a sixth day she held fast on the mountain. When the seventh day dawned I loosed a dove and let her go. She flew away, but finding no resting-place she returned. Then I loosed a swallow, and she flew away but finding no resting-place she returned. I loosed a raven, she saw that the waters had retreated, she ate, she flew around, she cawed, and she did not come back. Then I threw everything open to the four winds, I made a sacrifice and poured out a libation on the mountain top. Seven and again seven cauldrons I set up on their stands, I heaped up wood and cane and cedar and myrtle. When the gods smelled the sweet savour, they gathered like flies over the sacrifice. Then, at last, Ishtar also came, she lifted her necklace with the jewels of heaven that once Anu had made to please her. 'O you gods here present, by the lapis lazuli round my neck I shall remember these days as I remember the jewels of my throat; these last days I shall not forget. Let all the gods gather round the sacrifice, except Enlil. He shall not approach this offering, for without reflection he brought the flood; he consigned my people to destruction.'

"When Enlil had come, when he saw the boat, he was wrath and swelled with anger at the gods, the host of heaven, 'Has any of these mortals escaped? Not one was to have survived the destruction.' Then the god of the wells and canals Ninurta opened his mouth and said to the warrior Enlil, 'Who is there of the gods that devise without Ea? It is Ea alone who knows all things.' Then Ea opened his mouth and spoke to warrior Enlil, 'Wisest of gods, hero Enlil, how could you so senselessly bring down the flood?

> Lay upon the sinner his sin,
> Lay upon the transgressor his transgression,
> Punish him a little when he breaks loose,
> Do not drive him too hard or he perishes;
> Would that a lion had ravaged mankind
> Rather than the flood,
> Would that a wolf had ravaged mankind
> Rather than the flood,

> Would that famine had wasted the world
> Rather than the flood,
> Would that pestilence had wasted mankind
> Rather than the flood.

It was not I that revealed the secret of the gods; the wise man learned it in a dream. Now take your counsel what shall be done with him.'

"Then Enlil went up into the boat, he took me by the hand and my wife and made us enter the boat and kneel down on either side, he standing between us. He touched our foreheads to bless us saying, 'In time past Utnapishtim was a mortal man; henceforth he and his wife shall live in the distance at the mouth of the rivers.' Thus it was that the gods took me and placed me here to live in the distance, at the mouth of the rivers."

HAMMURABI'S CODE

The Sumerians were overrun after 2000 B.C. by successive waves of invaders from further up the Euphrates River. Among the most successful of these conquerors were the Babylonians who, under Hammurabi (ca. 1792–1750 B.C.) controlled the entire river valley. We remember them for their elaborate code of laws, one of the earliest. It is also the best mirror of their society.

This selection includes only about a fraction of Hammurabi's Code, but it is a fairly representative sample. What do these laws tell us about Babylonian society in the eighteenth century B.C.? To what extent were their legal concerns similar to, or different from, ours today?

THEFT

6. If a man has stolen goods from a temple, or house, he shall be put to death; and he that has received the stolen property from him shall be put to death.

8. If a patrician has stolen ox, sheep, ass, pig, or ship, whether from a temple, or a house, he shall pay thirtyfold. If he be a plebeian, he shall return tenfold. If the thief cannot pay, he shall be put to death.

14. If a man has stolen a child, he shall be put to death.

15. If a man has induced either a male or female slave from the house of a patrician, or plebeian, to leave the city, he shall be put to death.

From C. H. W. Johns, *Babylonian and Assyrian Laws, Contracts, and Letters.* New York: Scribner's, 1904.

21. If a man has broken into a house he shall be killed before the breach and buried there.

22. If a man has committed highway robbery and has been caught, that man shall be put to death.

23. If the highwayman has not been caught, the man that has been robbed shall state on oath what he has lost and the city or district governor in whose territory or district the robbery took place shall restore to him what he has lost.

MARRIAGE

128. If a man has taken a wife and has not executed a marriage-contract, that woman is not a wife.

129. If a man's wife be caught lying with another, they shall be strangled and cast into the water. If the wife's husband would save his wife, the king can save his servant.

130. If a man has ravished another's betrothed wife, who is a virgin, while still living in her father's house, and has been caught in the act, that man shall be put to death; the woman shall go free.

131. If a man's wife has been accused by her husband, and has not been caught lying with another, she shall swear her innocence, and return to her house.

138. If a man has divorced his wife, who has not borne him children, he shall pay over to her as much money as was given for her bride-price and the marriage-portion which she brought from her father's house, and so shall divorce her.

139. If there was no bride-price, he shall give her one mina of silver, as a price of divorce.

140. If he be a plebeian, he shall give her one-third of a mina of silver.

148. If a man has married a wife and a disease has seized her, if he is determined to marry a second wife, he shall marry her. He shall not divorce the wife whom the disease has seized. In the home they made together she shall dwell, and he shall maintain her as long as she lives.

149. If that woman was not pleased to stay in her husband's house, he shall pay over to her the marriage-portion which she brought from her father's house, and she shall go away.

153. If a man's wife, for the sake of another, has caused her husband to be killed, that woman shall be impaled.

154. If a man has committed incest with his daughter, that man shall be banished from the city.

155. If a man has betrothed a maiden to his son and his son has known her, and afterward the man has lain in her bosom, and been caught, that man shall be strangled and she shall be cast into the water.

156. If a man has betrothed a maiden to his son, and his son has not

known her, and that man has lain in her bosom, he shall pay her half a mina of silver, and shall pay over to her whatever she brought from her father's house, and the husband of her choice shall marry her.

186. If a man has taken a young child to be his son, and after he has taken him, the child discovers his own parents, he shall return to his father's house.

188, 189. If a craftsman has taken a child to bring up and has taught him his handicraft, he shall not be reclaimed. If he has not taught him his handicraft that foster child shall return to his father's house.

ASSAULT

195. If a son has struck his father, his hands shall be cut off.

196. If a man has knocked out the eye of a patrician, his eye shall be knocked out.

197. If he has broken the limb of a patrician, his limb shall be broken.

198. If he has knocked out the eye of a plebeian or has broken the limb of a plebeian's servant, he shall pay one mina of silver.

199. If he has knocked out the eye of a patrician's servant, or broken the limb of a patrician's servant, he shall pay half his value.

200. If a patrician has knocked out the tooth of a man that is his equal, his tooth shall be knocked out.

201. If he has knocked out the tooth of a plebeian, he shall pay one-third of a mina of silver.

LIABILITY

229. If a builder has built a house for a man, and has not made his work sound, and the house he built has fallen, and caused the death of its owner, that builder shall be put to death.

230. If it is the owner's son that is killed, the builder's son shall be put to death.

231. If it is the slave of the owner that is killed, the builder shall give slave for slave to the owner of the house.

232. If he has caused the loss of goods, he shall render back whatever he has destroyed. Moreover, because he did not make sound the house he built, and it fell, at his own cost he shall rebuild the house that fell.

237. If a man has hired a boat and a boatman, and loaded it with corn, wool, oil, or dates, or whatever it be, and the boatman has been careless, and sunk the boat, or lost what is in it, the boatman shall restore the boat which he sank, and whatever he lost that was in it.

238. If a boatman has sunk a man's boat, and has floated it again, he shall pay half its value in silver.

251. If a man's ox be a gorer, and has revealed its evil propensity as a gorer, and he has not blunted its horn, or shut up the ox, and then that ox has gored a free man, and caused his death, the owner shall pay half a mina of silver.

252. If it be a slave that has been killed, he shall pay one-third of a mina of silver.

THE STORY OF SI-NUHE

Si-nuhe was an Egyptian court official who fled Egypt around 1962 B.C. when the king, Amen-em-het I, died. We only have this, Si-nuhe's own account of his travels in Syria and his return. Since he and the new Pharoah, Sen-Usert I, seemed eager to forget the past when Si-nuhe returned, we do not know why he fled. It is likely, however, that the death of a king could be a trying time for his loyal officials.

What does Si-nuhe's story tell you about court life in ancient Egypt? What does it tell you about the ease or difficulty of travel in the ancient world? In what ways was Egyptian war and diplomacy different from today? Notice the Egyptian concern with death. Is this why Si-nuhe returns?

The Hereditary Prince and Count, Judge and District Overseer of the domains of the Sovereign in the lands of the Asiatics, real acquaintance of the king, his beloved, the Attendant Si nuhe. He says:

I was an attendant who followed his lord, a servant of the royal harem (and of) the Hereditary Princess, the great of favor, the wife of King Sen-User[1] in (the pyramid town) Khenem-sut, the daughter of King Amen-em-het[2] in (the pyramid town) Qanefru, Nefru, the lady of reverence.

Year 30, third month of the first season, day 7.[3] The god ascended to his horizon,[4] the King of Upper and Lower Egypt: Sehetep-ib-Re[5] was taken up to heaven and united with the sun disc. The body of the god

From James B. Pritchard, *Ancient Near Eastern Texts: Relating to the Old Testament*, second edition. Copyright 1950, 1955, © 1983 renewed by Princeton University Press. Excerpt, pp. 18–22, reprinted with permission of Princeton University Press.

1. Sen-Usert (or Sesostris) I, reigned 1971–1928 B.C. (for nine years reigned jointly with his father, Amen-em-het).

2. Amen-em-het I, reigned 1991–1962 B.C.

3. *Ca.* 1962 B.C., the date of Amen-em-het's death.

4. The dwelling of the sun-god in the sky. Since the Pharaoh was identified with the sun-god, his tomb is also called his "horizon."

5. The official name of Amen-em-het I.

merged with him who made him.[6] The Residence City was in silence, hearts were in mourning, the Great Double Doors[7] were sealed shut. The courtiers (sat) head on lap, and the people were in grief.

Now his majesty had sent an army to the land of the Temeh[8]-Libyans, with his eldest son as the commander thereof, the good god Sen-Usert, and even now he was returning and had carried off living captives of the Tehenu[8]-Libyans and all (kinds of) cattle without number.

The courtiers of the palace sent to the western border to let the King's Son know the events which had taken place at the court. The messengers met him on the road, and they reached him in the evening time. He did not delay a moment; the falcon[9] flew away with his attendants, without letting his army know it. Now the royal children who had been following him in this army had been sent for, and one of them was summoned.[10] While I was standing (near by) I heard his voice as he was speaking and I was a little way off. My heart was distraught, my arms spread out (in dismay), trembling fell upon all my limbs.[11] I removed myself by leaps and bounds to seek a hiding place for myself. I placed myself between two bushes, in order to cut (myself) off from the road and its travel.

I set out southward, (but) I did not plan to reach this Residence City, (for) I thought that there would be civil disorder, and I did not expect to live after him. I crossed Lake Ma'aty[12] near Sycamore,[12] and I came to Snefru Island.[12] I spent the day there on the edge of the fields. I came into the open light, while it was (still) day, and I met a man standing near by. He stood in awe of me, for he was afraid. When the time of the evening meal came, I drew near to Ox-town.[12] I crossed over in a barge without a rudder,[13] by aid of the west wind. I passed by the east of the quarry above Mistress-of-the-Red-Mountain.[14] I gave (free) road to my feet going northward, and I came up to the Wall-of-the-Ruler,[15] made to oppose the Asiatics and to crush the Sand-Crossers. I took a crouching position in a bush, for fear lest the watchmen upon the wall where their day's (duty) was might see me.

I set out at evening time, and when day broke I reached Peten. I

6. At death the Pharaoh was taken back into the body of his father, the sun-god.
7. The entrance to Pharaoh's palace.
8. The Temeh and Tehenu were Libyan tribes who frequently raided the Delta region.
9. The new king, Sen-Usert I.
10. This seems to refer to a plot to set up a rival king.
11. Note the relation of Si-nuhe's fright to the conversation of the summoned prince.
12. Localities unknown. Apparently Si-nuhe avoided the cultivated stretches of the Delta and crossed the Nile where it is a single stream, somewhere near the location of modern Cairo.
13. A broad vessel such as was employed in the transport of stone.
14. An elevation east of modern Cairo, a source for a kind of reddish-brown sandstone used in statues. The "mistress" is the goddess worshipped there.
15. A fortress on the eastern frontier along the general line of the present Suez Canal, meant to repel the Syrian nomads.

halted at the Island of Lem-wer.[16] An attack of thirst overtook me. I was parched, and my throat was dusty. I said: "This is the taste of death!" (But then) I lifted up my heart and collected myself, for I had heard the sound of the lowing of cattle, and I spied Asiatics. The sheikh among them, who had been in Egypt, recognized me.[17] Then he gave me water while he boiled milk for me. I went with him to his tribe. What they did (for me) was good.[18]

One foreign country gave me to another. I set off for Byblos[19] and approached Qedem,[20] and spent a year and a half there. Ammi-enshi[21]—he was a ruler of Upper Retenu[22]—took me and said to me: "Thou wilt do well with me, and thou wilt hear the speech of Egypt." He said this, for he knew my character, he had heard of my wisdom, and the people of Egypt who were there with him had borne witness for me.

Then he said to me: "Why hast thou come hither? Has something happened in the Residence City?" Then I said to him: "The King of Upper and Lower Egypt: Sehetep-ib-Re is departed to the horizon, and no one knows what might happen because of it." But I said equivocally: "I had come from an expedition to the land of Temeh, when report was made to me. My heart quailed; it carried me off on the way of flight. (Yet) no one had gossiped about me; no one had spat in my face; not a belittling word had been heard, nor had my name been heard in the mouth of the herald.[23] I do not know what brought me to this country. It was as though it might be a god."[24]

Then he said to me: "Well, what will that land be like without him, that beneficent god, the fear of whom pervaded foreign countries like (the fear of) Sekhmet[25] in a year of pestilence?" I spoke to him that I might answer him: "Well, of course, his son has entered into the palace and has taken the inheritance of his father. Moreover, he is a god without his peer. There is no other who surpasses him. He is a master of under-standing, effective in plans and beneficent of decrees. Going forth[26] and coming back are in conformance with his command. He it was who subdued the foreign countries while his father was in his palace, and he reported to him that what had been charged to him had been carried

16. Lakes on the Isthmus of Suez.
17. This indicates that Si-nuhe was well known in Egypt.
18. I.e., they treated me kindly.
19. The port of Lebanon from which the Egyptians imported wood.
20. (Or Kedemi): Semitic word for "the East" in general.
21. An Amorite name unfamiliar to the Egyptian scribe, who tried to egyptianize it to "Amu's son Enshi."
22. The highland country of northern Palestine and south-central Syria.
23. I.e., "There was no official charge against me."
24. I.e., a supernatural intervention.
25. A goddess associated with disease.
26. To war.

out. . . .[27] How joyful is this land which he has ruled! He is one who extends its frontiers. He will carry off the lands of the south, and he will not consider the northern countries (seriously), (for) he was made to smite the Asiatics and to crush the Sand-Crossers. Send to him! Let him know thy name! Do not utter a curse against his majesty. He will not fail to do good to the country which shall be loyal to him!"

Then he said to me: "Well, really, Egypt is happy that it knows that he is flourishing. Now thou art here. Thou shalt stay with me. What I shall do for thee is good."

He set me at the head of his children. He married me to his eldest daughter. He let me choose for myself of his country, of the choicest of that which was with him on his frontier with another country. It was a good land, named Yaa.[28] Figs were in it, and grapes. It had more wine than water. Plentiful was its honey, abundant its olives. Every (kind of) fruit was on its trees. Barley was there, and emmer [wheat]. There was no limit to any (kind of) cattle. Moreover, great was that which accrued to me[29] as a result of the love of me. He made me ruler of a tribe of the choicest of his country. Bread was made for me as daily fare, wine as daily provision, cooked meat and roast fowl, beside the wild beasts of the desert, for they hunted for me and laid before me, beside the catch of my (own) hounds. Many . . . were made for me, and milk in every (kind of) cooking.

I spent many years, and my children grew up to be strong men, each man as the restrainer of his (own) tribe. The messenger who went north or who went south to the Residence City[30] stopped over with me, (for) I used to make everybody stop over. I gave water to the thirsty. I put him who had stayed (back) on the road. I rescued him who had been robbed. When the Asiatics became so bold as to oppose the rulers of foreign countries,[31] I counseled their movements. This rule of (Re)tenu had me spend many years as commander of his army. Every foreign country against which I went forth, when I had made my attack on it, was driven away from its pasturage and its wells. I plundered its cattle, carried off its inhabitants, took away their food, and slew people in it by my strong arm, by my bow, by my movements, and by my successful plans. I found favor in his heart, he loved me, he recognized my valor, and he placed me at the head of his children, when he saw how my arms flourished.

---

27. A series of flattering epithets for Pharaoh is omitted here.

28. Yaa: the precise location of this place is not known, though it must have been in the general area of northern Palestine or southern Syria (Retenu). It was close enough to some main road so that Si-nuhe could entertain traveling Egyptians.

29. I.e., "the gifts which I received."

30. Of the Egyptian king.

31. I.e., of other foreign countries. The Egyptian term used here, *Heqaukhasut*, is the probable origin of the term "Hyksos." This may be an early reference to nomadic peoples who would later participate in the invasion of Egypt.

. . .

Now when the majesty of the King of Upper and Lower Egypt: Kheper-ka-Re, the justified,[32] was told about this situation in which I was,[33] then his majesty kept sending to me with presentations from the royal presence, that he might gladden the heart of this servant[34] like the ruler of any foreign country. The royal children in his palace let me hear their commissions.[35]

Copy of the decree which was brought to this servant about bringing him back to Egypt.

"The Hours: Living in Births; the Two Goddesses: Living in Births; the King of Upper and Lower Egypt: Kheper-ka-Re; the Son of Re: Amen-em-het,[36] living forever and ever. Royal decree to the Attendant Si-nuhe. Behold, this decree of the king is brought to thee to let thee know that:

"Thou hast traversed the foreign countries, starting from Qedem to (Re)tenu. One country gave thee to another, under the advice of thy (own) heart to thee. What hast thou done that anything should be done to thee? Thou has not cursed, that thy word should be punished. Thou has not spoken against the counsel of the nobles, that they speeches should be opposed. This plan (simply) carried away thy heart. It was in no heart against thee. This thy heaven which is in the palace[37] is firm and steadfast today. Her head is covered with the kingship of the land.[38] Her children are in the court.

"Mayest thou lay up treasures which they may give thee; mayest thou live on their bounty. Do thou return to Egypt, that thou mayest see the home in which thou didst grow up and kiss the ground at the Great Double Door and join with the courtiers. For today, surely, thou hast begun to grow old; thou hast lost (thy) virility. Recall thou the day of burial, the passing to a revered state,[39] when the evening is set aside for thee with ointments and wrappings from the hand of Tait.[40] A funeral procession is made for thee on the day of interment, a mummy case of gold, with head of lapis lazuli, with the heaven above thee,[41] as thou art

32. Sen-Usert I.
33. Perhaps this negotiation was undertaken by one of the envoys whom Si-nuhe was in the habit of entertaining as they passed through his domain.
34. Servant: polite expression for "I."
35. I.e., they also wrote to him.
36. Scribal error for Sen-Usert.
37. The queen.
38. I.e., she wears the insignia of rule.
39. Thy coming to an honored death. The following sentences describe embalming and burial.
40. The goddess of weaving.
41. The canopy over the hearse, or possibly the lid of the sarcophagus, which was thought to symbolize the sky-goddess, Nut.

placed upon a sledge,[42] oxen dragging thee and singers in front of thee, when the dance of the muu[43] is performed at the door of thy tomb, when the requirements of the offering table are summoned for thee and there is sacrifice beside thy offering stones, thy pillars[44] being hewn of white stone in the midst of (the tombs of) the royal children. It should not be that thou shouldst die in a foreign country. Asiatics should not escort thee. Thou shouldst not be placed in a sheep-skin when thy wall is made. This is (too) long to be roaming the earth. Give heed to sickness, that thou mayest return."[45]

This decree reached me as I was standing in the midst of my tribe. It was read to me. I put myself upon my belly; I touched the ground; I scattered it upon my hair. I went about my encampment rejoicing and saying: "How can this be done for a servant whom his heart led astray to barbarous countries? But the indulgence which saved me from death is really good! Thy ka[46] will let me effect the end of my body at home!"

Copy of the answer to this decree. The Servant of the Palace Si-nuhe says:

"In very good peace![47] This flight which this servant made in his ignorance is known by thy ka, O good god, Lord of the Two Lands,[48] whom Re loves and whom Montu, Lord of Thebes, favors! . . .[49]

"This is the prayer of this servant to his Lord, the saviour in the West:[50] The lord of perception, who perceives people, may he perceive[51] in the majesty of the palace that this servant was afraid to say it. It is (still) like something (too) big to repeat.[52] . . . Further, may thy majesty command that there be brought Maki from Qedem, Kenti-iaush from Khent-keshu, and Menus from the lands of the Fenkhu.[53] They are men exact and reliable, young men who grew up in the love of thee—not to mention (Re)tenu: it is thine, like thy (own) hands.[54]

"Now this flight which the servant made, it was not planned, it was not in my heart, I had not worried about it. I do not know what severed me from (my) place. It was after the manner of a dream, as if a man of the

42. The common means of transporting heavy loads.
43. A funerary dance.
44. The pillars of the tomb.
45. I.e., you have been following the nomadic life for too long. Remember that you are of an age when a sickness might carry you off and deprive you of burial in Egypt.
46. Usually, the force in a man which keeps him alive, his personality, but here merely a poetic expression for "thou."
47. May you read this writing.
48. Upper and Lower Egypt.
49. This translation omits the good wishes for the king which follow.
50. The realm of the dead.
51. I.e., may he perceive Si-nuhe's wish.
52. Si-nuhe feels that his case is too delicate to be stated directly.
53. It is unclear whether Si-nuhe suggests these Asiastics as reliable character witnesses, as hostages, or as escort. Fenkhu: perhaps Phoenicia.
54. I.e., Retenu is well-disposed toward Pharaoh.

Delta were to see himself in Elephantine,[55] or a man of the (northern) marshes in Nubia.[56] I had not been afraid. No one had run after me. I had not heard a belittling word. My name had not been heard in the mouth of the herald. And yet—my body shuddered, my feet were trembling, my heart led me on, and the god who ordained this flight drew me away. I was not at all stiff-backed formerly.[57] A man who knows his land should be afraid, (for) Re has set the fear of thee throughout the earth, and the dread of thee in every foreign country. Whether I am at home or whether I am in this place, thou art he who covers this horizon,[58] the sun disc rises at thy pleasure, the water in the River is drunk as thou wishest, and the air in the sky is breathed as thou biddest. This servant will hand over the viziership which this servant has exercised in this place."[59]

Then they came for this servant. . . . I was permitted to spend a day in Yaa handing over my property to my children, my eldest son being responsible for my tribe. My tribe and all my property were in his charge: my serfs, all my cattle, my fruit, and every pleasant tree of mine.

Then this servant came southward. I halted at the "Ways of Horus."[60] The commander there who was responsible for the patrol sent a message to the Residence to make (it) known. Then his majesty sent a capable overseer of peasants of the palace, with loaded ships in his train, carrying presentations from the royal presence for the Asiatics who had followed me, escorting me to the "Ways of Horus." I called each of them by his name.[61] Every butler was (busy) at his duties. When I started and set sail, the kneading and straining (of beer) was carried on beside me, until I had reached the town of Lisht.[62]

When day had broken, very early, they came and summoned me, ten men coming and ten men going to usher me to the palace.[63] I put my brow to the ground between the sphinxes,[64] while the royal children were waiting in a recess to meet me. The courtiers who usher into the audience hall set me on the way to the private chambers. I found his majesty upon the Great Throne in a recess of fine gold. When I was stretched out upon my belly, I knew not myself in his presence,[65] (although) this god greeted me pleasantly. I was like a man caught in the

---

55. An island in the first cataract of the Nile: the southern boundary of Egypt.
56. Region south of Egypt, now northern Sudan.
57. I.e., it was not insolence or presumption which led him astray.
58. I.e., can cause night to fall.
59. Si-nuhe maintains the flattering pretense that he has been ruling his part of Retenu on behalf of Pharaoh.
60. The Egyptian frontier station facing Sinai.
61. He paid the Asiatics the compliment of introducing them to Pharaoh.
62. The capital at that time, some distance south of the later Memphis.
63. Ten men were assigned to summon him and ten to escort him.
64. Or statues.
65. I.e., "I lost my presence of mind."

dark: my soul departed, my body was powerless, my heart was not in my body, that I might know life from death.

Then his majesty said to one of these courtiers: "Lift him up. Let him speak to me." Then his majesty said: "Behold, thou art come. Thou hast trodden the foreign countries and made a flight. (But now) elderliness has attacked thee; thou hast reached old age. It is no small matter that thy corpse be (properly) buried; thou shouldst not be interred by bowmen.[66] Do not, do not act thus any longer: (for) thou dost not speak when thy name is pronounced!" Yet (I) was afraid to respond, and I answered it with the answer of one afraid: "What is it that my lord says to me? I should answer it, (but) there is nothing that I can do: it is really the hand of a god. It is a terror that is in my belly like that which produced the fated flight. Behold, I am before thee. Thine is life. May thy majesty do as he pleases.

Thereupon the royal children were ushered in. Then his majesty said to the Queen: "Here is Si-nuhe, come as a Bedu,[67] (in) the guise of the Asiatics." She gave a very great cry, and the royal children clamored all together. Then they said to his majesty: "It is not really he, O Sovereign, my lord!" Then his majesty said: "It is really he!"[68] Now when they had brought with them their bead-necklaces, their rattles, and their sistra, then they presented them to his majesty.[69] . . . Loose the horn of thy bow and relax thy arrow![70] Give breath to him that was stifled! Give us our goodly gift in this sheikh Si-Mehit,[71] a bowman born in Egypt. He made a flight through fear of thee; he left the land through terror of thee. (But) the face of him who beholds thy face shall not blench; the eye which looks at thee shall not be afraid!"

Then his majesty said: "He shall not fear. He has no title to be in dread. He shall be a courtier among the nobles. He shall be put in the ranks of the courtiers. Proceed ye to the inner chambers of the morning (toilet), in order to make his position.[72]

So I went forth from the midst of the inner chambers, with the royal children giving me their hands. Thereafter we went to the Great Double Door. I was put into the house of a royal son, in which were splendid things. A cool room was in it, and images of the horizon.[73] Costly things

---

66. Foreigners.
67. Bedouin.
68. They do not recognize the formerly elegant courtier in the wild Bedouin.
69. Rattles and sistra: musical instruments. The large necklaces are the symbols of their goddess, Hathor (ancient sky-goddess and goddess of women). By reaching out these instruments to someone during a dance, the women thereby present him with the goddess's blessing.
70. I.e., set the man free.
71. A designation of Si-nuhe, on his return from Asia, as "Son of the North Wind."
72. Si-nuhe's new rank is to be established by a change of dress.
73. Painted decorations. The "cool room" may have been a bathroom or a cellar for preserving foods.

of the Treasury were in it. Clothing of royal linen, myrrh, and prime oil of the king and of the nobles whom he loves were in every room. Every butler was (busy) at his duties. Years were made to pass away from my body. I was plucked, and my hair was combed. A load (of dirt) was given to the desert, and my clothes (to) the Sand-Crossers. I was clad in fine linen and anointed with prime oil. I slept on a bed, I gave up the sand to them who are in it, and wood oil to him who is anointed with it. I was given a house which had a garden, which had been in the possession of a courtier. Many craftsmen built it, and all its wood (work) was newly restored. Meals were brought to me from the palace three or four times a day, apart from that which the royal children gave, without ceasing a moment.

There was constructed for me a pyramid-tomb of stone in the midst of the pyramid-tombs.74 The stone-masons who hew a pyramid-tomb took over its ground-area. The outline-draftsmen designed in it; the chief sculptors carved in it; and the overseers of works who are in the necropolis made it their concern.75 Its necessary materials were made from all the outfittings which are placed at a tomb-shaft.76 Mortuary priests were given to me. There was made for me a necropolis garden, with fields in it formerly (extending) as far as the town, like that which is done for a chief courtier. My statute77 was overlaid with gold, and its skirt was of fine gold. It was his majesty who had it made. There is no poor man for whom the like has been done.

(So) I was under the favor of the king's presence until the day of mooring had come.78 It has come (to its end), from beginning to end as it had been found in writing.

74. The members of Pharaoh's court are buried around his grave.
75. I.e., the best craftsmen who work on the royal pyramids are also employed on the pyramid of Si-nuhe.
76. I.e., the various offerings which a well-equipped tomb of this period contained.
77. The statue erected in his tomb.
78. I.e., the day of death.

3. THE ANCIENT CIVILIZATIONS OF ASIA

INDUS CIVILIZATION AND THE ARYAN INVASION

FRANCIS WATSON

Ancient Indus civilization, especially that of the two principal cities on the Indus River, Mohenjo-Daro and Harappa, rivaled that of the Middle East after 3000 B.C. It was completely destroyed, however, by the time of the Aryan invasion of about 1500 B.C. Consequently, Indian civilization today owes much more to the Aryan invaders than to the ancient cities of the Indus.

As you read this history of ancient India, note how ancient Indus civilization was similar to, and different from, the civilizations of the ancient Middle East. What were the new elements introduced by the Aryans?

From about 3000 B.C. in about a hundred sites so far uncovered, over a huge area of the Indus plain—almost a thousand miles from north to south—the pottery styles show a startling uniformity. The semi-isolated settlements had been succeeded by something very different: a homogenous realm of villages and townships, with the river as the axis of communication, and with an agricultural surplus sufficient to support two capital cities, more than 350 miles apart: Mohenjo-Daro in the south, Harappa in the north.

Standardization, an ordered society, and ten centuries of relatively stable conditions, are among the surprising features revealed by excavation of these two urban centres. Both made use of vast quantities of baked bricks, presupposing the existence of forests to provide firing fuel. The ground-plans of both were not only similar, but retained through successive phases of rebuilding a common principle, with a raised citadel, or acropolis, on the west, main streets laid out in grid-iron fashion, a network of lanes within each block, the better houses concealed in courtyards, and in both cities a clearly defined labourers' quarter. The great size of the granaries indicates a strong centralized authority, and the water-supply and drainage systems were extremely thorough. "No Indian city", writes Dr. Kosambi, "possessed anything of the sort until modern times; far too many still lack these amenities."

This civic sophistication sets the Indus civilization apart from its great contemporaries in Sumer and Akkad and Middle Kingdom Egypt. Its written language, which might dispel some of the mystery, remains undeciphered, and has survived only in brief seal-inscriptions apparently concerned with property or commerce. There seem to be no religious dedications, no names of rulers, and so far no dynastic tombs to shed light on a hierarchical system. The terracotta seals, of a type distinct from the Sumerian, are at once enigmatic and suggestive in the frequently consummate quality of their engraved images and in the subjects depicted, which include animals such as the elephant, tiger, rhinoceros and the Indian humped and dewlapped bull—as well as mythical beasts, emblems and figures. A horned deity depicted on some of the seals, seated in yogic posture, with erect phallus and accompanied by wild animals, has been seen as an early prototype of the Hindu god Shiva. The numerous small clay figurines of an earth-goddess, primitive by contrast with the seal-engravings, point to a popular fertility-cult; but the absence of monuments, religious or secular, is singular.

At Mohenjo-Daro the enormous stone bath on the citadel mound is presumed to have served ritual ablutions. Other evidence, such as the long conservation of a static pattern of life, has been used to support the argument for a dominant priesthood. All that we really know is that existence at this remote period must have been comfortable for an elite and was certainly highly organized. Humped cattle and buffaloes, goats, sheep and pigs, the camel and the elephant had all been domesticated, though not the horse (which has always, for some reason, presented breeding difficulties in India). The dog, first trained by Paleolithic hunters, left his urban traces at the Indus site of Chanhu-Daro, in footprints chasing those of a cat across the once wet surface of some brickwork. The domestic fowl, one of India's gifts to the world, had by this time been tamed from the jungle-fowl.

Another distinctive Indian product, cotton, was already in use for clothing, as well as wool. Barley and wheat were the chief food crops, and both meat and fish were eaten. Iron was as yet unknown. Copper (probably from Rajasthan east of the Indus) was extensively used for household implements, though some of them were still of stone. Upper-class luxury and advanced craftsmanship were displayed in adornments of gold and silver, ivory, jade, agate, crystal, lapis lazuli and other fine materials; and the absence of large works of art by which to distinguish the Indus culture is compensated, not only by the best of the seals, but by a number of small sculptures—a bronze dancing-girl, a male torso, heads in steatite, and others—each of which has won high admiration in our own day.

There is enough that is unique and indigenous about Harappa and Mohenjo-Daro to leave the question of influence from or upon the Sumerian culture an open one. Of a flourishing trade between the two there is firm evidence, both by land across the Iranian plateau and by sea from a port near the mouth of the Indus. Hugging the dangerous coastline to reach the Persian Gulf, Indian crews used a "compass-bird"—a crow which would fly when released towards the nearest point of land. The story that was later included in the Buddhist *Jatakas* of traders to Babylon using this device—exactly as recorded of Noah in the Bible and of Gilgamesh in the Sumerian epic—is pictorially confirmed on one of the Mesopotamian seals.

Recent excavations have shown the Indus civilization to have been wider in its extent and influence than was previously supposed; and the uniformity of the evidence over an immense area has promoted Sir Mortimer Wheeler to infer "something like an imperial status . . . the vastest political experiment before the Roman Empire." Its mysterious obliteration is thereby rendered all the more intriguing. However the people of the Indus cities met their doom, the Aryans who succeeded them were barbarians in comparison, though their self-given name meant "noble" or "free-born."

THE COMING OF THE ARYANS

From early in the second millennium B.C. the urban cultures of Western Asia were increasingly threatened by that recurrent instrument of history, the hardy nomads of the grasslands of Central Asia. In the words of the Mesopotamian chroniclers, "their onslaught was like a hurricane: a people who had never known a city." The tribes who brought their Aryan languages and their Aryan gods to Iran and India, while a separate wave flowed westwards into Europe, may not have been the sole executioners of the Indus civilization. Mohenjo-Daro in particular provides evidence of trouble and decay over several centuries before 1500 B.C., the date now roughly agreed for the first Aryan immigrations through the passes of the Hindu Kush. But the same site also illustrates, with a huddle of skeletons, the final drama of an overwhelmed defence. There is also, in the collection of Sankrit hymns called *Rig-Veda*, the earliest product of the Vedic tradition from which, in default of material remains, our knowledge of the next millennium has somehow to be gleaned. Renowned for the beauty of its invocations to the creative spirit of the natural world, this tradition is at the same time positive in the pride of conquest and the concept of racial and religious superiority.

The *Rig-Veda* was not at first committed to writing, but memorized. Almost a quarter of its hymns are addressed to the rain-god Indra, not simply as the seasonal banisher of drought but as the great storm-warrior and wielder of the thunderbolt. Irresistible in strength, gargantuan in appetite, fair-complexioned and bursting with rude vigour, Indra often calls to mind the deified hero of some Norse or Celtic myth. From details of his exploits, the horse-drawn chariot of the Aryans, holding a charioteer and a warrior, can be reconstructed as a prime factor of conquest in the plains. The horse, praised in splendid verses in the *Rig-Veda*, must have been as terrifying a novelty to the foe as it was to prove in the Spanish conquest of the Incas in the sixteenth century, but there is little evidence of its use independently of the chariot: effective cavalry had to wait the curiously late invention of the stirrup. "Destroyer of Citadels" is one of Indra's epithets, and in the Land of the Seven Rivers (later to be reduced by desiccation to the five which gave the Punjab its name) he assisted an Aryan chief by tearing to pieces "like old clothes" the defending forces of a place called Hariyupiya—surely Harappa? In his capacity as "Releaser of Waters," moreover, Indra is praised for feats suggesting the destruction of the dams now known to have been in use for flood control and irrigation in the basin of the Indus, which by shifting its course had caused Mohenjo-Daro to be rebuilt several times. "On circumstantial evidence," to quote Wheeler again, "Indra stands accused."

The Sanskrit vocabulary is rich in pejorative terms for the appearance, customs and character of the various peoples encountered by the invaders, whether as enemies in pitched battle, peasant communities overrun, cattle-raiders, refugees from defended cities, or wild forest-hunters. Often they were "noseless" or flat-faced demons, and always they were "godless" in their unseemly ways and their indifference to the Aryan pantheon, its rites and sacrifices. From the post-Vedic epics and *Puranas* (miscellaneous sacred texts) such fanciful opprobrium as the description of one-legged aborigines who shaded themselves with a single enormous foot found its way many centuries later, through Pliny and other classical writers, into the travel-lore of medieval Europe.

The generalized name of *dasas*, which began by meaning "enemies" and came to mean "subjects," at all times carried the signification of a darker-skinned race. It would be an over-simplification to suppose that the descendants of the Aryans are found today in the northern half of India and in the higher castes, and the indigenous (Dravidian) strain in the South, in the lower castes and among the tribes. But the persistence of a social prejudice in favour of a light (in matrimonial advertisements "wheaten") complexion cannot be overlooked. In this connection it is often pointed out that the word *varna*, as applied to the four-class system recognized from Vedic times, means "colour" ("caste" comes from the Portuguese and was not used before the sixteenth century). These four classes were of priests (*brahmans*), warriors (*kshatriyas*), peasant farmers (*vaishyas*) and serfs (*shudras*), and in theory the subjugated elements could be admitted into the Aryan system only at the lowest level. The religious sanction for a strict maintenance of the four divisions, however, is either a late Vedic text or, as some think, a subsequent interpolation at a period when miscegenation had gone so far as to threaten the whole system. There is a note almost of desperation in the invocation which lays one more task upon the mighty Indra: "O Indra, find out who is an Aryan and who is a Dasa, and separate them!"

Behind the advancing warriors, agricultural settlement accompanied and gradually gained over pastoral nomadism, in which wealth was at first entirely in cattle. Herds of oxen, sheep and goats gave the Aryans meat (taboos against beef or other flesh were not yet in operation), milk products, and wool for their few garments. The knowledge of cotton cultivation had vanished for the time being with the civilization of their predecessors, but barley and possibly wheat were grown at the first stage of settlement. *Soma*, the unidentified and sanctified potion used in ritual, was one of several intoxicants. Women appear to have had a respected status, and there is no reference to child-marriage. Games, dancing and chariot-races are mentioned in the early Vedas, which also include the lament of an unsuccessful gambler. Musical instruments were developed, and jewellery of some kind came to be worn by the more important Aryans, but no art-objects have survived for comparison either with those found in the Indus culture or with the admired "animal style" produced by the nomads of the Euro-Asian steppes. Their absence might be partly attributed to the burning of their dead by the Indo-Aryans, but simple burial was also practised.

The ways of these vigorous clans and families pushing in from the northwest differed totally from those that had characterized the long-established cities of the Indus valley. In this sense, as has been said, the newcomers were barbarians. But they were not primitive. They had no written language because they needed none, but the feat of memorizing and handing down an increasing body of oral "literature" has to be borne in mind as we peruse it for clues to their life and thought. After the loss of the characters used by the Indus civilization there is no evidence of a script until about the fourth century B.C., a thousand years later, though some use of writing must be presumed from perhaps a couple of centuries earlier. As spoken tongues, the sacred and elaborate Sanskrit and the "natural" vernaculars, generally called Prakrit and reflecting a degree of Aryan mingling with the indigenous peoples, existed side by side. Even after Sanskrit was fully mature, however, the priestly ban on the committal of the religious texts to writing was effective for many centuries. The oldest *known* manuscript of the *Rig-Veda* dates from the fifteenth century A.D.—nearly three thousand years after the assumed time of its composition—but the Vedic hymns are used today at Hindu wedding ceremonies, in an astonishing example of continuous tradition.

The Vedas:
1. The Rig-Veda—
Sacrifice as Creation

Indian Hinduism is rooted in the Vedic Age (1500–600 B.C.) which opened with the Aryan invasion after the disappearance of the ancient Harappa culture. The Vedas are the writings of the priests. They cover a wide variety of religious subjects and concerns: ritual, sacrifice, hymns, healing, incantations, allegories, philosophy, and the problems of everyday life. In general, the earliest Vedas (like the Rig-Veda) *are more concerned with the specifics of ritual and sacrifice. They are carefully composed, but reflect the needs and instruction of the priests during the Aryan conquest. The last of the Vedas (like the Upanishads) are in general more philosopical: less concerned with ritual and more speculative.*

This first selection is from the Rig-Veda. *What happened when Purusha was sacrificed? What is the meaning of this first sacrifice? How does this story support the role of the priests? How does it support the divisions of Indian society?*

Thousand-headed Purusha, thousand-eyed, thousand-footed—he having pervaded the earth on all sides, still extends ten fingers beyond it.

Purusha alone is all this—whatever has been and whatever is going to be. Further, he is the lord of immortality and also of what grows for food.

Such is his greatness; greater, indeed, than this is Purusha. All creatures constitute but one quarter of him, his three quarters are the immortal in heaven. . . . Being born, he projected himself behind the earth as also before it.

When the gods performed the sacrifice with Purusha as the oblation [religious offering], then the spring was its clarified butter, the summer the sacrificial fuel, and the autumn the oblation.

The sacrificial victim, namely, Purusha, born at the very beginning, they sprinkled with sacred water upon the sacrificial grass. With him as oblation the gods performed the sacrifice, and also the Sādhyas [a class of semidivine beings] and the rishis [ancient seers].

From that wholly offered sacrificial oblation were born the verses and the sacred chants; from it were born the meters; the sacrificial formula was born from it.

From it horses were born and also those animals who have double rows of teeth; cows were born from it, from it were born goats and sheep.

When they divided Purusha, in how many different portions did they arrange him? What became of his mouth, what of his two arms? What were his two thighs and his two feet called?

His mouth became the brāhman; his two arms were made into the rājanya; his two thighs the vaishyas; from his two feet the shūdra was born.

The moon was born from the mind, from the eye the sun was born; from the mouth Indra and Agni, from the breath the wind was born.

From the navel was the atmosphere created, from the head the heaven issued forth; from the two feet was born the earth and the quarters (the cardinal directions) from the ear. Thus did they fashion the worlds.

Seven were the enclosing sticks in this sacrifice, thrice seven were the fire-sticks made, when the gods, performing the sacrifice, bound down Purusha, the sacrificial victim.

With this sacrificial oblation did the gods offer the sacrifice. These were the first norms (dharma) of sacrifice. These greatnesses reached to the sky wherein live the ancient Sādhyas and gods.

The Vedas:
2. The Upanishads—
Brahman and Atman

The Upanishads, the "crown" and completion of the Vedic age, were more philosophical than the earlier Vedas. They treated sacrifice symbolically, preferring meditation, contemplation, and psychological inquiry to the details of a priestly ritual. The numerous gods of the early Vedas were replaced by a single, mysterious Brahman, which was equivalent to each and every interior self (atman).

This selection from the Chandogya Upanishad begins by comparing the chanting of the Gayatri morning offering with the Brahman. What is

From *The Upanishads* (Penguin Classics, 1965), translated by Juan Mascaro. Copyright © 1965 by Juan Mascaro. Reproduced by permission of Penguin Books Ltd., London.

meant by this comparison? What is the Brahman? This universal Brahman is identified with the atman, *or Spirit. What does this mean? What is the point of this identification?*

Great is the Gayatri, the most sacred verse of the Vedas; but how much greater is the Infinity of Brahman! A quarter of his being is this whole vast universe: the other three quarters are his heaven of Immortality.   (3.12.5)

There is a Light that shines beyond all things on earth, beyond us all, beyond the heavens, beyond the highest, the very highest heavens. This is the Light that shines in our heart.   (3.13.7)

All this universe is in the truth Brahman. He is the beginning and end and life of all. As such, in silence, give unto him adoration.

Man in truth is made of faith. As his faith is in this life, so he becomes in the beyond: with faith and vision let him work.

There is a Spirit that is mind and life, light and truth and vast spaces. He contains all works and desires and all perfumes and all tastes. He enfolds the whole universe, and in silence is loving to all.

This is the Spirit that is in my heart, smaller than a grain of rice, or a grain of barley, or a grain of mustard-seed, or a grain of canary-seed, or the kernel of a grain of canary-seed. This is the Spirit that is in my heart, greater than the earth, greater than the sky, greater than heaven itself, greater than all these worlds.

He contains all works and desires and all perfumes and all tastes. He enfolds the whole universe and in silence is loving to all. This is the Spirit that is in my heart, this is Brahman.

To him I shall come when I go beyond this life. And to him will come he who has faith and doubts not. Thus said Sandilya, thus said Sandilya.   (3.14)

The Vedas:
3. The Upanishads—
Karma

One of the speculations of the Upanishads concerned the effects of moral and immoral actions. Actions are karma. *Good actions bring good*

From *The Upanishads* (Penguin Classics, 1965), translated by Juan Mascaro. Copyright © 1965 by Juan Mascaro. Reproduced by permission of Penguin Books Ltd., London.

karma; bad actions increase bad karma. There is no divine judgment, confession, forgiveness, heaven, or hell. Instead good karma increases one's goodness. This is not only true in this life, but the next life as well.

This selection from the Brihad-aranyaka Upanishad summarizes the doctrine of karma. How does the "doer of good become good"? Is this an optimistic or pessimistic view of human nature? According to this view, are people in charge of their own destinies?

According as a man acts and walks in the path of life, so he becomes. He that does good becomes good; he that does evil becomes evil. By pure actions he becomes pure; by evil actions he becomes evil.

And they say in truth that a man is made of desire. As his desire is, so is his faith. As his faith is, so are his works. As his works are, so he becomes. It was said in this verse:

A man comes with his actions to the end of his determination.

Reaching the end of the journey begun by his works on earth, from that world a man returns to this world of human action.

Thus far for the man who lives under desire.

SHANG CHINA

DUN J. LI

The Shang Dynasty (c. 1766–c. 1122 b.c.) is the oldest Chinese dynasty that we know much about. It established an extensive civilization in the Yellow River valley in the north, centered at the capital city of Yin. This reading is by a modern historian.

How was Chinese civilization similar to, or different from, those of the Middle East and India? What effects did the system of Chinese writing have on Chinese society?

Shang originally was the name of a nomadic tribe, moving from place to place until it finally settled in Shangch'iu of modern Honan province. Through contacts with the more advanced Chinese tribes, it gradually adopted agriculture and acquired the sophisticated culture of a sedentary society. Meanwhile, it lost none of the vigor and vitality of a nomadic horde. In the eighteenth century b.c. a great leader emerged who,

Excerpted from Dun J. Li, *The Ageless Chinese: A History*, third edition. Copyright © 1978 Charles Scribner's Sons. Reprinted with the permission of Charles Scribner's Sons.

through diplomacy and warfare, annexed most of his neighboring states. This leader, T'ang, was not only noted for his military exploits, but even more so for his enlightened domestic policy. He ran an efficient government, worked hard for the welfare of his people, and was held in great esteem by them. In his struggle for supremacy, he promoted agricultural production to sustain his military campaigns, made alliances with those tribes that submitted to his will, and conquered those that resisted. As a showdown drew near with the Hsia, he successfully convinced most Chinese tribes as well as his own people how oppressive and corrupt the Hsia regime had become and why he had no choice except revolt. As a result, an increasing number of Chinese tribes switched their loyalty to him. Instead of rising up to meet the challenge, the last Hsia ruler, Chieh, became depraved and cruel. He reportedly killed his best ministers simply because they had offended him and he wasted manpower needlessly by building elaborate palaces for his concubines. As the military campaign progressed, more and more tribes joined T'ang's revolt. In the final battle Chieh was captured. After he had been exiled, the new dynasty, Shang, was formally established. The establishment of the dynasty was traditionally placed at 1766 B.C.

As the Shangs are closer to us than the Hsias in terms of time, we know a great deal more about them. Recent archaeological findings have further enriched our knowledge. For one thing, we know that they moved their capital often. This could have meant that they were not yet completely out of the pastoral stage or that they had repeatedly exhausted land fertility by constant cultivation. Both theories have perhaps an element of truth. Anyhow, agriculture was their main occupation. Crops included millet, wheat, and rice; millet seems to have been the main staple crop and was also used to make wine. Sericulture had been discovered before, and the silk produced was used to make clothes, kerchiefs, curtains, etc. For meat there were cattle, sheep, chicken, and hogs. Dogs had been domesticated. Other animals like oxen, horses, and elephants were used for transportation; we know that the nobility and the wealthy had carriages drawn by animals. On the battlefield, while common soldiers fought on foot, the nobles attacked each other in horse chariots. Elephants were sometimes used for charging the enemy's defense lines. As forests could still be found in most parts of North China, game was abundant, and hunting was the most popular sport among the nobles. Even around the capital city Yin (after 1401 B.C.) there were large undeveloped areas to which agriculture had not been extended. We know that in one hunting trip a Shang ruler bagged 348 deer, and in another, 113 boars.

As for shelter, a peasant's house was no more than a thatched hut; the whole family lived in one large, rectangular room, divided by wooden boards or thatched curtains to make kitchen and living quarters. The houses of the wealthy were more elaborate. Stone and bronze foundations have been found on the Yin ruins; columns must have been extensively used for supporting the main beams. Since no tiles or bricks have been found on these sites, it is presumed that even among the wealthy, thatched roofing was common. Walls were generally made of hardened earth; doors usually faced south to admit more sunlight.

During the Shang dynasty two of the most epochal events occurred, namely, the discovery of bronze metallurgy and the development of a written language. Though we cannot place the date when bronze metallurgy was discovered in China, it must have undergone a long process of development before it reached the perfection evidenced by the bronzes unearthed in the Yin ruins. Experts have opined that the technique of casting bronze in the Shang dynasty was even superior to the famed craftsmanship of the European Renaissance. The unearthed bronzes were of many kinds, mostly household utensils and religious implements. There were wine pots, cups, plates and dishes, drinking vessels, and food containers of various shapes and designs. There were also religious vessels covered with elaborate designs in incised lines or in high relief. One bronze piece, perhaps serving the same purpose as our lazy Susan, had a beautifully designed central column around which four sculptured dragons rotated. Bronze was also cast into military weapons. The points of spears, javelins, and arrows, together with swords and knives, were made of bronze, as were warriors' helmets. However, bronze did not replace stone completely, as some weapons were still made of stone or animal bones.

Though overshadowed by bronzes, other handicraft products of the Shangs were scarcely less impressive. Some of the glazed potteries were made of clay of the finest quality, with paintings or relief drawings of animals and geometrical patterns. Jade was carved into many shapes representing men, wild animals, birds, fishes, and frogs; stone was sculptured into statues of men, tigers, rabbits, and birds. There was also a variety of ornaments made of jade and precious stones used for women's hairdressing. Since none of these materials were produced in the areas in which they were found, trade must have been very extensive. Cowrie shells were used as a medium of exchange; coined money was not yet invented.

The Shangs were said to be a religious people. They believed in spirits who, they thought, existed everywhere: in the forests, mountains, rivers, fields, and even in one's own house. However, most of the spirits were those of harmless, deceased ancestors. After a man died, his spirit presumably left the body and was wafted into the air, but it would extend protection to the family if properly humored and worshipped. By means of sacrifices and by magic incantations the spirits could be summoned before a priest and could be persuaded to reveal what the future held for the family. The Shangs would not do anything important without consulting the spirits, whether it be making a trip or fighting a war. For the kings who had to make important decisions affecting the entire nation, religious rituals became exceedingly elaborate affairs. Sheep or cattle used for each sacrifice sometimes numbered three or four hundred. The method of offering them, whether it was burning in open flames, drowning in rivers, or burying underneath the ground, varied according to occasions; even the color and sex of the animals were carefully prescribed. Sometimes prisoners-of-war were slaughtered as sacrifices. It was believed that the spirits, carefully attended to, would make their wishes known through the oracle bones. To conjure oracles, a priest drilled a turtle shell or a piece of animal bone with a hand piercer on one side and then placed the hollowed points on top of a flame. The other side of the shell or bone began to crack, and the cracks formed various patterns. The priest would then interpret the meaning of the patterns according to a magic formula; his interpretations were the alleged oracles. Thousands of these oracle bones have been unearthed from the Yin ruins.

When these oracle bones were unearthed, the archaeologists were amazed that there were written inscriptions on them. The inscriptions indicated the questions asked by the priest, the answers, and sometimes even the eventual outcome. More than two thousand written characters of this script have been deciphered, and most of them have been identified with their modern counterparts in the Chinese written system. It is beyond any doubt that the Shell-Bone script was the forerunner of modern Chinese. In fact, the modern script can be traced all the way back to this ancient script through several stages of development. The large number of written characters in the Shell-Bone script implied an advanced and sophisticated society which used it; the number of Chinese characters commonly used in China today does not exceed five thousand. The period during which this ancient script flourished is placed between 1700 and 1100 B.C.; since it had already reached an advanced stage by then, it is reasonable to assume that the rudiments of a written language first appeared in China around 2000 B.C., if not earlier. Perhaps we are not in great error when we say that China entered the historical period four thousand years ago.

The Chinese language, the oldest surviving language in the world, is unique in the sense that it is non-phonetic. Interestingly, it is still used by the largest number of people in the world. It began with pictographs and ideographs, and after 4,000 years they still constitute a sizable portion of modern characters, even though they have been stylized, simplified, or both. When it is pointed out that each character can serve the purpose of an English letter or syllable besides being an independent word, it is easy to see what a versatile language Chinese is. On the other hand, since the language is not phonetic and since each character has to be memorized independently with regard to its pronunciation as well as its variety of meanings, Chinese is acknowledgedly one of the most difficult languages in the world. While a great deal could be said about the disadvantages of a non-phonetic language, the fact that in the Chinese language the written form (as contrary to pronunciation) counted most enabled it to spread to faraway places where it was adopted even though the pronunciation of the same item as indicated by a Chinese character was entirely different. In other words, after foreigners had adopted the written characters, they pronounced the characters not as the Chinese pronounced them but as they had been pronouncing those words which they then began to write in Chinese. Today, a Japanese, a Korean, and a Chinese might not be able to communicate with each other orally, but they could do so with a piece of paper and a pen, because a written Chinese character conveys the same (or approximately the same) meanings to all of them. The same is true of a southern and a northern Chinese who write the same characters but pronounce them differently. Had the phonetic part of the language not been detached from its written part to a considerable extent, many written languages would have been developed in China in view of the difficulties in communication and transportation of the ancient years. The sharing of a common written language meant a common heritage and a common identity for all Chinese despite great distances between them. When it is pointed out that the word *Chinese* is more a cultural than a racial term, we can easily see what an important role the language has played in the development of China as a nation.

II. THE CLASSICAL WORLD: 1000 B.C. TO A.D. 500

A sixth-century B.C. Greek vase showing a wedding procession.
(The Metropolitan Museum of Art, Rogers Fund, 1917.)

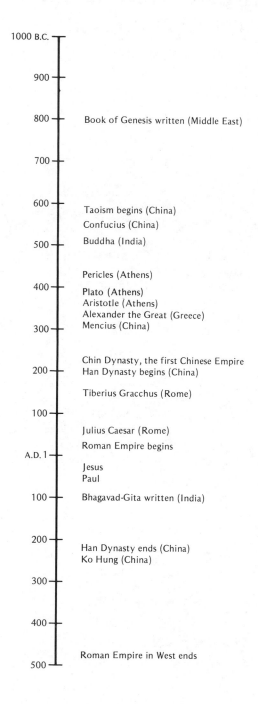

1000 B.C. —

900 —

800 — Book of Genesis written (Middle East)

700 —

600 — Taoism begins (China)
Confucius (China)
500 — Buddha (India)

Pericles (Athens)
400 — Plato (Athens)
Aristotle (Athens)
Alexander the Great (Greece)
300 — Mencius (China)

Chin Dynasty, the first Chinese Empire
200 — Han Dynasty begins (China)

Tiberius Gracchus (Rome)

100 —

Julius Caesar (Rome)
Roman Empire begins
A.D. 1 —
Jesus
Paul

100 — Bhagavad-Gita written (India)

200 — Han Dynasty ends (China)
Ko Hung (China)

300 —

400 —

Roman Empire in West ends
500 —

4. GREEK CIVILIZATION

THE DEFINITION OF GREEK CIVILIZATION TO 500 B.C.

WILLIAM H. McNEILL

In this brief excerpt from William H. McNeill's brilliant A World History, *Greek civilization is placed in a broad perspective that includes India and ancient Israel as well as Minoan Crete and Mycenae. McNeill argues that when we compare the experience of the ancient Greeks with that of the Indians or Hebrews, the uniqueness of Greece lies in its political organization into territorial states. What does he mean by that?*

What do you think of this idea? How were the experiences of the Indians, Hebrews, and Greeks similar? How were they different? Or was the Greek experience unusual? Can it still influence us today?

While India worked its way toward the definition of a new and distinctive civilization on one flank of the ancient Middle East, on its other flank another new civilization was also emerging; the Greek. The principal stages of early Greek history closely resemble what we know or can surmise about Indian development. But the end product differed fundamentally. The Greeks put political organization into territorial states above all other bases of human association, and attempted to explain the world and man not in terms of mystic illumination but through laws of nature. Thus despite a similar start, when fierce "tamers of horses"—like those of whom Homer later sang—overran priest-led agricultural societies, the Indian and Greek styles of civilization diverged strikingly by 500 B.C.

MYCENAEAN VIKINGS

One great difference existed from the start. The Aryans of India remained landsmen, whereas the earliest Greek invaders of the Aegean region took readily to the sea, infiltrating Knossos in Minoan Crete and establishing themselves among the Aegean islands as well as on the Greek mainland. The first Greek-speaking rulers of Knossos made very little change in the archaeological remains of Minoan civilization, although they did develop a new script (Linear B), which recorded an archaic form of the Greek language. About 1400 B.C., however, Knossos was destroyed, perhaps by some piratical raid launched from the new-sprung capital at Mycenae on the Greek mainland. For the next two hundred years a series of sea raids—alternating perhaps with more peaceable trade—carried Mycenaean ships to almost all the coasts of the Mediterranean. We know from Egyptian records of three separate attacks launched against Egypt by a coalition of "sea peoples" in which Mycenaean Greeks probably took a minor part. In the year 1190 B.C., however, the Egyptians successfully repelled the last of these ventures, and a remnant of the invading host settled in Palestine to become the Philistines of biblical history. A similar raid (traditionally dated 1184 B.C.) against Troy at the mouth of the Dardanelles became the focus around which Homer's tales of heroism clustered.

THE CITY-STATE

Soon after 1200 B.C. these far-flung enterprises came to an end. A new wave of invaders, Greek-speaking Dorians, came down from the north and overran the centers of Mycenaean power. With the Dorians or very soon after came iron, with all the usual political consequences. Aristocratic charioteers, who had controlled war and politics in the days of Mycenae's greatness, were overthrown by wandering tribes of iron-wielding warriors. Such groups were always ready to migrate to any new spot where better cropland or pasture could be found. The Dorian invasions therefore proceeded piecemeal, and involved many secondary displacements of peoples. In particular, refugees from the Greek mainland took ship and established a series of new settlements across the Aegean on the coast of Asia Minor. These regions were subsequently known as Ionia and, further north, Aeolia. For protection against the native inhabitants the Greek settlements clustered on defensible peninsulas and other suitable places on the coast. Since the refugees (like the Hebrews of the Exodus) had no pre-existing pattern of leadership or code of custom to which all unthinkingly subscribed, they had to invent a visible set of laws and system of government to assure effective co-operation in the new settlements. In so doing, they created the earliest Greek city-states.

Moses had faced a similar problem a century or two before, when he led the children of Israel from Egypt into the desert. The legislation with which he organized the Hebrew community in its new environment became the kernel of later Judaism. The self-governing city-states created by Greeks on the coast of Asia Minor had almost as great an importance in world history. For by inventing the city-state or *polis* (hence our word "politics"), the Greeks of Ionia established the proto-type from which the whole Western world derived its penchant for political organization into territorially defined sovereign units, i.e., into states. The supremacy of territoriality over all other forms of human association is neither natural nor inevitable, as the Indian caste principle may remind us. Hence, if we Westerners owe our religion to Hebrew refugees from Pharaoh, we also owe our politics to Greek refugees from the Dorians, who had to reorganize and rationalize their traditional society in order to survive in a new and hostile environment just about two centuries after Moses had led his followers out of Egypt into the desert.

Development on the mainland toward supremacy of the polis was slower. Semi-migratory tribes had first to settle permanently on some particular piece of land, and then had to combine with neighbors into a single territorial unit to constitute a polis. The line of evolution is fairly clear. Violence diminished, population grew, land became scarce and fixed farming became the rule. As the population settled down, local chieftains found it convenient to settle disputes by sitting in council under the presidency of a high king. When the full council could not be in session it often seemed desirable to appoint individuals to look after matters of common concern, and to check the king in any attempt he might make to extend his authority. In this fashion magistrates arose, who were appointed for a limited term and entrusted with a delegated and, in course of time, legally defined authority. In some of the emergent city-states the kingship itself became a magistracy; in other cases kingship remained hereditary in a particular family.

THE FUNERAL ORATION OF PERICLES

THUCYDIDES

The most famous statement of Greek loyalty to the city-state is the following account of the funeral speech of Pericles in the classic History of the Peloponnesian War *by the ancient historian Thucydides. The*

From *The History of Thucydides*, Book II, translated by Benjamin Jowett. New York: Tandy-Thomas, 1909.

speech commemorated the Athenian soldiers who had died in the battle against Sparta in 431 B.C.

Notice the high value placed on loyalty to Athens and service to the state. Here is the origin of patriotism. Pericles also insists that Athens is a democratic city-state. Notice his praise of Athenian freedom as well as public service. Could there be a conflict between personal freedom and public service? If so, how would Pericles resolve such a conflict? You might also notice that Pericles is commending Athenian citizen-soldiers who died defending not their home but the empire. Could there be a conflict between Athenian democracy and the ambitions of empire?

Most of those who have spoken here before me have commended the lawgiver who added this oration to our other funeral customs; it seemed to them a worthy thing that such an honour should be given at their burial to the dead who have fallen on the field of battle. But I should have preferred that, when men's deeds have been brave, they should be honoured in deed only, and with such an honour as this public funeral, which you are now witnessing. Then the reputation of many would not have been imperilled on the eloquence or want of eloquence of one, and their virtues believed or not as he spoke well or ill. For it is difficult to say neither too little nor too much; and even moderation is apt not to give the impression of truthfulness. The friend of the dead who knows the facts is likely to think that the words of the speaker fall short of his knowledge and of his wishes; another who is not so well informed, when he hears of anything which surpasses his own powers, will be envious and will suspect exaggeration. Mankind are tolerant of the praises of others as long as each hearer thinks that he can do as well or nearly as well himself, but, when the speaker rises above him, jealousy is aroused and he begins to be incredulous. However, since our ancestors have set the seal of their approval upon the practice, I must obey, and to the utmost of my power shall endeavour to satisfy the wishes and beliefs of all who hear me.

I will speak first of our ancestors, for it is right and seemly that now, when we are lamenting the dead, a tribute should be paid to their memory. There has never been a time when they did not inhabit this land, which by their valour they have handed down from generation to generation, and we have received from them a free state. But if they were worthy of praise, still more were our fathers, who added to their inheritance, and after many a struggle transmitted to us their sons this great empire. And we ourselves assembled here to-day, who are still most of us in the vigour of life, have carried the work of improvement further, and have richly endowed our city with all things, so that she is sufficient for herself both in peace and war. Of the military exploits by which our various possessions were acquired, or of the energy with which we or our fathers drove back the tide of war, Hellenic or

Barbarian [non-Greek], I will not speak: for the tale would be long and is familiar to you. But before I praise the dead, I should like to point out by what principles of action we rose to power, and under what institutions and through what manner of life our empire became great. For I conceive that such thoughts are not unsuited to the occasion, and that this numerous assembly of citizens and strangers may profitably listen to them.

Our form of government does not enter into rivalry with the institutions of others. We do not copy our neighbours, but are an example to them. It is true that we are called a democracy, for the administration is in the hands of the many and not of the few. But while the law secures equal justice to all alike in their private disputes, the claim of excellence is also recognised; and when a citizen is in any way distinguished, he is preferred to the public service, not as a matter of privilege, but as the reward of merit. Neither is poverty a bar, but a man may benefit his country whatever be the obscurity of his condition. There is no exclusiveness in our public life, and in our private intercourse we are not suspicious of one another, nor angry with our neighbour if he does what he likes; we do not put on sour looks at him which, though harmless, are not pleasant. While we are thus unconstrained in our private intercourse, a spirit of reverence pervades our public acts; we are prevented from doing wrong by respect for the authorites and for the laws, having an especial regard to those which are ordained for the protection of the injured as well as to those unwritten laws which bring upon the transgressor of them the reprobation of the general sentiment.

And we have not forgotten to provide for our weary spirits many relaxations from toil; we have regular games and sacrifices throughout the year; our homes are beautiful and elegant; and the delight which we daily feel in all these things helps to banish melancholy. Because of the greatness of our city the fruits of the whole earth flow in upon us; so that we enjoy the goods of other countries as freely as of our own.

Then, again, our military training is in many respects superior to that of our adversaries. Our city is thrown open to the world, and we never expel a foreigner or prevent him from seeing or learning anything of which the secret if revealed to an enemy might profit him. We rely not upon management or trickery, but upon our own hearts and hands. And in the matter of education, whereas they from early youth are always undergoing laborious exercises which are to make them brave, we live at ease, and yet are equally ready to face the perils which they face. And here is the proof. The Lacedaemonians come into Attica not by themselves, but with their whole confederacy following; we go alone into a neighbour's country; and although our opponents are fighting for their homes and we on a foreign soil, we have seldom any difficulty in overcoming them. Our enemies have never yet felt our united strength; the care of a navy divides our attention, and on land we are obliged to send our own citizens everywhere. But they, if they meet and defeat a part of our army, are as proud as if they had routed us all, and when defeated they pretend to have been vanquished by us all.

If then we prefer to meet danger with a light heart but without laborious training, and with a courage which is gained by habit and not enforced by law, are we not greatly the gainers? Since we do not anticipate the pain, although, when the hour comes, we can be as brave as those who never allow themselves to rest; and thus too our city is equally admirable in peace and in war. For we are lovers of the beautiful, yet simple in our tastes, and we cultivate the mind without loss of manliness. Wealth we employ, not for talk and ostentation, but when there is a real use for it. To avow poverty with us is no disgrace; the true disgrace is in doing nothing to avoid it. An Athenian citizen does not neglect the state because he takes care of his own household; and even those of us who are engaged in business have a very fair idea of politics. We alone regard a man who takes no interest in public affairs, not as a harmless, but as a useless character; and if few of us are originators, we are all sound judges of policy. The great impediment to action is, in our opinion, not discussion, but the want of that knowledge which is gained by discussion preparatory to action. For we have a peculiar power of thinking before we act and of acting too, whereas other men are courageous from ignorance but hestiate upon reflection. And they are surely to be esteemed the bravest spirts who, having the clearest sense both of the pains and pleasures of life, do not on that account shrink from danger. In doing good, again, we are unlike others; we make our friends by conferring, not by receiving favours. Now he who confers a favour is the firmer friend, because he would fain by kindness keep alive the memory of an obligation; but the recipient is colder in his feelings, because he knows that in requiting another's generosity he will not be winning gratitude but only paying a debt. We alone do good to our neighbours, not upon a calculation of interest, but in the confidence of freedom and in a frank and fearless spirit.

To sum up: I say that Athens is the school of Hellas, and that the individual Athenian in his own person seems to have the power of adapting himself to the most varied forms of action with the utmost versatility and grace. This is no passing and idle word, but truth and fact; and the assertion is verified by the position to which these qualities have raised the state. For in the hour of trial Athens alone among her contemporaries is superior to the report of her. No enemy who comes against her is indignant at the reverses which he sustains at the hands of such a city; no subject complains that his masters are unworthy of him. And we shall assuredly not be without witnesses; there are mighty monuments of our power which will make us the wonder of this and of succeeding ages; we shall not need the praises of Homer or of any other panegyrist whose poetry may please for the moment, although his representation of the facts will not bear the light of day. For we have compelled every land and every sea to open a path for our valour, and have everywhere planted eternal memorials of our friendship of our enmity. Such is the city of whose sake these men nobly fought and died; they could not bear the thought that she might be taken from them; and every one of us who survive should gladly toil on her behalf.

I have dwelt upon the greatness of Athens because I want to show you that we are contending for a higher prize than those who enjoy none of these privileges, and to establish by manifest proof the merit of these men whom I am now commemorating. Their loftiest praise has been already spoken. For in magnifying the city I have magnified them, and men like them whose virtues made her glorious. And of how few Hellenes can it be said as of them, that their deeds when weighed in the balance have been found equal to their fame! Methinks that a death such as theirs has been given the true measure of a man's worth; it may be the first revelation of his virtues, but is at any rate their final seal. For even those who come short in other ways may justly plead the valour with which they have fought for their country; they have blotted out the evil with the good, and have benefited the state more by their public services than they have injured her by their private actions. None of these men were enervated by wealth or hesitated to resign for pleasures of life, none of them put off the evil day in the hope, natural to poverty, that a man, though poor, may one day become rich. But, deeming that the punishment of their enemies was sweeter than any of these things, and that they could fall in no nobler cause, they determined at the hazard of their lives to be honourably avenged, and to leave the rest. They resigned to hope their unknown chance of happiness; but in the fact of death they resolved to rely upon themselves alone. And when the moment came they were minded to resist and suffer, rather than to fly and save their lives; they ran away from the word of dishonour, but on the battlefield their feet stood fast, and in an instant, at the height of their fortune, they passed away from the scene, not of their fear, but of their glory.

Such was the end of these men; they were worthy of Athens, and the living need not desire to have a more heroic spirit, although they may pray for a less fatal issue. The value of such a spirit is not to be expressed in words. Any one can discourse to you for ever about the advantages of a brave defence, which you know already. But instead of listening to him I would have you day by day fix your eyes upon the greatness of Athens, until you become filled with the love of her; and when you are impressed by the spectacle of her glory, reflect that this empire has been acquired by men who knew their duty and had the courage to do it, who in the hour of conflict had the fear of dishonour always present to them, and who, if ever they failed in an enterprise, would not allow their virtues to be lost to their country, but freely gave their lives to her as the fairest offering which they could present at her feast. The sacrifice which they collectively made was individually repaid to them; for they received again each one of himself a praise which grows not old, and the noblest of all sepulchres—I speak not of that in which their remains are laid, but of that in which their glory survives, and is proclaimed always and on every fitting occasion both in word and deed. For the whole earth is the sepulchre of famous men; not only are they commemorated by columns and inscriptions in their own country, but in foreign lands there dwells also an unwritten memorial of them, graven not on stone but in the hearts of men. Make them your examples, and, esteeming courage to be freedom and freedom to be happiness, do not weigh too nicely the perils of war. The unfortunate who has no hope of a change for the better has less reason to throw away his life than the prosperous who, if he survives, is always liable to a change for the worse, and to whom any accidental fall makes the most serious difference. To a man of spirit, cowardice and disaster coming together are far more bitter than death striking him unperceived at a time when he is full of courage and animated by the general hope.

Wherefore I do not now commiserate the parents of the dead who stand here; I would rather comfort them. You know that your life has been passed amid manifold vicissitudes; and that they may be deemed fortunate who have gained most honour, whether an honourable death like theirs, or an honourable sorrow like yours, and whose days have been so ordered that the term of their happiness is likewise the term of their life. I know how hard it is to make you feel this, when the good fortune of others will too often remind you of the gladness which once lightened your hearts. And sorrow is felt at the want of those blessings, not which a man never knew, but which were a part of his life before they were taken from him. Some of you are of an age at which they may hope to have other children, and they ought to bear their sorrow better; not only will the children who may hereafter be born make them forget their own lost ones, but the city will be doubly a gainer. She will not be left desolate, and she will be safer. For a man's counsel cannot have equal weight or worth, when he alone has no children to risk in the general danger. To those of you who have passed their prime, I say: Congratulate yourselves that you have been happy during the greater part of your days; remember that your life of sorrow will not last long, and be comforted by the glory of those who are gone. For the love of honour alone is ever young, and not riches, as some say, but honour is the delight of men when they are old and useless.

To you who are the sons and brothers of the departed, I see that the struggle to emulate them will be an arduous one. For all men praise the dead, and, however pre-eminent your virtue may be, hardly will you be thought, I do not say to equal, but even to approach them. The living have their rivals and detractors, but when a man is out of the way, the honour and good-will which he receives is unalloyed. And, if I am to speak of womanly virtues to those of you who will henceforth be widows, let me sum them up in one short admonition: To a woman not to show more weakness than is natural to her sex is a great glory, and not to be talked about for good or for evil among men.

I have paid the required tribute, in obedience to the law, making use of such fitting words as I had. The tribute of deeds has been paid in part; for the dead have been honourably interred, and it remains only that their children should be maintained at the public charge until they are grown up; this is the solid prize with which, as with a garland, Athens crowns her sons living and dead, after a struggle like theirs. For where the rewards of virtue are greatest, there the noblest citizens are enlisted in the service of the state. And now, when you have duly lamented, every one his own dead, you may depart.

THE REPUBLIC

PLATO

In the introduction to the funeral oration of Pericles, we suggested that by modern standards Athens was not very democratic. Service to the state, the empire, and (we might add) slavery were its limitations. From the standpoint of many ancient Athenians, however, Athens appeared to be too democratic. They worried that democracy meant the rule of the least capable or the mob. Plato was one of these conservative critics. His famous work, The Republic, *is an extended argument that "justice" is best achieved if the state is ruled by philosophers rather than the demos, or common people. Plato puts this argument in the mouth of Socrates, his teacher.*

The Republic begins, as do many of the other "dialogues" or discussions, with an account of how the group of friends got together and the discussion began. We might notice here that besides giving us a peek at educated male society in ancient Athens, these introductory discussions are also a testament to how much freedom of thought was enjoyed in the city-state. One might be tempted to argue against Plato that a city which encouraged all citizens to debate legislation in the assembly in democratic fashion also nurtured the wide-ranging intellectual discussions that Plato found so fruitful.

From *The Republic of Plato*, translated by F. M. Cornford. Copyright © 1941 by Oxford University Press. Reprinted by permission of Oxford University Press.

CHAPTER 1

SOCRATES. I walked down to the Piraeus yesterday with Glaucon, the son of Ariston, to make my prayers to the goddess. As this was the first celebration of her festival, I wished also to see how the ceremony would be conducted. The Thracians, I thought, made as fine a show in the procession as our own people, though they did well enough. The prayers and the spectacle were over, and we were leaving to go back to the city, when from some way off Polemarchus, the son of Cephalus, caught sight of us starting homewards and sent his slave running to ask us to wait for him. The boy caught my garment from behind and gave me the message.

I turned round and asked where his master was.

There, he answered; coming up behind. Please wait.

Very well, said Glaucon; we will.

A minute later Polemarchus joined us, with Glaucon's brother, Adeimantus, and Niceratus, the son of Nicias, and some others who must have been at the procession.

Socrates, said Polemarchus, I do believe you are starting back to town and leaving us.

You have guessed right, I answered.

Well, he said, you see what a large party we are?

I do.

Unless you are more than a match for us, then, you must stay here.

Isn't there another alternative? said I; we might convince you that you must let us go.

How will you convince us, if we refuse to listen?

We cannot, said Glaucon.

Well, we shall refuse; make up your minds to that.

Here Adeimantus interposed: Don't you even know that in the evening there is going to be a torch-race on horseback in honour of the goddess?

On horseback! I exclaimed; that is something new. How will they do it? Are the riders going to race with torches and hand them on to one another?

Just so, said Polemarchus. Besides, there will be a festival lasting all night, which will be worth seeing. We will go out after dinner and look on. We shall find plenty of young men there and we can have a talk. So please stay, and don't disappoint us.

It looks as if we had better stay, said Glaucon.

Well, said I, if you think so, we will.

Accordingly, we went home with Polemarchus.

At the home of Polemarchus, the participants meet a number of other old friends. After the usual greetings and gossip, the discussion begins in response to the question of Socrates: what is justice?

*Each of the participants poses an idea of justice that Socrates chal-
lenges. Then Socrates outlines an ideal state that would be based on
absolute justice. In the following selection he is asked how this ideal
could ever come about.*

CHAPTER 18

But really, Socrates, Glaucon continued, if you are allowed to go on like
this, I am afraid you will forget all about the question you thrust aside
some time ago: whether a society so constituted can ever come into
existence, and if so, how. No doubt, if it did exist, all manner of good
things would come about. I can even add some that you have passed
over. Men who acknowledged one another as fathers, sons, or brothers
and always used those names among themselves would never desert one
another; so they would fight with unequalled bravery. And if their
womenfolk went out with them to war, either in the ranks or drawn up
in the rear to intimidate the enemy and act as a reserve in case of need,
I am sure all this would make them invincible. At home, too, I can see
many advantages you have not mentioned. But, since I admit that our
commonwealth would have all these merits and any number more, if
once it came into existence, you need not describe it in further detail. All
we have now to do is to convince ourselves that it can be brought into
being and how.

This is a very sudden onslaught, said I; you have no mercy on my
shilly-shallying. Perhaps you do not realize that, after I have barely
escaped the first two waves, the third, which you are now bringing down
upon me, is the most formidable of all. When you have seen what it is
like and heard my reply, you will be ready to excuse the very natural
fears which made me shrink from putting forward such a paradox for
discussion.

The more you talk like that, he said, the less we shall be willing to let
you off from telling us how this constitution can come into existence; so
you had better waste no more time.

Well, said I, let be begin by reminding you that what brought us to this
point was our inquiry into the nature of justice and injustice.

True; but what of that?

Merely this: suppose we do find out what justice is, are we going to
demand that a man who is just shall have a character which exactly
corresponds in every respect to the ideal of justice? Or shall we be
satisfied if he comes as near to the ideal as possible and has in him a
larger measure of that quality than the rest of the world?

That will satisfy me.

If so, when we set out to discover the essential nature of justice and
injustice and what a perfectly just and a perfectly unjust man would be

like, supposing them to exist, our purpose was to use them as ideal patterns: we were to observe the degree of happiness or unhappiness that each exhibited, and to draw the necessary inference that our own destiny would be like that of the one we most resembled. We did not set out to show that these ideals could exist in fact.

That is true.

Then suppose a painter had drawn an ideally beautiful figure complete to the last touch, would you think any the worse of him, if he could not show that a person as beautiful as that could exist?

No, I should not.

Well, we have been constructing in discourse the pattern of an ideal state. Is our theory any the worse, if we cannot prove it possible that a state so organized should be actually founded?

Surely not.

That, then, is the truth of the matter. But if, for your satisfaction, I am to do my best to show under what conditions our ideal would have the best chance of being realized, I must ask you once more to admit that the same principle applies here. Can theory ever be fully realized in practice? Is it not in the nature of things that action should come less close to truth than thought? People may not think so; but do you agree or not?

I do.

Then you must not insist upon my showing that this construction we have traced in thought could be reproduced in fact down to the last detail. You must admit that we shall have found a way to meet your demand for realization, if we can discover how a state might be constituted in the closest accordance with our description. Will not that content you? It would be enough for me.

And for me too.

Then our next attempt, it seems, must be to point out what defect in the working of existing states prevents them from being so organized, and what is the least change that would effect a transformation into this type of government—a single change if possible, or perhaps two; at any rate let us make the changes as few and insignificant as may be.

By all means.

Well, there is one change which, as I believe we can show, would bring about this revolution—not a small change, certainly, nor an easy one, but possible.

What is it?

I have now to confront what we called the third and greatest wave. But I must state my paradox, even though the wave should break in laughter over my head and drown me in ignominy. Now mark what I am going to say.

Go on.

Unless either philosophers become kings in their countries or those who are now called kings and rulers come to be sufficiently inspired with a genuine desire for wisdom; unless, that is to say, political power and philosophy meet together, while the many natures who now go their several ways in the one or the other direction are forcibly debarred from doing so, there can be no rest from troubles, my dear Glaucon, for states, nor yet, as I believe, for all mankind; nor can this commonwealth which we have imagined ever till then see the light of day and grow to its full stature. This it was that I have so long hung back from saying; I knew what a paradox it would be, because it is hard to see that there is no other way of happiness either for the state or for the individual.

Socrates, exclaimed Glaucon, after delivering yourself of such a pronouncement as that, you must expect a whole multitude of by no means contemptible assailants to fling off their coats, snatch up the handiest weapon, and make a rush at you, breathing fire and slaughter. If you cannot find arguments to beat them off and make your escape, you will learn what it means to be the target of scorn and derision.

Well, it was you who got me into this trouble.

Yes, and a good thing too. However, I will not leave you in the lurch. You shall have my friendly encouragement for what it is worth; and perhaps you may find me more complaisant than some would be in answering your questions. With such backing you must try to convince the unbelievers.

I will, now that I have such a powerful ally.

Judging from the reaction of Glaucon, philosphers had no more prestige in ancient Greece than they do in modern America. They were often ridiculed in the popular comedies for their fuzzy impracticality.

By saying that philosophers should be kings, Plato (or Socrates) meant something very different, however. By "philosophers" he meant people with a deeper understanding, more profound wisdom, than that enjoyed by the common people. To explain that difference he turned to a parable of people in a cave whose only experience was the world of shadows, and he compared their understanding with those who had emerged into the light of the real world. This parable, perhaps the most famous in the history of philosophy, seems to undercut all of the claims of Greek democracy.

What is the meaning of the parable of the cave? Isn't Plato right when he suggests that some people only see the shadows? If so, should those people govern?

Perhaps Plato is making a distinction between common sense knowledge (what every day experience teaches) and wisdom (the flash of inspiration or enlightenment). If the latter is all that matters, then democratic quibbling is a waste of time. But so may be the carefully reasoned dialogues which Plato, and other Athenians, seem so much to

*enjoy. Does democracy, after all, mean accepting common sense and
even error as preferable to the rule of the wise?*

*Plato concludes with an additional argument that you might consider.
The value of philosophers as kings, he says, is not only that they know
"the truth," but also that they prefer philosophy to government. Thus,
they are good rulers because they do not enjoy it. Only those who have
nothing better to do, seek power for its own sake. Philosophy is
something better to do. What do you think of this line of argument?*

Next, said I, here is a parable to illustrate the degrees in which our
nature may be enlightened or unenlightened. Imagine the condition of
men living in a sort of cavernous chamber underground, with an
entrance open to the light and a long passage all down the cave. Here
they have been from childhood, chained by the leg and also by the neck,
so that they cannot move and can see only what is in front of them,
because the chains will not let them turn their heads. At some distance
higher up is the light of a fire burning behind them; and between the
prisoners and the fire is a track with a parapet built along it, like the
screen at a puppet-show, which hides the performers while they show
their puppets over the top.

I see, said he.

Now behind this parapet imagine persons carrying along various
artificial objects, including figures of men and animals in wood or stone
or other materials, which project above the parapet. Naturally, some of
these persons will be talking, others silent.

It is a strange picture, he said, and a strange sort of prisoners.

Like ourselves, I replied; for in the first place prisoners so confined
would have seen nothing of themselves or of one another, except the
shadows thrown by the fire-light on the wall of the Cave facing them,
would they?

Not if all their lives they had been prevented from moving their heads.

And they would have seen as little of the objects carried past.

Of course.

Now, if they could talk to one another, would they not suppose that
their words referred only to those passing shadows which they saw?

Necessarily.

And suppose their prison had an echo from the wall facing them?
When one of the people crossing behind them spoke, they could only
suppose that the sound came from the shadow passing before their eyes.

No doubt.

In every way, then, such prisoners would recognize as reality nothing
but the shadows of those artificial objects.

Inevitably.

Now consider what would happen if their release from the chains and
the healing of their unwisdom should come about in this way. Suppose

one of them set free and forced suddenly to stand up, turn his head, and walk with eyes lifted to the light; all these movements would be painful, and he would be too dazzled to make out the objects whose shadows he had been used to see. What do you think he would say, if someone told him that what he had formerly seen was meaningless illusion, but now, being somewhat nearer to reality and turned towards more real objects, he was getting a truer view? Suppose further that he were shown the various objects being carried by and were made to say, in reply to questions, what each of them was. Would he not be perplexed and believe the objects now shown him to be not so real as what he formerly saw?

Yes, not nearly so real.

And if he were forced to look at the fire-light itself, would not his eyes ache, so that he would try to escape and turn back to the things which he could see distinctly, convinced that they really were clearer than these other objects now being shown to him?

Yes.

And suppose someone were to drag him away forcibly up the steep and rugged ascent and not let him go until he had hauled him out into the sunlight, would he not suffer pain and vexation at such treatment, and, when he had come out into the light, find his eyes so full of its radiance that he could not see a single one of the things that he was now told were real?

Certainly he would not see them all at once.

He would need, then, to grow accustomed before he could see things in that upper world. At first it would be easiest to make out shadows, and then the images of men and things reflected in water, and later on the things themselves. After that, it would be easier to watch the heavenly bodies and the sky itself by night, looking at the light of the moon and stars rather than the Sun and the Sun's light in the day–time.

Yes, surely.

Last of all, he would be able to look at the Sun and contemplate its nature, not as it appears when reflected in water or any alien medium, but as it is in itself in its own domain.

No doubt.

And now he would begin to draw the conclusion that it is the Sun that produces the seasons and the course of the year and controls everything in the visible world, and moreover is in a way the cause of all that he and his companions used to see.

Clearly he would come at last to that conclusion.

Then if he called to mind his fellow prisoners and what passed for wisdom in his former dwelling–place, he would surely think himself happy in the change and be sorry for them. They may have had a practice of honouring and commending one another, with prizes for the man who had the keenest eye for the passing shadows and the best memory for the order in which they followed or accompanied one another, so that he could make a good guess as to which was going to come next. Would our released prisoner be likely to covet those prizes or to envy the men exalted to honour and power in the Cave? Would he not feel like Homer's Achilles, that he would far sooner "be on earth as a hired servant in the house of a landless man" or endure anything rather than go back to his old beliefs and live in the old way?

Yes, he would prefer any fate to such a life.

Now imagine what would happen if he went down again to take his former seat in the Cave. Coming suddenly out of the sunlight, his eyes would be filled with darkness. He might be required once more to deliver his opinion on those shadows, in competition with the prisoners who had never been released, while his eyesight was still dim and unsteady; and it might take some time to become used to the darkness. They would laugh at him and say that he had gone up only to come back with his sight ruined; it was worth no one's while even to attempt the ascent. If they could lay hands on the man who was trying to set them free and lead them up, they would kill him.

Yes, they would.

Every feature in this parable, my dear Glaucon, is meant to fit our earlier analysis. The prison dwelling corresponds to the region revealed to us through the sense of sight, and the fire-light within it to the power of the Sun. The ascent to see the things in the upper world you may take as standing for the upward journey of the soul into the region of the intelligible; then you will be in possession of what I surmise, since that is what you wish to be told. Heaven knows whether it is true; but this, at any rate, is how it appears to me. In the world of knowledge, the last thing to be perceived and only with great difficulty is the essential Form of Goodness. Once it is perceived, the conclusion must follow that, for all things, this is the cause of whatever is right and good; in the visible world it gives birth to light and to the lord of light, while it is itself sovereign in the intelligible world and the parent of intelligence and truth. Without having had a vision of this Form no one can act with wisdom, either in his own life or in matters of state.

So far as I can understand, I share your belief.

Then you may also agree that it is no wonder if those who have reached their height are reluctant to manage the affairs of men. Their souls long to spend all their time in that upper world—naturally enough, if here once more our parable holds true. Nor, again, is it at all strange that one who comes from the contemplation of divine things to the miseries of human life should appear awkward and ridiculous when, with eyes still dazed and not yet accustomed to the darkness, he is compelled, in a law-court or elsewhere, to dispute about the shadows of justice or the images that cast those shadows, and to wrangle over the notions of what is right in the minds of men who have never beheld Justice itself.

It is not at all strange.

No; a sensible man will remember that the eyes may be confused in two ways—by a change from light to darkness or from darkness to light; and he will recognize that the same thing happens to the soul. When he sees it troubled and unable to discern anything clearly, instead of laughing thoughtlessly, he will ask whether, coming from a brighter existence, its unaccustomed vision is obscured by the darkness, in which case he will think its condition enviable and its life a happy one; or whether, emerging from the depths of ignorance, it is dazzled by excess of light. If so, he will rather feel sorry for it; or, if he were inclined to laugh, that would be less ridiculous than to laugh at the soul which has come down from the light.

That is a fair statement.

If this is true, then, we must conclude that education is not what it is said to be by some, who profess to put knowledge into a soul which does not possess it, as if they could put sight into blind eyes. On the contrary, our own account signifies that the soul of every man does possess the power of learning the truth and the organ to see it with; and that, just as one might have to turn the whole body round in order that the eye should see light instead of darkness, so the entire soul must be turned away from this changing world, until its eye can bear to contemplate reality and that supreme splendour which we have called the Good. Hence there may well be an art whose aim would be to effect this very thing, the conversion of the soul, in the readiest way; not to put the power of sight into the soul's eye, which already has it, but to ensure that, instead of looking in the wrong direction, it is turned the way it ought to be.

Yes, it may well be so.

It looks, then, as though wisdom were different from those ordinary virtues, as they are called, which are not far removed from bodily qualities, in that they can be produced by habituation and exercise in a soul which has not possessed them from the first. Wisdom, it seems, is certainly the virtue of some diviner faculty, which never loses its power, though its use for good or harm depends on the direction towards which it is turned. You must have noticed in dishonest men with a reputation for sagacity the shrewd glance of a narrow intelligence piercing the objects to which it is directed. There is nothing wrong with their power of vision, but it has been forced into the service of evil, so that the keener its sight, the more harm it works.

Quite true.

And yet if the growth of a nature like this had been pruned from earliest childhood, cleared of those clinging overgrowths which come of gluttony and all luxurious pleasure and, like leaden weights charged with affinity to this mortal world, hang upon the soul, bending its vision downwards; if, freed from these, the soul were turned round towards true reality, then this same power in these very men would see the truth as keenly as the objects it is turned to now.

Yes, very likely.

Is it not also likely, or indeed certain after what has been said, that a state can never be properly governed either by the uneducated who know nothing of truth or by men who are allowed to spend all their days in the pursuit of culture? The ignorant have no single mark before their eyes at which they must aim in all the conduct of their own lives and of affairs of state; and the others will not engage in action if they can help it, dreaming that, while still alive, they have been translated to the Islands of the Blest.

Quite true.

It is for us, then, as founders of a commonwealth, to bring compulsion to bear on the noblest natures. They must be made to climb the ascent to the vision of Goodness, which we called the highest object of knowledge; and, when they have looked upon it long enough, they must not be allowed, as they now are, to remain on the heights, refusing to come down again to the prisoners or to take any part in their labours and rewards, however much or little these may be worth.

Shall we not be doing them an injustice, if we force on them a worse life than they might have?

You have forgotten again, my friend, that the law is not concerned to make any one class specially happy, but to ensure the welfare of the commonwealth as a whole. By persuasion or constraint it will unite the citizens in harmony, making them share whatever benefits each class can contribute to the common good; and its purpose in forming men of that spirit was not that each should be left to go his own way, but that they should be instrumental in binding the community into one.

True, I had forgotten.

You will see, then, Glaucon, that there will be no real injustice in compelling our philosophers to watch over and care for the other citizens. We can fairly tell them that their compeers in other states may quite reasonably refuse to collaborate: there they have sprung up, like a self-sown plant, in despite of their country's institutions; no one has fostered their growth, and they cannot be expected to show gratitude for a care they have never received. "But," we shall say, "it is not so with you. We have brought you into existence for your country's sake as well as for your own, to be like leaders and king-bees in a hive; you have been better and more thoroughly educated than those others and hence you are more capable of playing your part both as men of thought and as men of action. You must go down, then, each in his turn, to live with the rest and let your eyes grow accustomed to the darkness. You will then see a thousand times better than those who live there always; you will recognize every image for what it is and know what it represents, because you have seen justice, beauty, and goodness in their reality; and so you and we shall find life in our commonwealth no mere dream, as it is in most existing states, where men live fighting one another about shadows and quarrelling for power, as if that were a great prize; whereas in truth government can be at its best and free from dissension only where the destined rulers are least desirous of holding office."

Quite true.

Then will our pupils refuse to listen and to take their turns at sharing in the work of the community, though they may live together for most of their time in a purer air?

No; it is a fair demand, and they are fair-minded men. No doubt, unlike any ruler of the present day, they will think of holding power as an unavoidable necessity.

Yes, my friend; for the truth is that you can have a well-governed society only if you can discover for your future rulers a better way of life than being in office; then only will power be in the hands of men who are rich, not in gold, but in the wealth that brings happiness, a good and wise life. All goes wrong when, starved for lack of anything good in their own lives, men turn to public affairs hoping to snatch from thence the happiness they hunger for. They set about fighting for power, and this internecine conflict ruins them and their country. The life of true philosophy is the only one that looks down upon offices of state; and access to power must be confined to men who are not in love with it; otherwise rivals will start fighting. So whom else can you compel to undertake the guardianship of the commonwealth, if not those who, besides understanding best the principles of government, enjoy a nobler life than the politician's and look for rewards of a different kind?

There is indeed no other choice.

5. ROMAN CIVILIZATION

WAR, SLAVES, AND LAND REFORM: TIBERIUS GRACCHUS

APPIAN OF ALEXANDRIA

The enlargement of the Roman legions in the third and second centuries
B.C. undermined the old values of the Republic. Former citizen soldiers
lost their lands and became full-time professionals or poor urban workers
while wealthy landowners bought up farms and worked them with slaves.
In 133 B.C. Tiberius Gracchus, one of the tribunes (magistrates who
protected the plebeians), proposed a land reform bill that would return
surplus land to the poor and attempt to revive the tradition of small farms.
Appian of Alexandria describes what happened in his history of A.D. 150.
What, if anything, could have been done to avoid this tragedy?

The Romans, as they subdued the Italian nations successively in war, seized a part of their lands and built towns there, or established their own colonies in those already existing, and used them in place of garrisons. Of the land acquired by war they assigned the cultivated part forthwith to settlers, or leased or sold it. Since they had no leisure as yet to allot the part which then lay desolated by war (this was generally the greater part), they made proclamation that in the meantime those who were willing to work it might do so for a share of the yearly crops—a tenth of the grain and a fifth of the fruit. From those who kept flocks was required a share of the animals, both oxen and small cattle. They did these things in order to multiply the Italian race, which they considered the most laborious of peoples, so that they might have plenty of allies at home. But the very opposite thing happened; for the rich, getting possession of the greater part of the undistributed lands, and being emboldened by the lapse of time to believe that they would never be dispossessed, and adding to their holdings the small farms of their poor neighbors, partly by purchase and partly by force, came to cultivate vast tracts instead of single estates, using for this purpose slaves as laborers and herdsmen, lest free laborers should be drawn from agriculture into

From *The Roman History of Appian of Alexandria,* translated by Horace White. London: George Bell
& Sons, 1899.

the army. The ownership of slaves itself brought them great gain from the multitude of their progeny, who increased because they were exempt from military service. Thus the powerful ones became enormously rich and the race of slaves multiplied throughout the country, while the Italian people dwindled in numbers and strength, being oppressed by penury, taxes, and military service. If they had any respite from these evils they passed their time in idleness, because the land was held by the rich, who employed slaves instead of freemen as cultivators.

For these reasons the people became troubled lest they should no longer have sufficient allies of the Italian stock, and lest the government itself should be endangered by such a vast number of slaves. Not perceiving any remedy, as it was not easy, nor exactly just, to deprive men of so many possessions they had held so long, including their own trees, buildings and fixtures, a law was once passed with difficulty at the instance of the tribunes, that nobody should hold more than 500 jugera of this land, or pasture on it more than 100 cattle or 500 sheep. To ensure the observance of this law it was provided also that there should be a certain number of freemen employed on the farms, whose business it should be to watch and report what was going on. Those who held possession of lands under the law were required to take an oath to obey the law, and penalties were fixed for violating it, and it was supposed that the remaining land would soon be divided among the poor in small parcels. But there was not the smallest consideration shown for the law or the oaths. The few who seemed to pay some respect to them conveyed their lands to their relations fraudulently, but the greater part disregarded it altogether.

At length Tiberius Sempronius Gracchus, an illustrious man, eager for glory, a most powerful speaker, and for these reasons well known to all, delivered an eloquent discourse, while serving as tribune, concerning the Italian race, lamenting that a people so valiant in war, and blood relations to the Romans, were declining little by little in the pauperism and paucity of numbers without any hope of remedy. He inveighed against the multitude of slaves as useless in war and never faithful to their masters, and adduced the recent calamity brought upon the masters by their slaves in Sicily, where the demands of agriculture had greatly increased the number of the latter; recalling also the war waged against them by the Romans, which was neither easy nor short, but long-protracted and full of vicissitudes and dangers. After speaking thus he again brought forward the law, providing that nobody should hold more than 500 jugera of the public domain. But he added a provision to the former law, that the sons of the present occupiers might each hold one-half of that amount, and that the remainder should be divided among the poor by triumvirs, who should be changed annually.

This was extremely disturbing to the rich because, on account of the triumvirs, they could no longer disregard the law as they had done before; nor could they buy the allotments of others, because Gracchus had provided against this by forbidding sales. They collected together in groups, and made lamentation, and accused the poor of appropriating the results of their tillage, their vineyards, and their dwellings. Some said that they had paid the price of the land to their neighbors. Were they to lose the money with the land? Others said that the graves of their ancestors were in the ground, which had been allotted to them in the division of their fathers' estates. Others said that their wives' dowries had been expended on the estates, or that the land had been given to their own daughters as dowry. Money-lenders could show loans made on this security. All kinds of wailing and expressions of indignation were heard at once. On the other side were heard the lamentations of the poor—that they had been reduced from competence to extreme penury, and from that to childlessness, because they were unable to rear their offspring. They recounted the military services they had rendered, by which this very land had been acquired, and were angry that they should be robbed of their share of the common property. They reproached the rich for employing slaves, who were always faithless and ill-tempered and for that reason unserviceable in war, instead of freemen, citizens, and soldiers. While these classes were lamenting and indulging in mutual accusations, a great number of others, composed of colonists, or inhabitants of the free towns, or persons otherwise interested in the lands and who were under like apprehensions, flocked in and took sides with their respective factions. Emboldened by numbers and exasperated against each other they attached themselves to turbulent crowds, and waited for the voting on the new law, some trying to prevent its enactment by all means, and others supporting it in every possible way. In addition to personal interest the spirit of rivalry spurred both sides in the preparations they were making against each other for the day of the comitia.

What Gracchus had in his mind in proposing the measure was not wealth, but an increase of efficient population. Inspired greatly by the usefulness of the work, and believing that nothing more advantageous or admirable could ever happen to Italy, he took no account of the difficulties surrounding it. When the time for voting came he advanced many other arguments at considerable length and also asked them whether it was not just to divide among the common people what belonged to them in common; whether a citizen was not worthy of more consideration at all times than a slave; whether a man who served in the army was not more useful than one who did not; and whether one who had a share in the country was not more likely to be devoted to the public interests. He did not dwell long on this comparison between freemen and slaves, which he considered degrading, but proceeded at once to a review of their hopes and fears for the country, saying that the Romans had acquired most of their territory by conquest, and that they had hopes of occupying the rest of the habitable world, but now the question of greatest hazard was, whether they should gain the rest by having plenty of brave men, or whether, through their weakness and mutual jealousy, their enemies should take away what they already possessed. After exaggerating the glory and riches on the one side and the danger and fear on the other, he admonished the rich to take heed, and said that for the realization of these hopes they ought to bestow this very land as a free gift, if necessary, on men who would rear children, and not, by contending about small things, overlook larger ones; especially since they were receiving an ample compensation for labor expended in the undisputed title to 500 jugera each of free land, in a high state of cultivation, without cost, and half as much more for each son of those who had sons. After saying much more to the same purport and exciting the poor, as well as others who were moved by reason rather than by the desire for gain, he ordered the scribe to read the proposed law.

Marcus Octavius, another tribune, who had been induced by those in possession of the lands to interpose his veto (for among the Romans the tribune's veto always prevailed), ordered the scribe to keep silence. Thereupon Gracchus reproached him severely and adjourned the comitia to the following day. Then he stationed a sufficient guard, as if to force Octavius against his will, and ordered the scribe with threats to read the proposed law to the multitude. He began to read, but when Octavius again vetoed he stopped. Then the tribunes fell to wrangling with each other, and a considerable tumult arose among the people. The leading citizens besought the tribunes to submit their controversy to the Senate for decision. Gracchus seized on the suggestion, believing that the law was acceptable to all well-disposed persons, and hastened to the senate-house. There, as he had only a few followers and was upbraided by the rich, he ran back to the forum and said that he would take the vote at the comitia of the following day, both on the law and on the magistracy of Octavius, to determine whether a tribune who was acting contrary to the people's interest could continue to hold his office. And so he did, for when Octavius, nothing daunted, again interposed, Gracchus distributed the pebbles to take a vote on him first. When the first tribe voted to abrogate the magistracy of Octavius, Gracchus turned to him and begged him to desist from this veto. As he would not yield, the votes of the other tribes were taken. There were thirty-five tribes at that time. The seventeen that voted first angrily sustained this motion. If the eighteenth should do the same it would make a majority. Again did Gracchus, in the sight of the people, urgently importune Octavius in his present extreme danger not to prevent this most pious work, so useful to all Italy, and not to frustrate the wishes so earnestly entertained by the people, whose desires he ought rather to share in his character of tribune, and not to risk the loss of his office by public condemnation. After speaking thus he called the gods to witness that he did not willingly do any despite to his colleague. As Octavius was still unyielding he went on taking the vote. Octavius was forthwith reduced to the rank of a private citizen and slunk away unobserved.

Quintus Mummius was chosen tribune in his place, and the agrarian law was enacted. The first triumvirs appointed to divide the land were Gracchus himself, the proposer of the law, his brother of the same name, and his father-in-law, Appius Claudius, since the people still feared that the law might fail of execution unless Gracchus should be put in the lead with his whole family. Gracchus became immensely popular by reason of the law and was escorted home by the multitide as though he were the founder, not of a single city or race, but of all the nations of Italy. After this the victorious party returned to the fields from which they had come to attend to this business. The defeated ones remained in the city and talked the matter over, feeling bitterly, and saying that as soon as Gracchus should become a private citizen he would be sorry that he had done despite to the sacred and inviolable office of tribune, and had opened such a fountain of discord in Italy.

At the advent of summer the notices for the election of tribunes were given, and as the day for voting approached it was very evident that the rich were earnestly promoting the election of those most inimical to Gracchus. The latter, fearing that evil would befall if he should not be reelected for the following year, summoned his friends from the fields to attend the comitia, but as they were occupied with their harvest he was obliged, when the day fixed for the voting drew near, to have recourse to the plebeians of the city. So he went around asking each one separately to elect him tribune for the ensuing year, on account of the danger he had incurred for them. When the voting took place the first two tribes pronounced for Gracchus. The rich objected that it was not lawful for the same man to hold the office twice in succession. The tribune Rubrius, who had been chosen by lot to preside over the comitia, was in doubt about it, and Mummius, who had been chosen in place of Octavius, urged him to turn over the comitia to his charge. This he did, but the remaining tribunes contended that the presidency should be decided by lot, saying that when Rubrius, who had been chosen in that way, resigned, the casting of lots ought to be done over again for all. As there was much strife over this question, Gracchus, who was getting the worst of it, adjourned the voting to the following day. In utter despair he clothed himself in black, while still in office, and led his son around the forum and introduced him to each man and committed him to their charge, as if he were about to perish at the hands of his enemies.

The poor were moved with deep sorrow, and rightly so, both on their own account (for they believed that they were no longer to live in a free state under equal laws, but were reduced to servitude by the rich), and on account of Gracchus himself, who had incurred such danger and suffering in their behalf. So they all accompanied him with tears to his house in the evening, and bade him be of good courage for the morrow.

Gracchus cheered up, assembled his partisans before daybreak, and communicated to them a signal to be displayed in case of a fight. He then took possession of the temple on the Capitoline hill, where the voting was to take place, and occupied the middle of the assembly. As he was obstructed by the other tribunes and by the rich, who would not allow the votes to be taken on this question, he gave the signal. There was a sudden shout from those who saw it, and a resort to violence in consequence. Some of the partisans of Gracchus took position around him like body-guards. Others, having girded themselves, seized the fasces* and staves in the hands of the lictors and broke them in pieces. They drove the rich out of the assembly with such disorder and wounds that the tribunes fled from their places in terror, and the priests closed the doors of the temple. Many ran away pell-mell and scattered wild rumors. Some said that Gracchus had deposed all the other tribunes, and this was believed because none of them could be seen. Others said that he had declared himself tribune for the ensuing year without an election.

Under these circumstances the Senate assembled at the temple of Fides. It is astonishing to me that they never thought of appointing a dictator in this emergency, although they had often been protected by the government of a single ruler in such times of peril. Although this resource had been found most useful in former times few people remembered it, either then or later. After reaching the decision that they did reach, they marched up to the Capitol, Cornelius Scipio Nasica, the pontifex maximus [president of the guild of priests—Ed.], leading the way and calling out with a loud voice, "Let those who would save the country follow me." He wound the border of his toga about his head either to induce a greater number to go with him by the singularity of his appearance, or to make for himself, as it were, a helmet as a sign of battle for those who looked on, or in order to conceal from the gods what he was about to do. When he arrived at the temple and advanced against the partisans of Gracchus they yielded to the reputation of a foremost citizen, for they saw the Senate following with him. The latter wrested clubs out of the hands of the Gracchans themselves, or with fragments of broken benches or other apparatus that had been brought for the use of the assembly, began beating them, and pursued them, and drove them over the precipice. In the tumult many of the Gracchans perished, and Gracchus himself was caught near the temple, and was slain at the door close by the statues of the kings. All the bodies were thrown by night into the Tiber.

So perished on the Capitol, and while still tribune, Gracchus, the son of the Gracchus who was twice consul, and of Cornelia, daughter of that

---

* A bundle of rods with an axe projecting from it, carried by the lictors (public attendants) of magistrates as an emblem of criminal jurisdiction.—Ed.

Scipio who subjugated Carthage. He lost his life in consequence of a most excellent design, which, however, he pursued in too violent a manner. This shocking affair, the first that was perpetrated in the public assembly, was seldom without parallels thereafter from time to time. On the subject of the murder of Gracchus the city was divided between sorrow and joy. Some mourned for themselves and for him, and deplored the present condition of things, believing that the commonwealth no longer existed, but had been supplanted by force and violence. Others considered that everything had turned out for them exactly as they wished.

WOMEN AND ROMAN RELIGION

SARAH B. POMEROY

Roman religious cults, according to this modern historian, satisfied the political needs of the Roman state rather than the emotional needs of individuals. Roman women, therefore, often turned to the more satisfying Oriental religious cults. What were the differences between the native state cults of the Romans and the Oriental cults? What roles did women play in the state cults? Why did Oriental cults, like that of Isis, have greater appeal to women? Did Roman women have different religious needs than Roman men?

My dear, I truly desire to see you as soon as possible, and to die in your arms, since neither the gods whom you have piously worshiped nor the men whom I have always served have shown us any thanks.

> *Cicero to his wife, Terentia,*
> *Brundisium, April 29, 58 B.C.*

This division of labor—the cultivation of the heavenly powers by the woman and the care of the mundane by the man—would not come as a surprise to anyone familiar with Italian customs even today. But it is necessary to point out at once that Cicero has simplified the facts for rhetorical effect, and that the dichotomy is more ideal than real, for the life of a Roman man was also fraught with religious duties, while a

From *Goddesses, Whores, Wives, and Slaves* by Sarah Pomeroy. Copyright © 1975 by Schocken Books Inc. Reprinted by permission of Schocken Books Inc.

woman like Terentia was primarily concerned with the management of her family and finances. For Terentia, participation in religion could be both an obligation and a pleasure.

Roman religion was basically of two kinds: there were the native cults that supported and were supported by the state; and there were the imported Oriental cults—including that of Isis, the most intriguing of all Roman deities. Religion afforded an outlet for those whose lives were circumscribed in other ways: some cults—evidently the more popular— offered opportunities for joy and release. The Romans had festivals confined to women, analogous to the Thesmophoria of the Athenians, at which drunkenness, obscene jests, and lewd behavior were appropriate. They also had Mystery religions like those at Eleusis, which held out the comfort of a blessed resurrection. On the other hand, many cults that offered no particular pleasure to the worshiper had to be maintained in order to avert the wrath of a spurned deity. Often these cults had their own peculiar constellations of prescriptions for the devotee: abstinence from certain foods or from sex, and the punctilious performance of ritualized—but frequently inexplicable—ceremonies at designated times.

Among the numerous cults developed by the Romans to enlist divine aid for practical purposes were those designed to uphold ideals of female conduct. The Roman genius for organization is reflected in the categorizing of women and their desirable qualities and in the creation of cults appropriate to the categories. Women were ranked according to the class distinction between plebeians and patricians, by a moral standard segregating respectable women from those who followed disreputable professions, by age, and by whether they were slave or free. Marital status was also a fundamental subdivision by which women were ranked, including the following distinctions: young virgin, celibate adult, wife, wife married only once (*univira*), and widow.

The several cults of Fortuna (Luck or Fortune) that emerged from that goddess' patronage of women's lives show the Romans' use of religious sanctions to promote socially desirable behavior. Identifiable in the Roman pantheon by her rudder, globe, and cornucopia, Fortuna's significance for women centered on the last of her symbols, for she was the guarantor not only of the fruits of the earth but also of women's physical maturation and sexual fulfillment.

• • •

Vesta (Greek Hestia) was the goddess of the hearth, both public and domestic. The hearth with its undying flame symbolized the continuity of both family and community, and extinction of the fire was a grave matter. Tending the family hearth was the responsibility of the daughter of the household.

. . .

The priestesses of Ceres were the only women besides Vestals [virgin priestesses] who had the prestigious duty of administering a state cult.

Ceres was an agricultural divinity whose name shows the same root as the Latin verbs *creare* and *cresco*, meaning "to produce" and "to grow." Thus Ceres was an important goddess in earliest Rome, when the principal occupation was farming and religion was devoted to agrarian prosperity. The goddess Tellus (Mother Earth) was closely associated with Ceres in the realm of agriculture, and both goddesses were especially concerned with the production of grain.

Ceres and Tellus were concerned with human fecundity as well as the productivity of the fields. Both were goddesses of marriage, for it is clear that the chief objective of marriage was procreation. Thus brides, who would be thought at fault if the marriage proved sterile, customarily honored Ceres and Tellus. There was also a tradition that Ceres protected wives, since the laws attributed to Romulus by Plutarch state that if a husband divorces his wife for any reason other than poisoning his children, counterfeiting his keys, or adultery, half his property will belong to his wife and the other half be consecrated to Ceres, and that whoever puts away his wife must make a sacrifice to the infernal deities.

. . .

The cult of Isis was one of the many Oriental mystery religions that stand in dramatic contrast to the traditional cults of Roman religion. The foreign cult of the Greek goddess Demeter had been easily accepted by the Romans, who assimilated her to their own goddess Ceres. The cult of Ceres and some Fortuna cults were controllable, for they were confined to female devotees. Likewise, the cults of Ceres, Fortuna, and the Vestals were entwined with the interests of the state, rather than directed toward the benefit of particular individuals. The cult of Isis is unlike the others we have discussed. Through it the religious and emotional needs of women and men of the Hellenistic and Roman worlds could be expressed and satisfied. Isis met with official resistance from the Romans, but ended by having a larger sphere of influence in religious ideas than any of the cults we have previously considered.

Isis was a national divinity of ancient Egypt dating back at least to 2500 B.C., but she was a goddess with accretions of myths and rituals of many lands by the time she reached the shores of Italy at the end of the second century B.C. The cult of Isis had spread throughout the Mediterranean world, and easily adapted itself wherever it was carried. Unlike Roman cults, in which the details of worship and the categories of worshipers were rigidly prescribed, that of Isis was capable of unlimited flexibility. The goddess readily encompassed inconsistencies and mutually contradictory qualities. Thus she was identified with many other Mediterranean goddesses ranging from Astarte of Phoenicia, to Fortuna, Athena, Aphrodite, Hestia, Hera, Demeter, and Artemis. She was endowed with magical capabilities, could heal the sick, and promised blessed resurrection to her devotees after death.

Even more remarkable than her assimilation of the powers of female deities is Isis' acquisition of powers associated in the classical world with male divinities. She has the attributes traditionally assigned to the Indo-European sky god: dominion over lightning, thunder, and the winds. She is the creator, for she divided earth from heaven, assigned languages to nations, and invented alphabets and astronomy. Aretalo- gies [lists of virtues] surviving from antiquity give long lists of the attributes of the goddess; her epithets are innumerable, her powers limitless.

Owing to the influence of her worshipers in port cities such as Alexandria, Isis became a patroness of navigation and commerce. Her cult lent itself as well to philosophical interpretations. Plutarch explains the creativity of Isis with citations from Plato's *Timaeus*, and writes that the power of Isis "is concerned with matter which becomes and receives everything: light and dark, day and night, fire and water, life and death, beginning and end." Thus Isis could be all things to all people, a quality that greatly enhanced her popularity. She was a single supreme goddess behind many manifestations; the prerogatives of other goddesses ac- crued to her, and she was worshiped in varying ways, but she remained Isis. In this sense her religion was henotheistic,* but her worshipers were pagan and polytheistic, for they did not deny the existence of other divinities. An inscription found in Capua erected by a Roman senator described Isis succinctly as "you who are one and all" ("*te tibi una quae es omnia dea Isis*"). But in her omnipotence she was not threatening, for she was loving and merciful.

The impressive history of the expansion of the cult both before and after it migrated to Italy has been traced in detail by the meticulous study of archaeological and inscriptional evidence. However, examining the cult from the viewpoint of women's history allows new questions to be posed relating to women's role in the religion, the emotional appeal of a supreme female divinity, and the ascendancy of a mother goddess at a particular point of Roman history.

The worshipers of Isis were everywhere, of all ages and both sexes.

---

* Allowed the worship of one god without denying the existence of other gods.—Ed.

The only segment of society where Isis did not attract devotees was the Roman army, for whom the masculine god Mithras held more appeal. By contrast, the cult of Isis was especially attractive to women. Isis was a wife and mother, but she had also been a whore. Respectable women as well as prostitutes could identify with her. Isis also elevated the status of women. Male deities were sometimes worshiped in her temples, but in the Hellenistic and Roman worlds Isis was supreme among the Egyptian gods. Diodorus Siculus* reported that because of the example of Isis, the Egyptian queens had more honor than the kings, and that among commoners the wives ruled the husbands. No doubt the example of the domination of Cleopatra over Antony was fresh in the mind of Diodorus, who wrote in the time of Caesar and Augustus. Equality rather than domination is mentioned in a long hymm to Isis dating from the second century A.D. found in Oxyrhynchus, Egypt, which includes in its praises of the goddess that "she made the power of women equal to that of men."

However, the worship of Isis was by no means confined to women. Like the Mysteries of Demeter and Persephone at Eleusis, those of Isis appealed to men as well. There were also Mysteries of male gods; in paganism it was possible to have one's choice. It may be suggested that one specific avenue of appeal that a loving maternal divinity held within a rigid patriarchal society was that she was accessible to entreaty—she could be yielding and merciful.

· · ·

The story of the spiritual conversion of Lucius, told by Apuleius in the novel *The Golden Ass*, or *Metamorphoses*, in the second century A.D., illustrates on a larger scale the tenderness and closeness of Isis, and the love Lucius gave her in return. Lucius, a young man of a good family, meddled with the magic of Thessalian witches and was changed accidentally into an ass. He retained his human perceptions, and suffered vicissitudes, many of which included lewd and humiliating incidents, until, at last, by the agency of Isis, he was restored to human form. Isis visited him personally in dreams and invited him to be initiated into her Mysteries and to vow his life to her service. It is clear that the devotee had a private relationship with the goddess, and the worship of Isis suited the individualism of the Hellenistic and Roman worlds. Individuals were responsible for their own acts; they could be initiated, rewarded, forgiven, and granted eternal salvation. In contrast, traditional Roman religion was based on a communal responsibility, in which

* A Greek historian of the first century A.D.—Ed.

the unchastity of one Vestal jeopardized the entire population, while the expiation of her transgression would restore the favor of the gods to all.

The central myth of the Isis cult combines peculiarly Egyptian antecedents with Greco-Roman elements. According to one version, Isis and her brother Osiris had loved one another even within their mother's womb. Their marriage provided the paradigm for the brother-sister marriages common among Egyptian rulers. But Osiris, commonly identified with the sun, was killed and dismembered by his brother Set, god of darkness. Isis mourned and searched for the fragments of Osiris' body, and through her agency he was restored to life. But before his resuscitation Isis bore a child, and thus she is often depicted in visual representations nursing a baby. These portraits have led to comparisons between Isis with her infant Horus and the Virgin Mary with the baby Jesus. However, while Christian theologians held up Mary as a model of virginal maternity, the child Horus was clearly seen in the cult of Isis as being the offspring of his parents' union. The Isis myth also relates that when she searched for the pieces of Osiris' body, she failed to recover his phallus. Perhaps to compensate for that critical loss, Osiris is often represented as a phallus.

The emotional appeal of a divinity who has herself suffered such inestimable loss is undeniable. Worshipers could feel sympathy for and closeness to Isis, while they experienced only awe and fear in their distant relationships with most of the Olympian deities. Moreover, the worshiper could readily identify with Osiris—as Osiris suffered death and was born again, so the devotee of Isis could anticipate his own renewal after death. This appeal must have been especially potent among the most wretched members of society. Women were attracted, too, to the promises of exotic religions, as Juvenal disparagingly pointed out in his diatribe on women:

> And watch out for a woman who's a religious fanatic: in the summer, she'll fill the house with a coven of worshipers of strange oriental deities. Their minister will be a weird apparition, an enormous obscene eunuch, revered because he castrated himself with a jagged hunk of glass. He'll use his prophetic powers and solemnly intone the usual warning:
>
> > Beware the ides of September!
> > Beware the arrival of December!
> > Protect yourself! pledge me one
> > hundred eggs and a warm woolen cloak.
>
> He claims that whatever dangers threaten will be absorbed by the cloak and promises protection for the coming year.
>
> In the middle of winter, at dawn, she'll go down to the Tiber, break through the ice, and piously immerse herself three times to purify her body, and then she'll crawl on her bleeding knees halfway across Rome—to atone

for having slept with her husband the night before: this is the ritual prescribed by the deity in favor *this* month. If some Egyptian goddess instructs her to make a pilgrimage to the Nile, she'll leave at once, follow the river to its source, and return with a phial of sacred water to sprinkle on the temple (which, as you can see, desecrates one of our oldest historical landmarks). She actually believes that Isis speaks to her! As if any god would bother to talk with such a fool.

Women like this revere any Egyptian priest who cons his followers with elaborate rituals and meaningless taboos. He has them convinced that he has the power to obtain forgiveness for their sins. If they fail to abstain from marital relations on holy days, or if they owe a penance for violating the goddess' prohibitions, the goddess will reveal her displeasure by shaking her head; the priest, in tears, mumbling an empty litany, will intercede with the gods so that Osiris, bribed by a fat goose and a piece of cake, will forgive them.

· · ·

Social pleasure and sensual gratification were among the rewards of the devotees of Isis. Magnificent processions of worshipers and professional priests garbed in white linen proceeded to the edge of the sea to launch a sacred boat, accompanied by the rattle of the sistrum* and the music of the flute. This ceremony was called the Navigium Isidis, and took place on March 5 to inaugurate the season of navigation. The rite was more purposeful to the businessman than the agrarian-based rituals of Roman religion, while to an urban population it assured the protection of ships laden with grain from the provinces of the Empire, in particular from Egypt. Also of major importance were the Mysteries at which the worshipers reenacted the lamentation of Isis and her subsequent joy when she found the body of Osiris. Here the rite of Isis is directly parallel to the Eleusinian Mysteries at Athens: empathy with the woman who lost what was dear to her and found it again. At this time the devotees of Isis exchanged embraces, danced in the streets, and invited strangers to dinner parties.

For slaves and freedmen and anyone who lacked a family, the conviviality of the cult was attractive. The social order was precious to Romans, but disregarded by Isis; her cult was open to all. There was a professional body of male priests, but others, both men and women, could hold high office within the cult. Of twenty-six functionaries termed minister (*sacerdos*) in extant inscriptions of Italy, six are women, including one woman of senatorial rank and one daughter of a freedman. Frescoes of Herculaneum and Pompeii portray women participating fully in the ceremonies. In contrast, the state religion of Rome

---

* An Egyptian percussion instrument made of a looped metal frame with crossbars set in a handle.—Ed.

traditionally excluded slaves, freedmen, and of course women—with the exception of a few, including the six Vestals and two priestesses of Ceres—from its hierarchy, while those who did participate were carefully organized into separate categories.

Those Romans who idealized their traditional way of life nursed a hostility against foreigners and secret societies, fearing that their activities might erupt in antisocial behavior. No wonder that congregations such as those worshiping Isis could be considered potentially revolutionary, especially since so many votaries were those who had little stake in the perpetuation or revival of Roman traditions; worshipers were not viewed as part of a societal or governmental world and, as we have noted, the cult was oriented to the well-being of the individual.

THE ROMAN EMPIRE IN THE YEAR ONE

M. I. FINLEY

The Year One, this modern historian reminds us, was not a Roman date but a Christian one. And even if it was not the correct date for the beginning of Christianity, it was very close to the beginning of the Roman Empire (twenty-seven years after Octavian became the Emperor Augustus).

What was it like to be a Roman in this period of the early empire? What was it like to be a colonial subject? What were the accomplishments of Augustus? What were his failures? How did Roman rule come into conflict with the Jews? What, if anything, began in the Year One?

Decisive years, like decisive battles, are an old favourite with historians. Some—1492, 1776, 1914—are pretty obvious: knowledgeable contemporaries could not have escaped the feeling that something big was up, even though they could not have foreseen all the consequences. More often, however, great historical processes begin altogether invisibly, and only much later, looking back, is it possible to pin the critical date down. Such a year is the Year One. Indeed, of all the great years in history it is the oddest because no one alive at the time, or for centuries thereafter, had any idea that this was the Year One at all. If they ever used such a date, they would have meant by it the year in which the world was created, not what we mean by A.D. I.

How, for example, was a birth certificate, a marriage contract, a business agreement, dated in the Year One? There is no single answer to such a question, since for most of the purposes of ordinary living, local dates were used. In Rome a contract would be dated "in the consulship of C. Caesar son of Augustus and L. Aemilius Paullus son of Paullus." Elsewhere there were regnal years, or years of local officials, or of priesthoods. This may look like chaos to us, habituated as we are to a continuous, fixed calendar in use more or less all over the world, but it worked well enough. Only the learned were troubled, the men who wanted an exact answer to the question "How long ago?" or who wished to synchronize events in Greek and Roman history. A number of systems had been invented for their use. In Rome scholars commonly dated events from the legendary foundation of the city by Romulus in the year we call 753 B.C.; in Greece they used four-year units, Olympiads, beginning with the first Olympic Games in 776 B.C. In those two systems the Year One was, respectively, 754 A.U.C. (*ab urbe condita*) and the first year of the 195th Olympiad. No system was official: every scholar and historian was free to choose whichever he preferred, singly or in combination.

It is therefore hardly surprising that it took the Christians a long time to think up and introduce a scheme of their own. The honour goes to an eastern Greek-speaking monk, Dionysius Exiguus, who lived in Rome in the first half of the sixth century. He calculated that Christ was born in 754 A.U.C., called that the first "year of our Lord," *anno Domini*, and counted everything that preceded it as so many years *ante Christum*, "before Christ." His calculation was slightly inaccurate. The only real evidence is in two of the four Gospels, and unfortunately that is conflicting and irreconcilable. If Matthew is right in the way he dates the flight into Egypt, then Jesus was born in or shortly before the last year of the reign of King Herod the Great, who died in 4 B.C. But if Luke is right in linking the Nativity with a census—"And all went to enrol themselves, everyone to his own city"—then the date must be A.D. 6 or even 7. On neither account is A.D. 1 possible. Nevertheless, Dionysius's chronological scheme spread gradually, first in the west, more slowly in the east, until it achieved near universality. The Year One—whatever it really was—became a great year, for many the greatest year in all history.

If A.D. 6 is the right date, then Jesus was born in the newly established Roman province of Judaea. In that year the Romans deposed Herod's son Archelaus, took over Judaea, and sent in Syria's governor, Quirinius, with instructions to conduct the first census there. Galilee, on the other hand, was allowed to continue under the family of Herod for another generation. This rather confusing political situation was not untypical of districts on the eastern frontier of the Roman empire, where imperial policy fluctuated between backing local client-kings and ruling directly. After all, Palestine was a long way from Rome. Problems much nearer home were pressing: large forces were just then occupied with trying to incorporate the German territory between the Rhine and the Elbe. They were wiped out in A.D. 9 in a treacherous ambush by Arminius (Hermann), a German chieftain who had earlier served in the Roman auxiliary forces and been rewarded with Roman citizenship. That disaster in the Teutoburg Forest effectively settled the northern frontier of the empire on the Rhine-Danube line, subject to various later adjustments, including the conquest of Britain. The western frontier was the Atlantic Ocean; the southern was the Atlas Mountains, the Sahara, and the cataracts [steep rapids] of the Nile—though parts of northern Africa had the same shifting political history as Judaea.

The Roman Empire was an empire in the strictest possible sense. The "Roman people"—that is, Roman citizens who were concentrated very largely in Rome and central or northern Italy—ruled all the rest as subjects. The empire outside Italy was divided into what were called *provinciae*, which were not provinces in the way Ontario is now a province of Canada, but rather colonies in the way India or Nigeria were British colonies before they obtained their independence. The total area of the empire in A.D. 2 was nearly 1,250,000 square miles, the population perhaps 60,000,000. Whether anyone, in or out of government, actually knew the latter figure is much to be doubted. Although censuses were taken, they were irregular, and they came at different times in different provinces. Their sole purpose was to bring the tax rolls up to date: the tax collector, along with the soldier, was the most obvious and ubiquitous link between the provinces and Rome.

Rome had begun to acquire provinces as far back as the third century B.C., and the process never stopped until the second century of the Christian Era. Imperial expansion usually looks deceptive in its motivation because defence and strategy can so plausibly be adduced as the excuse: the farther the frontiers are extended, the farther the menaces—real or imaginary—are pushed back. But in antiquity in general, and among the Romans in particular, there seems to have been much less effort than in modern times to disguise or deny the open exploitation of empire. Whatever the reasons piously given for their conquest and incorporation in each individual instance, the right to profit directly from conquered lands was freely recognized. That meant not only taxes—in goods, services and money—for the state, but often great personal income, legal or illegal, for high officials and members of the tax-farming corporations. It was also in the interests of Rome that her empire be pacific and orderly, as well as reasonably well administered locally. To achieve the latter aim she depended chiefly on the local ruling classes, for she lacked the manpower to do otherwise, and they normally played the part assigned to them as a pro-Roman counter-weight in what could well have become a rebellious situation.

From the days when Rome first began to expand, her rulers had also adopted a policy of as much non-interference as possible in social and cultural institutions, although not so much from a broad theory or principle of toleration as from the much more elementary consideration, Why bother? Rome had no "mission"—that myth was imposed retro-spectively much later. She wished to rule successfully, and it was repeatedly demonstrated to her that minimum interference paid off—even though the Roman provincial governor retained virtually absolute power and did not hesitate to use it when he felt the need, including the imposition of the death penalty. Under normal conditions the upshot was that in their daily lives very large numbers of people were touched lightly indeed by Roman rule. That was particularly true in the eastern parts of the empire which had a high civilization of their own long before the Romans came. These areas remained very diverse, both among themselves and from the west—about as diverse as they had been in their days of independence. The calendar is fairly symptomatic, language even more so. Latin was of course the official language of the Roman state. But it was not the language spoken in the east or even in some western regions such as Sicily and Libya. There the ruling classes and the intellectuals tended to speak and write and think in Greek, the rest in their native tongues—in some places Greek, in others Aramaic or Egyptian or whatever. Educated Romans were more or less fluent in Greek, but their counterparts in the eastern provinces rarely troubled to know Latin equally well. When Josephus—Joseph ben Matthias, mem-ber of a Jewish priestly family, highly educated, born and bred in Judaea—wrote his *Jewish War*, a pro-Roman eyewitness account of the Roman capture of rebel Jerusalem and the destruction of the Temple in A.D. 70, his first version was in Aramaic, his second in Greek.

Josephus was a Pharisee, for whom the villains among his own people were the Zealots, who stirred up and led the revolt against Rome. His favourite word for the rebels is "bandits," so that bandits, Zealots, and lower classes are virtually synonymous in his books. The mighty Romans needed four years to quell the Jewish uprising—precisely because social revolt, the desire for independence and sectarian religious conflict were closely intertwined. This was an age of lavish living among relatively few men at one end of the scale, and extreme poverty among the many at the other end. The Gargantuan banquet given by the freedman Trimalchio in the *Satyricon* of Petronius is funny in the way it exaggerates; the account caricatures, but it does not invent out of whole cloth. The wealth of Herod the Great was a subject for neverending comment by Josephus. But the linen weavers of Tarsus, skilled free craftsmen whose products were sought after throughout the empire, could never afford the small fee charged for the acquisition of local citizenship in their own city.

Outside Judaea serious revolt was rare, for whatever reason. There was much unhappiness and much grumbling, but it takes more than that to make a lasting mark on the record: history tends to be the history of the winners, with the losers assigned the passive, largely unvoiced, faceless role of the people on whom the winners operated. Romans in the Year One were able to contemplate their position with much satisfaction. Not only were they the rulers of what they chose to believe was the civilized world, but they had emerged successfully from a long, desperately violent, and dangerous period of civil war. The republican machinery of government, led by the exclusive, oligarchical Senate— which had sent victorious Roman armies east, west, north and south and had carved out the greatest empire yet known—had broken down badly by the end of the second century B.C. Various attempts to mend it had failed, until Julius Caesar's great-nephew and adopted son, Octavian, finally replaced the old system by a monarchy—although the explicit terminology of kingship was carefully avoided and a republican façade reconstructed, with Senate, popular assembly, consuls, praetors and so on. But a façade is just that: its function is to conceal the reality behind it. In January of 27 B.C. the Senate formally ratified the position Octavian had won by arms and conferred on him a new name, Augustus, by which he has been known ever since. At the same time a euphemistic title was chosen for him, Princeps—before this a common Latin word which the dictionary defines as "the first, chief, principal, most distinguished person," hence lacking any of the undesirable overtones of *rex* (king). He was also Imperator, a military title he used often because it affirmed his special relationship with the base and guarantee of his power: the army, roughly half of it Roman citizens in the legions, the other half auxiliaries recruited chiefly in the less Romanized provinces.

Twenty-seven years later Augustus was firmly in control of an empire which he had considerably enlarged. Small stirrings of anti-monarchical sentiment were crushed, all lingering misunderstandings about the real nature of his rule removed. In 2 B.C. he had been given the title *pater patriae*, Father of the Nation, which recalled to Roman citizens the despotic authority of the Roman *pater* at least as much as paternal benevolence. He lived on to A.D. 14, with only one new honour to look forward to: his formal deification upon his death (like Julius Caesar before him). As important as these titular acquisitions were his open manoeuvrings to establish a royal dynasty: Augustus and no one else was going to choose his successor, and in the process he trampled on some of the most deeply rooted of Roman traditions. In 4 B.C. the Senate decreed that his two grandsons (and sons by adoption), Gaius and Lucius, should be designated consuls at the age of fifteen and that they should actually assume office when they were twenty. Each was entitled "Princeps of the Youth." This rigmarole was pure crown-princedom. In the Year One, Gaius, having become twenty, was duly elected consul along with his sister's husband, L. Ameilius Paullus. Then Augustus's luck ran out: Lucius died the next year, Gaius in A.D. 4. The sick, ageing emperor proceeded to adopt Tiberius, making it quite plain that he did so joylessly, and it was Tiberius who eventually succeeded him.

That Tiberius was able to take over smoothly and peacefully is a measure of the full extent of Augustus's success. Historians commonly and rightly call Augustus the "architect of the Roman Empire." In the days when imperialism was still a virtue and Roman imperialism the accepted model, he was regularly referred to with unmixed adulation. The pendulum has now swung back, though less for some, perhaps, than for others—E. M. Forster calls Augustus "one of the most odious of the world's successful men." It is hard to imagine anyone today reading without discomfort these lines[1]:

> And here, here is the man, the promised one you know of—
> Caesar Augustus, son of a god, destined to rule
> Where Saturn ruled of old in Latium, and there
> Bring back the age of gold: his empire shall expand
> Past Garamants and Indians to a land beyond the zodiac.

Virgil and Horace were the towering figures in the literary circle patronized by one of Augustus's closest and richest friends, Maecenas. (It was not for nothing that the very name of Maecenas became a common word in the languages of Europe.) Augustus thought of everything: public opinion was not to be neglected any more than finance, dynastic arrangements, food supply, or the army. Even the coinage was harnessed. When he was given the title *pater patriae*, for example, his chief mint, at Lugdunum (Lyons), began to issue silver coins carrying his portrait with the legend *pater patriae* on the obverse; on the reverse were his two young grandsons in togas, with emblems of priesthood and the legend, "Gaius and Lucius Caesar, sons [by adoption] of Augustus, consuls-designate, *principes* of the youth." Coins circulate rapidly, and public response was not slow. Poets picked up the theme; so did individuals and communities in dedicatory inscriptions on monuments.

Yet it would be a mistake to speak cynically of prostituted art. Neither Virgil nor Horace, who died in 19 and 8 B.C., respectively, nor the historian Livy, who in the Year One was still writing away on his vast epic history of Rome, had been bought in any real sense. Horace was the son of a rich ex-slave, while Virgil and Livy came from the propertied middle classes of northern Italy. These classes had suffered heavily in

---

1. From *The Aeneid of Virgil*, edited and translated by C. Day Lewis (London: The Hogarth Press, 1952; New York: Doubleday, Anchor Books ed., 1953).

the civil wars, but now there was peace again—the *pax Augusta*—and great hope for the future, both for Rome and for the empire. With renewed greatness would come moral regeneration. This last was a favourite theme of Augustus, expressed in a stream of legislation designed to curb excessively wasteful personal living, licentiousness and depravity in the upper classes. They were to be called back, these upper classes—not to the freedom and power they had had in the Republic, but to responsible participation in the army and the civil administration under the Princeps. Augustus himself, according to his Roman biographer Suetonius, listened to poetry recitals and readings from history, and he even enjoyed them "provided they were serious and the author of the first rank."

Moral crusades are never easy to judge: standards, motives and realities are too much like icebergs. Certainly the visible part of contemporary behaviour looked rotten enough, even allowing for differences between ancient and modern values. The banishment at different times for sexual depravity of Augustus's daughter and granddaughter is proof enough. A number of men of high rank were exiled with the former as her accomplices; the husband of the latter, L. Aemilius Paullus (who had been the second consul in the Year One), was executed. There is thus something altogether mysterious about both affairs. There is no particular reason to whitewash either of the Julias, but it is hard to avoid the implication that dynastic palace plotting was a more important element in the picture. Conspiracy was henceforth endemic in the empire, and it is not unimportant that it touched the heart of the regime as early as the reign of the founder himself.

One of the younger Julia's co-victims was the poet Ovid, sent off to Tomi (now Constanța) on the Black Sea, where he was forced to live out the remaining ten years of his life, grumbling, whining, and begging in the most toadying terms for a reprieve which never came. In a sense Ovid sums up in his own career the great paradox of the Rome of his day. What had he done to warrant such severe punishment? As far as we know, nothing—or at worst something trifling. But ten years earlier he had written the *Art of Love*, and throughout his brilliant career—he was enormously popular—he belonged to a circle of poets and intellectuals who gave only lip service to the glories of the new reign while they exulted in their own individuality and, sin of sins, in the delights of love when the Emperor was demanding moral regeneration. The *pax Augusta* was enforced by a military despotism; the literary renaissance was expected to stay pretty much in line; the rule of law could be broken at the ruler's whim.

It was not the brutality that disturbed anyone. The list of Augustus's massive philanthropies, which he himself compiled for posthumous publication, included the sponsorship of eight monster exhibitions in which about ten thousand gladiators fought, the largest number on record. These were now the most popular type of public show in the Empire. If the theatre was the characteristic secular building of classical Greek civilization, the amphitheatre was its Roman counterpart. What critics of the imperial system (the few whose voices we hear) attacked was not its brutality but the arbitrariness and the sycophancy it bred, the inevitable conspiratorial atmosphere.

Yet there *was* a great cultural renaissance under Augustus. And there was peace throughout the empire most of the time, peace without political freedom as the Greeks had once understood it, even without freedom in the more limited sense men had experienced in republican Rome, but more continuous peace than the Mediterranean world had perhaps ever known. The Roman and Italian response is well documented in literature and sculptured monuments, and is not hard to understand. But what of the "provincials," the subjects, and particularly what of the great mass of them who were not local magnates supporting Rome in return for benefits received? Part of the answer, for the east in particular, is that they began to worship Augustus as Saviour, Benefactor and God Manifest (Epiphanes), just as they had deified a succession of Ptolemies, Seleucids, and other rulers in the preceding centuries. Among the Romans themselves divinity had to wait until his death; in the meantime only his genius or *daemon*, the immortal spirit within him, could have an altar. But the east, with a different tradition, built temples to Augustus the god.

This ruler-cult should neither be underestimated nor misunderstood. It was cult in the strict sense, difficult as that may be to grasp today. At the same time it did not prove the existence of widespread popular enthusiasm for the ruler as a person, or of anything more positive than a recognition of the facts of life. Power had to be worshipped, that was self-evident: the power of natural forces, Fate or Fortune, the many gods and goddesses in their multiple attributes, and the great power on earth. To do otherwise was stupid and brought certain punishment, even though rewards for proper veneration were unfortunately far from guaranteed, at least in this life. In so one-sided a relationship, in a world in which there was little hope of material success for the majority of the free population (let alone the slaves), and in which the earthly power was now pretty close to despotism, fear rather than love was often the dominating emotion behind worship, at best fear and love together. Religion became increasingly centred on salvation in the next world, whereas it had once been chiefly concerned with life in this one.

However complicated the psychology, emperor worship was a binding force in the empire. The first manifestations were more or less spontaneous, but it would be naïve to imagine that Augustus or his advisers and successors were unaware of the value of the institution. Particularly zealous to foster it were the petty tyrants and client-kings who depended on Roman arms for their very existence, among them King Herod of

Judaea (who also, significantly, introduced the amphitheatre and glad-iators into his realm). Herod thereby set off a delayed chain reaction with the most far-reaching consequences. Where there were already many gods, to add the emperor to the pantheon was easy. The polytheistic religions of the eastern Mediterranean had been adding, combining, and altering their divinities and their rituals for millennia. A small minority of intellectuals rationalized the system into one or another kind of universal religion, in which the individual gods and their cults were all manifestations of one God. Everyone else was more literal-minded, with a take-it-or-leave-it approach that permitted one to pick and choose. It was physically impossible for anyone to participate in the observances of all the divinities. A policy of *laissez faire* prevailed, provided only that no one blasphemed against anyone else's gods and that cult did not become entangled with political opposition or create an excessive amount of vicious public immorality.

The Jews stood apart. Many now lived outside Judaea: there were particularly large communities in Egypt and elsewhere in North Africa, smaller ones in Asia Minor and in Rome itself. In the Diaspora they had become very much Hellenized: parts of the Old Testament had been translated into Greek by the middle of the third century B.C. because few could any longer understand Hebrew. In Palestine, by contrast, Helle-nization had been relatively negligible, restricted to small aristocratic circles and to certain districts. Yet wherever they were, Greek and other external influences left untouched the fundamental commandments:

> Thou shalt have no other gods before me. Thou shalt not make unto thee any graven image. . . .Thou shalt not bow down thyself to them, nor serve them: for I the Lord thy God am a jealous God.

Once before, in the second century B.C., there had been grave trouble over this question, when the Jews under the leadership of the Maccabees had rebelled successfully against Antiochus IV Epiphanes, the Greek ruler of Syria and Babylonia. Now Herod was trying to repeat the same sacrilege. There was an outcry and he quickly backed down, in time to avoid civil war but not an abortive attempt to assassinate him.

In the next generations the Romans were thus faced with a strange and to them distasteful and even unintelligible situation, with a people who would not play the rules of the game as they were understood by everyone else, who worshipped one God, an exclusive, jealous God. Opposition to emperor worship was to the Romans not so much a religious issue as a political offence, *contumacia*, insubordination, civil disobedience. Augustus and Tiberius made no attempt to force matters with the Jews, and under their immediate successors official policy was inconsistent. But Roman officials in the provinces, and the local populations, for reasons of their own, were far less tolerant and cautious; there were flare-ups against the Jews, ostensibly over imperial statues, in Egypt as well as in Palestine. The Jews themselves were right to be nervous about it. Jewish "extremists" played on these fears, and on social unrest, till finally they brought about the great revolt which the emperor Vespasian and his son Titus smashed in A.D. 70.

It is this complicated combination of motives and circumstances that explains why Jewish nationalism emerged and rebelled whereas Egyptian or Syrian or Greek did not, though widespread poverty, imperial taxation, and similar factors were equally present in these other areas. Economic misery and social unrest had long been turning people to religious salvation as the only promise for the future. In this instance religion drove men to political action (as druidism may also have done in Gaul in A.D. 21). To put the whole burden of explanation on emperor worship would be wrong: religious exclusiveness and alienness, in a world which otherwise found room for all varieties of cult and belief, bred misunderstanding, dislike, wild rumours, irrational hate, mob violence. It cannot be doubted that the destruction of Jerusalem was a popular measure, on the whole, with other peoples of the empire. Imperial Rome triumphed for the moment, only to discover that she was faced with the same problem under a new name, Christianity—a religion which was just as fiercely monotheistic and exclusive as Judaism, and even more dynamic in its proselytizing zeal. "Render unto Caesar the things that are Caesar's" did not extend to worship of Caesar for Christians any more than for the Jews.

Of course there were no Christians in the Year One. Not even a hundred or two hundred years later could anyone have foreseen how radically the balance was going to shift, that the invincible Roman Empire would turn out to be transitory while the still negligible Christian sect would one day bid for universality. To emperors and ordinary non-Christians alike, Christianity was a nuisance and no more. Early in the second century, Pliny the Younger, governor of the province of Bithynia, wrote to the emperor Trajan for advice on how to deal with men and women denounced to him for being Christians. "I have never participated in interrogations of Christians," was his significant opening remark, and his long letter confirms his ignorance on the subject. To test persons accused, he continued, he required them to call upon the gods, to sacrifice before the imperial statue and to revile the name of Christ— "none of which things, it is said, genuine Christians can be induced to do." Trajan in reply agreed that Christians must be punished, but "they should not be hunted out." Roman emperors never took so casual a view of problems they regarded as really serious.

Trajan, incidentally, was the last Roman expansionist. He conquered Dacia, roughly modern Transylvania in the loop of the lower Danube, and created a new province there. Then he embarked on an absurd campaign against the Parthian empire, the heirs of the Persians east of the Euphrates River. He had fleeting success, but Hadrian—who followed him on the throne—immediately and unavoidably gave up the new eastern gains. All in all, the frontiers of the Year One were not far from the absolute limits of the Roman world, except for adjustments, a few conquests, and the final elimination of client-kingdoms as in Judaea. Roman contacts through trade were something else again. Luxury goods moved back and forth across vast distances, and with the products some information and more misinformation. Even though silk came overland from China (the middlemen living in what is now Chinese Turkestan), it may safely be doubted if anyone within the Roman Empire had ever heard of the early Han dynasty or that it was about to come to an end just then (actually in A.D. 8). Trade with India and even Ceylon was more direct and on a considerably larger scale, chiefly by sea from Egypt. Indo-Roman trading stations existed as far away as Pondicherry; there was a drain of Roman coins to India and still farther east. Yet the knowledge of Indian life and civilization scattered in Roman literature is thin and unreliable, showing little advance over the reports brought back from the campaigns of Alexander the Great several centuries earlier. Similarly, there was trans-Sahara trade, especially for ivory, but almost total ignorance of the African continent below the desert.

The peoples the Romans knew best were of course their neighbours, the Armenians and Parthians immediately to the east, and, more important, the Germans beyond the Rhine and Danube. The latter were illiterate, organized in loose tribal federations rather than in more advanced political systems, and constantly on the move, both because their relatively primitive agricultural techniques exhausted the soil rapidly and because from time to time they were driven by invaders, such as the later Huns, who swept across the eastern and central European plains. Germans and Romans were in constant contact, sometimes hostile but more often neutral or even friendly, exchanging goods and occasionally ideas. It is hardly surprising that these less advanced peoples envied the superior Roman material standards and tried to share them, which meant trying to come into the empire.

Whatever the cultural influences going out—and they are visible in such far-flung places as Taxila in the Punjab, or among the Celts of Britain—it is easy (and sometimes too tempting) to exaggerate the reverse process, except in religion. Astrology from Babylon, the god Mithras, and the old Zoroastrian dual principle of Light and Darkness from Persia spread rapidly through the empire. Again one must not exaggerate; apart from these examples, the great matrix of religious innovation was *within* the empire, in its eastern regions: Egypt, Syria and Palestine, Asia Minor. And, of course, in the end the triumphant contribution from that area in this period was Christianity.

All this outruns the Year One by centuries, and it must be confessed that it was a decisive year only by convention, thanks to the slight error committed by Dionysius Exiguus. Nevertheless, the victory of Augustus and the birth of Christ between them marked out paths for the future, the impact of which cannot possibly be overstated. It is a commonplace to say that European civilization (and therefore American, too) has three roots, Greek, Roman and Judaeo-Christian. But it has become a commonplace because it is so obviously true. The Romanization of western Europe, for which the Augustan imperial settlement was essential, was one factor that eventually made the idea of Europe possible. The eastern half of the empire was fundamentally not Romanized, and in the end it broke away, from Rome and from Europe; but it produced and exported to Europe a second binding factor, a common and exclusive religion. These were not the only factors in subsequent European history, to be sure. In history, unlike biology, one must not ask too much of roots. They cannot explain everything. It is enough to understand how deep down they go and what they have contributed.

6. Judeo-Christian Tradition

THE BIBLE

The word "Bible" has different meanings for Jews and Christians. Jews use the word to mean just the Judaic writings that were composed between about 900 and 165 B.C., mainly in Hebrew, with some Aramaic. Christians use the word "Bible" to refer to both these writings (which they call the Old Testament) and the writings about Jesus and the early Christian church (the New Testament) that were written between about A.D. 50 and 100 in Greek, based in part on earlier Aramaic sources.

The Hebrew Bible is a rich collection of laws, history, poems, and prophecy. It reflects the life of a tribe of Hebrews, descended from a patriarch named Abraham, who may have left the ancient Mesopotamian city of Ur around 2000 B.C. These Hebrews were a nomadic, pastoral people (see Psalm 23), who practiced animal sacrifice (see Leviticus). Their wanderings took them across the Fertile Crescent to Egypt, which they fled about 1300 B.C. to settle in Canaan, or Palestine, where they built a kingdom (later divided) after 1000 B.C. around the city of Jerusalem.

Sometime between 2000 and 165 B.C., the Hebrews developed a radically different religion from that of their neighbors. The most striking element of this religion was its belief in one god (monotheism). This belief might be called the core message of the Bible. As such, it rings out from the first line of the first book, Genesis. The idea of a single creator God, not just a tribal ancestor or nature spirit, was unique. It meant the possibility of a single human story, and this is the story Genesis sets out to tell. Monotheism also implied a belief that the world was orderly and good. How are these ideas presented in Genesis? What does Genesis say about the relationship between God and humans? What is the relationship in Genesis between humans and nature?

Some scholars have suggested that we have two creation accounts here, a philosophical, "priestly" account written about 650 B.C. in 1:1 to 2:3, followed by an older, legendary, "story-telling" account written about 850 B.C., starting at 2:4. Do you see any evidence for this idea? How does the tone or meaning of Genesis change after 2:4? What does Genesis tell you about women in Hebrew society? What else does it tell you about the Hebrews?

All biblical selections are from the King James Version.

GENESIS

1

1 In the beginning God created the heaven and the earth. 2 And the earth was without form, and void; and darkness *was* upon the face of the deep. And the Spirit of God moved upon the face of the waters. 3 And God said, Let there be light: and there was light. 4 And God saw the light, and *it was* good: and God divided the light from the darkness. 5 And God called the light Day, and the darkness he called Night. And the evening and the morning were the first day.

6 And God said, Let there be a firmament in the midst of the waters, and let it divide the waters from the waters. 7 And God made the firmament, and divided the waters which *were* under the firmament from the waters which *were* above the firmament: and it was so. 8 And God called the firmament Heaven. And the evening and the morning were the second day.

9 And God said, Let the waters under the heaven be gathered together unto one place, and let the dry *land* appear: and it was so. 10 And God called the dry *land* Earth; and the gathering together of the water called he Seas: and God saw *it was* good. 11 And God said, Let the earth bring forth grass, the herb yielding seed, *and* the fruit tree yielding fruit after his kind, whose seed *is* in itself, upon the *earth*: and it was so. 12 And the earth brought forth grass, *and* herb yielding seed after his kind, and the tree yielding fruit, whose seed *was* in itself, after his kind: and God saw that *it was* good. 13 And the evening and the morning were the third day.

14 And God said, Let there be lights in the firmament of the heaven to divide the day from the night; and let them be for signs, and for seasons, and for days, and years: 15 And let them be for lights in the firmament of the heaven to give light upon the earth: and it was so. 16 And God made two great lights; the greater light to rule the day, and the lesser light to rule the night: *he made* the stars also. 17 And God set them in the firmament of the heaven to give light upon the earth, 18 And to rule over the day and over the night, and to divide the light from the darkness: and God saw that *it was* good. 19 And the evening and the morning were the fourth day.

20 And God said, Let the waters bring forth abundantly the moving creatures that hath life, and fowl *that* may fly above the earth in the open firmament of heaven. 21 And God created great whales, and every living creature that moveth. which the waters brought forth abundantly, after their kind, and every winged fowl after his kind: and God saw that *it was* good. 22 And God blessed them, saying, Be fruitful, and

multiply, and fill the waters in the seas, and let fowl multiply in the earth.   23 And the evening and the morning were the fifth day.

24 And God said, Let the earth bring forth the living creature after his kind, cattle, and creeping thing, and beast of the earth after his kind: and it was so.   25 And God made the beast of the earth after his kind, and cattle after their kind, and every thing that creepeth upon the earth after his kind: and God saw that *it was* good.

26 And God said, Let us make man in our image, after our likeness: and let them have dominion over the fish of the sea, and over the fowl of the air, and over the cattle, and over all the earth, and over every creeping thing that creepeth upon the earth.   27 So God created man in his *own* image, in the image of God created he him; male and female created he them.   28 And God blessed them, and God said unto them, Be fruitful, and multiply, and replenish the earth, and subdue it: and have dominion over the fish of the sea, and over the fowl of the air, and over every living thing that moveth upon the earth.

29 And God said, Behold, I have given you every herb bearing seed, which *is* upon the face of all the earth, and every tree, in the which *is* the fruit of a tree yielding seed; to you it shall be for meat.   30 And to every beast of the earth, and to every fowl of the air, and to every thing that creepeth upon the earth, wherein *there is* life, *I have given* every green herb for meat: and it was so.   31 And God saw every thing that he had made, and, behold, *it was* very good. And the evening and the morning were the sixth day.

2

1 Thus the heavens and the earth were finished, and all the host of them.   2 And on the seventh day God ended his work which he had made; and he rested on the seventh day from all his work which he had made.   3 And God blessed the seventh day, and sanctified it: because that in it he had rested from all his work which God created and made.

4 These *are* the generations of the heavens and of the earth when they were created, in the day that the Lord God made the earth and the heavens,   5 And every plant of the field before it was in the earth, and every herb of the field before it grew: for the Lord God had not caused it to rain upon the earth, and *there was* not a man to till the ground.   6 But there went up a mist from the earth, and watered the whole face of the ground.   7 And the Lord God formed man *of* the dust of the ground, and breathed into his nostrils the breath of life; and man became a living soul.

8 And the Lord God planted a garden eastward in Eden; and there he put the man whom he had formed.   9 And out of the ground made the Lord God to grow every tree that is pleasant to the sight, and good for food; and the tree of life also in the midst of the garden, and the tree

of knowledge of good and evil.   10 And a river went out of Eden to water the garden; and from thence it was parted, and became into four heads.   11 The name of the first *is* Pison: that *is* it which compasseth the whole land of Havilah, where *there* is gold;   12 And the gold of the land *is* good: there *is* bdellium and the onyx stone.   13 And the name of the second river *is* Gihon: the same *is* it that compasseth the whole land of Ethiopia.   14 And the name of the third river *is* Hiddekel: that *is* it which goeth toward the east of Assyria. And the fourth river *is* Euphrates.   15 And the Lord God took the man, and put him into the garden of Eden to dress it and to keep it.   16 And the Lord God commanded the man, saying, Of every tree of the garden thou mayest freely eat: 17 But of the tree of the knowledge of good and evil, thou shalt not eat of it: for in the day that thou eatest thereof thou shalt surely die.

18 And the Lord God said, *It is* not good that the man should be alone; I will make him a help meet for him.   19 And out of the ground the Lord God formed every beast of the field, and every fowl of the air; and brought *them* unto Adam to see what he would call them: and whatsoever Adam called every living creature, that *was* the name thereof.   20 And Adam gave names to all cattle, and to the fowl of the air, and to every beast of the field; but for Adam there was not found a help meet for him.   21 And the Lord God caused a deep sleep to fall upon Adam, and he slept; and he took one of his ribs, and closed up the flesh instead thereof.   22 And the rib, which the Lord God had taken from man, made he a woman, and brought her unto the man.   23 And Adam said, This *is* now bone of my bones, and flesh of my flesh: she shall be called Woman, because she was taken out of man.   24 Therefore shall a man leave his father and his mother, and shall cleave unto his wife: and they shall be one flesh.   25 And they were both naked, the man and his wife, and were not ashamed.

Genesis is both a history of the world and a history of Abraham's tribe. Thus, it accounts for how the God of Abraham is the Creator of the world. According to this account (Gen. 17:1–14), God made a special covenant (or agreement) with Abraham. What was the nature of this covenant? What does this account tell you about Hebrew society?

17

1 And when Abram was ninety years old and nine, the Lord appeared to Abram, and said unto him, I *am* the Almighty God; walk before me, and be thou perfect. 2 And I will make my covenant between me and thee, and will multiply thee exceedingly. 3 And Abram fell on his face: and God talked with him, saying, 4 As for me, behold, my covenant *is* with thee, and thou shalt be a father of many

nations. 5 Neither shall thy name any more be called Abram, but thy name shall be Abraham; for a father of many nations I have made thee. 6 And I will make thee exceeding fruitful, and I will make nations of thee, and kings shall come out of thee. 7 And I will establish my covenant between me and thee and thy seed after thee in their generations, for an everlasting covenant, to be a God unto thee and to thy seed after thee. 8 And I will give unto thee, and to thy seed after thee, the land wherein thou art a stranger, all the land of Canaan, for an everlasting possession; and I will be their God. 9 And God said unto Abraham, Thou shalt keep my covenant therefore, thou, and thy seed after thee in their generations. 10 This *is* my covenant, which he shall keep, between me and you and thy seed after thee; Every man child among you shall be circumcised. 11 And ye shall circumcise the flesh of your foreskin; and it shall be a token of the covenant betwixt me and you. 12 And he that is eight days old shall be circumcised among you, every man child in your generations, he that is born in the house, or bought with money of any stranger, which *is* not of thy seed. 13 He that is born in thy house, and he that is bought with thy money, must needs be circumcised: and my covenant shall be in your flesh for an everlasting covenant. 14 And the uncircumcised man child whose flesh of his foreskin is not circumcised, that soul shall be cut off from his people; he hath broken my covenant.

In the following selection from Exodus, the second book of the Bible, God has just led his "chosen people" out of bondage in Egypt. He renews the covenant with all of the "children of Israel." (Israel, also called Jacob, was the son of Isaac and grandson of Abraham.) Then God revealed his law, beginning with the Ten Commandments. What does this selection suggest about Hebrew society? What do you think the Hebrews expected to gain by following the covenant?

EXODUS

19

1 In the third month, when the children of Israel were gone forth out of the land of Egypt, the same day came they *into* the wilderness of Sinai. 2 For they were departed from Rephidim, and were come *to* the desert of Sinai, and had pitched in the wilderness; and there Israel camped before the mount. 3 And Moses went up unto God, and the Lord called unto him out of the mountain, saying, Thus shalt thou say to the house of Jacob, and tell the children of Israel; 4 Ye have seen what I did unto the Egyptians and *how* I bare you on eagles' wings, and brought you unto myself. 5 Now therefore, if ye will obey my voice

indeed, and keep my covenant, then ye shall be a peculiar treasure unto me above all people: for all the earth *is* mine: 6 And ye shall be unto me a kingdom of priests, and a holy nation. These *are* the words which thou shalt speak unto the children of Israel.

7 And Moses came and called for the elders of the people, and laid before their faces all these words which the Lord commanded him.   8 And all the people answered together, and said, All that the Lord hath spoken we will do. And Moses returned the words of the people unto the Lord.   9 And the Lord said unto Moses, Lo, I come unto thee in a thick cloud, that the people may hear when I speak with thee, and believe thee for ever. And Moses told the words of the people unto the Lord.

. . .

20

1 And God spake all these words, saying,

2 I *am* the Lord thy God, which have brought thee out of the land of Egypt, out of the house of bondage.   3 Thou shalt have no other gods before me.

4 Thou shalt not make unto thee any graven image, or any likeness *of any thing* that *is* in heaven above, or that *is* in the earth beneath, or that *is* in the water under the earth: 5 Thou shalt not bow down thyself to them, nor serve them: for I the Lord thy God *am* a jealous God, visiting the iniquity of the fathers upon the children unto the third and fourth *generation* of them that hate me;   6 And showing mercy unto thousands of them that love me, and keep my commandments.

7 Thou shalt not take the name of the Lord thy God in vain: for the Lord will not hold him guiltless that taketh his name in vain.

8 Remember the sabbath day, to keep it holy.   9 Six days shalt thou labor, and do all thy work: 10 But the seventh day *is* the sabbath of the Lord thy God: *in it* thou shalt not do any work, thou, nor thy son, nor thy daughter, thy manservant, nor thy maidservant, nor thy cattle, nor thy stranger that *is* within thy gates: 11 For in six days the Lord made heaven and earth, the sea, and all that in them *is*, and rested the seventh day: wherefore the Lord blessed the sabbath day, and hallowed it.

12 Honor thy father and thy mother: that thy days may be long upon the land which the Lord thy God giveth thee.

13 Thou shalt not kill.

14 Thou shalt not commit adultery.

15 Thou shalt not steal.

16 Thou shalt not bear false witness against thy neighbor.

17 Thou shalt not covet thy neighbor's house, thou shalt not covet thy

neighbor's wife, nor his manservant, nor his maidservant, nor his ox, nor his ass, nor any thing that *is* thy neighbor's.

18 And all the people saw the thunderings, and the lightnings, and the noise of the trumpet, and the mountain smoking: and when the people saw *it*, they removed, and stood afar off.

> The high moral tone of the Ten Commandments contrasts with the elaborate directions for animal sacrifice in Leviticus, a brief selection of which follows. Do these passages from Leviticus represent a different cultural stage in Hebrew history? Would you expect animal sacrifice to have increased or decreased in importance as the moral law developed?

LEVITICUS

1

1 And the Lord called unto Moses, and spake unto him out of the tabernacle of the congregation, saying, 2 Speak unto the children of Israel, and say unto them, If any man of you bring an offering unto the Lord, ye shall bring your offering of the cattle, *even* of the herd, and of the flock.

3 If his offering *be* a burnt sacrifice of the herd, let him offer a male without blemish: he shall offer it of his own voluntary will at the door of the tabernacle of the congregation before the Lord. 4 And he shall put his hand upon the head of the burnt offering; and it shall be accepted for him to make atonement for him. 5 And he shall kill the bullock before the Lord: and the priests, Aaron's sons, shall bring the blood, and sprinkle the blood round about upon the alter that *is by* the door of the tabernacle of the congregation. 6 And he shall flay the burnt offering, and cut it into his pieces. 7 And the sons of Aaron the priest shall put fire upon the altar, and lay the wood in order upon the fire: 8 And the priests, Aaron's sons, shall lay the parts, the head, and the fat, in order upon the wood that *is* on the fire which *is* upon the alter: 9 But his inwards and his legs shall he wash in water: and the priest shall burn all on the altar, *to be* a burnt sacrifice, an offering made by fire, of a sweet savor unto the Lord.

> Psalm 23, which follows, is attributed to King David, who ruled around 1000 B.C. It points backward in time to a day when the Hebrews were still shepherds. Who but shepherds would declare their Lord is "a shepherd"? What would farmers call their god? What would be the metaphor for a city god? Psalm 23 also points forward to a belief in a "for ever." You may have noticed that there has been no mention of an afterlife in the writings so far. Why?

PSALM 23

1 The Lord *is* my shepherd; I shall not want.

2 He maketh me to lie down in green pastures: He leadeth me beside the still waters.

3 He restoreth my soul: He leadeth me in the paths of righteousness for his name's sake.

4 Yea, though I walk through the valley of the shadow of death, I will fear no evil: for thou *art* with me; Thy rod and thy staff they comfort me.

5 Thou preparest a table before me in the presence of mine enemies: Thou anointest my head with oil; my cup runneth over.

6 Surely goodness and mercy shall follow me all the days of my life: And I will dwell in the house of the Lord for ever.

> *After the kingdoms of Israel and Judah were conquered, a new breed of Jewish thinkers, called* prophets, *tried to show how God had intended the conquest of His people as punishment for their transgressions. In the process these prophets reshaped God's message in significant ways. Instead of animal sacrifice or even ritual and law, they urged piety (religious feeling) and justice. One of the most eloquent of these prophets was Amos. This selection is Amos 5:21–24. How are these ideas different from those of Leviticus?*

AMOS

5

21 I hate, I despise your feast days, and I will not smell in your solemn assemblies.

22 Though you offer me burnt offerings and your meat offerings, I will not accept them: neither will I regard the peace offerings of your fat beasts.

23 Take thou away from me the noise of thy songs; for I will not hear the melody of thy viols.

24 But let judgment run down as waters, and righteousness as a mighty stream.

> *The last of the prophets was the author of the book of Daniel, written about 165 B.C. The author presents himself as a Daniel taken to Babylon in the sixth century B.C. In this way, he is able to present Hebrew history from 600 to 165 B.C. as if from the eye of God, divinely preordained. Seen in this light, the Babylonian, Median, Persian, and Greek conquests of the Jews take on a providential meaning. They are not unexpected disasters but part of a larger divine plan. Events seemed to be moving to history's ultimate struggle. The end would come not only to the Kingdom*

of Israel, Daniel declares, but to all earthly kingdoms. There would be a final catastrophe for Jew and Gentile alike, a Last Judgment and a new dawn.

This is the first explicit mention in the Bible of an end to history and an afterlife, central ideas in Christianity. Daniel predicted the apocalypse, the end of the world. When would the end come? The first answer is after "time, times, and a half." Then he alludes to "the time that the daily sacrifice shall be taken away, and the abomination that maketh desolate set up." This refers to the desecration of the Hebrew temple in Jerusalem by the Syrian king Antiochus Epiphanes in 168 B.C. When will the end come? Now Daniel is specific: 1,290 days after the desecration by Antiochus. That would be 164 B.C., which is why we know the book was written in 165 B.C. Why does the next line say, in effect, "blessed are those who wait 1,335 days?"

How is this selection from Daniel different from the other Bible selections you have read? In what ways is it similar? What function did this prophetic literature serve? Does it still today?

DANIEL

12

1 And at that time shall Michael stand up, the great prince which standeth for the children of thy people: and there shall be a time of trouble, such as never was since there was a nation *even* to that same time: and at that time thy people shall be delivered, every one that shall be found written in the book.   2 And many of them that sleep in the dust of the earth shall awake, some to everlasting life, and some to shame *and* everlasting contempt.   3 And they that be wise shall shine as the brightness of the firmament; and they that turn many to righteousness, as the stars for ever and ever.   4 But thou, O Daniel, shut up the words, and seal the book, *even* to the time of the end: many shall run to and fro, and knowledge shall be increased.

5 Then I Daniel looked, and, behold, there stood other two, the one on this side of the bank of the river, and the other on that side of the bank of the river.   6 And one said to the man clothed in linen, which *was* upon the waters of the river, How long *shall it be* to the end of these wonders?   7 And I heard the man clothed in linen, which *was* upon the waters of the river, when he held up his right hand and his left hand unto heaven, and sware by him that liveth for ever, that *it shall be* for a time, times, and a half; and when he shall have accomplished to scatter the power of the holy people, all of *these* things shall be finished.

8 And I heard, but I understood not: then said I, O my Lord, what *shall be* the end of these *things*?   9 And he said, Go thy way, Daniel: for

the words *are* closed up and sealed till the time of the end.   10 Many shall be purified, and made white, and tried; but the wicked shall do wickedly: and none of the wicked shall understand; but the wise shall understand.   11 And from the time *that* the daily *sacrifice* shall be taken away, and the abomination that maketh desolate set up, *there shall be* a thousand two hundred and ninety days.   12 Blessed *is* he that waiteth, and cometh to the thousand three hundred and five and thirty days.   13 But go thou thy way till the end *be*: for thou shalt rest, and stand in thy lot at the end of the days.

> *Jesus was a Jew, familiar with the Bible, including the book of Daniel. Some Jews, like the Essenes whom we have come to know through the recently discovered Dead Sea Scrolls, prepared for God's ending of a world polluted by Roman occupation in the same way that Daniel urged preparation in his time. The New Testament Gospels of Mark and Matthew show Jesus following the footsteps of John the Baptist, who taught preparation for the end. Matthew put John's role this way (Matt. 3:1–2):*
>
> > *In those days came John the Baptist, preaching in the wilderness of Judea, And saying, Repent ye: for the kingdom of heaven is at hand.*
>
> *Jesus is also quoted as preaching that the end of the world is at hand. But the author of Matthew (written about A.D. 70) quotes Jesus giving two very different, perhaps contradictory, messages. One is that people should immediately repent because the end is at hand. The other is that there will be plenty of time before the end comes. Find these different messages in the following selection (Matt. 24). How do you account for these differences? Is it possible that one of these messages is closer to the actual sayings of Jesus and the other was added later? Would the followers of Jesus be more likely to add the urgent message or the long-term view? Why?*

MATTHEW

24

1 And Jesus went out, and departed from the temple: and his disciples came to *him* for to show him the buildings of the temple.   2 And Jesus said unto them, See ye not all these things? verily I say unto you, There shall not be left here one stone upon another, that shall not be thrown down.   3 And as he sat upon the mount of Olives, the disciples came unto him privately, saying, Tell us, when shall these things be? and what *shall* be the sign of thy coming, and of the end of the world?   4 And Jesus answered and said unto them, Take heed that no

man deceive you. 5 For many shall come in my name, saying, I am Christ; and shall deceive many. 6 And ye shall hear of wars and rumors of wars: see that ye be not troubled: for all *these things* must come to pass, but the end is not yet. 7 For nation shall rise against nation, and kingdom against kingdom: and there shall be famines, and pestilences, and earthquakes, in divers places. 8 All these *are* the beginning of sorrows. 9 Then shall they deliver you up to be afflicted, and shall kill you: and ye shall be hated of all nations for my name's sake. 10 And then shall many be offended, and shall betray one another, and shall hate one another. 11 And many false prophets shall rise, and shall deceive many. 12 And because iniquity shall abound, the love of many shall wax cold. 13 But he that shall endure unto the end, the same shall be saved. 14 And this gospel of the kingdom shall be preached in all the world for a witness unto all nations; and then shall the end come.

15 When ye therefore shall see the abomination of desolation, spoken of by Daniel the prophet, stand in the holy place, (whoso readeth, let him understand,) 16 Then let them which be in Judea flee into the mountains: 17 Let him which is on the housetop not come down to take any thing out of his house: 18 Neither let him which is in the field return back to take his clothes. 19 And woe unto them that are with child, and to them that give suck in those days! 20 But pray ye that your flight be not in the winter, neither on the sabbath day: 21 For then shall be great tribulation, such as was not since the beginning of the world to this time, no, nor ever shall be. 22 And except those days should be shortened, there should no flesh be saved: but for the elect's sake those days shall be shortened. 23 Then if any man shall say unto you, Lo, here *is* Christ, or there; believe *it* not. 24 For there shall arise false Christs, and false prophets, and shall show great signs and wonders; insomuch that, if *it were* possible, they shall deceive the very elect. 25 Behold, I have told you before. 26 Wherefore if they shall say unto you, Behold, he is in the desert; go not forth: behold *he is* in the secret chambers; believe *it* not. 27 For as the lightning cometh out of the east, and shineth even unto the west; so shall also the coming of the Son of man be. 28 For wheresoever the carcass is, there will the eagles be gathered together.

29 Immediately after the tribulation of those days shall the sun be darkened, and the moon shall not give her light, and the stars shall fall from heaven, and the powers of the heavens shall be shaken: 30 And then shall appear the sign of the Son of man in heaven: and then shall all the tribes of the earth mourn, and they shall see the Son of man coming in the clouds of heaven with power and great glory. 31 And he shall send his angels with a great sound of a trumpet, and they shall gather together his elect from the four winds, from one end of heaven to the other. 32 Now learn a parable of the fig tree; When his branch

is yet tender, and putteth forth leaves, ye know that summer is nigh: 33 So likewise ye, when ye shall see all these things, know that it is near, *even* at the doors.   34 Verily I say unto you, This generation shall not pass, till all these things be fulfilled.   35 Heaven and earth shall pass away, but my words shall not pass away.

36 But of that day and hour knoweth no *man*, no, not the angels of heaven, but my Father only.   37 But as the days of Noe [Noah] *were*, so shall also the coming of the Son of man be.   38 For as in the days that were before the flood they were eating and drinking, marrying and giving in marriage, until the day that Noe entered into the ark,   39 And knew not until the flood came, and took them all away; so shall also the coming of the Son of man be.   40 Then shall two be in the field; the one shall be taken, and the other left.   41 Two *women shall* be grinding at the mill; the one shall be taken, and the other left.

PAUL AND HIS OPPONENTS

S.G. BRANDON

Paul's idea that Jesus was the savior of mankind was seriously challenged by the disciples of Jesus in Jerusalem. That is the thesis of this essay by S.G. Brandon, a professor of comparative religion at Manchester University and author of a number of books on Jesus. In fact, Brandon says, the victory of Paul's interpretation of Jesus as the son of God rather than a Jewish Messiah was quite accidental. Who were Paul's opponents? Why did Paul have such a difficult time convincing them? How did Paul's view of Jesus eventually win out? What difference did that make?

Whoever turns the pages of that collection of ancient Christian writings called the New Testament must surely conclude that Paul was the apostle par excellence of the early church. For no less than thirteen separate items of that collection are entitled "Epistles of Paul," whereas to no other apostle are more than two letters assigned. And that is not all: not only do the writings of Paul comprise a quarter of the whole content of the New Testament: the larger part of the Acts of the Apostles, which

S.G. Brandon, "Paul and His Opponents," in William L. Langer, ed., *Perspectives in Western Civilization*, vol. I. New York: American Heritage Publishing Company, 1972. First published in *Horizon*, Winter 1968. Copyright by the author.

sets out to record the early history of the Christian faith, is devoted to recounting his career.

But this impression of the primacy of Paul, both as a leader and a teacher in the early church, is strangely belied by the internal evidence of Paul's own writings. When we read many of these documents, we at once sense an atmosphere of great tension. Paul often appears profoundly concerned with what he regards as the pernicious influence of certain opponents who operate among his own converts; he sometimes uses the fiercest invective against them, but in a curiously oblique way, never naming them.

Herein lies one of the fundamental problems that beset our understanding of the origins of Christianity. How is it that Paul's own letters are so full of bitter controversy, yet the space given to his letters in the New Testament, as well as the evidence of the Acts, so signally attest his pre-eminence as the great leader and exponent of the faith, a position that is also abundantly confirmed in later Christian tradition?

An attempt to answer this question takes us into the intricate study of one of the most crucial episodes in the history of mankind. It is a field, too, where in recent years many new evaluations of traditional views have been taking place. The attempt is worth making, for it will afford an insight into the dramatic clash of two powerful personalities with whom lay the future of one of the world's greatest religions.

It is necessary at the outset to appreciate the nature of our chief sources of information about Paul and his career. His own writings, of course, are of primary importance; but since they mostly comprise letters dealing with specific situations among the Christian communities that he had founded in various places in the Roman Empire, their interpretation is no easy task. Paul rarely outlines the situation with which he is dealing, because it was obviously well known to his readers; consequently we are obliged to reconstruct the issue from passing references and allusions. Moreover, it must be remembered that the Epistles are essentially ex parte accounts of the basic conflict; we have no documents giving us the case of Paul's opponents, and our chief information about it must be inferred from Paul's own statements.

The Acts of the Apostles constitutes our secondary source of information. When it was written, some four decades separated it from the events it records; in the interval the destruction of Jerusalem by the Romans in A.D. 70 had decisively altered the internal situation of the church. The Acts, moreover, is clearly motivated by an apologetic purpose; it is concerned with tracing the triumphant spread of Christianity from its beginnings in Jerusalem to its establishment in Rome, the metropolis of the world. Thus it gives an idealized picture of the past, passing lightly over the conflicts and representing the leading figures as amicably disposed to each other. However, the evidence of the Acts can be of great value when carefully interpreted, and it does supply us with two precious facts about Paul: that he was a Hellenized Jew, being a native of the Cilician city of Tarsus, and that he enjoyed the privilege of Roman citizenship.

Both our sources are clear on one point of basic significance: Paul had never been an original disciple of Jesus but had joined the church sometime after the Crucifixion. Another important point on which the sources agree is that Paul was not converted to the new faith by the original community of disciples living in Jerusalem. His independence of the Jerusalem Christians at this crucial stage in his career was a matter of supreme importance to Paul, and it provides the key to the role that he was destined to play in the development of the new faith. Paul gives us his own account of the events that led up to his conversion in a context of great significance. He is writing to his converts in Galatia, who are in danger of being won over by his opponents, and he seeks to prove to them the greater authority of his own teaching. The passage is from Epistle to the Galatians (1:11–20).

> For I make known to you, brethren, as touching the gospel which was preached by me, that it is not after man. For neither did I receive it from man, nor was I taught it, but *it came to me* through revelation of Jesus Christ. For ye have heard of my manner of life in time past in the Jews' religion, how that beyond measure I persecuted the Church of God, and made havoc of it. And I advanced in the Jews' religion beyond many of mine own age among my countrymen, being more exceedingly zealous for the tradition of my fathers. But when it was the good pleasure of God, who separated me, *even* from my mother's womb, and called me through his grace, to reveal his Son in me, that I might preach him among the Gentiles; immediately I conferred not with flesh and blood. Neither went I up to Jerusalem to them which were apostles before me: but I went away in Arabia; and again I returned unto Damascus. Then after three years I went up to Jerusalem to visit Cephas, and tarried with him fifteen days. But other of the apostles saw I none, save James the Lord's brother. Now touching the things which I write unto you, behold, before God, I lie not.

The implications of this passage are immense. It informs us about three vital aspects of Paul's position. To defend his own teaching to his converts against that of his opponents Paul asserts that he had not derived it from any human source and, in particular, that he did not owe it to the original apostles at Jerusalem. This teaching, moreover, he claimed had been communicated to him directly by God for the express purpose of revealing "his Son in me, that I might preach him among the Gentiles." In other words, Paul maintains that his teaching was especially designed to be intelligible to those who were not Jews. He therefore admits by implication that his teaching differed from the tradition of the original apostles of Jerusalem, and he defends its novelty by claiming for it a direct divine origin.

We begin to perceive, then, the outlines of a truly amazing situation in the Christian church within some two decades of the Crucifixion. Paul is anxious to assert his independence of the Jerusalem apostles and to explain that his teaching has been divinely revealed for the Gentiles. Since he evidently had to defend his teaching against certain opponents, it becomes necessary to attempt to identify these opponents and the cause of their hostility to Paul.

In two separate writings Paul refers to these opponents and their rival teaching in very remarkable terms. In his Galatian letter (1:6–9) he writes in admonition to his converts:

> I marvel that ye are so quickly removing from him that called you in the grace of Christ unto a different gospel; which is not another *gospel*: only there are some that trouble you, and would pervert the gospel of Christ. But though we, or an angel from heaven, should preach any gospel other than that we preached unto you, let him be anathema. As we have said before so say I now again: If any man preacheth unto you any gospel other than that which ye received, let him be anathema.

The extraordinary language used here is paralleled in another passage, which occurs in the Second Epistle to the Corinthians (11:3–6). A situation had apparently developed among his converts in the Greek city of Corinth similar to that with which Paul sought to deal in Galatia. He writes:

> But I fear lest by any means, as the serpent beguiled Eve in his craftiness, your minds should be corrupted from the simplicity and the purity that is toward Christ. For if he that cometh preacheth another Jesus, whom we did not preach, or if ye received a different spirit, which he did not receive, or a different gospel, which ye did not accept, ye do well to bear with *him*. For I reckon that I am not a whit behind the very chiefest apostles. But though I be rude in speech, yet *am* I not in knowledge; nay, in everything we have made *it* manifest among all men to you-ward.

Paul's language in both these passages is as amazing as it is significant. Paul does in fact attest to the presence in the Church of two rival interpretations of the faith. For the references to "another Jesus" and "a different gospel" must mean that Paul's opponents were teaching a different version of the meaning of the person and roles of Jesus from Paul's version.

But who *were* these opponents? Obviously they were not some obscure sect of heretics; otherwise Paul would surely have repudiated them with all that vehemence of utterance of which he was capable. Clearly they were men who could operate effectively enough within Paul's own mission-field to cause him profound concern. But, curiously, Paul never explicitly names them or questions their authority. He does, however, give a clue to their identity in the latter of the passages just quoted, when he significantly adds, after referring to this rival teaching, "I reckon that I am not a whit behind the very chiefest apostles." In view of the facts just considered, and of Paul's concern to assert his independence of the Jerusalem apostles, there can indeed be little doubt that those opponents who taught "another Jesus" were either the leaders of the church in Jerusalem or their emissaries. In his Galatian epistle, describing a later visit to Jerusalem, Paul gives more details of these leaders. They formed a kind of triumvirate of what he calls *stuloi* (pillars); their names are James, Cephas, and John. The order in which these names are given is significant. James was certainly the leader; he precedes Cephas, i.e., Peter, who had apparently been the leader of the apostles during the lifetime of Jesus. The fact that James was the brother of Jesus (Galatians 1:19) probably accounts, at least in part, for this pre-eminence. But a mystery seems to surround this James. According to the Gospels, he had not been an original disciple—indeed he had actually been unsympathetic to Jesus. The Acts is strangly silent about his antecedents; it represents him suddenly, without explanation, as the head of the church of Jerusalem. How he ousted Peter from the leadership of the new movement remains a veiled episode in the Christian documents. His blood relationship to Jesus obviously gave him great prestige, but it is evident that he was also a man of strong character and ability. In his Galatian letter Paul tells of a dispute at Antioch over whether Jewish Christians might eat with Gentile believers; Peter, who had agreed with Paul on the matter, had later withdrawn on the arrival of emissaries from James—surely a significant act of submission.

It was, then, the teaching of the Jerusalem church, presided over by James, from which Paul differed and again which he tacitly directs his innuendo by describing it as a "different gospel" that taught "another Jesus." But how did this Jerusalem gospel differ so radically from that of Paul? In brief, since it is certain that the Jerusalem Christians continued to worship in the Temple at Jerusalem and to practice the ritual customs of Judaism, it is evident that they did not regard their faith in Jesus as inconsistent with Jewish orthodoxy or as separating them from their national religion. To them Jesus was the promised Messiah of Israel. His death by crucifixion was a problem, since there was no expectation that the Messiah should die—rather he was to be the mighty champion who would free Israel from subjugation to a heathen conqueror. But Jesus' death could be explained as a martyr's death for Israel at the hands of the Romans. And it was believed that God had raised him from this death, so that he might soon return with supernatural power to "restore the kingdom to Israel." Such, then, was the "gospel" of the Jerusalem Christians, it was conceived essentially in terms of Jewish thought, and it was calculated to emphasize and maintain that claim to a unique spiritual status and destiny that characterized Judaism. According to the evidence of the Acts, a considerable number of priests and Pharisees had, significantly, been won to the new movement.

If such was the "gospel of Jerusalem," what was Paul's version of the new faith? It would seem that before his conversion Paul was scandalized by the new movement because it taught "a crucified Messiah." On his conversion, whatever the true nature of that mysterious episode may be, Paul became convinced that the crucified Jesus was alive and of divine status. But he still had to explain to himself the apparent scandal of the Crucifixion. It was at this point, so it would seem, that Paul came to differ fundamentally from the Jerusalem Christians and to assert his original independence of them. To him the death of Jesus could not be just a martyr's death for Israel; it must have some more profound and universal meaning. It was in his attempt to interpret this meaning that Paul surely drew, though unconsciously, on his Hellenistic background.

This Hellenistic background teemed with religious cults and esoteric philosophies that promised salvation of various kinds. Consciously Paul would have vigorously rejected them as the service of false gods or "philosophy and vain deceit." But he could not have escaped their influence, since they reflected the aspirations and fears of contemporary Greco-Roman society and provided the current religious vocabulary. Two ideas of key importance that these cults and philosophies severally enshrined and propagated were those of the savior-god and of the fallen state of man. The classic pattern of the savior-god was afforded by the ancient Egyptian deity Osiris. The initiates of his mysteries believed that he had once died and risen again to life and that by ritual assimilation with him they too could win immortal life. The various esoteric philosophies that can be described as Gnostic taught that each human being was compounded of an immortal soul imprisoned in a physical body. This unhappy condition was due to an original fall of the soul from its abode of light and bliss and its involvement in matter. By thus becoming incarnated in this world the soul had also become subject to the demonic powers that inhabited the planets and controlled the world. From this state of perdition it could be rescued by acquiring a proper knowledge (gnosis) of its nature; emancipated from its involvement in matter, it would ascend through the celestial spheres to its original home.

Such ideas were foreign to orthodox Judaism. Hence it is significant that Paul, seeking to interpret the meaning of the Crucifixion, does so in terms that presuppose that mankind is enslaved by demonic powers, from whom they are redeemed through the death and resurrection of a divine savior. Thus he writes: "So we also, when we were children, were held in bondage under the *stoicheia* of the world. But when the fulness of the time came, God sent forth his Son, born of a woman, born under the law, that he might redeem them which were under the law, that we might receive the adoption of sons." The word *stoicheia*, which the

Revised Standard Version translates as "elemental spirits," means in this context the demonic powers that were identified with the astral phenomena. Consequently Paul here envisages the human situation as one of subjection to these demonic powers until redemption is won by the incarnated Son of God. Paul clearly regards the crucifixion of Jesus as achieving this redemption, but of the way in which this was achieved he is not clear. Sometimes he invokes the concepts of the Jewish sacrificial cultus, thereby implying that the death of Jesus was a sacrifice; but who demanded it and to whom it was made, he is not explicit. A more coherent conception, which links up with the thought of the Galatian passage just quoted, is found in his First Epistle to the Corinthians (2:7–8): "But we speak God's wisdom in a mystery, *even* the *wisdom* that hath been hidden, which God foreordained before the *aeons* unto our glory; which none of the *archontes* of this *aeon* knoweth; for had they known it, they would not have crucified the Lord of glory." In this passage Paul professes to explain the Crucifixion as an event, arranged for in a divine plan conceived before the *aeons*, whereby the *archontes* of this *aeon* were led, unwittingly, to crucify a supernatural being called "the Lord of glory." Since "*archontes* of this *aeon*" is in effect an alternative designation for the demonic powers described as the *stoicheia* in the Galatian letter, a further phase of Paul's interpretation of the death of Jesus can be discerned. In other words, the hold that the demonic powers had over mankind was broken when they were deceived into crucifying the "Lord of glory."

By employing ideas and terminology current in the Greco-Roman world, Paul thus fashioned an interpretation, intelligible to his Gentile converts, of a movement that was in origin and essence Jewish. But that was not all. Whereas the rite of circumcision was the form of initiation into the spiritual privileges of Judaism, baptism was adopted as the means of entry into the church of Christ. Paul's explanation of it is also indicative of the milieu of syncretistic faith and practice upon which he drew. He writes to the Christians in Rome:

> Or are ye ignorant that all we who were baptized into Christ Jesus were baptized into his death? We were buried therefore with him through baptism into death: that like as Christ was raised from the dead through the glory of the Father, so we also might walk in newness of life. For if we have become united with *him* by the likeness of his death, we shall be also *by the likeness* of his resurrection.

In other words, according to Paul, in baptism the neophyte was ritually assimilated to Christ in his death in order to be one with him in his resurrection. When Paul wrote, for nearly three thousand years in Egypt resurrection from death had been sought by ritual assimilation with the dying-rising god Osiris.

Such, then, was the gospel with which Paul believed that he had been divinely entrusted for preaching to the Gentiles. In effect it replaced the presentation of Jesus as the Messiah of Israel by that of Jesus as the divine savior of mankind; and it presupposed that all men, whether Jew or Gentile, were equally in need of the same kind of salvation.

Such a gospel diverged fundamentally from the teaching of the Jerusalem Christians, and it was obnoxious to them. For not only did it equate the Jew with the Gentile, thereby robbing the former of his cherished sense of spiritual superiority; it made the Messiah of Israel into the savior of those heathen who had done him to death and who daily opposed his people.

When the Jerusalem leaders understood the nature and implications of Paul's teaching, they set about opposing it. They were in a strong position to do this: whereas they could repudiate Paul as a latecomer to the faith, he could not openly challenge their authority as the original disciples and eyewitnesses of Jesus. Accordingly they sent out their emissaries among Paul's converts, asserting that theirs was the original and authentic version of the faith.

As his letters eloquently attest, the activities of these Jerusalem emissaries seriously threatened Paul's position, undermining his authority with his converts and causing them to accept a "different gospel" and "another Jesus." The situation eventually became so serious that Paul resolved to go to Jerusalem in an attempt to negotiate some *modus vivendi* with the authorities there. He sought to strengthen his case by taking with him a delegation of his Gentile converts and a considerable sum of money, which he had collected from his churches for the support of the mother church of Jerusalem. Paul seems to have known that a visit to Jerusalem might be dangerous for him, and according to the narrative of the Acts, he received several divine warnings of impending danger. To have persisted in going against such advice surely attests that he felt the need to achieve an understanding with the Jerusalem leaders was urgent.

The outcome of the visit is recorded in Acts 21; its testimony must be evaluated in terms of that apologetic purpose that, as we have already noticed, inspires the work.

Paul was received by James in the presence of the elders of the Jerusalem church and is represented as reporting on the success of his work among the Gentiles. Paul's coming to Jerusalem must clearly have embarrassed the Christians there, and James comes quickly to the point about the matter.

> Thou seest, brother, how many thousands there are among the Jews of them that have believed; and they are all zealous for the law; and they have been informed concerning thee, that thou teachest all the Jews which are among the Gentiles to forsake Moses, telling them not to circumcise their children,

neither to walk after the customs. What is it therefore? They will certainly hear that thou art come.

The accusation was in fact a calumny, but it represented a plausible deduction from the logic of Paul's teaching. Reference to it by James was an astute move to solve the difficulty that Paul's visit had created. Accordingly he proposes a test of Paul's Jewish orthodoxy:

> Do therefore this that we say to thee: We have four men which have a vow on them; these take, and purify thyself with them; and be at charges for them, that they may shave their heads: and all shall know that there is no truth in the things whereof they have been informed concerning thee; but that thou thyself also walkest orderly, keeping the law.

Paul was placed in a dilemma. James had shrewdly detected the weakness of his position, in that while the logic of his teaching negated the peculiar spiritual claims of Judaism, he still endeavored himself to remain an orthodox Jew. Now James challenged him to give a public demonstration of his orthodoxy, for the ceremony in which Paul should take part, i.e., the discharge of the so-called Nazarite vow, was performed in the Temple. To refuse the test was tantamount to a declaration of apostasy from his native faith: but to accept it was to admit the validity of Judaism on the order of the Jerusalem church.

Paul felt obliged to submit, but the sequel was disastrous to his cause. While performing the rites in the Temple courts, he was set upon by a Jewish mob and only rescued from death by the intervention of the Roman guard from the nearby fortress of the Antonia. To escape subsequent trial and certain condemnation by the Jewish authorities, Paul invoked his right as a Roman citizen to be tried before the imperial tribunal. After recording his survival from shipwreck en route to Rome, the narrative of the Acts finally leaves Paul a prisoner there. What was his ultimate fate is unrecorded. According to ancient tradition he suffered martyrdom in Rome, and there is much reason for thinking that his appeal to Caesar did not prove successful.

The arrest of Paul probably took place in the year 55, and from that date he seems to have been removed from personal contact with his converts. What, then, was the fate of his work?

It would seem reasonable to conjecture, since Paul had previously felt his position to be gravely threatened by the Jerusalem Christians, that after his arrest the defeat of his cause was inevitable. His converts would have been left defenseless against the propaganda of the Jerusalem emissaries. That this did actually happen seems to be confirmed by the prophecy that is attributed to Paul when he took his farewell of the elders of the church of Ephesus: the prophecy is recorded by the author of Acts, who knew what had happened:

I know that after my departure grievous wolves shall enter in among you, not sparing the flock; and from among your own selves shall men arise, speaking perverse things to draw away the disciples after them.

If this situation had continued, without doubt Paul's interpretation of Christianity would have perished, and the faith evoked by Jesus would have remained but the belief of a small messianic sect within the fold of Judaism. But this was not to be. In the year 66 the Jewish nationalists raised the standard of revolt against Roman rule in Judaea. After four years of bitter warfare, the Jewish state was overthrown, Jerusalem ruined and its Temple destroyed. In the course of that cataclysm the Christian church of Jerusalem disappeared.

In consequence of these tremendous events the future of Christianity was completely changed. The hold of the mother church of Jerusalem was broken, and the Gentile churches were left to work out their own destiny. This signal overthrow of Jewish Christianity led, understandably, to a rehabilitation of Paul's reputation as the great exponent of the faith. When the author of Acts wrote his story of the beginnings of the Church, magnifying the part played by Paul, others were searching for Paul's writings as the inspired teaching of a revered master and saint. Eventually the *Corpus Paulinum* was formed, becoming one of the earliest components of the New Testament, but bearing also within it evidence both of the eclipse and the rehabilitation of Paul in the mind of the Church. For the formation of Christian theology this rehabilitation was definitive. From Paul's teaching has stemmed the foundational doctrine of Christianity; namely, the incarnation of the Son of God, in the person of Jesus of Nazareth, to be the savior of mankind.

THE SIGNIFICANCE OF CHRISTMAS

ERNEST JONES

Ernest Jones is known as the student, friend, and biographer of Sigmund Freud and as an important psychologist himself. In this essay he brings a rich background in the classics, a knowledge of anthropology, and Freudian psychological theory to bear on an important and interesting question. Why, according to Jones, did Christianity succeed over Mithraism and other popular religions of the Roman empire? What

From *Psycho-Myth, Psycho-History*, Vol. II, by Ernest Jones. New York: Hillstone, 1974.

elements of popular pagan culture and human psychological need did Christianity satisfy most effectively?

To ask why we keep Christmas is to ask a good question, i.e., one which one does not usually ask because of taking something for granted. Yet a moment's reflection will show that there is much worth in asking the question. To begin with, we might wonder why Christmas is the only one of the Christian religious festivals that makes any appeal to people who are not Christians. If someone becomes a sceptic or atheist he is apt to lose interest in the important Christian dates; he is likely to forget what ideas are commemorated by the words Epiphany, Whitsun, Advent or Palm Sunday; Eastertide loses its emotional significance and becomes merely a Spring holiday. But Christmas commonly retains as much meaning as ever. And the same is often true of people with other religions who live in contact with Christians. I remember when crossing to America a couple of years ago in December finding that nearly half of the passengers were American Jews rushing through in order to be "home for Christmas"; and no doubt the same observation could be made in any other year. There must therefore be something in the idea of Christmas that appeals to far more than interest in the date, or even the fact, of Christ's birth.

Perhaps we ought to begin further back in our inquiry and raise the question of why mankind keeps festivals at all on particular dates. It was Sir Isaac Newton, in 1730, who first drew attention to the astronomical associations of Christmas and other festivals. Many years ago General Furlong, the distinguished anthropologist, in his famous *Rivers of Life*, took the trouble to collect the dates of festivals in all parts of the world and to construct a curve indicating the times of year in which they most often occurred. The curve revealed the unmistakable fact that by far the greatest number of festivals was held at one or other of the four cardinal points in the earth's journey round the sun. The most favoured times are those of the summer and winter solstice, towards the end of June and December respectively, when the sun begins to wane or wax, when the days begin to shorten or lengthen. The times of year next in favour are those of the spring or autumn equinox, towards the end of March or of September. There can be little doubt that man has always tended, sometimes even consciously so, to associate his aspirations and emotions with these fundamental changes relating to the source of all life, the sun. It is well known how extensively the idea of the sun has permeated the religions of the world, He being the most visible and striking emblem of both the life-giving and the life-destroying forces of the universe.

We can further divide the innumerable religious festivals of the world into two broad groups, happy and unhappy ones or—to speak more accurately—into cheerful and solemn ones. There are festivals of celebration, of rejoicing; there are occasions of sheer merriment and they have at times passed over into bacchanalian orgies. Christmas plainly belongs to this group. On the other hand there are festivals which mark man's periodic need to search his heart, to make a serious review of his position in the Universe or to question his purpose in life and take a strict account with himself. The former group indicate moods of easy conscience, the latter of uneasy conscience.

To get back to the particular festival of Christmas. Before trying to ascertain what it stands for it is necessary to know something of its historical background. Literally, of course, it signifies the date of Christ's birthday. But actually we have no knowledge of what time of the year that fell on, and even the year itself is uncertain, so there must have been some other reason for choosing a particular day on which to celebrate it. In spite of hints in the New Testament that the birth took place at the beginning of the Jewish New Year, i.e., at about the time of the autumn equinox, there was in early Christian times a number of sects who proclaimed the spring equinox as the most suitable date. Most Christians, however, seem at first to have regarded the matter of His physical birth as too mundane or even desecrating a thought to dwell on; in A.D. 245, for instance, Origen declared it to be a sin even to think of celebrating the birthday of Christ "as if he were a King Pharaoh." They confined their attention to the date when the Holy Spirit took possession of Him; that was His real Divine birth. This moment they regarded as the occasion of His baptism, and to commemorate it they chose the date of 6th January, now called Epiphany. We do not know why they chose that date, but it was one when many festivals were held in the Ancient World—probably on astronomical grounds, it being the first day on which the morning hours begin to lengthen. Epiphany and Baptism were for many centuries closely associated. By the fourth century the date of 6th January was universally accepted in the Eastern World as the time to celebrate the birth of Christ, whether the human or the divine one, and, in the oldest Christian nation, (the Armenian), that is still the date adhered to.

The theological controversies on the nature of Christ decided, however, that His divinity began at birth, so that attention was directed there. Discarding some earlier forgeries we can say that the first authentic date when Christmas Day was recorded in connection with the physical birth of Christ was A.D. 354. The matter seems to have been settled in A.D. 329 at a Council known by the name of Dionysius the Little. In A.D. 400 an Imperical rescript ordered all theatres to be closed on that day (as well as at Epiphany and Easter), and in the course of the fifth century 25th December was firmly established in both East and West as the proper time to celebrate the anniversary of Christ.

The reasons why the festival was established at all, and why that particular date was selected for the purpose, are both interesting and complex. A Syrian writer of the period (a Christian) is quoted for the following frank description of the motives. "The reason why the fathers transferred the celebration of 6th January to 25th December was this. It was a custom of the heathen to celebrate on the same 25th December the birthday of the Sun, at which they kindled lights in token of festivity. In these solemnities and festivities the Christians also took part. Accordingly when the doctors of the Church perceived that the Christians had a leaning to this festival, they took counsel and resolved that the true Nativity should be solemnized on that day." This political reason had of course to be defined by the Church, and both St. Augustine and the Pope Leo the Great found it necessary to rebuke Christians for still associating Christmas with the rebirth of the Sun. The fact remains that the date had already been established in innumerable pagan religions in just this sense. The 25th December was the birthday of many a Persian, Phoenician, Egyptian, and even Teutonic Sun-God. And the decision was in line with the general syncretizing activities of the Church in the early centuries when it was combating paganism: it cannot be coincidence that—to quote a few examples—the date of Easter coincides with the similar celebration of the Phrygian god Attis (so popular in Rome) at the vernal equinox; that the festival of the Assumption of the Virgin in August has replaced the festival of the goddess Diana; the festival of St. George in April has replaced the ancient festival of the goddess Pales (one which the Romans later combined with that of Dea Roma); that the festival of St. John the Baptist in June has succeeded to the water festivals of Adonis in midsummer; that the feast of All Souls in November continues the Keltic Feast of the Dead at that time (the beginning of their New Year), and so on.

The matter was, however, a good deal more complex than the Syrian writer supposed, and can be elucidated only by considering the life-and-death struggle that Christianity was going through in the first three or four centuries in Rome. When faith in the orthodox Roman religion began to wane a number of competing Oriental ones crowded in to secure the succession, one of which was the Christian one. The general characteristic of them was the theme of a young Saviour-God who dies, either periodically or once for all, and thereby assures the eternal salvation (from the wrath of the Almighty) of those who believe in him. The series included Attis, Osiris, Adonis, Mithra, and Jesus himself. With all of them except the last two mentioned the belief in a powerful Mother Goddess, whose help secured the reassuring Resurrection of the dying God, played an important part. And it was just those two that were ahead in the struggle for general acceptance, the only two, incidentally, in which the young God died only once and afterwards reigned in heaven. There is little doubt that Mithraism, the religion especially of the army, was the most dangerous rival to Christianity, and the issue of the conflict between the two faiths appears for a time to have hung in the balance. There was much similarity in their beliefs, rituals and moral aspirations: virginity, baptism, holy communion, purity, etc. But Mithraism had one serious weakness, on which the Christians seized and thereby ensured their ultimate success. Its attitude and beliefs were exclusively masculine. In its ritual the young God took up the challenge of the wrathful father, slew him and reigned in his stead, whereas in Christianity he submits in a more feminine fashion to the will of the Father and by sacrificing himself assuages His wrath. Consistently with this solution Mithraism made the conflict one entirely between two males; there was no feminine element, no goddess, in its theology, and women were excluded from its worship. Christianity here saw its chance and incorporated from the other religions the element that had been missing in both itself and Mithraism. Isis, Cybele, Rhea, Astarte and the rest began a new lease on life. Mary, who had been little but the necessary vehicle for the begetting of a son, was rapidly raised in status and from being the Mother of God was given in the fourth century the exalted title of Queen of Heaven. Her virginal conception, the usual belief then attaching to the birth of heroes and gods, had long been established. From then on the increasing Mariolatry demanded that more attention be paid, not only to her intercessory and saving powers, but especially her maternal role. Mother and Infant, resembling Isis and Horus, began to play a more central part in Christianity, and it still does in Roman Catholicism, so that the circumstances of the birth, including its date and the appropriate festival, assumed a cardinal importance. One might even wonder whether Christianity would have survived had it not instituted the festival of Christmas with all that it signified!

In the crisis the Roman Christians would not have been long in doubt about choosing the actual date. It was indeed dictated by the situation. In the Julian calendar 25th December was reckoned as the winter solstice and hence as the Nativity of the Sun when the day begins to lengthen and the power of the sun to increase. In Eastern countries the pagan celebrants of the Nativity had retired to inner shrines or caves, from which at midnight they issued with cries of "The Virgin has brought forth! The light is waxing!" The Egyptians even represented the new-born sun by the image of an infant which on his birthday, the winter solstice, they exhibited to the worshippers. The Virgin who thus bore a son on that day was of course the great Oriental Mother-Goddess, who had many forms and names in different countries. Mithra after conquering the sun had become a Sun-God himself with the title of Solus Invictus, and his festival, the Mithrakana, was appropriately celebrated on 25th December. If, therefore, the Christians had to compete with such a formidable rival they had to assert that it was *their* God who had been born on that significant date, and surely of a Heavenly Virgin.

From the vast importance of the sun in earlier days one might suppose that man was anxiously concerned lest he might fail them, since it was evident that without his heat and light life could not go on. This might occasionally have been so, to judge by the anxiety displayed during an eclipse and the human efforts (tom-toms, etc.) made to assist him in his fight with the monster apparently swallowing him. But I am persuaded that the case was really otherwise, and that the sun was on the contrary much more a source of security. One must remember that, in the East particularly, celestial phenomena were observed with astonishing accuracy, and that the motions of the stars and planets were known in great detail; astronomy was in fact the first of the sciences. Those people knew perfectly well that the sun would wax after 25th December just as surely as he would wane before then and that day would infallibly follow night. Uncertain human happenings could therefore be referred to his activities as a means of obtaining reassurance. We still say, as an expression of the utmost certainty, "It is sure as the sun will rise tomorrow." The sun, therefore, belonged to the external absolutes of the universe, like God, and human uncertainties that could be brought into association with him, or better still identification, would to that extent be dispelled.

Comparative anthropology has clearly shown that man has always tended to identify the changes in the sun's apparent powers with the most vital of his own activities. The waxing young sun of spring brings times for confident rejoicing which culminate in the mad triumph of Midsummer Eve, the German's Johannisnacht. Then the bonfires shoot upward and proclaim the apothegm of human and divine power. How wise were the Fathers of the Revolution to choose the beginning of July to declare their independence and thus provide a whole nation with the opportunity of perpetuating man's delight in the crackling of fire at that time of the year! On the other hand, the diminishing strength of the sun arouses by association the deep fears man always nurses of his own failing powers, of impotence, old age, and death—with the terrors of what may follow this. The re-birth of the sun, therefore, has often been the greatest reassurance he can receive of eternal hope, always provided—and that was vital—that he was identified with the Deity. That a God, however powerful, should periodically, (most often annually), die, to be constantly re-born, is the central theme of many religions. It is fitting that this re-birth should take place on what, according to Bede, the pagan Anglo-Saxons called "Mother-Night," i.e., Christmas Eve, the date from which their new year commenced. The Sun and the God may die, but they will surely be eternally re-born, so all is well.

The most natural expression of the re-birth idea is the association with a new-born babe, and to Christians it is the birth of the babe Jesus that is the central emblem of all that Christmas stands for. In the Roman Catholic Church, in particular, there is no moment of the year in which the Madonna and Babe are more adored; they can occupy the centre of interest to the exclusion of all other theological preoccupations. In Catholic countries Christmas is little else; the more mundane accompaniments and ceremonies of Northern Christmases are postponed to another date.

The feeling, however, that Christmas is in some deep sense a pagan festival has evinced itself with a strange persistence throughout the ages. The Western Church was responsible for its incorporation in the Christian religion, and the Eastern Church for long protested against what they regarded as a pagan innovation. Behind this word "pagan" surely lies the idea of Mother-Goddess worship, the attraction of which so often seduced the patriarchal monotheistic Hebrews and indeed the Christian Church itself. It is perhaps fundamentally what Protestantism protested against, following the Hebrew prophets. Our own Puritans have felt very strongly on the matter, and an Act of Parliament in 1644 forbade the celebration of Christmas as being a heathen festival, until the Merry Monarch once more sanctioned it. To this day many Protestant sects, notably in Scotland, look distinctly askance at Christmas as being something alien to the pure faith. Ever since the Reformation this attitude of suspicion has connected Christmas with what has often been called the "paganism" of the Roman Catholic Church. An amusing example is recorded of a fanatical member of Parliament moving that, in order to eliminate any association with the Mass, the word itself be purified by being changed to Christ-tide; by way of answer, however, he was exhorted to initiate the change by altering his own name from Thomas Massey Massey to Thotide Tidey Tidey!

To return to the concept of the sacrificial God. It is probably that this was preceded by the custom of sacrificing a king from time to time, either when he grew old or even, as Frazer has expounded in his *Golden Bough*, annually.

However much such a king may have acquiesced in the proceeding, sharing the belief of his people that it would accrue to the good of the community, it was inevitable that he should also feel some objection to it; so it was not surprising that an alternative procedure should be sought for. Two were found. One was to displace his majesty to the skies in the form either of a God like Adonis or an actual Sun-God. That the Sun should decline almost to death every year and then arise refreshed in his glory and strength was a solution satisfying to all concerned and was a relatively innocent form of regicide (i.e., parricide). The other, and perhaps more obvious, solution was to provide a substitute, a mock king. Here we touch on the vast theme of the scapegoat in mythology. In Babylonia, for example, the king originally had to die at the end of his year's rule, ostensibly so as to go and help the God Marduk in his periodical struggle with the monsters of chaos in the regions below, but after a time a criminal was set up for a few days as a "mock king" and then executed in the king's stead. The periodical rebellion against authority (ultimately the Father) implied in the ceremony is attested by the general license of the rejoicings and by the curious reversal of slaves and masters so characteristic of the Roman Saturnalia (15th December to 1st January) and before that the Persian Sacaea and the Babylonian Zagmuk festivals. Relics of the mock king idea have persisted into historical times. In the early centuries of our era the Roman soldiers stationed in the Balkans had the custom of choosing by lot one of their number to preside over the Saturnalia as king of the revels. After he was feted and boisterously paid court to he had to complete his career by standing at the altar and killing himself. St. Dasius is said to have achieved his fame (and martyrdom) by refusing to play this part on the ground of its being a pagan custom. In parts of central Europe a troupe of masqueraders are still headed by a "fool" or "wild man" who leads their carol singing, but with less lethal results than formerly. In the Middle Ages the "Feast of Fools" was similarly presided over by someone who was given the various titles of "Lord of Misrule," "Abbot of Unreason," "King of the Bean," etc., and who reigned from All Hallows' Eve till Christmas. His position was abrogated in Scotland by Act of Parliament in 1555. A mock service was held in the Church, with an imitation Mass, robes were worn inside out and music sheets held upside down—a general reversal very reminiscent of the Satanic Black Mass and like that indicating a violent reaction against divine authority. The only trace left of it all nowadays is the license of kissing anyone encountered under the mistletoe, as part of the jollification of a Merry Christmas.

Perhaps the last emblem of the sacrificed god or king was the ceremony of the boar's head at the Christmas banquet, thus turning it into a totemistic feast. For the boar, sacred to the God Frey in the north and to others in the East, is one of the patriarchal symbols in the unconscious; in his parricidal ritual Mithra slew sometimes a bull, sometimes a boar. And he was treated as a royal personage, his entry to the banqueting hall being preceded by a flourish of trumpets and similar rituals. In the Balkans and in Scandinavia cakes or loaves in the form of a pig are still sold at Christmas, reminding the anthropologist how long the impulse to cannibalistic parricide persists in the folklore of the people.

The many other constituents of the Christmas festival accord with its significance as just described. Some date from Rome, but more have been added as Christianity advanced northward and in doing so incorporated pre-existing customs and rituals. Some of them have just been mentioned. Others are the Yule log, cut down by a young man and burned ceremoniously to rekindle the sun; holly and evergreens to show that there is still life in nature; the Christmas tree, which was added only in the seventeenth century but which has an ancient tradition from the days of tree worship (may trees, etc.); the Christmas candles which replace the old Feast of Lights. All life will surely be somehow renewed and one need not fear extinction.

It is hard to determine how and when Christmas became so predominantly the children's festival it now is—at least in Northern countries. The birth of a babe is, it is true, its central feature, and in this connection it is interesting that to receive a present—which is what Christmas means to children—is in the unconscious mind always associated with the idea of the birth of a baby—the primordial gift *par excellence*. Oddly enough, in Catholic countries this custom is usually postponed to 1st January, such as with the French *étrennes* on the *jour de l'an*. The giver, Father Christmas—evidently Father Time himself—has in the past century got fused with the figure of St. Nicholas, the Archbishop of Myra, the children's saint, famous for his habit of giving presents; and Santa Klaus—the American corruption of the Dutch Colonists' San Nicolaas— is now his accepted name in all English-speaking countries. In Germany he was identified, as Knecht Rupprecht, with Odin himself, the god who sacrificed himself by hanging on a tree, his side pierced by a spear, for nine days; and so St. Nicholas wears his broad-brimmed hat and rides his white horse. In Holland hay has to be put out for the white horse on 6th December, St. Nicholas' own Day; on this day also Perchta, the companion of Odin, comes to inspect households to see if they have been properly managed.

Historically expressed, the festival of Christmas is thus a fusion of many strains of pagan customs and beliefs, but one which Christianity has inspired with a fresh spiritual significance. Psychologically it represents the ideal of resolving all family discord in a happy reunion, and to this it owes its perennial attraction. These two points of view are seen to be identical when one remembers that the ultimate significance of all religions is the attempted solution on a cosmic stage of the loves and hatreds that take their source in the complicated relations of children and parents.

7. Indian Civilization

THE BHAGAVAD-GITA

The Bhagavad-Gita *is the best-known work in Hindu religious literature. It is part of a larger epic called the* Mahabharata, *a story of two feuding families that may have had its origins in the Aryan invasion of 1500 B.C. The* Bhagavad-Gita *is a philosophical interlude that interrupts the story just before the great battle between the two families. It poses some fundamental questions about the nature of life, death, and proper religious behavior. It begins as the leader of one of the battling armies, Arjuna, asks why he should fight his friends and relatives on the other side. The answer comes from none other than the god Krishna, who has taken the form of Arjuna's charioteer.*

What is Krishna's answer? What will happen to the people Arjuna kills? What will happen to Arjuna? What would happen to Arjuna if he refused to fight the battle? What does this selection tell you about Hindu ideas of life, death, and the self?

LORD KRISHNA

You grieve for those beyond grief,
and you speak words of insight;
but learned men do not grieve
for the dead or the living.

Never have I not existed,
nor you, nor these kings;
and never in the future
shall we cease to exist.

Just as the embodied self
enters childhood, youth, and old age,
so does it enter another body;
this does not confound a steadfast man.

Contacts with matter make us feel
heat and cold, pleasure and pain.
Arjuna, you must learn to endure
fleeting things—they come and go!

When these cannot torment a man,
when suffering and joy are equal
for him and he has courage,
he is fit for immortality.

Nothing of nonbeing comes to be,
nor does being cease to exist;
the boundary between these two
is seen by men who see reality.

Indestructible is the presence
that pervades all this;
no one can destroy
this unchanging reality.

Our bodies are known to end,
but the embodied self is enduring,
indestructible, and immeasurable;
therefore, Arjuna, fight the battle!

He who thinks this self a killer
and he who thinks it killed,
both fail to understand;
it does not kill, nor is it killed.

It is not born,
it does not die;
having been,
it will never not be;
unborn, enduring,
constant, and primordial,
it is not killed
when the body is killed.

Arjuna, when a man knows the self
to be indestructible, enduring, unborn,
unchanging, how does he kill
or cause anyone to kill?

As a man discards
worn-out clothes
to put on new
and different ones,
so the embodied self
discards

its worn-out bodies
to take on other new ones.

Weapons do not cut it,
fire does not burn it,
waters do not wet it,
wind does not wither it.

It cannot be cut or burned;
it cannot be wet or withered;
it is enduring, all-pervasive,
fixed, immovable, and timeless.

It is called unmanifest,
inconceivable, and immutable;
since you know that to be so,
you should not grieve!

If you think of its birth
and death as ever-recurring,
then too, Great Warrior,
you have no cause to grieve!

Death is certain for anyone born,
and birth is certain for the dead;
since the cycle is inevitable,
you have no cause to grieve!

Creatures are unmanifest in origin,
manifest in the midst of life,
and unmanifest again in the end.
Since this is so, why do you lament?

Rarely someone
sees it,
rarely another
speaks it,
rarely anyone
hears it—
even hearing it,
no one really knows it.

The self embodied in the body
of every being is indestructible;
you have no cause to grieve
for all these creatures, Arjuna!

Look to your own duty;
do not tremble before it;
nothing is better for a warrior
than a battle of sacred duty.

The doors of heaven open
for warriors who rejoice
to have a battle like this
thrust on them by chance.

If you fail to wage this war
of sacred duty,
you will abandon your own duty
and fame only to gain evil.

People will tell
of your undying shame,
and for a man of honor
shame is worse than death.

> In this next passage from the Bhagavad-Gita, Krishna reveals a deeper
> meaning to his message to Arjuna. Not only must Arjuna act like a warrior
> because that is his caste, but he must also act without regard to the
> consequences of his action. What does Krishna seem to mean by this?
> How does one do "nothing at all even when he engages in action"? In
> what sense is this advice "religious"?

Abandoning attachment to fruits
of action, always content, independent,
he does nothing at all
even when he engages in action.

He incurs no guilt if he has no hope,
restrains his thought and himself,
abandons possessions,
and performs actions with his body only.

Content with whatever comes by chance,
beyond dualities, free from envy,
impartial to failure and success,
he is not bound even when he acts.

When a man is unattached and free,
his reason deep in knowledge,
acting only in sacrifice,
his action is wholly dissolved.

The Bhagavad-Gita *taught many lessons for many different people. Those, like Arjuna, who were required to act in the world might benefit from a doctrine of action (*karma*) that showed them how to keep their spiritual distance while acting. But far more people in Indian society, as in any other, found consolation in devotion rather than philosophy. In the following passage Krishna encourages devotion (*bhakti*). These lines influenced the development in the Middle Ages of bhakti sects of devotion to Shiva, the destroyer, and Vishnu, the restorer. How did Krishna encourage devotion to other gods (or incarnations) as well as himself? How is devotion like sacrifice? What, according to Krishna, does one gain by devotion or sacrifice? What would have been the appeal of this doctrine?*

When devoted men sacrifice
to other deities with faith,
they sacrifice to me, Arjuna,
however aberrant the rites.

I am the enjoyer
and the lord of all sacrifices;
they do not know me in reality,
and so they fail.

Votaries of the gods go to the gods,
ancestor-worshippers go to the ancestors,
those who propitiate ghosts go to them,
and my worshippers go to me.

The leaf or flower or fruit or water
that he offers with devotion,
I take from the man of self-restraint
in response to his devotion.

Whatever you do—what you take,
what you offer, what you give,
what penances you perform—
do as an offering to me, Arjuna!

You will be freed from the bonds of action,
from the fruit of fortune and misfortune;
armed with the discipline of renunciation,
your self liberated, you will join me.

I am impartial to all creatures,
and no one is hateful or dear to me;

but men devoted to me are in me,
and I am within them.

If he is devoted solely to me,
even a violent criminal
must be deemed a man of virtue,
for his resolve is right.

His spirit quickens to sacred duty,
and he finds eternal peace;
Arjuna, know that no one
devoted to me is lost.

If they rely on me, Arjuna,
women, commoners, men of low rank,
even men born in the womb of evil,
reach the highest way.

How easy it is then for holy priests
and devoted royal sages—
in this transient world of sorrow,
devote yourself to me!

Keep me in your mind and devotion,
sacrifice to me, bow to me,
discipline your self toward me,
and you will reach me!

BUDDHISM: 1. GOTAMA'S DISCOVERY

One of the traditional stories told about the Buddha (who grew up in northern India around 500 B.C.) is the following account of how he discovered old age, sickness, and death. According to the story, at the birth of the Buddha wise men predicted that he would be either a prince

From *Life of Gotama the Buddha*, translated by E. H. Brewster, as quoted in *Buddhism* by Clarence H. Hamilton (New York: 1952). London: Routlege & Kegan Paul, reprint of 1926 edition.

like his father or a wandering hermit. His father tried to insure the first result by keeping him content within the palace and unaware of human suffering. Eventually, however, the young prince decided to see the world beyond the palace gates.

What did he see? What did it mean to him? What did it mean to the later Buddhists who told this story? What important idea of Buddhism did it contain? In what ways were these ideas similar to, or different from, the ideas that Prince Gotama [Gautama] Siddartha (later the Buddha) learned when reciting the Vedas and the Gita?

Now the young lord Gotama, when many days had passed by, bade his charioteer make ready the state carriages, saying: "Get ready the carriages, good charioteer, and let us go through the park to inspect the pleasaunce [a recreation place attached to a mansion—Ed.]." "Yes, my lord," replied the charioteer, and harnessed the state carriages and sent word to Gotama: "The carriages are ready, my lord; do now what you deem fit." Then Gotama mounted a state carriage and drove out in state into the park.

Now the young lord saw, as he was driving to the park, an aged man as bent as a roof gable, decrepit, leaning on a staff, tottering as he walked, afflicted and long past his prime. And seeing him Gotama said: "That man, good charioteer, what has he done, that his hair is not like that of other men, nor his body?"

"He is what is called an aged man, my lord."

"But why is he called aged?"

"He is called aged, my lord, because he has not much longer to live."

"But then, good charioteer, am I too subject to old age, one who has not got past old age?"

"You, my lord, and we too, we all are of a kind to grow old; we have not got past old age."

"Why then, good charioteer, enough of the park for today. Drive me back hence to my rooms."

"Yea, my lord," answered the charioteer, and drove him back. And he, going to his rooms, sat brooding sorrowful and depressed, thinking, "Shame then verily be upon this thing called birth, since to one born old age shows itself like that!"

Thereupon the rāja sent for the charioteer and asked him: "Well, good charioteer, did the boy take pleasure in the park? Was he pleased with it?"

"No, my lord, he was not."

"What then did he see on his drive?"

(And the charioteer told the rāja all.)

Then the rāja thought thus: We must not have Gotama declining to rule. We must not have him going forth from the house into the homeless state. We must not let what the brāhman soothsayers spoke of come true.

So, that these things might not come to pass, he let the youth be still more surrounded by sensuous pleasures. And thus Gotama continued to live amidst the pleasures of sense.

Now after many days had passed by, the young lord again bade his charioteer make ready and drove forth as once before. . . .

And Gotama saw, as he was driving to the park, a sick man, suffering and very ill, fallen and weltering in his own water, by some being lifted up, by others being dressed. Seeing this, Gotama asked: "That man, good charioteer, what has he done that his eyes are not like others' eyes, nor his voice like the voice of other man?"

"He is what is called ill, my lord."

"But what is meant by ill?"

"It means, my lord, that he will hardly recover from his illness."

"But I am too, then, good charioteer, subject to fall ill; have I not got out of reach of illness?"

"You, my lord, and we too, we are all subject to fall ill; we have not got beyond the reach of illness."

"Why then, good charioteer, enough of the park for today. Drive me back hence to my rooms." "Yea, my lord," answered the charioteer, and drove him back. And he, going to his rooms, sat brooding sorrowful and depressed, thinking: Shame then verily be upon this thing called birth, since to one born decay shows itself like that, disease shows itself like that.

Thereupon the rāja sent for the charioteer and asked him: "Well, good charioteer, did the young lord take pleasure in the park and was he pleased with it?"

"No, my lord, he was not."

"What did he see then on his drive?"

(And the charioteer told the rāja all.)

Then the rāja thought thus: We must not have Gotama declining to rule; we must not have him going forth from the house to the homeless state; we must not let what the brāhman soothsayers spoke of come true.

So, that these things might not come to pass, he let the young man be still more abundantly surrounded by sensuous pleasures. And thus Gotama continued to live amidst the pleasures of sense.

Now once again, after many days . . . the young lord Gotama . . . drove forth.

And he saw, as he was driving to the park, a great concourse of people clad in garments of different colours constructing a funeral pyre. And seeing this he asked his charioteer: "Why now are all those people come together in garments of different colours, and making that pile?"

"It is because someone, my lord, has ended his days."

"Then drive the carriage close to him who has ended his days."

"Yea, my lord," answered the charioteer, and did so. And Gotama saw the corpse of him who had ended his days and asked: "What, good charioteer, is ending one's days?"

"It means, my lord, that neither mother, nor father, nor other kinsfolk will now see him, nor will he see them."

"But am I too then subject to death, have I not got beyond reach of death? Will neither the rāja, nor the ranee, nor any other of my kin see me more, or shall I again see them?"

"You, my lord, and we too, we are all subject to death; we have not passed beyond the reach of death. Neither the rāja, nor the ranee, nor any other of your kin will see you any more, nor will you see them."

"Why then, good charioteer, enough of the park for today. Drive me back hence to my rooms."

"Yea, my lord," replied the charioteer, and drove him back.

And he, going to his rooms, sat brooding sorrowful and depressed, thinking: Shame verily be upon this thing called birth, since to one born the decay of life, since disease, since death shows itself like that!

Thereupon the rāja questioned the charioteer as before and as before let Gotama be still more surrounded by sensuous enjoyment. And thus he continued to live amidst the pleasures of sense.

Now once again, after many days . . . the lord Gotama . . . drove forth.

And he saw, as he was driving to the park, a shaven-headed man, a recluse, wearing the yellow robe. And seeing him he asked the charioteer, "That man, good charioteer, what has he done that his head is unlike other men's heads and his clothes too are unlike those of others?"

"That is what they call a recluse, because, my lord, he is one who has gone forth."

"What is that, 'to have gone forth'?"

"To have gone forth, my lord, means being thorough in the religious life, thorough in the peaceful life, thorough in good action, thorough in meritorious conduct, thorough in harmlessness, thorough in kindness to all creatures."

"Excellent indeed, friend charioteer, is what they call a recluse, since so thorough is his conduct in all those respects, wherefore drive me up to that forthgone man."

"Yea, my lord," replied the charioteer and drove up to the recluse. Then Gotama addressed him, saying, "You master, what have you done that your head is not as other men's heads, nor your clothes as those of other men?"

"I, my lord, am one whose has gone forth."

"What, master, does that mean?"

"It means, my lord, being thorough in the religious life, thorough in the peaceful life, thorough in good actions, thorough in meritorious conduct, thorough in harmlessness, thorough in kindness to all creatures."

"Excellently indeed, master, are you said to have gone forth since so thorough is your conduct in all those respects." Then the lord Gotama bade his charioteer, saying: "Come then, good charioteer, do you take the carriage and drive it back hence to my rooms. But I will even here cut off my hair, and don the yellow robe, and go forth from the house into the homeless state."

"Yea, my lord," replied the charioteer, and drove back. But the prince Gotama, there and then cutting off his hair and donning the yellow robe, went forth from the house into the homeless state.

Now at Kapilavatthu, the rāja's seat, a great number of persons, some eighty-four thousand souls, heard of what prince Gotama had done and thought: Surely this is no ordinary religious rule, this is no common going forth, in that prince Gotama himself has had his head shaved and has donned the yellow robe and has gone forth from the house into the homeless state. If prince Gotama has done this, why then should not we also? And they all had their heads shaved and donned the yellow robes; and in imitation of the Bodhisat [Buddha] they went forth from the house into the homeless state. So the Bodhisat went forth from the house into the homeless state. So the Bodhisat went up on his rounds through the villages; towns and cities accompanied by that multitude.

Now there arose in the mind of Gotama the Bodhisat, when he was meditating in seclusion, this thought: That indeed is not suitable for me that I should live beset. 'Twere better were I to dwell alone, far from the crowd.

So after a time he dwelt alone, away from the crowd. Those eighty-four thousand recluses went one way, and the Bodhisat went another way.

Now there arose in the mind of Gotama the Bodhisat, when he had gone to his place and was meditating in seclusion, this thought: Verily, this world has fallen upon trouble—one is born, and grows old, and dies, and falls from one state, and springs up in another. And from the suffering, moreover, no one knows of any way of escape, even from decay and death. O, when shall a way of escape from this suffering be made known—from decay and from death?

BUDDHISM:
2. THE BUDDHA'S FIRST SERMON

This is said to be the Buddha's first sermon, delivered shortly after he achieved enlightenment. It contains the essence of Buddhist thought: the four noble truths, the eightfold path, and the middle way. The middle way is the path between the extremes of the pursuit of pleasure and the pursuit of pain. It is defined by an eightfold path, an eight step path to a peaceful mind (right concentration). The four noble truths might be summarized as the following:

1. *Life is sorrow.*
2. *Sorrow is the result of selfish desire.*
3. *Selfish desire can be destroyed.*
4. *It can be destroyed by following the eightfold path.*

What do these ideas mean? What was considered the value of a "middle way"? In what ways did the eightfold path offer a spiritual discipline? What answers did the four noble truths provide?

Thus I have heard. Once the Lord was at Vrānasī, at the deer park called Iwipatana. There he addressed the five monks:

There are two ends not to be served by a wanderer. What are these two? The pursuit of desires and of the pleasure which springs from desire, which is base, common, leading to rebirth, ignoble, and unprofitable; and the pursuit of pain and hardship, which is grievous, ignoble, and unprofitable. The Middle Way of the Tathāgata avoids both these ends. It is enlightened, it brings clear vision, it makes for wisdom, and leads to peace, insight, enlightenment, and Nirvāna. What is the Middle Way? . . . It is the Noble Eightfold Path—Right Views, Right Resolve, Right Speech, Right Conduct, Right Livelihood, Right Effort, Right Mindfulness, and Right Concentration. This is the Middle Way. . . .

And this is the Noble Truth of Sorrow. Birth is sorrow, age is sorrow, disease is sorrow, death is sorrow; contact with the unpleasant is sorrow, separation from the pleasant is sorrow, every wish unfulfilled is sorrow—in short all the five components of individuality are sorrow.

And this is the Noble Truth of the Arising of Sorrow. It arises from craving, which leads to rebirth, which brings delight and passion, and seeks pleasure now here, now there—the craving for sensual pleasure, the craving for continued life, the craving for power.

And this is the Noble Truth of the Stopping of Sorrow. It is the complete stopping of that craving, so that no passion remains, leaving it, being emancipated from it, being released from it, giving no place to it.

And this the Noble Truth of the Way which Leads to the Stopping of Sorrow. It is the Noble Eightfold Path—Right Views, Right Resolve, Right Speech, Right Conduct, Right Livelihood, Right Efforts, Right Mindfulness, and Right Concentration.

BUDDHISM:
3. THE STORY OF ISIDĀSĪ, A BUDDHIST NUN

Buddhism, like Christianity, was a monastic religion. One of its ideals was the renunciation of the everyday world in favor of a life of poverty and devotion in a monastery. There were mendicant (begging) nuns as well as monks in Buddhism.

In this selection a Buddhist nun, Isidāsī, explains why she became a mendicant nun. How was she rejected by three husbands? Why did she decide to become a nun? What were her previous lives? What did they have to do with her decision to renounce the world? What does Isidāsī's story say about Buddhist ideas of karma and reincarnation?

In the city of Pātaliputta, treasured
on earth for its glorious flowers,
there were two mendicant nuns
of the Buddha's own Sakya clan.
One was Isidāsī, the other was Bodhī,
both of them morally pure,
skilled in meditation, wise,
and freed from painful vices.
They begged alms, ate their food,
washed their bowls,
and found a secret place
to rest and share their stories.

"You're still beautiful, Isidāsī.
Your youth hasn't faded.
What vision of evil drove you
to renounce the world?"

From *Ballads of Early Buddhist Nuns* in *Zero*, Vol. V, translated from the *Pali Therigatha* by Barbara Stoler Miller. Reprinted by permission of Barbara Stoler Miller.

In that secret place she told her tale
to teach the truth of Buddha's way.
Isidāsī said to Bodhī,
"Hear why I am a mendicant nun:

In the great city of Ujjenī
my father was a merchant of high repute.
I was his only daughter,
deeply loved and pampered.
A wealthy merchant sent noblemen
from the city of Sāketa
to arrange a marriage, and my father
gave me to be his son's wife.
Day and night I humbled myself
to honor my in-laws—
my training made me bow
my head down at their feet.
When I saw my husband's
sisters and brothers
I cringed and crept away
to free my seat for them.
I kept fresh-cooked food and drink
and spiced pickles ready
to serve their demands.
I woke early every morning
to scrub my hands and feet
before I crossed the threshold
to beg my husband's blessing.
Like a slave girl,
I took combs and scented oils
and my mirror
to groom him.
I cooked his rice gruel,
I washed his bowl,
I waited on this husband
like a mother doting on her son.
Though I was diligent and humble,
meticulous and virtuous
in serving him,
my husband despised me.
He begged his parents,
'Give me your leave.
I must go away. I will not stay
in this house with Isidāsī!'

'Don't speak this way, son!
Isidāsī is intelligent and wise,
diligent, meticulous.
Doesn't she please you, son?'
'She does me no harm,
but I will not stay with Isidāsī.
I detest her! Enough!
Give me leave, I must go away.'
My husband's parents heard
his words and questioned me,
'How did you offend him?
Confide what really happened.'
'I committed no offense or harm
or ever answered his cruel words.
I don't know what I did
to make this husband hate me.'
They took me back
to my father's house.
'To keep our precious son
we sacrifice this goddess.'

Then my father married me
into another wealthy house.
The second merchant took me
for half the first bride price.
I lived in that house
for barely a month,
serving him like a slave
until he sent me back.
Then my father snared an ascetic
begging for alms; he said,
'Be my daughter's husband!
Throw away your robe and pot!'
He stayed for two weeks
before he told my father,
'Give me my robe and pot and cup!
I'll beg for alms again.'
My parents and my family
beseeched him,
'What have we neglected?
Quickly, name your every want!'
He answered, 'I only want
enough to feed myself.

I will not stay in this house
with Isidāsī!'
They dismissed him and he left.
I brooded in my solitude:
'I'll tell them I'm going to die
unless I become a mendicant nun.'
And the great nun Jinadattā
came begging alms
at my father's house—she was
disciplined, wise, morally pure.
I rose when I saw her
and gave her my seat,
bowed at her feet
and offered her a meal.
I served her fresh-cooked food
and drink and spiced pickles.
When she had eaten, I said,
'Lady, I want to be a nun.'
My father argued, 'My child,
you may follow the Buddha's way
by giving food and drink
to holy men and brahmin priests.'
I pleaded in tears,
begging his blessing,
'I must destroy
the evil I have done!'
My father blessed me then,
'Attain enlightenment
and the Buddha's way
that leads to liberation!'
I bid farewell to my parents
and became a mendicant nun.
After only seven days
I reached the triple wisdom.
I know my former seven births
that ripened into this one.
I'll recount them.
Listen carefully!

In the city of Ekakaccha
I was a wealthy goldsmith,
intoxicated by youth's wine,
seducing other men's wives.
I died and boiled in hell
for some time; tormented,

I rose from my tortures
and entered a monkey's belly.
Seven days after my birth
the troop's leader castrated me;
this was the fruit
of seducing other men's wives.
Then I died again,
spent time in the forest of Sindh,
and entered the belly
of a wild, blind, lame goat.
I suffered twelve years
as a worm-ridden, sickly,
castrated goat
for seducing other men's wives.
When I died again, I was born
to a cattle-trader's cow,
a calf the color of coppery lac [resin],
castrated in the twelfth month.
I pulled a plough and cart,
wretched, blind, and sickly,
for seducing other men's wives.
I died again on the road
to be born an androgyne
in a slave girl's house
for seducing other men's wives.
At thirty I died and was born
a female in a carter's family,
out-caste, indigent, enslaved
by money-lenders' loans.
A caravan trader claiming
interest on a loan
dragged me screaming
from my family.
When I was sixteen
the son of this merchant
noticed my maiden youth
and took me.
He had another wife
who was moral and virtuous,
in love with her husband.
I sowed discord with her.
The fruit of seven former lives
made three husbands scorn me,
though I served them like a slave—
I have ended all this now.

INDIAN CAVE SANCTUARIES

RICHARD LANNOY

Richard Lannoy is a modern historian of Indian culture. In this selection from his richly suggestive book The Speaking Tree, *he calls our attention to the importance of sculptured caves in Indian culture and religion from the time of the Upanishads, the Buddha, and the rise of city kingdoms in northern India (around 500 B.C.) until the development of Hindu temple architecture one thousand years later.*

How were these caves similar to, and different from, Christian monasteries? What was the appeal of the "retreat to the forest" in Indian culture of this period? Why did people choose to create caves? How did the caves combine elements of monasticism and fertility cults?

THE ART OF THE CAVE SANCTUARIES

For a thousand years almost all the most important sculptural monuments were *caves*. This is the most singular fact about Indian art, and distinguishes it from that of other civilizations. . . . In order to understand the function of these caves in society at the time, the meaning of the word "monastic" should be made clear. Though Indian monasticism does resemble similar Christian institutions, the two arose under quite different historical conditions and were organized on lines that are as dissimilar as the doctrines of Christianity and Indian religion themselves. . . . The Indian cave sanctuaries, in spite of their relative inaccessibility up precipitous ledges and through jungle infested with wild beasts, were well-known centres of pilgrimage in which numerous members of the society had at least a spiritual, if not a financial, interest. For this very reason they are the very opposite of forbiddingly austere retreats for ascetic monks, and their art reflects the interests of the entire society, from king to commoner. Human beings generally wish to be free of labour, to be beautiful and sexually satisfied in the most luxurious and varied way they can imagine. This motive, however, like every other basic human impulse, was originally contained within an all-inclusive religious system and completely at one with it. It was the kind of movement instigated by the Buddha and other "protestant" reformers which sought to "purify" religion of these aspects. In this respect the

Buddha's own views were not observed for long, and the later cave sanctuaries are the product of a return to a more permissive outlook.

One final point should be made clear in order to describe the focal role of the cave sanctuaries in the life of the people as a whole. The Buddhist *vibāra*, or monastery, as it still is in Buddhist countries, was an important centre of social life in the villages, a kind of "clubroom" or "village hall," the venue of the secular as well as the sacred, even though the monks and nuns were themselves celibate and took their vows seriously.

THE RETREAT TO THE FOREST

In a clean, level spot, free from pebbles, fire, and gravel,
By the sound of water and other propinquities
Favourable to thought, not offensive to the eye,
In a hidden retreat protected from the wind, one should practise Yoga.
Fog, smoke, sun, fire, wind,
Fire-flies, lightning, a crystal, a moon—
These are the preliminary appearances,
Which produce the manifestation of Brahmā in Yoga.

To understand the motivation for the creation of this most important Indian monumental art—the cave sanctuaries—we must briefly retrace our steps to that watershed in history, the period between the sixth and third centuries B.C. During that time, when society became increasingly differentiated, the intellectual climate of India was characterized not only by early Buddhism, but by the rise of sophism, the schools of metaphysics, and the ascetic sects. The new urban man felt increasingly alienated from nature; social discipline called for by new productive techniques created a sense of anxiety among the more individualistic non-conformists. At all such periods of inner crisis and difficulty, man retreated into the forest to test his own strength and recover the sense of identity with his surroundings. At this moment of spiritual crisis in India, the Upanishads (from which the above quotation is taken) and "forest books" were composed by mystics who retreated to the solitude of the forest, to wrestle with their inner selves and seek union through Nature with the All. "These high-minded men," writes the dramatist Bhāsa in *The Vision of Vasavadatta*, "make their home in the forest to escape from the brutalities of a town." Similarly, the Buddhist monks were enjoined to pass a period of time each year (the monsoon months) residing in a place of permanent shelter, preferably in forest caves.

This idea of the retreat to the solitude of nature became one of the most persistent and important traits in the development of Indian culture, owing to the prestige which renunciation conferred; the practice evolved in accordance with the pattern of priestly education of the

Brahmans. The novice withdrew to the forest retreat of his chosen teacher for a period of twelve years or more. The most significant feature of this life, and the one which should be emphasized if the ethos of the forest retreat is to be fully grasped, is that the novice gathered, though *never produced*, food for his guru. The ideal of a carefree, simpler pattern of life in which there was no need to engage in hard productive labour for survival, had in itself a profound emotional appeal (even among kings). Though this needs no further explanation, as it still remains the dream of urban man even in the most industrially advanced societies, it should be remembered that the co-existence of food-collecting tribes alongside industrious food-producing communities gave to the archaic Indian ideal of the forest retreat a very concrete and specific connotation. The surviving tribal life, with its sense of collective unity, abundantly evident, aroused in the city-dwellers ancestral memories of times in the not too distant past when society was not split into antagonistic classes and castes, nor condemned to unremitting labour. The pattern continues to the present day. As many observers have noted, there is a very marked contrast between the Hindu, caste-ridden Indian village society, with its poverty, its careworn ethos of hard labour on exhausted soil, its tabu-ridden family relationships, on the one hand, and on the other, a carefree, colourful, joyous, extraverted tribal way of life in the refreshing environment of the forest. But envy for these communities by social misfits in the caste system takes a much stronger form too, as it has since very ancient times: a hankering for the less organized, the less rationalized, even the relatively lawless state. Just as the Dantes, Rousseaus, and Thoreaus of India developed their inner orientation in the forest retreat, so too have its Robin Hoods found shelter and strength there. The romanticism of the *dacoit*, or bandit, and other forms of anarchic social protest, also figure among the components of forest nostalgia. In recent times these types of idealized banditry, "robbing the rich to pay the poor," have been linked with the cult of "old gods" and the revalorization of primitive customs. The *thaggi*, a celebrated sect of bandits finally suppressed in the nineteenth century, were worshippers of the aboriginal black goddess of destruction, Kālī. In the ancient period we are dealing with, the contemplative sects who retreated to the forest turned once more to the "old gods," the mother goddesses, the tree and snake deities of the forest tribes.

If the ideal surroundings for the Buddhist sanctuaries were indeed the kind of thickly forested ravine generally selected, why did they not *build*, instead of resorting to the exceedingly slow technique of excavating from the living rock.

Why *caves*?

Curiously enough, no writer has attempted more than a hesitant and partial answer to the question, which is fundamental to a full understanding of Indian art. For it is here that India makes its most original contribution to the language of form, and here too that the Indian artist succeeded in projecting the totality of a people's ideals, a community of feeling shared by the entire society. There is nothing in the history of Indian culture which attains the same grandeur of vision; other examples, whatever the medium of expression, seem fragmentary in comparison, mere facets of the unitary whole. Certainly so consistent a preference for mining permanent structures directly from the earth deserves some attempt at an explanation.

Permanence, aesthetic unity, shelter which would be cool in summer, security, and refuge are all obvious needs of the monastic communities which the caves served. A peasant cave-builder in Lin Ling village, northern Shansi, where many homes are excavated from the hillside for practical convenience, told Jan Myrdal that a cave "is a good dwelling and one that is easy to keep warm in winter, while it is always cool in summer. And you never need to think about maintenance." But these practical issues are not sufficient to explain excavation on such an ostentatious scale, over so long a period. . . .

I would tentatively suggest that the detailing of the cave architecture may reflect not only nostalgia for wooden construction, but a conscious recreation of a primitive ethos, integrally part of the fertility theme. The sheer difficulty of detailed execution suggests a more compulsive motivation than adaptation of an available vernacular style. Furthermore, the incorporation of this symbolism, along with rites of death and rebirth which originally belonged to the cult of a mother goddess, lies at the root of the transformation of early Buddhist doctrine into a devotional religion. Numerous examples of this "prestige of beginnings" will be cited. To some extent, the continuity of every civilization is assured by nostalgia for old ways; in India this nostalgia is an integral part of a system, of which one cardinal feature is *rites* which restore to the society its sense of primal innocence and unity. The *rites* performed in the cave sanctuaries were based on the symbolism of the Eternal Return.

The conjunction of monasticism and fertility cults is significant. We are dealing with a mode of living integrally linked with the symbolism of initiatory rites of death and rebirth, where *mortification* of the flesh precedes initiation into an enhanced mode of life. Such rites are accompanied by the enactment of body-destruction and self-annihilation fantasies. The conjunction of death and fertility cults figures in a number of ancient societies; the cult of Yamāī, the mother and death goddess of Kālī, is but one example. There are certain Indus Valley figurines which represent a "grim embodiment of the mother-goddess who is also guardian of the dead—an underworld deity concerned alike with the corpse and the seed corn buried beneath the earth." In Mediterranean antiquity the myth of the maiden goddess carried off to the bridal chamber of the underworld deity is widespread, notably in Orphism.

Erotic art came to be associated with fertility cults and death and regeneration rites, in both ancient India and Greece. The symbol of the sepulchral phallus was common in classical antiquity. In the Hindu cave shrines the sanctum contains no sculptural decoration of imagery except the stone *lingā* (ancient symbol of cosmic energy as a conceptualized phallus). In view of the great prominence of erotic imagery in the cave sanctuaries it is worth remembering that, as Professor Siegfried Giedion puts it, "in prehistory it was the concept of fertility rather than the sexual act which gave birth to their symbols." Indian art preserves in unbroken sequence the evolution of fertility symbols from the pre-Harappan to the erotic imagery of later periods. This was accomplished during a period of two or three thousand years, but even then the original traits of the pre-Aryan fertility cults were never entirely lost, although the emphasis in devotional religion and in the cults of divine love was remote from tribal orgiasticism.

E.M. Forster's symbol of the Marabar Caves has acquired a popular significance quite independent of its legitimate and intended role within the fictional scheme of *A Passage to India*. This is probably because the modern world is fascinated by the inclusive field of echoing resonance which the Indian cave world conjures up in the imagination. The technological environment in which we now live creates a highly complex field of interconnectedness, and in this vortex we seek the reassurance of far simpler types of wrap-around environment. I doubt if Forster's young readers today have the slightest sympathy with Mrs. Moore's total disorientation subsequent to hearing the echo in the Marabar Caves. From what I have seen of their rapturous response to the perfect echoing acoustics of Cave VI at Ajantā, they regard the Indian cave world, the psychedelic lights-show, and total theatre as kindred media. As Mrs. Moore's train meanders through the countryside, taking her away from the hated Marabar, she is filled with loathing when the same minaret [a tower attached to a mosque—Ed.] looms up outside the train window again and again, each time viewed from a different angle, depending on the twists and turns of the railway line. This multiple perspective on a single object is seen through the eyes of Mrs. Moore as yet another irritating feature of a country which consistently upsets the Western equilibrium. Both the echoing cave and the multiple minaret are vivid examples of the aesthetic dysphoria which the nonsequential, intuitive, tactile culture of India often induces in Europeans of an older generation conditioned by rationalism and Euclidean space.

8. Chinese Civilization

THE *ANALECTS* OF CONFUCIUS

Not much is known about the life of Confucius. He was born about 551 B.C., orphaned at an early age, became a minor official and teacher and then travelled widely to give advice to princes. He died in 479 B.C. at the age of 70. His teachings are not religious, but they are very moral. He seems to have believed that the moral life was the most worthy goal one could have. The ideal moral character for Confucius was "the gentleman." The most important virtue of the gentleman is jen (humanity or benevolence). He must also demonstrate chung (doing his best) and shu (knowing what other people want). These are highly social ideals. Confucianism became the moral code of Chinese culture for thousands of years. Whether practiced or honored in the breach, interpreted in various ways, enshrined as official orthodoxy, or sometimes villified, probably no set of ideas has influenced so many people in the history of the world.

What kind of people are these ideas likely to produce? Are there certain groups in society who would find these ideas more appealing? In what ways are these ideas different from those which you have been taught in your own moral education? What, if anything, do these ideas of morality have to do with religion?

ON EDUCATION

II,15 The Master said, " 'He who learns but does not think, is lost.' He who thinks but does not learn is in great danger."

II,17 The Master said, "Yu, shall I teach you what knowledge is? When you know a thing, to recognize that you know it, and when you do not know a thing, to recognize that you do not know it. That is knowledge."

VII,1 The Master said, "I have 'transmitted what was taught to me without making up anything of my own.' I have been faithful to and loved the Ancients. In these respects, I make bold to think, not even our old P'eng can have excelled me."

VII,2 The Master said, "I have listened in silence and noted what was

From *Analects of Confucius*, translated by Arthur Waley. London: George Allen & Unwin, 1958. Reprinted by permission.

said. I have never grown tired of learning nor wearied of teaching others what I have learnt. These at least are merits which I can confidently claim."

XIII,9 When the Master was going to Wei, Jan Ch'iu drove him. The Master said, "What a dense population!" Jan Ch'iu said, "When the people have multiplied, what next should be done for them?" The Master said, "Enrich them." Jan Ch'iu said, "When one has enriched them, what next should be done for them?" The Master said, "Instruct them."

XV,35 The Master said, "When it comes to Goodness one need not avoid competing with one's teacher."

ON GOODNESS

I,3 The Master said, " 'Clever talk and a pretentious manner' are seldom found in the Good."

I,6 The Master said, "A young man's duty is to behave well to his parents at home and to his elders abroad, to be cautious in giving promises and punctual in keeping them, to have kindly feelings towards everyone, but seek the intimacy of the Good. If, when all that is done, he has any energy to spare, then let him study the polite arts."

IV,3,4 Of the adage, "Only a Good Man knows how to like people, knows how to dislike them," the Master said, "He whose heart is in the smallest degree set upon Goodness will dislike no one."

VII,15 The Master said, "He who seeks only coarse food to eat, water to drink and bent arm for pillow, will without looking for it find happiness to boot. Any thought of accepting wealth and rank by means that I know to be wrong is as remote from me as the clouds that float above."

XII,2 Jan Yung asked about Goodness. The Master said, "Behave when away from home as though you were in the presence of an important guest. Deal with the common people as though you were officiating at an important sacrifice. Do not do to others what you would not like yourself. Then there will be no feelings of opposition to you, whether it is the affairs of a State that you are handling or the affairs of a Family."

XV,23 Tzu-kung asked saying, "Is there any single saying that one can act upon all day and every day?" The Master said, "Perhaps the saying about consideration: 'Never do to others what you would not like them to do to you.' "

ON THE GENTLEMAN

II,13 Tzu-kung asked about the true gentleman. The Master said, "He does not preach what he practices till he has practiced what he preaches."

III,7 The Master said, "Gentlemen never compete. You will say that in archery they do so. But even then they bow and make way for one another when they are going up to the archery-ground, when they are coming down and at the subsequent drinking bout. Thus even when competing, they still remain gentlemen."

IV,5 "Wealth and rank are what every man desires; but if they can only be retained to the detriment of the Way he professes, he must relinquish them. Poverty and obscurity are what every man detests; but if they can only be avoided to the detriment of the Way he professes, he must accept them. The gentleman who ever parts company with Goodness does not fulfill that name. Never for a moment does a gentleman quit the way of Goodness. He is never so harried but that he cleaves to this; never so tottering but that he cleaves to this."

IV,16 The Master said, "A gentleman takes as much trouble to discover what is right as lesser men take to discover what will pay."

VI,25 The Master said, "A gentleman who is widely versed in letters and at the same time knows how to submit his learning to the restraints of ritual is not likely, I think, to go far wrong."

VIII,2 . . . The Master said, "When gentlemen deal generously with their own kin, the common people are incited to Goodness. When old dependents are not discarded, the common people will not be fickle."

IX,13 The Master wanted to settle among the Nine Wild Tribes of the East. Someone said, "I am afraid you would find it hard to put up with their lack of refinement." The Master said, "Were a true gentleman to settle among them there would soon be no trouble about lack of refinement."

XII,16 The Master said, "The gentleman calls attention to the good points in others; he does not call attention to their defects. The small man does just the reverse of this."

XV,18 The Master said, "A gentleman is distressed by his own lack of capacity; he is never distressed at the failure of others to recognize his merits."

XV,20 The Master said, " 'The demands that a gentleman makes are upon himself; those that a small man makes are upon others.' "

XV,21 The Master said, "A gentleman is proud, but not quarrelsome, allies himself with individuals, but not with parties."

X,6 A gentleman does not wear facings of purple or mauve, nor in undress does he use pink or roan. In hot weather he wears an unlined gown of fine thread loosely woven, but puts on an outside garment before going out-of-doors. With a black robe he wears black lambskin; with a robe of undyed silk, fawn. With a yellow robe, fox fur. On his undress robe the fur cuffs are long; but the right is shorter than the left. His bedclothes must be half as long again as a man's height. The thicker kinds of fox and badger are for home wear. Except when in mourning, he wears all his girdle-ornaments. Apart from his Court apron, all his skirts are wider at the bottom than at the waist. Lambskin dyed black and a hat of dark-dyed silk must not be worn when making visits of condolence. At the Announcement of the New Moon he must go to Court in full Court dress.

ON FILIAL PIETY

II,5 Meng I Tzu asked about the treatment of parents. The Master said, "Never disobey!" When Fan Ch'ih was driving his carriage for him, the Master said, "Meng asked me about the treatment of parents and I said, 'Never disobey!' " Fan Ch'ih said, "In what sense did you mean it?" The Master said, "While they are alive, serve them according to ritual. When they die, bury them according to ritual and sacrifice to them according to ritual."

II,7 Tzu-yu asked about the treatment of parents. The Master said, " 'Filial sons' nowadays are people who see to it that their parents get enough to eat. But even dogs and horses are cared for to that extent. If there is no feeling of respect, wherein lies the difference?"

ON RITUAL AND MUSIC

III,3 The Master said, "A man who is not Good, what can he have to do with ritual? A man who is not Good, what can he have to do with music?"

III,4 Lin Fang asked for some main principles in connexion with ritual. The Master said, "A very big question. In ritual at large it is a safe rule always to be too sparing rather than too lavish; and in the particular case of mourning-rites, they should be dictated by grief rather than by fear."

VIII,2 The Master said, "Courtesy not bounded by the prescriptions of ritual becomes tiresome. Caution not bounded by the prescriptions of ritual becomes timidity, daring becomes turbulence, inflexibility becomes harshness."

VIII,8 The Master said, "Let a man be first incited by the *Songs*, then given a firm footing by the study of ritual, and finally perfected by music."

ON GOVERNMENT BY MORAL FORCE

I,5 The Master said, "A country of a thousand war-chariots cannot be administered unless the ruler attends strictly to business, punctually observes his promises, is economical in expenditure, shows affection towards his subjects in general, and uses the labour of the peasantry only at the proper times of year."

II,3 The Master said, "Govern the people by regulations, keep order among them by chastisements, and they will flee from you, and lose all self-respect. Govern them by moral force, keep order among them by ritual and they will keep their self-respect and come to you of their own accord."

XII,11 Duke Ching of Ch'i asked Master K'ung about government. Master K'ung replied saying, "Let the prince be a prince, the minister a minister, the father a father and the son a son." The Duke said, "How true! For indeed when the prince is not a prince, the minister not a minister, the father not a father, the son not a son, one may have a dish of millet in front of one and yet not know if one will live to eat it."

XII,19 Chi L'ang-tzu asked Master K'ung about government, saying, "Suppose I were to slay those who have not the Way in order to help on those who have the Way, what would you think of it?" Master K'ung replied saying, "You are there to rule, not to slay. If you desire what is good, the people will at once be good. The essence of the gentleman is that of wind; the essence of small people is that of grass. And when a wind passes over the grass, it cannot choose but bend."

XIII,6 The Master said, "If the ruler himself is upright, all will go well even though he does not give orders. But if he himself is not upright, even though he gives orders, they will not be obeyed."

XIII,10 The Master said, "If only someone were to make use of me, even for a single year, I could do a great deal; and in three years I could finish off the whole work."

XIII,11 The Master said, " 'Only if the right sort of people had charge of a country for a hundred years would it become really possible to stop cruelty and do away with slaughter.' How true the saying is!"

ON PUBLIC OPINION

II,19 Duke Ai asked, "What can I do in order to get the support of the common people?" Master K'ung replied, "If you 'raise up the straight and set them on top of the crooked,' the commoners will support you. But if you raise the crooked and set them on top of the straight, the commoners will not support you."

II,20 Chi L'ang-tzu asked whether there were any form of encouragement by which he could induce the common people to be respectful and loyal. The Master said, "Approach them with dignity, and they will respect you. Show piety towards your parents and kindness toward your children, and they will be loyal to you. Promote those who are worthy, train those who are incompetent; that is the best form of encouragement."

XII,7 Tzu-kung asked about government. The Master said, "Sufficient food, sufficient weapons, and the confidence of the common people." Tzu-kung said, "Suppose you had no choice but to dispense with one of these three, which would you forgo?" The Master said, "Weapons." Tzu-kung said, "Suppose you were forced to dispense with one of the two that were left, which would you forgo?" The Master said, "Food. For from of old death has been the lot of all men; but a people that no longer trusts its rulers is lost indeed."

ON RELIGION

III,11 Someone asked for an explanation of the Ancestral Sacrifice. The Master said, "I do not know. Anyone who knew the explanation could deal with all things under Heaven as easily as I lay this here"; and he laid his finger upon the palm of his hand.

V,12 Tzu-kung said, "Our Master's views concerning culture and the outward insignia of goodness, we are permitted to hear; but about Man's nature and the ways of Heaven he will not tell us anything at all."

VII,20 The Master never talked of prodigies, feats of strength, disorders or spirits.

VII,34 When the Master was very ill, Tzu-lu asked leave to perform the Rite of Expiation. The Master said, "Is there such a thing?" Tzu-lu answered saying, "There is. In one of the Dirges it says, 'We performed rites of expiation for you, calling upon the sky-spirits above and the earth-spirits below.'" The Master said, "My expiation began long ago!"

XI,11 Tzu-lu asked how one should serve ghosts and spirits. The Master said, "Till you have learnt to serve men, how can you serve ghosts?" Tzu-lu then ventured upon a question about the dead. The Master said, "Till you know about the living, how are you to know about the dead?"

CONFUCIANISM: THE MENCIUS

MENCIUS

Confucianism is more than the writings of Confucius. It is a tradition that includes the thought of many of his followers as well. Second only to Confucius is Mencius, who lived during the fourth century B.C. In opposition to those who urged political manipulation, Mencius directed Confucians toward a more optimistic view of human nature and a richer regard for the rewards of benevolence.

What is Mencius's reason for saying that human nature is fundamentally good? What is benevolence? Are people born benevolent, or do they have to develop it? How is this philosophy different from Buddhism?

6. Mencius said, "No man is devoid of a heart sensitive to the suffering of others. Such a sensitive heart was possessed by the Former Kings and this manifested itself in compassionate government. With such a sensitive heart behind compassionate government, it was as easy to rule the Empire as rolling it on your palm.

"My reason for saying that no man is devoid of a heart sensitive to the suffering of others is this. Suppose a man were, all of a sudden, to see a young child on the verge of falling into a well. He would certainly be moved to compassion, not because he wanted to get in the good graces of the parents, nor because he wished to win the praise of his fellow villagers or friends, nor yet because he disliked the cry of the child. From this it can be seen that whoever is devoid of the heart of compassion is not human, whoever is devoid of the heart of shame is not human, whoever is devoid of the heart of courtesy and modesty is not human, and whoever is devoid of the heart of right and wrong is not human. The heart of compassion is the germ of benevolence; the heart of shame, of dutifulness; the heart of courtesy and modesty, of observance of the rites; the heart of right and wrong, of wisdom. Man has these four germs just as he has four limbs. For a man possessing these four germs to deny his own potentialities is for him to cripple himself; for him to deny the potentialities of his prince is for him to cripple his prince. If a man is able to develop all these four germs that he possesses, it will be like a fire starting up or a spring coming through. When these are fully developed, he can take under this protection the whole realm within the Four Seas, but if he fails to develop them, he will not be able even to serve his parents."

7. Mencius said, "Is the maker of arrows really more unfeeling than the maker of armour? He is afraid lest he should fail to harm people, whereas the maker of armour is afraid lest he should fail to protect them. The case is similar with the sorcerer-doctor and the coffin-maker. For this reason one cannot be too careful in the choice of one's calling.

"Confucius said, "The best neighbourhood is where benevolence is to be found. Not to live in such a neighbourhood when one has the choice cannot by any means be considered wise." Benevolence is the high honour bestowed by Heaven and the peaceful abode of man. Not to be benevolent when nothing stands in the way is to show a lack of wisdom. A man neither benevolent nor wise, devoid of courtesy and dutifulness, is a slave. A slave ashamed of serving is like a maker of bows ashamed of making bows, or a maker of arrows ashamed of making arrows. If one is ashamed, there is no better remedy than to practice benevolence. Benevolence is like archery: an archer makes sure his stance is correct before letting fly the arrow, and if he fails to hit the mark, he does not hold it against his victor. He simply seeks the cause within himself."

TAOISM:
THE TAO TE CHING

LAO TZU

When Indian missionaries brought Buddhism to China, they initially met strong resistance from Confucianism. What do you imagine were some of the points of disagreement between Buddhists and Confucians?

Eventually the Buddhists were successful by using the language of a very different Chinese philosophical tradition, Taoism. Lao Tzu may or may not have been an actual contemporary of Confucius, but the Tao Te Ching *was written around the sixth century B.C., and Taoism remained an alternative vision to the dominant Confucianism. In what ways are the ideas expressed in the* Tao Te Ching *different from those of Confucianism? Might a person easily follow both Confucianism and Taoism, or would these philosophies appeal to different people? Compared to Confucianism, are these Taoist ideas more "religious"? Which set of ideas do you find more appealing? Why?*

From *The Way and Its Power, A Study of the Tao Te Ching* by Arthur Waley. London: George Allen & Unwin, 1934. Reprinted by permission.

CHAPTER 1

The Way that can be told of is not an Unvarying Way;
The names that can be named are not unvarying names.
It was from the Nameless that Heaven and Earth sprang;
The named is but the mother that rears the ten thousand creatures,
    each after its kind.
Truly, "Only he that rids himself forever of desire can see the
    Secret Essences";
He that has never rid himself of desire can see only the Outcomes.
These two things issued from the same mould, but nevertheless are
    different in name.
This "same mould" we can but call the Mystery.
Or rather the "Darker than any Mystery,"
The Doorway whence issued all Secret Essences.

CHAPTER II

It is because every one under Heaven recognizes beauty as beauty,
    that the idea of ugliness exists.
And equally if every one recognized virtue as virtue, this would
    merely create fresh conceptions of wickedness.
For truly "Being and Not-being grow out of one another;
Difficult and easy complete one another.
Long and short test one another;
High and low determine one another.
The sounds of instrument and voice give harmony to one another.
Front and back give sequence to one another."
Therefore the Sage relies on actionless activity,
Carries on wordless teaching,
But the myriad creatures are worked upon by him; he does not
    disown them.
He rears them, but does not lay claim to them,
Controls them, but does not lean upon them,
Achieves his aim, but does not call attention to what he does;
And for the very reason that he does not call attention to what he
    does
He is not ejected from fruition of what he has done.

CHAPTER III

If we stop looking for "persons of superior morality" (hsien) to put in
power, there will be no more jealousies among the people.
If we cease to set store by products that are hard to get, there will be

no more thieves. If the people never see such things as excite desire, their hearts will remain placid and undisturbed.

Therefore the Sage rules

> By emptying their hearts
> And filling their bellies,
> Weakening their intelligence
> And toughening their sinews
> Ever striving to make the people knowledgeless and desireless.

Indeed he sees to it that if there be any who have knowledge, they dare not interfere. Yet through his actionless activity all things are duly regulated.

CHAPTER IV

The Way is like an empty vessel
That yet may be drawn from
Without ever needing to be filled.
It is bottomless; the very progenitor of all things in the world.
In it all sharpness is blunted,
All tangles untied,
All glare tempered,
All dust smoothed.
It is like a deep pool that never dries.
Was it too the child of something else? We cannot tell.
But as a substanceless image it existed before the Ancestor.

CHAPTER VIII

The highest good is like that of water. The goodness of water is that it benefits the ten thousand creatures; yet itself does not scramble, but is content with the places that all men disdain. It is this that makes water so near to the Way.

And if men think the ground the best place for building a house
   upon,
If among thoughts they value those that are profound,
If in friendship they value gentleness,
In words, truth; in government, good order;
In deeds, effectiveness; in actions, timeliness—
In each case it is because they prefer what does not lead to strife,
And therefore does not go amiss.

CHAPTER IX

Stretch a bow to the very full,
And you will wish you had stopped in time;
Temper a sword-edge to its very sharpest,
And you will find it soon grows dull.
When bronze and jade fill your hall
It can no longer be guarded.
Wealth and place breed insolence
That brings ruin in its train.
When your work is done, then withdraw!
Such is Heaven's Way.

CHAPTER XI

We put thirty spokes together and call it a wheel;
But it is on the space where there is nothing that the utility of the
  wheel depends.
We turn clay to make a vessel;
But it is on the space where there is nothing that the utility of the
  vessel depends.
We pierce doors and windows to make a house;
And it is on these spaces where there is nothing that the utility of
  the house depends.
Therefore just as we take advantage of what is, we should recognize
  the utility of what is not.

CHAPTER XII

The five colours confuse the eye,
The five sounds dull the ear,
The five tastes spoil the palate.
Excess of hunting and chasing Makes minds go mad.
Products that are hard to get
Impede their owner's movements.
Therefore the Sage
Considers the belly not the eye.
Truly, "he rejects that but takes this."

CHAPTER XVIII

It was when the Great Way declined
That human kindness and morality arose;

It was when intelligence and knowledge appeared
That the Great Artifice began.
It was when the six near ones were no longer at peace
That there was talk of "dutiful sons";
Nor till fatherland was dark with strife
Did we hear of "loyal slaves."

CHAPTER XIX

Banish wisdom, discard knowledge,
And the people will be benefited a hundredfold.
Banish human kindness, discard morality,
And the people will be dutiful and compassionate.
Banish skill, discard profit,
And thieves and robbers will disappear
If when these three things are done they find life too plain and
    unadorned,
Then let them have accessories;
Give them Simplicity to look at, the Uncarved Block to hold,
Give them selflessness and fewness of desires.

KO HUNG'S
AUTOBIOGRAPHY

*Ko Hung lived between A.D. 283 and 343, a time of social and political
unrest. As he is at pains to make clear, his career was not particularly
noteworthy. But his struggles of everyday life are brought to us vividly in
this revealing autobiography. Rarely do we get to know someone from so
long ago so well. What does Ko Hung's autobiography tell you about
Chinese life in the period? What effects did the Confucian and Taoist
classics have on someone like Ko Hung? What was it like to be Ko Hung?*

I was my father's third son. Because I was born late, my parents spoiled
me and did not make me study. When I was thirteen my father passed
away, so I was left without his guidance and had to endure the hardships
of hunger and cold. I took on the farming chores myself. Having no

inheritance whatsoever, I had only stars to look upon and the grass to tread on.

Since our family library had been completely lost in the repeated wars, there was nothing I could read in my leisure after farming. I was therefore forced to shoulder my satchel and walk long distances to borrow books. Because I could rarely get an entire book from one household, this task was rather time-consuming. Moreover, I had to cut firewood and sell it in order to buy paper and writing brushes and do my copying by the light of fires amidst the fields and gardens. For these reasons, I was not introduced to literature at an early age. And because I constantly lacked paper, I would write on both sides of each sheet; as a result, no one could decipher my writing.

Not until I was sixteen did I start reading the *Classic of Filial Piety*, the *Analects*, the *Classic of Poetry*, and the *Classic of Changes*. As I was too poor to travel far in search of teachers and learned friends, I was shallow in my knowledge and understanding. Although I could not understand the profundity of books, I was avid to read them; I would silently recite the texts and carefully memorize the key points. The books that I went through ranged from the classics, histories, and the various philosophical treatises to short, miscellaneous essays—altogether nearly ten thousand chapters. Because I was slow and forgetful by nature, because I did not have many ideas or a set goal, my knowledge was meager and I had doubts about many points. Nevertheless, in my writings I have found occasion to cite these sources.

I never became a pure scholar of Confucianism or fit to be a teacher. In fact, I only glanced at the River Chart, the Lo Text, and the apocryphal books. I was not fond of astrology, arithmetic, the nine divisions of the sky, the three treasures of man, the "great union," the "flying talismans," and such things. I wanted no part of these arts because they cause people much trouble but have little to offer. In my later years I studied the methods of divination based on observation of the wind and the air, the auspicious and inauspicious elements, and the cycle of the agents. I learned only the main ideas, however, and not the fine points of practice. I figured that people who specialize in these arts are all employed by others, and therefore practicing them was no different from taking public office. Since I was not pressed by circumstances to struggle with such matters, I saw more to gain in studying philosophy. Thus I gave them up.

According to the *Imperial Library Catalog* and the *Treatise on Bibliography*, there were 13,299 volumes of books in all [in the Han], and since the Wei dynasty [220–265], all genres of literature have doubled in quantity. Realizing this made me aware of how many books I had never seen. Since so many books were not available in the area south of the Yangtze River, I decided to go to the capital to search for rare works. However, it so happened that there was a rebellion, and I had to turn back midway, much to my regret.

Now that I am approaching my fortieth year, my life-long ambitions are waning; I think only of further reducing my ambitions and converting my actions into nonaction. All that I do is till my fields to eke out a living, and my efforts to achieve broad learning diminish day by day. I am an unrefined person; my nature is dull, my speech slow, and my appearance ugly. I never try to hide my shortcomings. I wear a soiled hat, dirty shoes, and worn-out clothes but am not embarrassed by them. Clothing styles change quickly and frequently. Sometimes people all of a sudden wear broad collars and wide belts; at other times they dress up in tightly fitted clothes with long, slender sleeves. Sometimes robes are so long that they sweep the ground, while at other times they are too short to cover the feet. I, however, stick with one style and do not follow the whims of the world.

When I speak I am straightforward and matter-of-fact, never sarcastic or playful. If I am not in the company of the right kind of people, I keep silent all day. This is why people call me "the scholar who embraces simplicity," a sobriquet which I have adopted for my writings.

I was born with a weak constitution and further was subjected to many illnesses. Thus, on top of being too poor to afford carriages or horses, I am too feeble to travel on foot. Anyway, travel is something that does not appeal to my nature: the corrupt custom of discarding the fundamental and pursuing the trivial, of placing too much emphasis on making friends and paying visits, makes me apprehensive. For these reasons, I have lived in quiet seclusion in my humble residence and have not rushed to visit others. I am not even acquainted with the rich and influential people who reside nearby.

My clothes do not protect me from the cold, my roof does not keep me from the rain, my food does not save me from being weak, and I am not known outside of my own house—yet none of this causes me worry. I am too poor to keep a servant, my bamboo fences have crumbled, thorny thistles grow thick in my yards, and weeds block the steps. To go out of my gate I have to push away the bushes; to get into my room I have to brush aside the tall grass. People unsympathetically criticize me for aiming at the faraway and ignoring the close-at-hand, when the truth of the matter is that I do not have anyone to do the housework.

Being ignorant of the etiquette for visiting superiors, I never pay visits to high officials. I do, however, make an effort to go and express my condolences to families who have lost an elderly member and to visit the seriously ill. Yet, though I intend to present myself on every such occasion, I often fail to do so because of my own frequent illnesses. I am often criticized on this account, and I admit my own faults, but they do not worry me; I am fully sympathetic toward the bereaved and the ill, but my own illnesses prevent me from carrying out my intentions. As long as I do not have a bad conscience, why should I argue with those who do not understand me? Those who are discerning, nevertheless, do forgive me, for they know that I am not trying to cultivate an image of loftiness for myself.

Most people in this world enjoy having intimate friends and are given to probing into others' secrets. Yet I find it quite a task to know someone well. (The sages also found it difficult.) Casual acquaintances who are congenial in conversation but poles apart in spirit do more harm than good. Although I cannot cut off all contacts as Chu Kung-shu did, I pay no special attention to a person until I have cleared away all my doubts about him and have come to know him thoroughly. Although this is one more reason why I am disliked by so many, I will not change my ways.

Those who hasten to chase after distinguished personages and wait deferentially at the gates of influential families all hate me for being different from them. They slander me, saying that I am haughty and that I disregard established custom. I, however, base my behavior on my conscience and do not listen to others' praise or slander.

It troubles me how nowadays people often pride themselves on their own strong points and despise others on account of their shortcomings. I admit that my abilities as a scholar are slight, yet whenever I talk with someone, I estimate his knowledge and keep the conversation within that limit; I do not deliberately direct it to what he does not know. Whenever I argue a point with a scholar, I bring forth my main points. If he should be too prejudiced by his own opinions to comprehend my ideas, I merely explain the direction of my ideas in general terms, in order to inspire him, not pressing so hard that he is trapped by his own arguments. If he thinks the matter over thoroughly on his own, often he realizes his mistakes and comes to the correct understanding. If I judge that it is useless to talk to someone, even though he comes to me with questions, I often say that I do not know the answer in order to avoid wasting words.

By nature I have a deep aversion to bothering officials and superiors. In the course of my life I have saved several good friends who were in distress, and in these cases I forced myself to speak with the officials in power. Yet I never let these friends know what I did for them, for it was because I could not bear to see them wronged that I secretly assisted them. Otherwise, even when my closest relatives, who would gladly do me favors, are in power, I never trouble them with written or oral requests. It is true that when I run out of food or desperately need medicine, I appeal to my friends and accept their help if they offer it. Whenever I have received favors from others, I have repaid them in subtle ways over a long period of time, so that they were not aware of it. Yet I do not lightly accept gifts from those who are not the right kind of people. When I have food for ten days, I share it with people who are in need; however, if I do not have enough for myself, I do not give away my own food—for I do not ostentatiously display little acts of virtue. Sometimes the good-natured common people of the village offer me wine and food. Even though they are not my equals, I do not decline their invitations, and later I repay them at my leisure. I once explained my motives by remarking that Shihyun's refusal to accept food from his own brothers and Master Hua's keeping himself aloof from his over-friendly company were but hypocritical acts performed to win a reputation and were not in accordance with the broad-mindedness required of people in high positions.

Those I abhor are the unprincipled men who do not work diligently at the principal occupations of farming and silk production but instead use unethical means to obtain undue profits. Such men control public opinion and sell their recommendations for gain. They use the power of their positions to extort money. Sometimes they accept bribes from the guilty and consequently wrong those who are in the right; at other times they harbor criminals fleeing for their lives. They appropriate corvée labor* for their own purposes, thereby interfering with the public good; or they hoard currency or commodities to force the value up; or they dominate the markets to rob the commoners of their profit; or they encroach on others' land, destroying the livelihood of the orphaned and the weak; or they wander from one government office to another to look for profits to be made. In this way they impress their wives and concubines, angle for fame, and seek offices. I will have nothing to do with such people. For these reasons, the vulgar sort hate me since I dislike them, and it is only natural that we should become alienated. In my alley there are no traces of carriages and horses; in my livingroom there are no incompatible guests; my courtyard is so quiet one can set up bird nets; on my furniture dust accumulates.

Since the time I was old enough to understand things, I have never uttered a word concerning others' faults or private affairs. This comes naturally to me, for I do not even make fun of the defects of servants or little children. I never discuss my opinions of people's characters, nor do I like to criticize people on their selection of friends. When I am forced by my elders to give my evaluations, then I mention only a person's excellent qualities, or in evaluating his writing ability, raise only his good points. Because I never criticize others' shortcomings, I have never offended anyone through criticism. Occasionally I am asked by the higher-ups to give my opinion of officials, clerks, or common citizens. If the person is superior in morality and ability, I report on his achievements; if he is greedy, violent, stupid, or narrow-minded, I reply that I do not know him. As a result, I have been rather severely critized for being overcautious and for failing to distinguish good from bad and

---

*Labor exacted in lieu of taxes, especially for the construction of roads.—Ed.

black from white. However, I have never cared to change my ways. I have often observed that those who are fond of discussing others' personalities are not always fair in their comparisons and critiques. Those who are praised by them take it for granted and are not particularly grateful to them; whereas those who are offended regard them with a hatred more ferocious than that caused by a blood feud. I am therefore even more cautious and no longer talk about other people. I even leave the evaluation of the younger members of my own family and lineage to others. When people criticize me for this, I answer as follows: "It should be far easiest for me to evaluate myself. But if someone asks me to compare myself with other men, ancient and modern, I do not know who to consider my equal. How can I then take another person and give an evaluation of him?"

During the T'ai-an period [302–303], Shih Ping led a revolt in six provinces which brought about the decline of the dynasty. The rightful rulers of the state were disobeyed and the loyalist army was opposed. The Commander-in-Chief asked me to take the position of Commandant and lead troops. After repeated pleadings, I agreed, taking into account that the country was endangered by the rebels, that the ancients saw it as one's obligation to act in emergencies, and that martial law was not to be challenged freely. Thus, I drafted several hundred men and joined other regiments in an attack on a rebel general. On the day I broke into the rebel's city, money and silk were stored in heaps and valuables and curios covered the ground. All the other regiments set their soldiers loose upon the riches, and they loaded cart after cart, basket after basket. I alone gave orders that my soldiers were not to leave their positions. By beheading those who collected loot, I made sure no one else dared to set down their staffs. As expected, several hundred rebels burst forth to ambush us. As the other brigades were out looting, there were no troops to speak of, and those there were were all so heavily laden with booty, they had no will to fight. Frightened and confused, many were killed or wounded, and defeat was imminent. Only my men maintained enough discipline to avoid casualties. I was thus instrumental in saving the other regiments from a disastrous defeat. Later, in another battle, we settled a minor commander of the rebels, seized large quantities of armor, and took many heads. When I reported our victory to headquarters, the Commander-in-Chief conferred on me the title of Wave-Conquering General. All the generals were awarded, according to custom, a hundred bolts of cloth, which they sealed up or sent home. I was the only one to distribute it among my officers, soldiers, and needy friends. I exchanged the last ten bolts for meat and wine and feasted my men, earning me much praise and attention.

When the rebellion was suppressed, I discarded my weapons and armor and set out for Lo-yang in the hope of obtaining rare books. I did not at all intend to be rewarded for my military deeds, having long admired Lu Lien for not accepting gold from Liaoch'eng, and Pao-hsü for refusing a reward for saving Ch'u. Yet it so happened that while I was on my way, the capital was plagued by a major rebellion, blocking the route to the north. Furthermore, Ch'en Min staged an uprising in Chiang-tung, cutting off my return route. Moreover, at that time an old friend of mine, Chi Chün-tao of Ch'iao-kuo, was appointed as the governor of Kuang-chou, and he petitioned the throne to appoint me as his military councillor. Although this position was not what I wanted, it provided a way to escape south, so I forced myself to accept it. I was ordered to leave early in order to draft soldiers. After I left, Chi Chün-tao was killed, so I stayed at Kuang-chou, where I was frequently offered positions by the authorities. I declined them all, thinking that riches and high positions may be attained gradually but should not be amassed quickly. Besides, the trivialities one has to attend to in such posts are quite bothersome.

Honor, high posts, power, and profit are like sojourning guests: there is no way of keeping them when they are due to depart. Prosperity and glory will all come to an end, just like the spring flowers that quickly wither away. When I chance to have them, I do not rejoice; nor do I grieve when I lose them. They are not worth all the regret and blame, worry and anxiety they cause. Furthermore, I figure that I am by nature lazy and untalented. With these two characteristics, even if I could cringe, kneel, and rush about in the mundane world, I would certainly fail to obtain fame or high position—which is beside the fact since I could never bring myself to do so! It is better for me to cultivate the Way of the Taoists, Ch'ih Sung-tzu and Prince Ch'iao, and depend solely on myself.

I am hoping to ascend a famous mountain where I will regulate my diet and cultivate my nature. It is not that I wish to abandon worldly affairs, but unless I do so, how can I practice the abstruse and tranquil Way? Besides, to comprehend these matters is truly difficult, requiring considerable discussion and questioning. For these reasons, I neither visit nor send letters to powerful officials. However, even those scholars who refrain from visiting others cannot refuse to receive callers, who invariably become an obstacle to concentration. It is not that the Way is found in the mountains and forests; the reason the ancient practitioners of the Way always had to enter the mountains and forests was that they wished to be away from the noise of the world and keep their minds tranquil. Now I am about to fulfill an old wish; I will leave my hometown and go to Mount Sung in order to walk in the paths of Fang-p'ing and Master Liang.

Fortunately, I have put my mind to it and completed my philosophical works, including the *Inner Chapters* and the *Outer Chapters*. Now I only need to finish the selection and rearrangement to make it ready for later readers. When I was fifteen or sixteen I thought that my poetry, prose-poems, and miscellaneous writings were good enough to be circulated. At the age of twenty I carefully looked through those writings and found them very unsatisfactory. It was not that I had become more talented, but that I was a little better read and was able to differentiate between the beautiful and the ugly. Thereupon I threw out most of my writings, retaining less than one-tenth. Today, besides my philosophical works, I have another one hundred-odd volumes. I am not quite finished editing them yet, and it grieves me that I do not have the time to work on them.

When other people finish writing something, they are immediately satisfied. Being untalented and slow-witted, I have never been able to satisfy myself. Whenever I compose something, I feel that with every change of wording I can further improve it. Yet, because of my laziness, and because of the volume of my works, I have not been able to go over them enough times. When I passed twenty, I figured that it would be better to establish the tenets of my own philosophy than to waste my energy and time writing short, trivial compositions. Thus I now have a draft of my philosophical writings. It was written during a time of warfare and rebellion. As I wandered from place to place, homeless, some of my works were lost. Still, I never abandoned my writing brush. This continued for more than a decade, until 304, when my works were finally completed. They consisted of twenty chapters of the *Inner Chapters*, fifty chapters of the *Outer Chapters*, one hundred chapters of stone inscriptions, eulogies, poetry, and free verse, and thirty chapters of military strategies and proclamations, memorials, and commentaries. I also wrote ten chapters of *Biographies of Immortals*, ten dealing with those who are normally not recorded, and ten chapters of *Biographies of Recluses,* dealing with those who are lofty-minded and seek no place in officialdom. In addition, I made selections from the Five Classics, seven histories, the philosophers, military treatises, esoteric skills, and miscellaneous strange events. These totaled 310 chapters. I also made a separate index of my anthology. My *Inner Chapters* belong to the Taoist school, as they discuss immortals, longevity medicines, ghosts and devils, transformations, the nature and extension of human life, and the aversion of evil and misfortune. My *Outer Chapters*, which discuss the success and failure of men and the good and evil in the world, belong to the Confucian school.

At the end of the autobiographical notes to his *Records*, Emperor Wen of Wei [r. 220–227] mentioned such arts as playing chess and fencing. This gave me the idea to do something similar. But rather than boast of my own modest skills, I will give an account of what I do not know. I am physically clumsy and slow by nature and have few amusements or hobbies. As a child, I could not compete with other children in throwing tiles or wrestling. Throughout my life, I have never tried cock-fighting, drake-fighting, dog-racing, or horse-racing. Whenever I see people engaged in gambling, I try not to even glance at them; but if I have to watch, I do not pay close attention. Thus, to this day, I do not know how many rows there are on a chessboard, or the names of the chessmen. Another reason for my aversion is that I object to the way chess disturbs people's thoughts and wastes their time: this trivial art makes officials reduce their political undertakings, scholars ignore their studies, commoners forget their crops, and merchants lose their business. When engaged in a game at the marketplace, the players are fired up inside and worried in appearance. They lose their sense of righteousness and shame and become rivals; they take each other's money and develop hatreds and feuds. Long ago, the gaming of Duke Min of Sung and the Crown Prince of Wu led to their violent deaths and rebellion; the seven feudal states were overthrown as a result and the dynasty nearly toppled. This example provides an obvious lesson for all later generations.

I have often observed the players in a chess game. Overwhelmed by shame and anger, they hit and kick each other and abuse each other with foul language, much to the detriment of their friendship. Since grudges can start from small matters, it is not worth doing things which can cause so many regrets. Confucius warned against sleeping during the day, a sentiment that I do not fully share. Sleeping during the day produces no benefit, but neither does it cause resentments or give rise to quarrels and lawsuits. Even the Sage had to wear out the binding string of his books three times before he had completely familiarized himself with the classics. How then can an ordinary person of our time learn everything? I believe that playing all the games there are is less worthwhile than reading a short essay. Thus, finding no pleasure in games, I do not play them. Only the vulgar sort are attracted to them.

When I was young, I learned archery, but my strength was not up to drawing a bow as heavy as Yen Kao's. I studied it because archery is one of the six arts of a gentleman, and enables a person to defend himself against bandits and robbers and to hunt for birds and animals. When I was in the army, I myself shot at pursuring horsemen, who fell at the flicker of my bowstring. By killing two rebels and one horse, I escaped death myself. I also received instruction on sword-and-shield, single sword, and double lances. For all of these are verbal formulae and essential skills needed to defeat the opponents. There are also secret methods that are as clever as magic and, used against the unknowing, guarantee victory every time. Later, I also learned the art of the seven-foot staff, which can be used to defeat people with daggers and lances. However, this is also a trivial art of no urgency; it does not have to be used any more than the unicorn's horn or the phoenix's spur. Besides the above-mentioned, I hardly know anything else. . . .

Because I am untalented and unlearned, whether I restrain myself or indulge freely, my practices are always ill-suited to the times, my actions against the ways of the world, utterances out of tune with the customary, my steps out of line with the majority. At home, I do not have the advantage of being rich, like Chin and Chang; out in the world, I do not have friends in high office. Although the road I have traveled is broad, I do not have the feet of a unicorn; although the universe is wide, I do not have the wings of the great roc. Thus, I have not been able to soar high like a hawk, helping to govern our country, nor have I been able to bring glory to my parents or to be remembered by posterity. My qualities are not entrusted to official historians to record; my words are not inscribed on bells and tripods. For these reasons, on finishing my writings, I composed this autobiographical chapter—although it will not make up for any failure on my part, at least it will be preserved for the future.

III. THE TRADITIONAL WORLD: 500 to 1500

Enlarged detail of an illustration from the Japanese *Tale of Genji*.
(The Metropolitan Museum of Art, Fletcher Fund, 1955.)

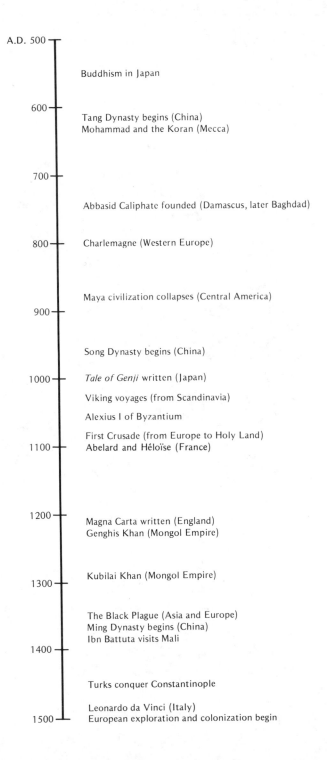

A.D. 500

Buddhism in Japan

600

Tang Dynasty begins (China)
Mohammad and the Koran (Mecca)

700

Abbasid Caliphate founded (Damascus, later Baghdad)

800

Charlemagne (Western Europe)

Maya civilization collapses (Central America)

900

Song Dynasty begins (China)

1000

Tale of Genji written (Japan)

Viking voyages (from Scandinavia)

Alexius I of Byzantium

First Crusade (from Europe to Holy Land)
1100   Abelard and Héloïse (France)

1200   Magna Carta written (England)
Genghis Khan (Mongol Empire)

Kubilai Khan (Mongol Empire)
1300

The Black Plague (Asia and Europe)
Ming Dynasty begins (China)
Ibn Battuta visits Mali
1400

Turks conquer Constantinople

Leonardo da Vinci (Italy)
1500   European exploration and colonization begin

9. Hindu-Buddhist Civilization

BUDDHISM IN CHINA

PAUL THOMAS WELTY

In this selection, a modern scholar of Asia, Paul Thomas Welty, discusses the expansion of Buddhism. The spread of Buddhism from India to China was similar to the spread of Christianity during the same period through the Roman Empire and Europe. Both religions could spread beyond their original settings because they were universal rather than tribal or local. They both preached salvation more than adherence to particular rites — a message that could be understood by all, regardless of particular language and cultural traditions. Buddhism in its Mahayana (or universal, salvationist form) was similar to Christianity not only in offering a savior god and heaven, but also in offering them equally to all people, women as well as men, poor as well as wealthy.

There were important differences as well between the spread of Buddhism and Christianity. Buddhism was five hundred years older than Christianity. As a result, Buddhism had a highly developed philosophy, a number of different sects, and a vast body of written literature. The translation of this body of literature (the sutras) from Sanskrit or Pali into Chinese, Korean, and Japanese (without dictionaries) was a far more formidable task than that faced by Christians in the Roman Empire and Barbarian Europe.

How did the Buddhist missionaries accomplish this task? What was the role of pilgrim monks in bringing Buddhism to China? How did Buddhism adapt to the new environment? How was the Bodhisattva different from the Buddha? Why do you think Mahayana Buddhism was more popular than the older Hinayana Buddhism? How did the Chinese adapt Buddhism to their own needs?

Thou perfect master, Who shinest upon all things and all men,
As gleaming moonlight plays upon a thousand waters at the same time!
Thy great compassion does not pass by a single creature.
Steadily and quietly sails the great ship of compassion across the sea of
    sorrow,
Thou are the Great Physician for a sick and impure world,
In pity giving the invitation to the Paradise of the West.
    —Prayer From Mass for the Dead

"Buddhism in China" from *The Asians: Their Heritage and Their Destiny* by Paul Thomas Welty © 1953, 1966, 1970, 1973, 1976 by Harper & Row, Publishers, Inc. Reprinted by permission of Harper & Row, Publishers, Inc.

When Buddhism passed from India to China, Korea, Tibet, and Japan, it changed from a religion demanding much of man to a religion of compassion promising much to man if he were faithful and devoted. This form of Buddhism is known as Mahayana Buddhism.

Mahayana Buddhism follows the example and heart of the Buddha more than his rigid teaching. It is concerned with the Buddha who, after his enlightenment, spent the remaining forty-five years of his life telling others about the path of freedom. His followers interpret this action as a social goal and ideal.

The story spread that, ages before, he had taken a vow to become enlightened in order to rescue suffering humanity. Before he was enlightened, he was a *Bodhisattva*, that is, one striving for enlightenment to fit himself to aid his fellow men. By heroic deeds in previous existences, he accumulated the merit which resulted in his enlightenment in his final rebirth. A Buddha is not accessible to human beings once he has entered Nirvana, but there are those, Bodhisattvas, who defer entrance into Nirvana and remain behind on earth in order to help those who suffer. Buddhas and Bodhisattvas are both enlightened beings. The difference between them is that Buddhas are those who have entered into Nirvana, while Bodhisattvas continue their cycle of birth and rebirth in order to gain merit for others and guide them to enlightenment.

According to Mahayana Buddhism, the true follower of Buddha is one who follows the example of Buddha and becomes a Bodhisattva. Anyone who is moved by the suffering of others and seeks enlightenment for their benefit may become a Bodhisattva of Buddha. Buddhahood and Bodhisattva are stages open to all—merchant, banker, farmer, lawyer, or laborer. This spirit is caught in a poem:

> O that I might become for all beings the soother of pain!
>
> O that I might be for all of them that ail the remedy, the physician, the nurse, until the disappearance of illness!
>
> O that by raining down food and drink I might soothe the pangs of hunger and thirst, and that in times of famine I might myself become drink and food!
>
> O that I might be for the poor an inexhaustible treasure!
>
> All my incarnations to come, all my goods, all my merits, past and present and future, I renounce with indifference, so that the end of all beings may be attained.

There are few great Bodhisattvas; and with the exception of Gautama Buddha who stayed on earth for many rebirths, Buddhas are beings in the heavens rather than on earth. The common people began to rely upon the merits of those whose compassion and pity were conceived to

be infinite. Buddhas and Bodhisattvas became deities who were worshiped, adored, and prayed to. They were clothed in all the formal
garments of an organized religion. Examples of these are: Kuan-yin
(Japanese, Kwannon), the Goddess of Mercy; Wen-shu, the Lord of
Wisdom; and Ti-ts'ang, who goes to hell (which the Chinese added to
Buddhism) to save the suffering ones. These Bodhisattvas are found
under other names in Japan, Korea, and Tibet.

AMITABHA: THE COMPASSIONATE BUDDHA

The greatest and most popular god is the Buddha Amitabha (O-mi-t'o in
China, Amid in Japan). Ages before, he had taken a vow to save others,
and through his good deeds done in countless ages, he created the "Pure
Land" or "Western Paradise," a heaven where all will go who call upon
his name. There, in the western part of the universe, he reigns with his
faithful in perfect happiness.

> It is called the Land of Supreme Happiness because all beings there do not
> suffer from any mental or physical pain and only enjoy pleasure and
> happiness of all kinds.
> In this land of Supreme Happiness there are seven lakes, all adorned with
> gems. The lakes are filled with water which possess the eight good quali-
> ties. . . . The bottoms of the lakes are strewn with golden sand. On the four
> sides of the lakes there are paths and steps of gold, silver, beryl, and crystal,
> white corals, red pearls, and diamonds. In the lakes the lotus flowers grow as
> big as wheels of chariots. . . .
> In this land of Supreme Happiness the musical instruments of heaven are
> often played on grounds of gold. Three times a day and three times a night
> Mandarava flowers drop down like rain. . . .

Thus is described the Western Heaven which is ruled over by a
Buddha of infinite compassion, Amitabha Buddha. All good Chinese
Buddhists, those who call with faith and constancy upon the name of
Amitabha Buddha, go to this magnificent place.

Another well-known compassionate being is Kuan-yin, the Goddess of
Mercy, who also is ready and willing to succor the afflicted who seek her
aid. . . . Kuan-yin has sometimes been compared to the Madonna of the
Christian faith. These two merciful beings are representatives of
Mahayana Buddhism who captured the imagination and loyalty of the
Chinese people in the past and who, along with the Western Heaven
described above, continue to hold a favorite place in the hearts of
millions of Chinese today.

All of the Buddhas and Bodhisattvas are the physical embodiments of
Mahayana mercy and compassion. Mahayana Buddhism is a religion of
compassion because it does not require man to rely solely upon himself

for salvation. Prayer and worship, absent from the literal teaching of Gautama Buddha, are an integral part of Mahayana Buddhism. Prayers are said continually to the various Bodhisattvas requesting them to aid the petitioner in his efforts to obtain salvation. The verse addressed to Amitabha which heads this chapter is from the *Mass for the Dead* and vividly illustrates the deep faith of the people in his infinite mercy. The emotion, the hope, the humanity of Mahayana Buddhism were preferred by the Tibetans, Chinese, Koreans, and Japanese to the middle way and self-discipline of Hinayana Buddhism.*

BUDDHISM BECOMES CHINESE

Buddhism in China played down its foreign elements and made itself as Chinese as possible. The abstract concept of Nirvana—the state or condition of desirelessness—was minimized, and a concrete place of happiness, like the Western Heaven of Amitabha Buddha, was given prominence.

It built on the foundations of the other ideologies popular during the early part of the Christian era. Since Taoism was popular among the commoners and intellectuals alike, Buddhists used Taoism as an instrument of conversion by taking over Taoist terms, writing commentaries on Taoist books, and identifying Buddhism with Taoist teaching and practice. The common elements in Taoist and Buddhist doctrine were deliberately stressed over and over again. At times, indeed, the truth was stretched in order make Taoism and Buddhism agree. They honored Confucianism by speaking of a Bodhisattva as being an incarnation of Confucius, by naming a temple after Confucius, and by stressing the virtue of filial piety as an aspect of Buddhist teaching. Buddhist monks pointed out the similarities between Confucian and Buddhist morality, even going so far as to set up ancestral tablets in a special hall to honor the memory of their dead monks.

Buddhism attracted the scholar class because of its speculative nature and enticed the common people because of its ritual and ceremonial observances. Its appeal was reinforced by the literary labors of numerous Indian and Chinese Buddhist missionaries who made a determined effort to translate Buddhist literature into Chinese and to relate Buddhism to the observances and attitudes of the Chinese. Two Chinese Buddhist pilgrims famous for their travels between China and India are Fa-Hsien, who left China in A.D. 399 and spent fifteen years in India,

---

*Hinayana Buddhism, also sometimes called Theravada Buddhism, was (and is) more common in Southeast Asia, especially Burma, Thailand, Laos, Cambodia, and Ceylon (now Sri Lanka). Hinayana Buddhists tried to practice the disciplines of the Buddha instead of worshipping him like a god. Even today, one sees many more monks and monasteries in Hinayana Buddhist countries. See the next selection.—Ed.

and Hsuan-tsang, who left China in A.D. 629 and lived for sixteen years in India. Both of these famous travelers carried Buddhist books and manuscripts back to China with them. It is said that Hsuan-tsang and his pupils translated more than a thousand volumes into Chinese.

Buddhism showed its desire to co-exist peacefully with the rulers by not developing an administrative machinery in the monastic order and by not attempting to wrest the administrative machinery of the country from the Confucian scholars.

By showing itself not as an exclusive religion but as a complement to other Chinese beliefs, Buddhism penetrated and permeated Chinese life and became as Chinese as the native philosophies of Confucianism and Taoism. The Chinese were never thereafter at any particular period either Confucianist, Taoist, or Buddhist—they were all three simultaneously.

Buddhism was a tremendous intellectual force in China. It gave the Chinese a new look at the universe, at the individual, and at life. It provided the Chinese with a new literature and stimulated the production of new forms of music and religious art. It influenced Chinese painting and architecture, brought to China a message of justice and hope, and imbued the Chinese with a love and respect for all living things. It also served as a vehicle for carrying the culture of India and China to Korea and Japan.

HINDUISM AND BUDDHISM IN SOUTHEAST ASIA

JOHN F. CADY

In this selection, John F. Cady, a modern historian of Southeast Asia, discusses the differing appeal of Mahayana and Theravada (or Hinayana) Buddhism. While Mahayana Buddhism passed easily into China, the older tradition, Theravada Buddhism, spread through Southeast Asia (modern Burma, Cambodia, Laos, and Thailand, but not Vietnam). The cultures of Southeast Asia were also heavily influenced by Hinduism. In fact, we might speak of the "Indianization" of Southeast Asia as a general phenomenon. India, especially in the Gupta Age (c. A.D. 320–550) was the

From *Southeast Asia: Its Historical Development* by John F. Cady. New York: McGraw-Hill Book Company, copyright © 1964. Reprinted by permission of McGraw-Hill Book Company.

cultural center of southern Asia and the Buddhist monastery at Nolanda in India remained the educational center into the seventh century.

What were the differing appeals of Theravada and Mahayana Buddhism in Southeast Asia? Why did Hinduism appeal to different groups than Buddhism? How did Indian culture influence or change the indigenous cultures of Southeast Asia?

HINDUISM AS IT AFFECTED SOUTHEAST ASIA

Hinduism as a cultural system was far too complex and deeply rooted in the context of India itself to be capable of transfer to Southeast Asia in any complete way. It included many sects and many philosophical systems; its religious values were relative to time and place, to a person's social level, and also to his intellectual and spiritual capacity to discern. Its cohesion in India derived from tenacity of social custom and from the organized caste structure in particular. Hinduism was thus a religious accumulation derived from all periods of India's history; primitive cults of fertility, hero reverence, and sun worship were combined with Aryan governmental practices and overlaid with an elaborate system of philosophical speculation. Hinduism countenanced almost every level of religious belief from crude animism to metaphysical monism.

Hinduism could be transferred, therefore, only in a selective way. Sophisticated Indians affirmed the mystical principle that the phenomenal world was illusion (*maya*) and that the ultimate reality of all life was Brahma, the indestructible soul of the universe. Failure to realize the soul's potential identity with the absolute essence (through mystical and ascetic exercises) bound an individual to phenomenal existence in a physical body through an endless series of rebirths. Persons of inferior spiritual capacities conceived their relative levels of truth in more tangible symbols. Moral and social duties in India thus varied according to caste status, itself determined by karma, or the law of deeds, which derived its character from previous existences. Neither the full philosophical implications of Brahmanism nor the full scope of the caste system proved capable of transference to Southeast Asian peoples. Southeast Asia's matrilineal tradition also rejected for the most part the severe restraints imposed by Hinduism upon women, such as seclusion, suttee, and child marriage.

For persons unable to grasp the truth of Brahma, the Hindu pantheon provided two rival gods, each capable of theoretical embodiment in many variant forms. Śiva [Shiva], the destroyer, personified the principle of attrition, the malevolent or destructive aspects of time which devours all, neither compassionate nor forgiving. His wives, especially Parvati and Kālī, assumed the role of the universal mother. The *linga*, or phallic symbol, was widely employed. During the development of Hinduism in India, Śiva worship absorbed a large number of pre-Aryan spirit cults. It did the same in Southeast Asia, where an easy accommodation was made to indigenous animistic worship of the godlings of forest, rivers, and mountains and of the earth goddess of fertility and to various expressions of supernatural malevolence.

The second god, Vishnu, and his favorite wife, Lakshmi, represented the more optimistic principles of restoration and prosperity. Krishna and Rama, the heroes of the *Bhagavad Gita* (*Song of the Blessed One*) and of the *Ramayana* epic respectively, were conceived as incarnations of Vishnu. Rama represented ideal kingship, and his wife, Sita, represented the highest pattern of motherhood. For various reasons, Vishnu found less wide acceptance than Śiva among the peoples of Southeast Asia. Cult practices appropriate to both gods were nevertheless widely copied. Images of Śiva and Vishnu, whether used in India or in Southeast Asia, could be symbolic intellectual principles to the sophisticated and at the same time crude idols to the simpler folk. In the Hinduized states, the divine rulers were frequently represented as *avatars* (reincarnations) of either Śiva or Vishnu.

Three other religio-political principles borrowed from Hindu culture were widely appropriated in Southeast Asia, often in combination. The first of these was derived from the idea that magical astrological forces emanating from the cardinal points of the compass and from heavenly bodies determined the destiny of individuals and states. Indian cosmology identified Mount Meru, the abode of the gods, as the cosmic center of the universe (Jambudvipa), around which the sun, moon, and stars revolved. Mount Meru was allegedly protected by eight guardian gods and surrounded by seven concentric rings of mountains and eight ocean belts separating it from the four man-inhabited islands located at the cardinal points of the compass. The city of the gods occupied the mountain's central summit. Buddhist as well as Hindu countries in Southeast Asia demanded as an important requirement for stable governmental authority the location of the royal palace at the exact center of the universe, magically determined by learned astrologers. The divine authority of Southeast Asian rulers was thus derived not only from their status as divine reincarnations but also in large measure from their occupancy of a palace conceived as a mundane Mount Meru.

Buddhist rulers as well as Hindu princes frequently identified themselves as agents or reincarnations of the ancient storm god Indra (derived from Rudra, the Aryan god of sky and storm), representing kingly authority and power. Thus the Pyu capital at Old Prome (Śrikshetra) was allegedly built by Indra. Its gates, each protected by a sacrificed guardian spirit, numbered thirty-two, a multiple of eight and four, and the thirty-two provinces of the Pyu state plus the capital corresponded to the thirty-three gods, including Indra, who were supposed to reside on Mount Meru. Preoccupation with the numbers four, eight, sixteen, and thirty-two as attributes of the famous Mount

Meru was a persistent legacy of all Southeast Asian courts. The same symbolism for kingly authority has been identified in the fourteenth-century Pegu state of the Mons. Burma's coronation building at Pagan was designated "Indra's palace," and around the enthroned Burmese king eight Brahman priests served as specialists in cosmologic magic and acted as counterparts of the eight guardian gods of Mount Meru. The royal regalia—crown, sword, and white umbrella—also symbolized magical authority under the Indian tradition of royalty. Kings of Burma and Thailand normally had a palace of four walls, with gates in multiples of fours, plus four major queens, four chief ministers, and four assistant ministers.

A third symbol of royalty was the multiple-headed Naga snake, traditional god of the soil. The fabulous role of the Naga spirit was to combine the magical resources of soil fertility with the royal principle of ownership and sovereignty over the land. In peninsular Southeast Asia it was widely applied and identified immediately with the indigenous fertility god of the soil. Kings often attributed their credentials as rulers to the alleged marriage of an ancestor with the beauteous daughter of the Naga snake. The royal symbol of the Naga's head has been long used in Thailand and Cambodia, and somewhat less frequently in Burma.

INDIAN BUDDHISM IN ITS VARIANT FORMS

Buddhism appeared in India during the sixth century B.C. as part of a protest against the presumptuous claims of Brahman priestly superiority and the degrading implications of caste. It was associated with the teachings and personality of Gautama, a Kshatriya-caste prince of the minor Indian state of Oudh. In revulsion against the brutality of warfare and suppression, Gautama left his throne and his family and became an ascetic and mendicant. His Buddhahood, or enlightenment, provided a new interpretation of life and destiny. It was based on characteristic Hindu premises of maya [illusion] and karma, but the new faith emphasized moral principles of conduct as affording an escape from the otherwise endless and burdensome gyrations of the wheel of existence.

Gautama's message was for ordinary men. It afforded a practical moral approach to life, not dependent on spells or priestly magic. Life's suffering, he affirmed, stemmed from desire, which could be conquered by following the meritful eightfold path of right belief, aspiration, speech, action, honest livelihood, sustained mental exertion, alertness, and serenity. Buddhist teachings provided the inspiration for the splendid reign of Emperor Asoka in the third century B.C., and they became the basis of much of the ethical appeal which India's culture later held out to leading peoples of Southeast Asia.

In its original interpretations, Buddhism placed everyone on his own, with no possibility of borrowed merit. It condemned outright as sinful or criminal such deeds as stealing, deceit, adultery, murder, and drinking of intoxicants. Buddhism accepted much Hindu legend, mythology, and folklore. It affirmed the principle of the sacredness of all life with its corollary obligation of *ahinsa*, noninjury to men and animals. The Buddhist goal of Nirvana, a merging with the absolute essence, thus ending life's cycle of suffering existences, corresponded to the Hindu principle of Brahma, except that the Buddhist path to the goal was one of righteous living, serenity, and peace, theoretically available to all men. By implication, Buddhism rejected priestly magic and the elaborate Hindu pantheon of the gods, but it was not dogmatic and was therefore subject to reinterpretation. It was missionary in spirit, not because it presumed to set forth any final or exclusive statement of truth, but rather because its message was broadly humanitarian and its appeal intended for all stations and races of men.

Some indication of the spirit and teachings of orthodox Indian Buddhism as it developed at the famous Nalanda monastery in the Ganges Valley can be gleaned from the writings of the Chinese pilgrim I-Ching, who visited the place during the last quarter of the 600's. The monastery at the time housed three thousand monks and had two hundred villages assigned to its support. The recluse-scholars were free of administrative responsibilities and of concern for providing food and clothing needs. According to I-Ching, Buddhism favored forest contemplation over the "noisy pursuit of fame and profit" and also deprecated land cultivation, which carried the hazards of taking the lives of creatures living in the soil. Drinking water must be strained, not to purify it for human consumption, but to avoid the possible sin of swallowing live organisms present in the water. The monks were nevertheless permitted to accept pieces of silken cloth presented to them, since, in I-Ching view, there was really no point in being over-meticulous about the sin of taking the life of the silkworm. The Buddhist view was lugubrious but not hopeless:

> Life here below . . . is but a dungeon for beings who have gone astray but look eagerly for the shore of Nirvana, which is the open gate of enlightenment and quietude. The ship of the Law should be manned ready for the sea of suffering, and the lamp of wisdom should be held up during the long period of darkness. . . . Each individual must himself be responsible for the results of his own practices, whether good or bad.

The variant form of Buddhism called Mahayana (greater vehicle) developed to its full expression in the middle Ganges area during Gupta times. It succeeded by the mid-seventh century in entirely supplanting in India the simpler Hinayana, or Theravada (teacher's), sect, only to succumb itself to Hinduism in time. The Mahayana system included three innovations which were important in strengthening its impact on Southeast Asia. In the first place, it posited the not unreasonable proposition that Gautama was only the most recent of a long series of Enlightened Ones and that other Buddhas would doubtless follow him. It also affirmed the possibility of the transference of merit of Buddhist saints about to enter into Nirvana, who generously elected to endure life's suffering a little longer in order to help struggling brethren along the path. They drew aid, as it were, from a kind of Buddhist treasury of grace. A third idea closely associated with the other two established the Bodhisattva status of near divinity for a meritful ruler who could be presumed to qualify as an emergent Buddha. This idea was perennially popular with the rulers of Buddhist countries of Southeast Asia, who frequently aspired to the pretensions of Bodhisattva status as a kind of substitute for royal divinity denied to them as a reincarnation (avatar) of Śiva, Vishnu, or Indra. Mahayana Buddhism in Southeast Asia frequently degenerated into corrupted and magical forms. In Java and Cambodia in particular, Buddhist courts found the transition fairly easy back to Śiva or Vishnu worship as providing a more effective religious sanction to the authority of the divine ruler.

In its acceptability to the peoples of Southeast Asia Buddhism was strong where Hinduism was weak, and vice versa. As a revealed faith repudiating caste and race, Buddhism could be transmitted by Indian missionary devotees and also by Southeast Asian converts and pilgrims. It was also a trader's religion. Hinduism, on the other hand, could be transmitted only by high-caste immigrants, Kshatriya or Brahman. Hinduism buttressed royal authority through the system of divine kingship, synthetically achieved by priestly intervention. Apart from the indispensable services of Brahman advisers at coronations, they assisted the rulers as clerks and scribes, as astrologers and numerologists, and also in the development of larger-scale systems of administration, revenue, and military operation. Buddhism, by contrast, could contribute little to political authority or government, except insofar as kings might choose to exploit the Bodhisattva principle. On the other hand, Hinduism was unable to attract the degree of popular acceptance so widely accorded to the more democratic Buddhist faith. Caste was not transferable in its full sense to the peoples of Southeast Asia. Lacking popular roots, the Hindu cult was dependent on royal favor and therefore on the vagaries of rulership, such as war, economic disaster, or governmental decay. Although remnants of the Hindu cultural impact long survived in many areas of Southeast Asia, the vitality of Śiva and Vishnu worship ebbed away not long after direct cultural contact was lost with sources in India.

THE PROCESS OF INDIANIZATION

The several attempted explanations of the process of Indianization in the various regions of Southeast Asia vary rather widely. They agree only in the conclusions that it was accomplished by peaceful and nonpolitical means, that Indian culture was ingratiating and assimilable in terms of indigenous traditions, and that it proved particularly attractive to local ruling princes.

. . .

Whereas Hinduization was mainly an aristocratic process, Buddhism involved cultural transfer at popular levels. Pilgrimages of Southeast Asian monks and scholars to Indian mainland monasteries and, in the case of the Hinayana sect, to Ceylon were commonplace. Endowed hostelries were established periodically at convenient points in India such as Negapatam and Nalanda for the care and entertainment of such pilgrims. Southeast Asian Buddhist scholars trained in India or Ceylon could be called back home to fill prominent posts at court or in monasteries. The vogue of Buddhism in early Southeast Asia coincided with the visits of large numbers of such pilgrims to India in Gupta and post-Gupta times. It is more than likely that the vast majority of the hundreds of Buddhist scholars whom the Chinese pilgrim I-Ching found studying at Śrivijaya during his visits from 671 to 695 were indigenous Malays or Javanese. It is also highly probable that some Southeast Asian students visiting India may have advanced Brahman pretensions when they returned.

SOUTHEAST ASIAN APPROPRIATION OF INDIAN CULTURE

Several final questions concern the thoroughness of the Indianizing process. Did Hinduism and Buddhism overwhelm the indigenous culture patterns, or were they merely an accretion added as a veneer to the traditional systems? Did contributions from India provide Southeast Asia with a cultural base from which further progress was possible?

The broad cultural gaps between cosmopolitan port cities dependent for food on imported grain, the court-oriented capitals with their Indianized atmosphere and their highly articulate symbolization of political authority, and the rural villages producing food and forest products under traditional social and religious patterns were never completely closed. The history of the region, in fact, drew its dynamics from just such contrasting situations. The alien trader vied with the local potentate; rulers who were bent on personal glorification and monument construction were forced in time to come to terms with a people wincing under heavy tax and *corvée* exactions (unpaid labor in lieu of taxes, particularly for road construction—Ed.) and the burdens of warfare. Even so, the impact of Indian culture was massively impressive down to the time of its diminution in the late thirteenth century. It demonstrated its genius for incorporating local deities and religious practices, reinterpreting them as variants of the great Vedic tradition. Thus, indigenous traditions concerned with worship of the lord of the mountain became part of the Devaraja cult, with Śiva as lord of the mountain and the ruler as an emanation of Śiva. The process generated in time a measure of cultural homogeneity, a kind of synthesis developed from a profusion of crude animistic practices reinterpreted on a higher level.

THE INTRODUCTION OF BUDDHISM INTO JAPAN: THE *CHRONICLES OF JAPAN (NIHONGI)*

The Chronicles of Japan *(Nihongi) is one of the oldest primary sources for Japanese history. Written in Chinese in A.D. 720 by Japanese in the court of the reigning Yamato family, it is a valuable source of information about Japan in the sixth century.*

The following two selections, the first from the year 538 and the second from 584, concern the introduction of Buddhism. How was Buddhism first introduced into Japan? What seems to have been the initial appeal of the new religion? How was the fate of the new religion determined? What seems to have happened between 538 and 584?

[A.D. 538], Winter, 10th month. King Syong of Paekche[1] sent [two envoys] with a present to the Emperor of an image of [the Buddha] in gold and copper, several flags and umbrellas, and a number of volumes of Sutras. Separately he presented a memorial in which he lauded the merit of diffusing abroad religious worship, saying:—"This doctrine is amongst all doctrines the most excellent. But it is hard to explain, and

From *Nihongi: Chronicles of Japan from the Earliest Times, Vol. II,* translated by W. G. Aston. London: George Allen & Unwin, 1896, 1956. Reprinted by permission.
  1. Paekche was one of the three main Korean kingdoms.

hard to comprehend. Even the Duke of Chou and Confucius had not attained to a knowledge of it. This doctrine can create religious merit and retribution [karma] without measure and without bounds, and so lead on to a full appreciation of the highest wisdom. Imagine a man in possession of treasures to his heart's content, so that he might satisfy all his wishes in proportion as he used them. Thus it is with the treasure of this wonderful doctrine. Every prayer is fulfilled and naught is wanting. Moreover, from distant India it has extended hither to the three [kingdoms of Korea], where there are none who do not receive it with reverence as it is preached to them.

"Thy servant, therefore, Syong, King of Paekche, has humbly despatched a retainer to transmit it to the Imperial Country [of Japan], and to diffuse it abroad throughout the home provinces, so as to fulfil the recorded saying of Buddha: 'My law shall spread to the East.' "

This day the Emperor, having heard to the end, leaped for joy, and gave command to the envoys, saying:—"Never from former days until now have we had the opportunity of listening to so wonderful a doctrine. We are unable, however, to decide of ourselves." Accordingly he inquired of his ministers one after another, saying:—"The countenance of this Buddha which has been presented by the Western frontier state is of a severe dignity, such as we have never at all seen before. Ought it to be worshipped or not?" The Oho-omi [chief of the Soga clan] addressed the Emperor, saying:—"All the Western frontier lands without exception do it worship. Shall [our land of] Yamato alone refuse to do so?" [The chiefs of the Mononobe and Nakatomi clans] addressed the Emperor jointly, saying:—"Those who have ruled the Empire in this our state have always made it their care to worship in spring, summer, autumn, and winter the 180 [Shinto] gods of heaven and earth, and the gods of the land and of grain. If just at this time we were to worship in their stead foreign deities, it may be feared that we should incur the wrath of our national gods."

The Emperor said:—"Let [the image] be given to [the Oho-omi], who has shown his willingness to take it, and, as an experiment, make him to worship it."

The Oho-omi knelt down and received it with joy. He enthroned it in his house at Oharida, where he diligently carried out the rites of retirement from the world, and on that score purified his house at Muku-hara and made it a temple. After this a pestilence was rife in the land, from which the people died prematurely. As time went on it became worse and worse, and there was no remedy. [The chiefs of the Mononobe and Nakatomi clans] addressed the Emperor jointly, saying:—"It was because thy servants' advice on a former day was not approved that the people are dying thus of disease. If thou dost now retrace thy steps before matters have gone too far, joy will surely be the result! It will be well promptly to fling it away, and diligently to seek happiness in the future."

The Emperor said:—"Let it be done as you advise." Accordingly officials took the image of Buddha and abandoned it to the current of the Canal of Naniha. They also set fire to the Temple, and burnt it so that nothing was left. Hereupon, there being in the heavens neither clouds nor wind, a sudden conflagration consumed the Great Hall (of the Palace).

. . .

[A.D. 584], Autumn, 9th month. [A man] who had come from Paekche had a stone image of [the Bodhisattva] and an image of Buddha. This year [a Soga clansman named] Mumako Sukune, having asked for these two Buddhist images, sent [three retainers] in all directions to search out persons who practised Buddhism. Upon this he only found in the province of Harima a man [of Korean origin], who from a Buddhist priest had become a layman again. So the Oho-omi made him teacher, and caused him to receive [three young women] into religion . . . Mumako Sukune, still in accordance with the Law of Buddha, reverenced the three nuns, and gave orders to provide them with food and clothing. He erected a Buddhist temple on the east side of his dwelling, in which he enshrined the stone image of [the Bodhisattva]. He insisted on the three nuns holding a general meeting to partake of [a vegetarian meal]. At this time [the father of one of the nuns] found a Buddhist relic on [top of] the food, and presented it to Mumako Sukune. Mumako Sukune, by way of experiment, took the relic, and placing it on the middle of a block of iron, beat it with an iron sledge-hammer, which he flourished aloft. The block and the sledge-hammer were shattered to atoms, but the relic could not be crushed. Then the relic was cast into water, where it floated on the water or sank as one desired. In consequence of this, Mumako Sukune held faith in Buddhism and practised it unremittingly. [He] built another Buddhist temple at his house in Ishikaha. From this arose the beginning of Buddhism.

10. East Asian Civilizations

CHINESE ANCESTRAL RITES

SSU-MA KUANG

Rituals to demonstrate reverence for the ancestors were practiced by the Chinese nobility as early as the Shang dynasty. The guides to such rituals, the Record of Ritual *and the* Ceremonies and Rituals, *were composed for the practice by noble families in the classical period. With the growth of empire and the spread of the rituals to other classes, new guides were needed. One of these was the guide by the historian and conservative statesman Ssu-ma Kuang (1019–1086), part of which follows. What kind of society is this practice likely to produce? What do we do as carefully and deliberately in our own society?*

All ancestor worship should be conducted in the second month of a season [the first month being reserved for imperial ceremonies].

First, the master of the household, his younger brothers, sons, and grandsons, dressed in their formal attire, attend to the divination of an auspicious day for the ceremony. This is done outside of the Image Hall. The master of the household stands facing west, and all the others file behind him in one line, ordered according to their ranks in the family, from north to south. A table is set in front of the master on which are placed incense burners, incense boxes, and milfoil [a strong-scented Eurasian herb] stalks. The master inserts his official tablet in his girdle, lights the incense, and addresses the diviner as follows:

"I would like to present a yearly offering to my ancestors on such-and-such a day. Please determine whether it is an auspicious day."

Then he steps back and hands the milfoil stalks to the diviner, who then performs the divination, facing west. If the proposed date turns out to be inauspicious, then the master of the household names another. When finally an auspicious day is found, all present enter the Image Hall. The master now stands facing north, with his sons and grandsons in file behind him as before, except that now they are ordered according to their ranks from west to east.

The master inserts the official tablet in his girdle, advances to light the incense, then returns to his former position. The deliverer of prayers now comes out from the left of the master, turns to face east, inserts his official tablet in his girdle, takes out the written prayer from his breast pocket, and kneels down to read: "Your filial grandson, officially entitled such-and-such, will on such-and-such a day offer the yearly sacrifice to his departed grandparents. This is to report to you that the date has been found auspicious and that the offering will be made." He then puts the prayer sheet away in his pocket, takes out his official tablet, and rises. After he has returned to his former position, the master of the household bows to the memorial tablets of the ancestors, and everyone exists.

Three days before the date set for the ceremony, the master of the household leads all the male members of the family (above ten years of age) to the outer quarters of the house to observe abstinence, while the women do so in the inner quarters. Thus, although there is wine-drinking, there is no disorder. Meat-eating is allowed, but strong-smelling foods such as onion, leek, and garlic are prohibited. During this period the family members do not attend funerals, nor do they listen to music. All inauspicious and unclean matters are avoided, so that everyone can concentrate on the memory of the departed ancestors.

On the day before the ceremony, the master organizes all the male members of the family and the assistants to dust and sweep the place where the sacrifice will be held, to wash and clean the utensils and containers, and to arrange the furniture. The places for the departed ancestors are so arranged that each husband and wife are side by side, arranged according to proper ranking from west to east, and all facing south. The mistress of the house supervises the women of the household in cleaning the cooking utensils and preparing the food, which should include five kinds of vegetables and five kinds of fruits and not more than fifteen dishes of the following sorts: red stew, roast meat, fried meat, ribs, boiled white meat, dried meat, ground meat, special meats other than pork or lamb, foods made of flour. (If the family is poor, or if certain items cannot be obtained at a particular location or time, then merely include several items from each category, that is, vegetable, fruit, meat, flour-foods, and rice-foods.)

The assistants prepare a basin with a stand for washing hands and set it on the southeastern side of the eastern steps. To the north of the stand is set a rack of towels for drying hands. (These are for the relatives.) Then, on the east side of the eastern steps another basin and some towels are set; these, however, are without a stand or a rack. (These are for the assistants.)

On the day of the ceremony, all members of the family rise early and put on formal attire. The master and the mistress lead the assistants to the hall for the ceremony. In front of every seat, on the south side of the table, the assistants place vegetables and fruits, and on the north side, wine cups, spoons, chopsticks, teacups and saucers, and sauce bowls. Next they put a bottle of water and a bottle of wine on a table above the eastern steps. To its east is placed a table with a decanter, wine cups, knives, and towels on it. An incense table is placed in the center of the hall, with an incense burner and an incense box on it. An ash bowl is set on the east side, and a burner, a water bottle, an incense ash ladle, and a pair of tongs are set on the west side. Water is poured into the washing basins.

In the morning, when the cook reports that all the foods have been prepared, the master and mistress go to the Image Hall together. Two assistants carry the memorial tablets in a bamboo basket, and, with the master taking the lead and the mistress following him, all the members of the family form two rows, the men on the left-hand side and the women on the right-hand side. In this order they proceed to the hall of the ceremony. The basket is then placed at the top of the western steps, to the west of the burner.

The master and mistress now wash their hands and carry the memorial tablets to the seats: those of the male ancestors first, those of the female ones next. Afterwards, the master leads all the men in the family to form one line, from west to east according to their ranks, below the eastern steps, all facing north. The mistress, likewise, leads all the women in the same order, from east to west, below the western steps, also facing north. The assistants to the ceremony form another line, from west to east, behind the men. When all have taken their proper positions, they bow together to greet the spirits of the ancestors.

The master then ascends the eastern steps and goes to the south of the incense table. He puts his official tablet in his girdle and lights the incense. Then he bows and returns to his former position. The deliverer of prayers and the assistants to the ceremony now wash and dry their hands. One assistant ascends the steps, opens the wine bottle, wipes the mouth of the bottle, and pours the wine into the decanter. Then he takes the wine cup, fills it with wine from the decanter, and makes a libation toward the west.

The cook and servants have by now put the foods for offering on a table placed on the east side of the washing basin and towel rack. The men now wash their hands. Then, following the example of the master, they put down their official tablets and hold up bowls of meat—the master ascends from the eastern steps, all the others from the western steps—and place them in front of the memorial tablets of the ancestors, to the north of the vegetables and fruits. Afterwards, they take up their official tablets and return to their former positions. Now the women wash and dry their hands. Led by the mistress, they first carry the foods made of flour, ascend the western steps, and set them down to the north of the meats. Then they carry the foods made of rice, ascend the western steps, and set them down to the north of the foods made of flour. Afterwards they descend and return to their former positions.

The master now ascends the eastern steps, goes to the wine table, and turns to face west. An assistant takes the wine cup of the great-grandfather in his left hand and that of the great-grandmother in his right hand; another assistant, in the same manner, holds the cups of the grandparents and a third holds the cups of the parents. The three assistants now go to the master, who, after putting his official tablet away in his girdle, pours wine into the cups. With these cups in their hands, the assistants walk slowly back to the tablets to set them down in their former positions. The master takes out his official tablet again, approaches the seats of his great-grandparents, facing north. One assistant now takes the wine cup of the great-grandfather and stands on the left side of the master; another holds the cup of the great-grandmother and stands on the right side of the master. The master, putting away his official tablet, kneels and receives the cup of the great-grandfather, offers a libation, and returns the cup to the assistant, who puts it back where it was. The master then takes out his official tablet, prostrates himself on the floor, then rises and steps back a little.

The deliverer of prayers steps out from the left of the master, turns to face east, puts away his official tablet, takes out the written prayer, kneels down and reads:

> On such-and-such a day, of such-and-such a month, of such-and-such a year, your filial great-grandson, officially titled as such-and-such, presents the soft-haired sacrifice (for lamb; if a pig is offered, then he should say "hard-haired" sacrifice) and good wine in the yearly offering to his great-grandfather, officially titled such-and-such, and great-grandmother (give honorary title here). O that you enjoy the food!

He then rolls up the prayer sheet and puts it back into his pocket. Then he takes out his official tablet and rises. The master bows to the memorial tablets.

Next they proceed with the same ceremony at the seats of the grandparents and those of the parents, except that the prayer is slightly modified, so that for the grandparents it reads: "Your filial grandson presents the yearly offerings . . ." and for the parents, "Your filial son . . ," etc.

When this first round of offerings is completed, the deliverer of prayers and the master descend and return to their former positions. Now the second round of offering begins. (This is usually performed by the mistress herself or some close relative). The offerer washes her hands if she has not done so already, ascends through the western steps, pours the wine and offers libations, just as the master has done. The only difference is that there is no reading of prayers.

When this second round of offerings is completed, the master ascends the eastern steps, takes off his official tablet, holds the decanter, and fills all the wine cups. Then he takes up his official tablet again and steps back to stand on the southeast side of the incense table, facing north. The mistress ascends the western steps, places spoons in the bowls of millet, and straightens the chopsticks. The handles of the spoon should point to the west. She now goes to stand on the southwest side of the incense table and faces north. The master bows twice at the memorial tablets and the mistress bows four times.

One assistant now removes the tea leaves and another ladles soup for the ancestors, both starting from the western end. When this is done they leave, and the deliverer of prayers closes the door for the ancestors to dine in private. The master now should stand on the east side of the closed door, facing west, with all male members of the family in a file behind him; the mistress stands on the west side of the closed door and faces east, with all female members of the family in a file behind her. In this manner all persons wait for the duration of a meal. Then the deliverer of prayers ascends and approaches the door, facing north. He coughs three times to warn the ancestors before opening the door.

The assistants now go to the north of the table with the water, and the master comes in to take his position, facing west. The deliverer of prayers ascends the western steps and approaches the seat of the great-grandfather. He puts his official tablet in his girdle and raises the wine cup, slowly walks to the right of the master, turns to face south, and offers the cup to the master, who, after putting his official tablet away in the girdle, kneels down to receive the cup and to sip the wine.

An assistant then hands a container over to the deliverer of prayers, who uses a spoon to take a few grains of millet from the bowl of each ancestor and puts them in the container. He then carries the container and walks up to the left of the master, turns to face north, and offers the master this blessing: "Your grandfather commands me to confer many blessings on you, the filial grandson, enabling you to receive prosperity from Heaven, your fields to produce abundantly, and you to live a long life."

The master places the wine cup in front of him, takes up his official tablet, prostrates himself on the floor, rises, and bows. Then he puts his official tablet away in his girdle and kneels to receive the millet. He tastes a little of it, then puts the rest in his left sleeve. An assistant is standing on his right side, and the master gives the container of the millet to him. The master then folds the edge of his left sleeve over his fingers, takes up the wine cup, and drinks from it. Another assistant is standing on his right side, to whom the master gives the cup. On the left side of the master another assistant is holding a plate. He now puts the plate on the floor, and the master lets the millet fall from his sleeve into the plate,which is then carried out. The master takes up his official tablet, prostrates himself, rises, and goes to stand at the top of the eastern steps, facing west. After the master receives the blessed millet, the deliverer of prayers holds up his official tablet and steps back to the top of the western steps, facing east. When the master has taken his position at the top of the eastern steps, the deliverer of prayers announces the completion of the ceremony. Then he descends and takes his former position. All present bow to the memorial tablets, except for the master, for he has received the blessing. Afterwards, the master descends and bows with everyone else to bid the ancestors farewell.

The ceremony having been completed, the master and mistress ascend to take down the memorial tablets and put them back into the bamboo basket, the tablets of the female ancestors being taken down first, then those of the male ancestors. Two assistants carry the basket to the Image Hall, followed by everyone in the family in the same manner as when the tablets were brought out.

At this point the mistress returns to supervise the removal of the offerings. The wine that remains in the cups, together with that in the decanter, is poured into a pot and sealed. This is the "blessed wine."

The assistants bring the offered foods back to the kitchen, where they are removed from the special containers into ordinary bowls and plates, and the special containers are carefully washed and put away under the supervision of the mistress. A small portion is taken from each item of the offered foods, and put into food boxes, which are sealed together with some "blessed wine," and dispatched, with a letter, to relatives and friends who are ardent observers of rites and rituals. This activity the master supervises. (The food sample is precious because it is left by the ancestors' spirits; it does not have to be rich in itself.)

The assistants now help set up the feast. The men and women are seated separately; the master and all the other male members of the family in the main hall, the mistress and the other female members of the family in the inner quarters. Tables and chairs are set; fruits, vegetables, sauces, wine cups, spoons, chopsticks, and knives are all placed in their proper places. Then wine is poured into decanters, and the hot foods that were offered to the spirits are warmed up.

First, the master of the household takes his seat, and all the other male members of the family offer their good wishes to him. They should stand according to their ranks in the family, just as during the preceding ceremony, and for both men and women the right side ranks higher than the left side. The eldest among them (either a younger brother of the master or his eldest son) stands a trifle ahead of everyone else. An assistant holds the wine decanter and stands on his right. Another assistant holds the wine cup and stands on his left. This eldest of the males then sticks his official tablet in his girdle, kneels, and takes the decanter in his right hand and the wine cup in his left. He then pours the wine and offers good wishes: "Now that the memorial ceremonies have been completed, our ancestors have been offered good food. We wish that you will receive all the five blessings, protect our lineage, and benefit our family."

NEO-CONFUCIANISM: 1. THE WESTERN INSCRIPTION

CHANG TSAI

As you have read, Confucianism was a system of ethics which had very little to say about religion. The appeal of Buddhism in China caused some Confucianists to search for a Confucian equivalent. They read the Taoist and Buddhist literature and reshaped Confucianism into a philosophical, religious, and ethical whole which has been called "new" or "Neo-Confucianism." One of the most celebrated essays in Neo-Confucian literature is the Western Inscription by Chang Tsai (1017–1073). Notice how he broadens the traditional idea of respect for parents into a larger vision of love for all. Notice also how the approach of Chang Tsai resembles Buddhist or Taoist religious thought. How might these ideas be more satisfying than traditional Confucianism?

Heaven is my father and Earth is my mother, and even such a small creature as I finds an intimate place in their midst.

Therefore that which fills the universe I regard as my body and that which directs the universe I consider as my nature.

All people are my brothers and sisters, and all things are my companions.

The great ruler (the emperor) is the eldest son of my parents (Heaven and Earth), and the great ministers are his stewards. Respect the aged–this is the way to treat them as elders should be treated. Show deep love toward the orphaned and the weak—this is the way to treat them as the young should be treated. The sage identifies his character with that of Heaven and Earth, and the worthy is the most outstanding man. Even those who are tired, infirm, crippled, or sick; those who have no brothers or children, wives or husbands, are all my brothers who are in distress and have no one to turn to.

When the time comes, to keep himself from harm—this is the care of a son. To rejoice in Heaven and to have no anxiety—this is filial piety at its purest.

He who disobeys [the Principle of Nature] violates virtue. He who destroys humanity is a robber. He who promotes evil lacks (moral) capacity. But he who puts his moral nature into practice and brings his physical existence into complete fulfillment can match (Heaven and Earth).

One who knows the principles of transformation will skillfully carry forward the undertakings (of Heaven and Earth), and one who penetrates spirit to the highest degree will skillfully carry out their will.

Do nothing shameful in the recesses of your own house and thus bring no dishonor to them. Preserve your mind and nourish your nature and thus (serve them) with untiring effort.

NEO-CONFUCIANISM: 2. THE GREAT LEARNING

This essay was influential far beyond its size. It was selected by a number of Neo-Confucianists, most notably Chu Hsi (1130–1200), as the most important of the Confucian works on education. As such it became one of the core readings for the Chinese civil service examinations from 1315 until 1905. Notice how it makes personal ethics an intrinsic part of good public policy. What kind of public officials were these ideas likely to produce?

The Way of learning to be great (or adult education) consists in manifesting the clear character, loving the people, and abiding (*chih*) in the highest good.

Only after knowing what to abide in can one be calm. Only after having been calm can one be tranquil. Only after having achieved tranquility can one have peaceful repose. Only after having peaceful repose can one begin to deliberate. Only after deliberation can the end be attained. Things have their roots and branches. Affairs have their beginnings and their ends. To know what is first and what is last will lead one near the Way.

The ancients who wished to manifest their clear character to the world would first bring order to their states. Those who wished to bring order

Wing-Tsit Chan, trans., *A Source Book in Chinese Philosophy*. Copyright © 1963 by Princeton University Press. Excerpts, pp. 86–87, reprinted with permission of Princeton University Press.

to their states would first regulate their families. Those who wished to regulate their families would first cultivate their personal lives. Those who wished to cultivate their personal lives would first rectify their minds. Those who wished to rectify their minds would first make their wills sincere. Those who wished to make their wills sincere would first extend their knowledge. The extension of knowledge consists in the investigation of things. When things are investigated, knowledge is extended; when knowledge is extended, the will becomes sincere; when the will is sincere, the mind is rectified; when the mind is rectified, the personal life is cultivated; when the personal life is cultivated, the family will be regulated; when the family is regulated, the state will be in order; and when the state is in order, there will be peace throughout the world. From the Son of Heaven down to the common people, all must regard cultivation of the personal life as the root or foundation. There is never a case when the root is in disorder and yet the branches are in order. There has never been a case when what is treated with great importance becomes a matter of slight importance or what is treated with slight importance becomes a matter of great importance.

THE CHINESE CIVIL SERVICE EXAM SYSTEM

ICHISADA MIYAZAKI

The Chinese civil service examination system originated fourteen hundred years ago, making it by far the first in the world. As a device for insuring government by the brightest young men, regardless of class or social standing, it may also be viewed as one of the world's earliest democratic systems.

It was not perfect. Like democratic systems in the West only 200 years ago, it excluded women. The system also put enormous pressure on young boys of ambitious families.

This selection consists of two passages from a book by a noted modern Japanese historian of China. The first passage concerns the elaborate early preparations for the exams. What did young boys have to learn? In what ways was their education different from your own? What effects did the examination system have on the goals and values of young people?

From *China's Examination Hell* by Ichisada Miyazaki, translated by Conrad Schirokauer. New Haven: Yale University Press, 1981.

The second passage is an evaluation of the system. What was the examination system supposed to accomplish? Did it succeed? What were, or still are, the alternatives?

PREPARING FOR THE EXAMINATIONS

Competition for a chance to take the civil service examinations began, if we may be allowed to exaggerate only a little, even before birth. On the back of many a woman's copper mirror the five-character formula "Five Sons Pass the Examinations" expressed her heart's desire to bear five successful sons. Girls, since they could not take the examinations and become officials but merely ran up dowry expenses, were no asset to a family; a man who had no sons was considered to be childless. People said that thieves warned each other not to enter a household with five or more girls because there would be nothing to steal in it. The luckless parents of girls hoped to make up for such misfortune in the generation of their grandchildren by sending their daughters into marriage equipped with those auspicious mirrors.

Prenatal care began as soon as a woman was known to be pregnant. She had to be very careful then, because her conduct was thought to have an influence on the unborn child, and everything she did had to be right. She had to sit erect, with her seat and pillows arranged in exactly the proper way, to sleep without carelessly pillowing her head on an arm, to abstain from strange foods, and so on. She had to be careful to avoid unpleasant colors, and she spent her leisure listening to poetry and the classics being read aloud. These preparations were thought to lead to the birth of an unusually gifted boy.

If, indeed, a boy was born the whole family rejoiced, but if a girl arrived everyone was dejected. On the third day after her birth it was the custom to place a girl on the floor beneath her bed, and to make her grasp a tile and a pebble so that even then she would begin to form a lifelong habit of submission and an acquaintance with hardship. In contrast, in early times when a boy was born arrows were shot from an exorcising bow in the four directions of the compass and straight up and down. In later times, when literary accomplishments had become more important than the martial arts, this practice was replaced by the custom of scattering coins for servants and others to pick up as gifts. Frequently the words "First-place Graduate" were cast on those coins, to signify the highest dream of the family and indeed of the entire clan.

It was thought best for a boy to start upon his studies as early as possible. From the very beginning he was instructed almost entirely in the classics, since mathematics could be left to merchants, while science and technology were relegated to the working class. A potential grand official must study the Four Books, the Five Classics, and other Confucian works, and, further, he must know how to compose poems and write essays. For the most part, questions in civil service examinations did not go beyond these areas of competence.

When he was just a little more than three years old, a boy's education began at home, under the supervision of his mother or some other suitable person. Even at this early stage the child's home environment exerted a great effect upon his development. In cultivated families, where books were stacked high against the walls, the baby sitter taught the boy his first characters while playing. As far as possible these were characters written with only a few strokes.

· · ·

First a character was written in outline with red ink on a single sheet of paper. Then the boy was made to fill it in with black ink. Finally he himself had to write each character. At this stage there was no special need for him to know the meanings of the characters.

After he had learned in this way to hold the brush and to write a number of characters, he usually started on the *Primer of One Thousand Characters*. This is a poem that begins:

> Heaven is dark, earth is yellow,
> The universe vast and boundless . . .

It consists of a total of two hundred and fifty lines, and since no character is repeated, it provided the student with a foundation of a thousand basic ideograms.

Upon completing the *Primer*, a very bright boy, who could memorize one thing after another without difficulty, would go on to a history text called *Meng Ch'iu* (*The Beginner's Search*) and then proceed to the Four Books and the Five Classics normally studied in school. If rumors of such a prodigy reached the capital, a special "tough examination" was held, but often such a precocious boy merely served as a plaything for adults and did not accomplish much in later life. Youth examinations were popular during the Sung dynasty, but declined and finally were eliminated when people realized how much harm they did to the boys.

Formal education began at about seven years of age (or eight, counting in Chinese style). Boys from families that could afford the expense were sent to a temple, village, communal, or private school staffed by former officials who had lost their positions, or by old scholars who had repeatedly failed the examinations as the years slipped by. Sons of rich men and powerful officials often were taught at home by a family tutor in an elegant small room located in a detached building, which stood in a courtyard planted with trees and shrubs, in order to create an atmosphere conducive to study.

A class usually consisted of eight or nine students. Instruction centered on the Four Books, beginning with the *Analects*, and the process of learning was almost entirely a matter of sheer memorization. With their books open before them, the students would parrot the teacher, phrase by phrase, as he read out the text. Inattentive students, or those who amused themselves by playing with toys hidden in their sleeves, would be scolded by the teacher or hit on the palms and thighs with his fan-shaped "warning ruler." The high regard for discipline was reflected in the saying, "If education is not strict, it shows that the teacher is lazy."

Students who had learned how to read a passage would return to their seats and review what they had just been taught. After reciting it a hundred times, fifty times while looking at the book and fifty with the book face down, even the least gifted would have memorized it. At first the boys were given twenty to thirty characters a day, but as they became more experienced they memorized one, two, or several hundred each day. In order not to force a student beyond his capacity, a boy who could memorize four hundred characters would be assigned no more than two hundred. Otherwise he might become so distressed as to end by detesting his studies.

Along with the literary curriculum, the boys were taught proper conduct, such as when to use honorific terms, how to bow to superiors and to equals, and so forth—although from a modern point of view their training in deportment may seem somewhat defective, as is suggested by the incident concerning a high-ranking Chinese diplomat in the late Ch'ing dynasty who startled Westerners by blowing his nose with his fingers at a public ceremony.

It was usual for a boy to enter school at the age of eight and to complete the general classical education at fifteen. The heart of the curriculum was the classics. If we count the number of characters in the classics that the boys were required to learn by heart, we get the following figures:

Analects	11,705
Mencius	34,685
Book of Changes	24,107
Book of Documents	25,700
Book of Poetry	39,234
Book of Rites	99,010
Tso Chuan	196,845

The total number of characters a student had to learn, then, was 431,286.

The *Great Learning* and the *Doctrine of the Mean*, which together with the *Analects* and the *Mencius* constitute the Four Books, are not counted separately, since they are included in the *Book of Rites*. And, of course, those were not 431,286 *different* characters: most of the ideographs would have been used many times in the several texts. Even so, the task of having to memorize textual material amounting to more than 400,000 characters is enough to make one reel. They required exactly six years of memorizing, at the rate of two hundred characters a day.

After the students had memorized a book, they read commentaries, which often were several times the length of the original text, and practiced answering questions involving passages selected as examination topics. On top of all this, other classical, historical, and literary works had to be scanned, and some literary works had to be examined carefully, since the students were required to write poems and essays modeled upon them. Anyone not very vigorous mentally might well become sick of it all halfway through the course.

Moreover, the boys were at an age when the urge to play is strongest, and they suffered bitterly when they were confined all day in a classroom as though under detention. Parents and teachers, therefore, supported a lad, urging him on to "become a great man!" From ancient times, many poems were composed on the theme, "If you study while young, you will get ahead." The Sung emperor Chen-tsung wrote such a one:

> To enrich your family, no need to buy good land:
> Books hold a thousand measures of grain.
> For an easy life, no need to build a mansion:
> In books are found houses of gold.
> Going out, be not vexed at absence of followers:
> In books, carriages and horses form a crowd.
> Marrying, be not vexed by lack of a good go-between:
> In books there are girls and faces of jade.
> A boy who wants to become a somebody
> Devotes himself to the classics, faces the window, and reads.

In later times this poem was criticized because it tempted students with the promise of beautiful women and riches, but that was the very reason it was effective.

Nonetheless, in all times and places students find shortcuts to learning. Despite repeated official and private injunctions to study the Four Books and Five Classics honestly, rapid-study methods were devised with the sole purpose of preparing candidates for the examinations. Because not very many places in the classics were suitable as subjects for examination questions, similar passages and problems were often repeated. Aware of this, publishers compiled collections of examinations answers, and a candidate who, relying on these compilations, guessed successfully during the course of his own examinations could obtain a good rating without having worked very hard. But if he guessed wrong he faced unmitigated disaster because, unprepared, he would have submitted so bad a paper that the officials could only shake their heads and fail him. Reports from perturbed officials caused the government to issue frequent prohibitions of the publication of such collections of model answers, but since it was a profitable business with a steady demand, ways of issuing them surreptitiously were arranged, and time and again the prohibitions rapidly became mere empty formalities.

AN EVALUATION OF THE EXAMINATION SYSTEM

Did the examination system serve a useful purpose? . . .

The purpose of instituting the examinations, some fourteen hundred years ago under the Sui rulers, was to strike a blow against government by the hereditary aristocracy, which had prevailed until then, and to establish in its place an imperial autocracy. The period of disunion lasting from the third to the sixth century was the golden age of the Chinese aristocracy: during that time it controlled political offices in central and local governments. . . .

The important point in China, as in Japan, was that the power of the aristocracy seriously constrained the emperor's power to appoint officials. He could not employ men simply on the basis of their ability, since any imperial initiative to depart from the traditional personnel policy evoked a sharp counterattack from the aristocratic officials. This was the situation when the Sui emperor, exploiting the fact that he had reestablished order and that his authority was at its height, ended the power of the aristocracy to become officials merely by virtue of family status. He achieved this revolution when he enacted the examination system (and provided that only its graduates were to be considered qualified to hold government office), kept at hand a reserve of such officials, and made it a rule to use only them to fill vacancies in central and local government as they occurred. This was the origin of the examination system.

The Sui dynasty was soon replaced by the T'ang, which for the most part continued the policies of its predecessor. Actually, as the T'ang was in the process of winning control over China, a new group of aristocrats appeared who hoped to transmit their privileges to their descendants. To deal with this problem the emperor used the examination system and favored its *chin-shih* [highest degree winner] trying to place them in important posts so that he could run the government as he wished. The consequence was strife between the aristocrats and the *chin-shih*, with the contest gradually turning in favor of the latter. Since those who gained office simply through their parentage were not highly regarded, either by the imperial government or by society at large, career-minded aristocrats, too, seem to have found it necessary to enter officialdom through the examination system. Their acceptance of this hard fact meant a real defeat for the aristocracy.

. . .

The T'ang can be regarded as a period of transition from the aristocratic government inherited from the time of the Six Dynasties to the purely bureaucratic government of future regimes. The examination system made a large contribution to what was certainly a great advance for China's society, and in this respect its immense significance in Chinese history cannot be denied. Furthermore, that change was begun fourteen hundred years ago, at about the time when in Europe the feudal system had scarcely been formed. In comparison, the exam ination system was immeasurably progressive, containing as it did a superb idea the equal of which could not be found anywhere else in the world at that time.

This is not to say that the T'ang examination system was without defects. First, the number of those who passed through it was extremely small. In part this was an inevitable result of the limited diffusion of China's literary culture at a time when printing had not yet become practical and hand-copied books were still both rare and expensive, thus restricting the number of men able to pursue scholarly studies. Further-more, because the historical and economic roots of the new bureaucratic system were still shallow, matters did not always go smoothly and sometimes there were harsh factional conflicts among officials. The development of those conflicts indicates that they were caused by the examination system itself and constituted a second serious defect.

As has been indicated, a master-disciple relationship between the examiner and the men he passed was established, much like that between a political leader and his henchmen, while the men who passed the examination in the same year considered one another as classmates and helped one another forever after. When such combinations became too strong, factions were born.

. . .

These two defects of the examination system were eliminated during the Sung regime. For one thing, the number of men who were granted degrees suddenly rose, indicating a similar rise in the number of candidates. This was made possible by the increase in productive power and the consequent accumulation of wealth, which was the underlying reason that Chinese society changed so greatly from the T'ang period to the Sung. A new class appeared in China, comparable to the bourgeoisie in early modern Europe. In China this newly risen class concentrated hard on scholarship, and with the custom of this group, publishers prospered mightily. The classic books of Buddhism and Confucianism were printed; the collected writings of contemporaries and their dis-courses and essays on current topics were published; and the government issued an official gazette, so that in a sense China entered upon an age of mass communications. As a result learning was so widespread that candidates for the examinations came from virtually every part of the land, and the government could freely pick the best among them to form a reserve of officials.

In the Sung dynasty the system of conducting the examinations every three years was established. Since about three hundred men were selected each time, the government obtained an average of one hundred men a year who were qualified for the highest government positions. Thus the most important positions in government were occupied by *chin-shih*, and no longer were there conflicts between men who differed in their preparatory backgrounds, such as those between *chin-shih* and non–*chin-shih* that had arisen in the T'ang period.

Another improvement made during the Sung period was the establishment of the palace examination as the apex of the normal examination sequence. Under the T'ang emperors the conduct of the examinations was completely entrusted to officials, but this does not mean that emperors neglected them, because they were held by imperial order. It even happened that Empress Wu (r. 684–705) herself conducted the examinations in an attempt to win popularity. . . .

The position of the emperor in the political system changed greatly from T'ang times to Sung. No longer did the emperor consult on matters of high state policy with two or three great ministers deep in the interior of the palace, far removed from actual administrators. Now he was an autocrat, directly supervising all important departments of government and giving instructions about every aspect of government. Even minor matters of personnel needed imperial sanction. Now the emperor resembled the pivot of a fan, without which the various ribs of government would fall apart and be scattered. The creation of the palace examination as the final examination, given directly under the emperor's personal supervision, went hand in hand with this change in his function in the nation's political machinery and was a necessary step in the strengthening of imperial autocracy.

Thus, the examination system changed, along with Chinese society as a whole. Created to meet an essential need, it changed in response to that society's demand. It was most effective in those early stages when, first in the T'ang period, it was used by the emperor to suppress the power of the aristocracy, and then later, in the Sung period, when the cooperation of young officials with the *chin-shih* was essential for the establishment of imperial autocracy. Therefore, in the early Sung years *chin-shih* enjoyed very rapid promotion; this was especially true of the first-place *chin-shih*, not a few of whom rose to the position of chief councilor in fewer than ten years.

JAPAN:
THE TALE OF GENJI

LADY MURASAKI SHIKIBU

The Tale of Genji is, by most measures, the world's first novel. It was written by Murasaki Shikibu, a woman at the Japanese court, probably in the first decade after the year 1000. While Japanese men were still using a dated form of Chinese for official documents, women like Lady Murasaki were fashioning the Japanese language into an effective and contemporary medium of communication. As ladies of the court, they also had the leisure and experience for writing intriguing, richly evocative stories. This novel is about Prince Genji, an attractive, talented, and sensitive son of the emperor, and his loves.

This selection tells of one of Prince Genji's many flirtations. It is probably of greater interest to us, however, for the light it sheds on the imperial court in the Heian Period (794–1185) in Japanese history. Notice the luxury of surroundings and the elaborate cultivation of sentiments enjoyed by the court nobility. Notice the immediate role of dance, music, and poetry in their lives. How was their idea of a "good time" different from your own? What might account for the difference? In what ways were the relationships of men and women similar to, or different from, others you are aware of?

About the twentieth day of the second month the Emperor gave a Chinese banquet under the great cherry-tree of the Southern Court. Both Fujitsubo and the Heir Apparent were to be there. Kokiden, although she knew that the mere presence of the Empress was sufficient to spoil her pleasure, could not bring herself to forego so delightful an entertainment. After some promise of rain the day turned out magnificent; and in full sunshine, with the birds singing in every tree, the guests (royal princes, noblemen and professional poets alike) were handed the rhyme words which the Emperor had drawn by lot, and set to work to compose their poems. It was with a clear and ringing voice that Genji read out the word "Spring" which he had received as the rhyme-sound of his poem. Next came To no Chujo who, feeling that all eyes were upon him and determined to impress himself favourably on his audience, moved with the greatest possible elegance and grace; and when on receiving his rhyme he announced his name, rank, and titles, he took great pains to speak pleasantly as well as audibly. Many of the other gentlemen were rather nervous and looked quite pale as they came forward, yet they acquitted themselves well enough. But the professional poets, particularly owning to the high standard of accomplishment which the Emperor's and Heir Apparent's lively interest in Chinese poetry had at that time diffused through the Court, were very ill at ease; as they crossed the long space of the garden on their way to receive their rhymes they felt utterly helpless. A simple Chinese verse is surely not much to ask of a professional poet; but they all wore an expression of the deepest gloom. One expects elderly scholars to be somewhat odd in their movements and behaviour, and it was amusing to see the lively concern with which the Emperor watched their various but always uncouth and erratic methods of approaching the Throne. Needless to say a great deal of music had been arranged for. Towards dusk the delightful dance known as the Warbling of Spring Nightingales was performed, and when it was over the Heir Apparent, remembering the Festival of Red Leaves, placed a wreath on Genji's head and pressed him so urgently that it was impossible for him to refuse. Rising to his feet he danced very quietly a fragment of the sleeve-turning passage in the Wave Dance. In a few moments he was seated again, but even into this brief extract from a long dance he managed to import an unrivalled charm and grace. Even his father-in-law who was not in the best of humour with him was deeply moved and found himself wiping away a tear.

"And why have we not seen To no Chujo?" said the Heir Apparent. Whereupon Chujo danced the Park of Willow Flowers, giving a far more complete performance than Genji, for no doubt he knew that he would be called upon and had taken trouble to prepare his dance. It was a great success and the Emperor presented him with a cloak, which everyone said was a most unusual honour. After this the other young noblemen who were present danced in no particular order, but it was now so dark that it was impossible to discriminate between their performances.

Then the poems were opened and read aloud. The reading of Genji's verses was continually interrupted by loud murmurs of applause. Even the professional poets were deeply impressed, and it may well be imagined with what pride the Emperor, to whom at times Genji was a source of consolation and delight, watched him upon such an occasion as this. Fujitsubo, when she allowed herself to glance in his direction, marvelled that even Kokiden could find it in her heart to hate him. "It is because he is fond of me; there can be no other reason," she decided at last, and the verse, "Were I but a common mortal who now am gazing at the beauty of this flower, from its sweet petals not long should I withhold the dew of love," framed itself on her lips, though she dared not utter it aloud.

It was now very late and the banquet was over. The guests had scattered. The Empress and the Heir Apparent had both returned to the Palace—all was still. The moon had risen very bright and clear, and Genji, heated with wine, could not bear to quit so lovely a scene. The people at the Palace were probably all plunged in a heavy sleep. On such a night it was not impossible that some careless person might have left some door unfastened, some shutter unbarred. Cautiously and stealthily he crept towards Fujitsubo's apartments and inspected them. Every bolt was fast. He sighed; here there was evidently nothing to be done. He was passing the loggia of Kokiden's palace when he noted that the shutters of the third arch were not drawn. After the banquet Kokiden herself had gone straight to the Emperor's rooms. There did not seem to be anyone about. A door leading from the loggia into the house was standing open, but he could hear no sound within. "It is under just such circumstances as this that one is apt to drift into compromising situations," thought Genji. Nevertheless he climbed quietly on to the balustrade and peeped. Everyone must be asleep. But no; a very agreeable young voice with an intonation which was certainly not that of any waiting-woman or common person was softly humming the last two lines of the *Oborozuki-yo*.[1] Was not the voice coming towards him? It seemed so, and stretching out his hand he suddenly found that he was grasping a lady's sleeve. "Oh, how you frightened me!" she cried. "Who is it?" "Do not be alarmed," he whispered. "That both of us were not content to miss the beauty of this departing night is proof more clear than the half-clouded moon that we were meant to meet," and as he recited the words he took her gently by the hand and led her into the house, closing the door behind them. Her surprised and puzzled air fascinated him. "There is someone there," she whispered tremulously, pointing to the inner room. "Child," he answered, "I am allowed to go wherever I please and if you send for your friends they will only tell you that I have every right to be here. But if you will stay quietly here . . ." It was Genji. She knew his voice and the discovery somewhat reassured her. She thought his conduct rather strange, but she was determined that he should not think her prudish or stiff. And so because he on his side was still somewhat excited after the doings of the evening, while she was far too young and pliant to offer any serious resistance, he soon got his own way with her.

Suddenly they saw to their discomfiture that dawn was creeping into the sky. She looked, thought Genji, as though many disquieting reflections were crowding into her mind. "Tell me your name," he said. "How can I write to you unless you do? Surely this is not going to be our only meeting?" She answered with a poem in which she said that names are

1. A famous poem by Oye no Chisato (ninth century): "What so lovely as a night when the moon though dimly clouded is never wholly lost to sight!"

of this world only and he would not care to know hers if he were resolved that their love should last till worlds to come. It was a mere quip and Genji, amused at her quickness, answered, "You are quite right. It was a mistake on my part to ask." And he recited the poem: "While still I seek to find on which blade dwells the dew, a great wind shakes the grasses of the level land." "If you did not repent of this meeting," he continued, "you would surely tell me who you are. I do not believe that you want. . . ." But here he was interrupted by the noise of people stirring in the next room. There was a great bustle and it was clear that they would soon be starting out to fetch Princess Kokiden back from the palace. There was just time to exchange fans in token of their new friendship before Genji was forced to fly precipitately from the room. In his own apartments he found many of his gentlemen waiting for him. Some were awake, and these nudged one another when he entered the room as though to say, "Will he never cease these disreputable excursions?" But discretion forbad them to show that they had seen him and they all pretended to be fast asleep. Genji too lay down, but he could not rest. He tried to recall the features of the lady with whom he had just spent so agreeable a time. Certainly she must be one of Kokiden's sisters. Perhaps the fifth or sixth daughter, both of whom were still unmarried. The handsomest of them (or so he had always heard) were Prince Sochi's wife and the fourth daughter, the one with whom To no Chujo got on so badly. It would really be rather amusing if it did turn out to be Chujo's wife. The sixth was shortly to be married to the Heir Apparent. How tiresome if it were she! But at present he could think of no way to make sure. She had not behaved at all as though she did not want to see him again. Why then had she refused to give him any chance of communicating with her. In fact he worried about the matter so much and turned it over in his mind with such endless persistency that it soon became evident he had fallen deeply in love with her. Nevertheless no sooner did the recollection of Fujisubo's serious and reticent demeanour come back to his mind than he realized how incomparably more she meant to him than this light-hearted lady.

That day the after-banquet kept him occupied till late at night. At the Emperor's command he performed on the thirteen-stringed zithern and had an even greater success than with his dancing on the day before. At dawn Fujitsubo retired to the Emperor's rooms. Disappointed in his hope that the lady of last night would somewhere or somehow make her appearance on the scene, he sent for Yoshikiyo and Koremitsu with whom all his secrets were shared and bade them keep watch upon the lady's family. When he returned next day from duty at the Palace they reported that they had just witnessed the departure of several coaches which had been drawn up under shelter in the Coutyard of the Watch. "Among a group of persons who seemed to be the domestic attendants of those for whom the coaches were waiting two gentlemen came threading their way in a great hurry. These we recognized as Shii no Shosho and Uchuben, so there is little doubt that the carriages belonged to Princess Kokiden. For the rest we noted that the ladies were by no means ill-looking and that the whole party drove away in three carriages." Genji's heart beat fast. But he was no nearer than before to finding out which of the sisters it had been. Supposing her father, the Minister of the Right, should hear anything of this, what a to-do there would be! It would indeed mean his absolute ruin. It was a pity that while he was about it he did not stay with her till it was a little lighter. But there it was! He did not know her face, but yet he was determined to recognize her. How? He lay on his bed devising and rejecting endless schemes. Murasaki too must be growing impatient. Days had passed since he had visited her and he remembered with tenderness how low-spirited she became when he was not able to be with her. But in a moment his thoughts had returned to the unknown lady. He still had her fan. It was a folding fan with ribs of hinoki-wood and tassels tied in a splice-knot. One side was covered with silverleaf on which was painted a dim moon, giving the impression of a moon reflected in water. It was a device which he had seen many times before, but it had agreeable associations for him, and continuing the metaphor of the "grass on the moor" which she had used in her poem, he wrote on the fan—"Has mortal man ever puzzled his head with such a question before as to ask where the moon goes to when she leaves the sky at dawn?" And he put the fan safely away. It was on his conscience that he had not for a long while been to the Great Hall; but fearing that Murasaki too might be feeling very unhappy, he first went home to give her her lessons. Every day she was improving not only in looks, but also in amiability of character. The beauty of her disposition was indeed quite out of the common. The idea that so perfect a nature was in his hands, to train and cultivate as he thought best, was very attractive to Genji. It might however have been objected that to receive all her education from a young man is likely to make a girl somewhat forward in her manner.

First there was a great deal to tell her about what had happened at the Court entertainments of the last few days. Then followed her music lesson, and already it was time to go. "Oh, why must he always go away so soon?" she wondered sadly, but by now she was so used to it that she no longer fretted as she had done a little while ago.

At the Great Hall he could, as usual, scarcely get a word out of Aoi. The moment that he sat idle a thousand doubts and puzzles began to revolve in his mind. He took up his zithern and began to sing:

> Not softlier pillowed is my head
> That rests by thine, unloving bride,
> Than were those jagged stones my bed
> Through which the falls of Nuki stride.

At this moment Aoi's father came by and began to discuss the unusual success of the recent festivities. "Old as I am," he said—"and I may say that I have lived to see four illustrious sovereigns occupy the Throne, I have never taken part in a banquet which produced verses so spirited or dancing and music so admirably performed. Talent of every description seems at present to exist in abundance; but it is creditable to those in authority that they knew how to make good use of it. For my part I enjoyed myself so much that had I but been a few years younger I would positively have joined in the dancing!" "No special steps were taken to discover the musicians," answered Genji. "We merely used those who were known to the government in one part of the country and another as capable performers. If I may say so, it was Chujo's Willow Dance that made the deepest impression and is likely always to be remembered as a remarkable performance. But if you, Sir, had indeed honoured us, a new lustre would have been added to my Father's reign." Aoi's brothers now arrived and leaning against the balustrade gave a little concert, their various instruments blending delightfully.

Fugitive as their meeting had been, it had sufficed to plunge the lady whose identity Prince Genji was now seeking to establish into the depths of despair; for in the fourth month she was to become the Heir Apparent's wife. Turmoil filled her brain. Why had not Genji visited her again? He must surely know whose daughter she was. But how should he know which daughter? Besides, her sister Kokiden's house was not a place where, save under very strange circumstances, he was likely to feel at all at his ease. And so she waited in great impatience and distress; but of Genji there was no news.

About the twentieth day of the third month her father, the Minister of the Right, held an archery meeting at which most of the young noblemen and princes were present. It was followed by a wistaria feast. The cherry blossom was for the most part over, but two trees, which the Minister seemed somehow to have persuaded to flower later than all the rest, were still an enchanting sight. He had had his house rebuilt only a short time ago when celebrating the initiation of his granddaughters, the children of Kokiden. It was now a magnificent building and not a thing in it but was of the very latest fashion. He had invited Genji when he had met him at the Palace only a few days before and was extremely annoyed when he did not appear. Feeling that the party would be a failure if Genji did not come, he sent his son Shii no Shosho to fetch him, with the poem: "Were my flowers as those of other gardens never should I have ventured to summon you." Genji was in attendance upon the Emperor and at once showed him the message. "He seems very pleased with himself and his flowers," said His Majesty with a smile; adding, "as he has sent for you like this, I think you had better go. After all your half-sisters are being brought up at his house, and you ought not to treat him quite as a stranger." He went to his apartments and dressed. It was very late indeed when at last he made his appearance at the party. He was dressed in a cloak of thin Chinese fabric, white outside but lined with yellow. His robe was of a deep wine-red colour with a very long train. The dignity and grace with which he carried this fancifully regal attire in a company where all were dressed in plain official robes were indeed remarkable, and in the end his presence perhaps contributed more to the success of the party than did the fragrance of the Minister's boasted flowers. His entry was followed by some very agreeable music. It was already fairly late when Genji, on the plea that the wine had given him a headache, left his seat and went for a walk. He knew that his two stepsisters, the daughters of Kokiden, were in the inner apartments of the palace. He went to the eastern portico and rested there. It was on this side of the house that the wistaria grew. The wooden blinds were raised and a number of ladies were leaning out of the window to enjoy the blossoms. They had hung bright-coloured robes and shawls over the windowsill just as is done at the time of the New Year dancing and other gala days and were behaving with a freedom of allure which contrasted very oddly with the sober decorum of Fujitsubo's household. "I am feeling rather overpowered by all the noise and bustle of the flower-party," Genji explained. "I am very sorry to disturb my sisters, but I can think of nowhere else to seek refuge . . ." and advancing towards the main door of the women's apartments, he pushed back the curtain with his shoulder. "Refuge indeed!" cried one of the ladies, laughing at him. "You ought to know by now that it is only poor relations who come to seek refuge with the more successful members of their family. What pray have you come to bother us for?" "Impertinent creatures!" he thought, but nevertheless there was something in their manner which convinced him they were persons of some consequence in the house and not, as he at first supposed, mere waiting-women. A scent of costly perfumes pervaded the room; silken skirts rustled in the darkness. There could be little doubt that these were Kokiden's sisters and their friends. Deeply absorbed, as indeed was the whole of this family, in the fashionable gaieties of the moment, they had flouted decorum and posted themselves at the window that they might see what little they could of the banquet which was proceeding outside. Little thinking that his plan could succeed, yet led on by delightful recollections of his previous encounter, he advanced towards them chanting in a careless undertone the song:

> At Ishikawa, Ishikawa
> A man from Koma [Korea] took my belt away . . .

But for "belt" he substituted "fan" and by this means he sought to discover which of the ladies was his friend. "Why, you have got it wrong! I never heard of *that* Korean," one of them cried. Certainly it was not she. But there was another who though she remained silent seemed to him to be sighing softly to herself. He stole towards the curtain-of-state behind which she was sitting and taking her hand in his at a venture he whispered the poem: "If on this day of shooting my arrow went astray, 'twas that in dim morning twilight only the mark had glimmered in my view." And she, unable any longer to hide that she knew him, answered with the verse: "Had it been with the arrows of the heart that you had shot, though from the moon's slim bow no brightness came would you have missed your mark?" Yes, it was her voice. He was delighted, and yet . . .

11. Islamic Civilization

THE KORAN:
1. SCRIPTURE AND LITERATURE

JAMES KRITZECK

The following is an introduction to the Koran by a leading modern interpreter of Islam. What is the Koran? How was it written? Why is it so difficult to understand in translation? What were the main elements of Mohammad's religion? What was appealing, and unappealing, to those who heard Mohammad's message? What changes were occasioned by Mohammad's move from Mecca to Medina?

"That inimitable symphony, the very sounds of which move men to tears and ecstasy," wrote Marmaduke Pickthall, describing the Koran. "As tedious a piece of reading as I ever undertook, a wearisome, confused jumble, crude, incondite—nothing but a sense of duty could carry any European through the Koran," was Thomas Carlyle's verdict. How could two sensitive and intelligent men of very similar backgrounds differ so markedly concerning a book which everyone knows is a world classic? The answer is complicated, but it can be made simple: Pickthall read Arabic and Carlyle did not.

For all of the world's Moslems, the Koran is the greatest work of literature. For almost everyone else it is, literally, a closed book. One would be hard pressed to find a single non-Moslem friend who has actually read it from cover to cover. Why is that? The Koran is not a long book; it is shorter than the New Testament. It is readily available in a variety of translations which are accurate enough, some of which have been issued in inexpensive editions. Is the Koran worth reading? To start with, what is it?

The Koran is the collection of formal utterances of Mohammed the prophet of Islam. He was born in Mecca about 570 and was orphaned soon after his birth. The family into which he was born was part of a prominent tribe, but indications are that it was in straitened circumstances. Little reliable information has come down to us concerning

Mohammed's youth. He became a trader, perhaps participated in caravans to Syria, and when he was about twenty-five, married a wealthy merchant's widow some years his senior.

Mecca at that time, it is important to note, was no mere desert oasis, but a bustling and prosperous center of commerce on the major north-south caravan route, and its sanctuaries were places of religious pilgrimage for many neighboring tribes. Mohammed began by following the beliefs and customs which were commonly adhered to by his tribe and by most Arabians. However, he soon became disgusted with polytheism and the morality which went along with it and gave careful (but probably concealed) audience to the worship and disputation of Jews and Christians, who lived in Arabia in considerable numbers. He seems to have accepted their general religious tradition and pattern without feeling inclined to embrace either Judaism or Christianity. When he was about forty years old he experienced his first "revelation" and a call to prophethood. These revelations, which continued to occur at intervals during the rest of his life, constitute the Koran.

Mohammed proved himself a prophet in an important sense of the Hebrew term: he was not a man who *foretold*, but a man who *told forth*. He did not claim to be divine; that is the very last thing he would ever have claimed and the very last claim he would ever have recognized. Rather he claimed to be the reciter of a "recitation" (*qur'ān*, or Koran, means "recitation") unmistakably within the tradition of the Hebrew prophets. Mohammed preached; he did not write. Indeed, one of the principal bits of evidence adduced by Moslems for the divine origin of the Koran is the doubtful fact, and even more doubtful compliment, than their prophet was illiterate.

The Koran was not put together in written form until well after Mohammed's death. A special point must be made of the form in which it was put together, since that helps to explain why even well-meaning non-Moslems never get very far in reading it. Its one hundred fourteen chapters, except for the first, are arranged roughly in order of length; many of the chapters must themselves have been compilations. There was no good reason, apart from a rare rabbinical custom, for doing such a thing—and every reason for doing otherwise. The chapters vary in length from thousands of words to only a line or two, and generally speaking the longer ones are of a later period than the shorter ones. One is reading the Koran, therefore, in roughly the reverse order of that in which it was composed. This is a serious obstacle for any book to have to overcome.

For the Moslems, on the other hand, it is no obstacle at all, only a trivial complaint characteristic of infidels. The nature of their claim for the Koran (which is the Koran's claim for itself) fully accounts for this attitude. There is absolutely no doctrine of inspiration in Islam. The

Koran must be believed to have no human author at all, but rather to be, syllable for syllable, the very dictation of God. That dictation, through an angel customarily identified as Gabriel, was "taken" by Mohammed's memory and then confidently set adrift in other men's memories. From the evidence of the final text, it must be granted that those memories were excellent. Nevertheless, by comparison with the claims advanced for the Koran, those advanced by Jews and Christians for the books of the Bible seem very modest.

When the Moslem legists forbade translations of the Koran, they recognized something important for us to recognize. The most difficult things to translate from any language are those captivating little nuances, lying somewhere between prose and poetry, which catch perfectly the beauty of that language. The Koran was composed entirely of such prose-poetry, in a form called *saj'*. Moslem sages contend that it is untranslatable, and they have no idea how right they are. It is regarded as a foolish cliché to say of a work that "it loses everything in translation." In the case of the Koran, this is true. No translation can convey more than the barest suggestion of what it is in the Koran that can "move men to tears and ecstasy."

So much for that. The Koran is still a book which can be read, if one is dogged enough, in a single day. One is likely to get further along with it, for the reason already given, if one starts at the back. Above all, one must bear in mind constantly while reading it that it is supposed to have been "spoken" by God to mankind through Mohammed. The *saj'* and many individual features, which will be noted in due course, are common to the book as a whole. However, among the chapters a distinction can be made between those composed at Mecca and those composed later at Medina. The distinction has sometimes been exaggerated by commentators but holds up well enough for the novice.

At Mecca, for some twelve years, Mohammed preached a religion which was quite simple and easy for anyone familiar with the Judaeo-Christian tradition to understand. For his polytheistic countrymen, of course, it was neither so simple nor so easy to understand. It was a religion of one God who created man, subsidized him with the goods of this world, revealed himself through the prophets and "messengers," and intends to judge him, rewarding good and punishing evil, in a life hereafter. Through Islam, this God wished to re-emphasize the fundamentals of what had become, in man's hands, a confused and contentious religious structure.

The themes and forms of the Meccan chapters are, from a literary standpoint, probably the most attractive in the book. The first chapter to be revealed, according to Islamic tradition, was "The Clot" (Koran 96). Each chapter has a title, usually taken from some striking reference within it, and all but one begin with the invocation, "In the name of God, the Merciful, the Compassionate":

> Recite: In the name of your Lord who created,
> created man from a clot.
> Recite: And your Lord is most generous,
> who taught by the pen,
> taught man what he did not know.
>
> No, but man is rebellious
> because he sees himself grown rich.
> Indeed, the return is to your Lord.
>
> Have you seen him who forbids a servant to pray?
> Have you seen if he was rightly guided or ordered piety?
> Have you seen if he called [piety] a lie and turned his back on it?
> Did he know that God sees?
>
> No, if he does not desist, we shall seize him by the forelock,
> a lying, sinful forelock!
> So let him call his council.
> We shall call the guards of hell.
>
> No, do not obey him,
> but fall down and draw near.

This chapter is obviously a conglomeration of editorial layers, and requires a great deal of explanation. It is more than likely that everything after the first five lines was added later, and everything after the first eight was aimed against a particular enemy. Most of the early Meccan chapters are simpler. Usually they begin with an interesting but harmless oath ("by the daylight," "by the fig and the olive," "by the city"), go on to indict some form of evil-doing, warn of judgment, frighteningly describe hell, and call men to repentance. "The Chargers" (100) is one of the most beautiful of them, though it, also, is difficult:

> By the snorting chargers,
>   the fire-strikers,
>   the plunder-raiders at daybreak,
>   the dust-raisers
>   centering in it all together!
>
> Man is indeed ungrateful to his Lord,
> and he himself is a witness to that:
> he is strong in his love of goods.
>
> Does he not know that when
>   what is in the graves will be torn out

and what is in the breasts will be made to appear,
on that day their Lord will be an expert on them?

That chapter was chosen because it is an especially brilliant example of the rhythmic *saj'*. It sounds, insofar as its sound can be represented by the Roman alphabet, something like this:

Waal aadiYAATi DAB-han,
    faal mooriYAATi KAD-han,
    faal mogheeRAATi SUB-han,
    fa atharna beehee NAK-an
    fa wasatna beehee JAM-an!

Innal inSAANa lee rubbeehee la-kaNOOD,
wa innahoo ala THAAlika la-shaHEED:
wa innahoo lee hobbil khair la-shaDEED.

Afalaa yalamoo itha
    bothira maa fill koBOOR
    wa hossila maa fis soDOOR,
inna rubbahom beehim yawma-ithin la-khaBEER?

Such clever combinations of repetition and variation of sound give these chapters their special lilt. They are brief, lively, menacing, full of crisp and startling imagery. Some of them are built entirely around strange words, presumably as strange to their first audiences as they are to us. It has been shown that in this respect they resemble the oracular pronouncements of the Arabian soothsayers, although Mohammed took an extremely harsh stand against them—and, indeed, against all mere poets. "The Striking" (101) is an example:

The "Striking"!—what is the "Striking"?
What could convey to you what the "Striking" is?
It is the day when people will be like scattered moths
and the mountains will be like carded wool!

Then, as for him whose scales [of merit] are heavy,
he will be in a pleasing life.
But as for him whose scales are light,
he will be a son of—"Bereft"!
And what could convey to you what "Bereft" is?—
Raging fire!

During this period, Mohammed liked to appeal, though somewhat vaguely, to the authority of the Bible for his teachings: "All this is written in earlier scriptures, the scriptures of Abraham and Moses" (87.18). As he then saw it, his was mainly a confirming scripture for the Arabs, who were without a scripture: "Before [the Koran], the book of Moses was revealed, a guide and blessing to all men. This book confirms it. It is revealed in the Arabic tongue" (46.12). Later, when Jews and Christians proved unwilling to accept his claim in sufficient numbers, he emphasized that they had deformed God's pure religion and that the Koran invalidated their scriptures, which had been corrupted. He represented Ishmael, the father of the Arabs according to Jewish lore, as coheir with Isaac to God's covenant with Abraham.

The chapters of the later Meccan period already betray something of this conflict. They also tend to be somewhat longer and to take on more ambitious substance. Entire stories from the Old Testament (such as that of Joseph) are narrated in general conformity with the Hebrew versions. Although there is only one indisputable quotation from the Bible in the Koran (that of Psalm 37.29 in 21.105), the Bible is paraphrased in almost every chapter after the early Meccan period. Some of the more trenchant chapters, for example "Unity" (112), bespeak Islam's disassociation from Christianity:

> Say: He is God—One!
>> God—the eternally sought after!
> He did not have a son
> and was no one's son.
> And there is no one equal to Him.

In Mecca, Mohammed's message was first met with indifference, then countered with opposition. The Meccans, and in particular Mohammed's wealthier relatives who profited from the pilgrimage trade to the pagan shrine of the Ka'bah, took his monotheistic warning very much to heart, but not in the manner he intended. They planned the elimination of his small sect. Some new material, aimed at coming to terms with these opponents, was introduced into the Koran. Three pagan goddesses, for instance, were acknowledged to be "daughters of God," whose cults might therefore be expected to continue. But such devices neither convinced nor placated the Meccans, and Mohammed himself soon regretted these "Satanic suggestions" and repudiated them. Ultimately a good many verses of the Koran were abrogated in this fashion. "The Unbelievers" (109) is said to have been revealed at this time:

> Say: O unbelievers!
>> I do not worship what you worship
>> and you do not worship what I worship;
>> and I shall not worship what you worship
>> and you will not worship what I worship.
> You have your religion and I have mine.

By 621, Islam's prospects seemed bleak. Mohammed had sent about eighty of his followers to Abyssinia, and indications are that some differences of opinion within his community, as well as the Meccan persecution, prompted that action. He had lost the encouraging presence of his first wife and the protective presence of his guardian, who, as chief of the Hashimite clan, had prevented violent steps being taken against him. Just as the situation was growing desperate, a miracle happened. Two of the principal tribes in Medina, a city some distance north of Mecca, had been feuding for years. Some of their members had heard Mohammed preach and sought him as mediator to end the feud. The Moslems left Mecca unobtrusively in small groups, and finally Mohammed himself fled.

The year of that "emigration" (al-Hijrah, or Hegira), 622, was later chosen as the commencement of the Islamic era. Although it might appear strange that it was selected in preference to the year of Mohammed's birth or that of his first revelation, it was actually an appropriate choice. For it was at Medina that Islam became a state—and ultimately a world empire and a world religion. That transformation did not, of course, take place overnight, but it took place rapidly. Mohammed proved himself a clever and farsighted statesman, as well as a religious leader. His conciliation was successful, and the expansion of his community began.

The style of the Meccan chapters of the Koran had been fitting for the blunt warnings and succinct preaching which were necessary there. At Medina, however, Mohammed became a lawgiver. The basic saj' form did not change in the Medinan chapters, but it was stretched tight to accommodate the lengthy and detailed prescriptions which now came forth. Certainly any legal portion of a typical Medinan chapter, such as the following from "Women" (4.11–12), provides a sharp contrast with any early Meccan chapter:

> God enjoins you [as follows] concerning [inheritance for] your children: A male shall get twice as much as a female. If there are more than two females, then they shall get two thirds of the estate; but if there is only one, then she shall get half. Parents shall get a sixth each, provided the deceased has a child; if he has no child and his parents are his only heirs, then his mother shall get a third. If he has more than one brother, then his mother shall get a sixth— after payment of legacies and debts.

It is really unfair to choose a passage like this one, but it was not chosen to typify the content of all the Medinan chapters.

Mohammed tried to secure the support of Jewish communities in the vicinity of Medina by incorporating into Islam many elements of Jewish law and ritual. Those which remained within it (for example, the prohibition of pork, the regulations concerning fasting and circumcision) are too numerous to list. It is more important to note that at some point Mohammed broke violently with the past. Islam assumed its own direction of prayer, Mecca (previously it had been Jerusalem), and its own "sabbath," Friday.

Some authorities have professed to sense in this period a greater appreciation of Christianity on Mohammed's part. He regarded the Gospel (in the singular) as a book revealed to Christ, which would indicate that he knew very little about it. The position that he had taken concerning Christ seems to have prevented him from inquiring into the New Testament. He denied original sin, so the incarnation became, in his eyes, the most wicked of blasphemies. Why he kept referring to Jesus as "the Messiah" is therefore something of a mystery, unless (as is quite possible) he had no idea of everything that title implied. Surprisingly enough, he affirmed the virgin birth (19.17–26) in words very similar to St. Luke's. According to one tradition, he even asserted the immaculate conception. What is most surprising of all, perhaps, is that he believed in the ascension of Jesus, while denying his crucifixion:

> [The Jews] declared: "We have put to death the Messiah, Jesus the son of Mary, the apostle of God." But they did not kill him, nor did they crucify him. They only thought they did. . . . But God took him up to himself (4.156–158).

A clearer indication of greater friendliness toward Christians would be the following verse:

> You will discover that those who are most implacable in their hatred of the [Moslems] are the Jews and the pagans, while those nearest to them in affection are those who profess to be Christians. That is because there are priests and monks among them, and they are free of pride (5.85).

Ultimately, however, both the Jews and the Christians, as "people of the Book" (i.e., the Bible), were accorded a status as privileged minorities within the Islamic state, or, more accurately, "protected" minorities, in return for payment of special taxes.

Against other non-Moslems the Koran ordered warfare, a holy warfare (*jihād*) against unbelievers. Mohammed spent much of the rest of his life in directing military campaigns against trading caravans and neighboring tribes, all with the general goals of consolidating and extending his community and of forcing the Meccans, his most formidable enemies, into submission. Not all of these expeditions ended in victory, and many of the victories were hard won. Tribal alliances gradually emerged as almost as effective a means of attaining these goals as warfare.

Mohammed's actions during these later years are usually regarded by non-Moslems as, at best, unbecoming to him. In Islamic terms, on the other hand, they appear both necessary and consistent. The fire of warning had simply been translated, by Koranic direction, into the fire of action. Toward the end, Mohammed was assured of final victory in "The Assistance" (110):

> When God's assistance comes, and victory,
> and you see the people entering God's religion in droves,
> then glorify your Lord with praise and ask His forgiveness.
> Indeed, He is a forgiver.

In 631, Mecca capitulated and the way was prepared for further expansion. A few months later, in 632, Mohammed died in the arms of his favorite wife, Aishah, whose father succeeded him as his first "successor" (*khalīfah*, hence caliph). Within a century, after one of the most remarkable series of military conquests in history, Moslems had carried the Koran into the valleys of France and the steppes of Central Asia.

The Koran stands at the beginning of Islamic literature, but it stands apart, pre-eminent without being dominant. All but a few [Moslems] would agree that it represents divine truth as well as superlative literary style—the personal style of God.

For Moslems the Koran is no more literature because it is scripture, than it is scripture because it is literature. It is both scripture and literature at the same time, in a manner absolutely unique to itself. The classical legists formulated it in the concept of "inimitability" (*i'jāz*), a formulation which in time found its way into several of the Islamic creeds. The important thing, however, was not so much its "inimitability" (its style was in fact consciously imitated by such poets as Abu Nuwas and Al-Maarri and was even, upon occasion, criticized by Moslems) as its singular claim, so unhesitatingly accepted by so many persons. For them, first and foremost, the Koran is God's word.

By the same token, the literary style of the Koran has seldom engaged Moslem thinkers except in illustration of its divine nature or for ancillary purposes. For the Koran is everything to the devout Moslem: It is history, sacred and profane; it is prayer; it is a code of civil and religious law; it is a guide to conduct and meditation. "Everything is in a clear book" (11.6). When the first tortuous theological debates were over, the Koran was formally declared the "uncreated" Word of God, on a par with the divine presence itself. The non-Moslem may be captivated by its beauty, may discern its sharply characterized styles and manifold literary subtleties, but he can never fully understand or appreciate how the Koran has superintended all genuine Moslem thought and fashioned the Moslem soul.

THE KORAN:
2. SELECTIONS

As James Kritzec pointed out in the previous reading, the Koran is a closed book for those who are unfamiliar with Islam or Arabic. Much is lost in translation. There is more poetic repetition and less direct statement than Westerners are used to. Chapters are titled after key words (like "clot") that seem better designed to jog the memory than reveal a meaning. Then they are arranged according to length.

Because of these difficulties for the Western reader, we have taken passages out of their original context and organized them according to more familiar categories. Numbers indicating original chapter and verse appear at the end of each selection.

What are some of the main messages contained in these selections? In what ways does the Koran continue the teachings of Judaism and Christianity, and to what extent does it depart from these? What kind of society would these teachings create?

THE OPENING

In the name of God, the Compassionate, the Merciful!

Praise be to God, Lord of the Universe, the Compassionate, the
  Merciful!
Ruler on the Day of Judgment!
You alone we worship and You alone we call on for help.
Guide us along the Straight Road, the road of those whom You
  have favoured, with whom You are not angry, nor who are
  lost!   (1:1–7)

MUHAMMAD'S FIRST CALL

In the name of God, the Compassionate, the Merciful!

Read in the name of your Lord Who creates, creates man from a
  clot!
Read, for your Lord is most Generous; Who teaches by means of
  the pen, teaches man what he does not know.   (96:1–5)

From *The Qur'an: Selections from the Noble Reading*, second revised edition, translated by T. B. Irving. Copyright © 1980 by T. B. Irving. Published by Lawrence Press, Cedar Rapids, Iowa. Reprinted by permission of the author. See also: *The Qur'an: The First American Version*, translated by T. B. Irving. Brattleboro, Vermont: Amana Books, 1985.

THE WARNING

In the name of God, the Compassionate, the Merciful!

You who are wearing a cloak,
   stand up and warn!
Magnify your Lord,
   purify your clothing
   and steer clear of filth.
Do not give so much away
   in order to receive more;
   be patient with your Lord!
For when the trumpet shall sound
It will be a fearful day
   for unbelievers.   (74:1–9)

THE MESSAGE

The Day of Judgment is fixed
The trumpets shall sound
and the multitudes shall come.
The gates of heaven shall open
and the mountains will disappear.

Hell waits in ambush,
a home for the rebellious.
They will live there for ages
without shade or drink . . .

As for the righteous, they shall
have gardens and vineyards
and maidens for companions
and an overflowing cup.   (78:17–34)

BELIEFS

SAY: "We believe in God and what has been sent
down to us, and what was sent down to Abraham,
Ishmael, Isaac, Jacob and their descendants, and
what was given Moses, Jesus and the prophets
by their Lord. We do not differentiate between
any one of them, and are committed to [live at]
peace with Him."   (3:95)

SAY: God speaks the truth. So
follow the religion of Abraham, the
upright. He was not one of the
idol worshipers.   (3:95)

Of the People of the Book
there is a staunch community
who recite the word of God every night,
falling prostrate before him.   (3:113)

They believe in God and the Last Day.
They demand right conduct and forbid indecency.
They compete with each other in good works.
They are the righteous.   (3:113–114)

THE WOMEN'S OATH

O Prophet, whenever believing women come to swear allegiance to you,
saying they will not associate anything with God, nor steal nor misbehave
sexually, nor kill their children, nor give any (cause for) slander they
may invent between their hands or legs, nor disobey you in any decent
matter; then accept their allegiance and seek forgiveness from God for
them. God is Forgiving, Merciful.   (60:12)

THE MESSIAH IS NOT GOD

Those who say that God is Christ the son of Mary have disbelieved.
Christ himself said: "Children of Israel, serve God Who is my Lord as
well as your Lord." God will ban the Garden to anyone who associates
anything else with God; his lodging will be the Fire.

Wrongdoers will have no supporters. Those who say: "God is the third
of three," have disbelieved! There is no deity except God Alone. If they
do not stop saying what they say, painful torment will afflict those of
them who disbelieve. Why do they not turn towards God and seek His
forgiveness? God is Forgiving, Merciful.   (5:72–74)

HOLY WAR (*JIHAD*)

Fight in the cause of God against those who fight against you, but do not
begin hostilities. Surely, God loves not the aggressors. Once they start
the fighting, kill them wherever you meet them, and drive them out
from where they have driven you out; for aggression is more heinous

than killing. But fight them not in the proximity of the Sacred Mosque unless they fight you therein; should they fight you even there, then fight them: such is the requital of these disbelievers. Then if they desist, surely God is Most Forgiving, Ever Merciful. Fight them until all aggression ceases and religion is professed for the pleasure of God alone. If they desist, then be mindful that no retaliation is permissible except against the aggressors. (2:190–193)

Do not account those who are slain in the cause of God, as dead. Indeed, they are living in the presence of their Lord and are provided for. They are jubilant over that which god has bestowed upon them of His bounty, and rejoice for those who have not yet joined them out of such as they left behind, because on them shall come no fear, nor shall they grieve. They rejoice at the favour of God and His bounty, and at the realisation that God suffers not the reward of the faithful to be lost. (3:169–171)

SUFISM:
1. RĀBI'A

Islam is fundamentally an intense monotheism. A deep emotional commitment to God takes precedence over everything else. Sometimes this commitment is so all consuming that the Muslim feels intoxicated or overwhelmed by God. This is the case with a kind of Islam, Sufism, two brief examples of which follow.

The first is a poem by one of the earliest Sufis, a woman mystic named Rābi'a from Basra (d. 801, or 185 by the Muslim calendar). Her poem is preceded by a few anecdotes about her life. Notice her sense of losing her self and her image of divine love as selfless or pure. What does she mean by these ideas? Why is "selfish love" thinking of God with every thought? And why is that inadequate, according to her?

Her hand was sought in marriage by a number of pious men, but she declined all offers, declaring, "The contract of marriage is for those who have a phenomenal existence. But in my case, there is no such existence, for I have ceased to exist and have passed out of self. I exist in God and am altogether His. I live in the shadow of His command. The marriage

From *Sufism: An Account of the Mystic Islam* by A. J. Arberry. New York: Harper & Row, 1950. Reprinted by permission, of George Allen & Unwin.

contract must be asked for from Him, not from me." Rābi'a was overwhelmed by the consciousness of the near presence of God; once, when ill, she said to a visitor who asked her what her sickness might be, "By God, I know of no cause for my illness, except that Paradise was displayed to me, and I yearned after it in my heart; and I think that my Lord was jealous for me, and so reproached me; and only He can make me happy." Close to this saying is the mood of her celebrated prayer: "O God! if I worship Thee in fear of Hell, burn me in Hell; and if I worship Thee in hope of Paradise, exclude me from Paradise; but if I worship Thee for Thine own sake, withhold not Thine Everlasting Beauty!" With her name is generally associated the first enunciation in Sufism of the doctrine of Divine Love, which later came to be so dominant a feature of the movement: her short poem on this theme is one of the most often quoted in Sufi literature.

> Two ways I love Thee: selfishly, And next, as worthy is of Thee.
> 'Tis selfish love that I do naught Save think on Thee with every thought.
> 'Tis purest love when Thou dost raise The veil to my adoring gaze.
> Not mine the praise in that or this: Thine is the praise in both, I wis.

SUFISM:
2. AL-HALLAJ

Al-Husayn ibn Mansur al-Hallaj was one of the best known, and most controversial, Sufis. Like Rābi'a, he embraced self-extinction in God. Like her he sought a mystical union with God. But as the following selections from those who knew him show, he pushed the idea of dependence on God as far as this world allows. He was then imprisoned and brutally executed in Baghdad in 922. While the theocratic state agreed that there was no god but God, they could not allow anyone to maintain that, since God was the only reality, God also existed in him. Notice how Al-Hallaj's deep religious devotion leads him to beliefs that seem self-destructive. Are they self-destructive? Is it possible to be so religious, and survive?

I saw Hallaj in the Qatica market once. He was weeping bitterly and crying: Hide me from God, you people! Hide me from God! He took me

From *Anthology of Islamic Literature* by James Kritzeck. Copyright © 1964 by James Kritzeck. Reprinted by permission of Henry Holt and Company.

from myself and has not given me back; and I cannot perform the service I should do in His Presence for my fear of His leaving me alone again. He will leave me deserted, abandoned! and woe for the man who knows himself outcast after that Presence!

I entered unannounced into Hallaj's room one day (says Ibn Fatik); someone had been in before me. Hallaj was in prayer, and his brow pressed to the ground. He was saying: O Thou Whose Closeness girds my very skin, Whose Mystery spurns me far away as lie all things in time from the Eternal, Thou shinest so before me that I think Thou art all these things; and then Thou dost deny Thyself in me, till I declare Thou art nothing here. And this can neither be Thy Distance, for that would fortify my selfhood, nor Thy Closeness, for that would help me; neither Thy War, for that would destroy me, nor Thy Peace, for that would comfort me.

Then, noticing my presence, he raised himself. Come in, you do not disturb me, said he.

So I went farther in and sat down in front of him. His eyes glowed like burning coals, and they were bloodshot.

My dear son, he said, I hear people are going about saying I am a saint, and others saying that I am impious. I prefer those who call me impious; and so does God.

How so, master? I said.

They call me a saint because they respect me; but the others call me impious out of zeal for their religion. A man who is zealous for his religion is dearer to me, and dearer to God also, than a man who venerates a creature. What will you say yourself, Ibrahim, on the day when you see me hanging on the gibbet, and killed, and burned? Yet that will be the happiest day of all my life.

Well, don't stay here, he said presently. Go, and into the Grace of God.

> When the giving of Love is entire,
> And What Love cries to is bygone in the stress of its crying,
> Then a man verifies What passion testifies:
> Prayer is Unbelief Once one knows.

Hallaj went one day into the Mosque of Mansur and cried: Gather round, and listen to what I have to tell.

And a great crowd assembled: lovers and followers of his, and haters and critics too.

You ought to know this, said Hallaj: God has made me your outlaw. Kill me.

People in the crowd began to weep; but Abd al-Wudud the Sufi pressed nearer to him and said: Shaykh, how could we kill a man who prays and fasts and recites the Word?

Shaykh, said Hallaj, the motive that really stays you from shedding my blood has nothing to do with Prayer or fasting or reciting the Word. So why not kill me? You will have your reward for it, and I shall come to my peace. For you it will be your Holy War; for me it will be my Martyrdom.

12.   Byzantine Civilization

BYZANTIUM AND ITS SPHERE

J. M. ROBERTS

In this selection a modern historian introduces Byzantine civilization. In what ways was Byzantine civilization different from the Western Roman? What were the Byzantine empire's sources of strength? What were its weaknesses?

In 1453, nine hundred years after Justinian [the emperor who codified Roman law and built the great St. Sophia church], Constantinople fell to an infidel army. "There has never been and there never will be a more dreadful happening," wrote one Greek scribe. It was indeed a great event. No one in the West was prepared; the whole Christian world was shocked. More than a state, Rome itself was at an end. The direct descent from the classical Mediterranean civilization had been snapped at last; if few saw this in quite so deep a perspective as the literary enthusiasts who detected in it retribution for the Greek sack of Troy, it was still the end of two thousand years' tradition. And if the pagan world of Hellenistic culture and ancient Greece were set aside, a thousand years of Christian empire at Byzantium itself was impressive enough for its passing to seem an earthquake.

This is one of those subjects where it helps to know the end of the story before beginning it. Even in their decline Byzantine prestige and traditions had amazed strangers who felt through them the weight of an imperial past. To the end its emperors were *augusti* and its citizens called themselves "Romans." For centuries, St. Sophia had been the greatest of Christian churches, the orthodox religion it enshrined needing to make even fewer concessions to religious pluralism as previously troublesome provinces were swallowed by the Moslems. Though in retrospect it is easy to see the inevitability of decline and fall, therefore, this was not how the men who lived under it saw the eastern empire. They knew, consciously or unconsciously, that it had great powers of evolution. It was a great conservative *tour de force* which had survived many extremities and its archaic style was almost to the end able to cloak important changes.

None the less, a thousand years brought great upheavals in both east and west; history played upon Byzantium, modifying some elements in its heritage, stressing others, obliterating others, so that the empire was in the end very different from Justinian's while never becoming wholly distinct from it. There is no clear dividing line between antiquity and Byzantium. The centre of gravity of the empire had begun to shift eastward before Constantine and when his city became the seat of world empire it was the inheritor of the pretensions of Rome. The office of the emperors showed particularly sharply how evolution and conservatism could combine. Until 800 there was no formal challenge to the theory that the emperor was the secular ruler of all mankind. With the coronation of a western emperor in that year, whatever might be said of the exact relationship of his power to that of the East, the uniqueness of the imperial purple had gone. Yet Byzantium continued to cherish the fantasy of universal empire; there would be emperors right to the end and their office was one of awe-inspiring grandeur. Still theoretically chosen by Senate, army and people, they had none the less an absolute authority. While the realities of his accession might determine for any particular emperor the actual extent of his power—and sometimes the dynastic succession broke under the strains—he was *autocrat* as a western emperor never was. Respect for legal principle and the vested interests of bureaucracy might muffle the emperor's will in action, but it was always supreme in theory. The heads of all the great departments of state were responsible to no one but him. This authority explains the intensity with which Byzantine politics focused at the imperial court, for it was there, and not through corporate and representative institutions such as evolved slowly in the West, that authority could be influenced.

This autocratic power had its harsh side. The *curiosi* or secret police informers who swarmed through the empire were not there for nothing. But the nature of the imperial office also laid obligations on the emperor. Crowned by the Patriarch of Constantinople, the emperor had the enormous authority, but also the responsibilities, of God's representative upon earth. The line between lay and ecclesiastical was always more blurred in the East than in the West. Though this meant that there was in the East nothing like the western opposition of Church and State there was a continuing pressure upon God's vice-regent to act appropriately, to show *philanthropia*, a love of mankind, in his acts. The purpose of the autocratic power was the preservation of mankind and of the conduits by which it drew the water of life—orthodoxy and the Church. Appropriately most of the early Christian emperors were canonized—just as pagan emperors had been deified. Other traditions than the Christian also affected the office, as this suggested. Byzantine emperors were to receive the ritual prostrations of oriental tradition and the images of them which look down from their mosaics show their heads surrounded by the nimbus in which the last pre-Christian emperors were depicted, for it was part of the cult of the sun god. (Some representations of Sassanid* rulers have it, too.) It was, none the less, above all as a Christian ruler that the emperor justified his authority.

The imperial office itself thus embodied much of the Christian heritage of Byzantium. That heritage also marked the eastern empire off sharply from the West at many other levels. There were, in the first place, the ecclesiastical peculiarities of what came to be called the Orthodox Church. Islam, for example, was sometimes seen by the eastern clergy less as a pagan religion than a heresy. Other differences lay in the Orthodox view of the relationship of clergy to society; the coalescence of spiritual and lay was important at many levels below the throne. One symbol of it was the retention of a married clergy; the Orthodox priest, for all his reputed holiness, was never to be quite the man apart his western Catholic colleague became. This suggests the great rôle of the Orthodox Church as a cementing force in society down to modern times. Above all, no sacerdotal authority as great as that of the papacy would emerge. The focus of authority was the emperor, whose office and responsibility towered above the equally ranked bishops. Of course, so far as social regulation went, this did not mean that Orthodoxy was more tolerant than the Church of the medieval West. Bad times were always liable to be interpreted as evidence that the emperor had not been doing his Christian duty—which included the harrying of such familiar scapegoats as Jews, heretics and homosexuals.

Distinction from the West was in part a product of political history, of the gradual loosening of contact after the division of the empires, in part a matter of an original distinction of style. The Catholic and Orthodox traditions were on divergent courses from early times, even if at first the divergence was only slight. At an early date Latin Christianity was somewhat estranged by the concessions the Greeks had to make to Syrian and Egyptian practice. Yet such concessions had also kept alive a certain polycentrism within Christendom. When Jerusalem, Antioch and Alexandria, the other three great patriarchates of the East, fell into Arab hands, the polarization of Rome and Constantinople was accentuated. Gradually, the Christian world was ceasing to be bilingual; a Latin west came to face a Greek east. It was at the beginning of the seventh century that Latin finally ceased to be the official language of the army and of justice, the two departments where it had longest resisted Greek. That the bureaucracy was Greek-speaking was to be very important. When the eastern Church failed among Moslems, it opened a new missionary field and won much ground among the pagans to the north.

*Persian dynasty (c. 224–640) before the Arab invasion.—Ed.

Eventually, southeastern Europe and Russia owed their evangelizing to Constantinople. The outcome—among many other things—was that the Slav peoples would owe to their teachers not only the creation of a literature and written language based on Greek, but many of their most fundamental political ideas. And because the West was Catholic, its relations with the Slav world were sometimes hostile, so that the Slav peoples came to view the western half of Christendom with deep reservations. This lay far in the future and takes us further afield than we need go for the present.

The distinctiveness of the eastern Christian tradition could be illustrated in many ways. Monasticism, for example, remained closer to its original forms in the East and the importance of the Holy Man has always been greater there than in the more hierarchically aware Roman Church. The Greeks, too, seem to have been more disputatious than Latins; the Hellenistic background of the early Church had always favoured speculation and the eastern Churches were open to oriental trends, always susceptible to the pressures of many traditional influences. Yet this did not prevent the imposition of dogmatic solutions to religious quarrels.

Some of these were about issues which now seem trivial or even meaningless. Inevitably, a secular age such as our own finds even the greatest of them difficult to fathom simply because we lack a sense of the mental world lying behind them. It requires an effort to recall that behind the exquisite definitions and logic-chopping of the Fathers lay a concern of appalling importance, nothing less than that mankind should be saved from damnation.

• • •

One major source of division and difficulty for the empire in the earlier part of this period was, as so often before, religion. This plagued the empire and held back its recovery because it was so often tangled with political and local issues. The outstanding example was a controversy which embittered feelings for over a century, the campaign of the iconoclasts.

The depicting of the saints, the Blessed Virgin and God Himself had come to be one of the great devices of Orthodox Christianity for focusing devotion and teaching. In late antiquity such images, or icons, had a place in the West, too, but to this day they occupy a special place in Orthodox churches where they are displayed in shrines and on special screens to be venerated and contemplated by the believer. They are much more than mere decoration, for their arrangement conveys the teachings of the Church and (as one authority has said) provides "a point of meeting between heaven and earth," for the faithful amid the icons can feel surrounded by the whole invisible Church, by the departed, the saints and angels, and Christ and His mother themselves. It is hardly surprising that something concentrating religious emotion so intensely should have led in paint or mosaic to some of the highest achievements of Byzantine (and, later, Slav) art.

Icons had become prominent in eastern churches by the sixth century. There followed two centuries of respect for them and in many places growing popular devotion to them, but then their use came to be questioned. Interestingly, this happened just after the caliphate had mounted a campaign against the use of images in Islam, but it cannot be inferred that the iconoclasts took their ideas from Moslems. The critics of the icons claimed that they were idols, perverting the worship due to God to the creations of men. They demanded their destruction or expunging and set to work with a will with whitewash, brush and hammer.

Leo III favoured such men. There is still much that is mysterious about the reason why imperial authority was thrown behind the icono-clasts, but he acted on the advice of bishops, and Arab invasions and volcanic eruptions were no doubt held to indicate God's disfavour. In 730, therefore, an edict forbade the use of images in public worship. A persecution of those who resisted followed; enforcement was always more marked at Constantinople than in the provinces. The movement reached its peak under Constantine V and was ratified by a council of bishops in 754. Persecution became fiercer, and there were martyrs, particularly among monks, who usually defended icons more vigorously than did the secular clergy. But iconoclasm was always dependent on imperial support and there were ebbings and flowings in the next century. Under Leo IV and Irene, his widow, persecution was relaxed and the "iconophiles" (lovers of icons) recovered ground, though this was followed by renewed persecution. Only in 843, on the first Sunday of Lent, a day still celebrated as a feast of Orthodoxy in the eastern Church, were the icons finally restored.

What was the meaning of this strange episode? There was a practical justification, in that the conversion of Jews and Moslems was said to be made more difficult by Christian respect for images, but this does not take us very far. Once again, a religious dispute cannot be separated from factors external to religion, but the ultimate explanation probably lies in a sense of religious precaution, and given the passion often shown in theological controversy in the eastern empire, it is easy to understand how the debate became embittered. No question of art or artistic merit arose: Byzantium was not like that. What was at stake was the feeling of reformers that the Greeks were falling into idolatry in the extremity of their (relatively recent) devotion to icons and that the Arab disasters were the first rumblings of God's thunder; a pious king, as in the Israel of the Old Testament, could yet save the people from the consequences of sin by breaking the idols. This was easier in that the process suited the mentalities of a faith which felt itself at bay. It was notable that iconoclasm was particularly strong in the army. Another fact which is suggestive is that icons had often represented local saints and holy men; they were replaced by the uniting, simplifying symbols of eucharist and cross, and this says something about a new, monolithic quality in Byzantine religion and society from the eighth century onwards. Finally, iconoclasm was also in part an angry response to a tide which had long flowed in favour of the monks who gave such prominence to icons in their teaching. As well as a prudent step towards placating an angry God, therefore, iconoclasm represented a reaction of centralized authority, that of emperor and bishops, against local pieties, the independence of cities and monasteries, and the cults of holy men.

Iconoclasm offended many in the western Church but it showed more clearly than anything yet how far Orthodoxy now was from Latin Christianity. The western Church had been moving, too; as Latin culture was taken over by the Germanic peoples, it drifted away in spirit from the churches of the Greek east. The iconoclast synod of bishops had been an affront to the papacy, which had already condemned Leo's supporters. Rome viewed with alarm the emperor's pretensions to act in spiritual matters. Thus iconoclasms drove deeper the division between the two halves of Christendom. Cultural differentiation had now gone very far—not surprisingly when it could take two months by sea to go from Byzantium to Italy and by land a wedge of Slav peoples soon stood between two languages.

Contact between East and West could not be altogether extinguished at the official level. But here, too, history created new divisions. The appearance of an empire in the West, where a Frankish king was crowned "emperor" by the Pope of Rome in 800, was a challenge to the Byzantine claim to be the legatee of Rome. Distinctions within the western world did not much matter in Constantinople; the Byzantine officials identified a challenger in the Frankish realm and thereafter indiscriminately called all westerners "Franks," a usage which was to spread as far as China. The two states failed to cooperate against the Arab and offended one another's susceptibilities. The Roman coronation was in part a response to the assumption of the title of emperor at Constantinople by a woman, Irene, an unattractive mother who had blinded her own son. But the Frankish title was only briefly recognized in Byzantium; later emperors in the West were regarded only as kings. Italy divided the two Christian empires, too, for the remaining Byzantine lands there came to be threatened by Frank and Saxon as much as they had ever been by Lombards. In the tenth century the manipulation of the papacy by Saxon emperors made matters worse.

Of course the two Christian worlds could not altogether lose touch. One German emperor of the tenth century had a Byzantine bride and

German art of the tenth century was much influenced by Byzantine themes and techniques. But it was just the difference of two cultural worlds that made such contacts fruitful, and as the centuries went by, the difference became more and more palpable. The old aristocratic families of Byzantium were replaced gradually by others drawn from Anatolian and Armenian stocks. Above all, there was the unique splendour and complication of the life of the imperial city itself, where religious and secular worlds seemed completely to interpenetrate one another. The calendar of the Christian year was inseparable from that of the court; together they set the rhythms of an immense theatrical spectacle in which the rituals of both Church and State displayed to the people the majesty of the empire. There was some secular art, but the art constantly before men's eyes was overwhelmingly religious. Even in the worst times it had a continuing vigour, expressing the greatness and omnipresence of God, whose vice-regent was the emperor. Ritualism sustained the rigid etiquette of the court about which there proliferated the characteristic evils of intrigue and conspiracy. The public appearance of even the Christian emperor could be like that of the deity in a mystery cult, preceded by the raising of several curtains from behind which he dramatically emerged. This was the apex of an astonishing civilization which showed half the world for perhaps half a millennium what true empire was. When a mission of pagan Russians came to Byzantium in the tenth century to examine its form of the Christian religion as they had examined others, they could only report that what they had seen in Hagia Sophia [St. Sophia] had amazed them. "There God dwells among men," they said.

MONASTICISM

THEODORE OF STUDIUS

Monasticism was an important force in Byzantine society. It was always torn between those who favored a hermit life apart from other members of society and those who preferred monastic communities. Theodore of Studius (d. 826) followed St. Basil (d. 379) in favoring the later, more social form of monasticism.

In this letter to a pupil, however, Theodore shows how severe even the more social form of monasticism could be. What advice does he give his

From *Theodore of Studium(s): His Life and Times*, trans. by A. Gardner. London: Edward Arnold, 1905.

pupil? What seems to be his greatest concern? What were the advantages in this form of behavior? What were the disadvantages?

Since, by the good pleasure of God, you have been promoted, my spiritual child Nicolas, to the dignity of abbot, it is needful for you to keep all the injunctions in this letter. Do not alter without neccessity the type and rule that you have received from your spiritual home, the monastery. Do not acquire any of this world's goods, nor hoard up privately for yourself to the value of one piece of silver. Be without distraction in heart and soul in your care and your thought for those who have been entrusted to you by God, and have become your spiritual sons and brothers;—and do not look aside to those formerly belonging to you according to the flesh, whether kinsfolk, or friends, or companions. Do not spend the property of your monastery, in life or death, by way of gift or of legacy, to any such kinsfolk or friends. For you are not of the world, neither have you part in the world. Except that if any of your people come out of ordinary life to join our rule, you must care for them according to the example of the Holy Fathers. Do not obtain any slave nor use in your private service or in that of the monastery over which you preside, or in the fields, man who was made in the image of God. For such an indulgence is only for those who live in the world. For you should yourself be as a servant to the brethren like-minded with you, at least in intention, even if in outward appearance you are reckoned to be master and teacher. Have no animal of the female sex in domestic use, seeing that you have renounced the female sex altogether, whether in house or fields, since none of the Holy Fathers had such, nor does nature require them. Do not be driven by horses and mules without neccessity, but go on foot in imitation of Christ. But if there is need, let your beast be the foal of an ass.

Use all care that all things in the brotherhood be common and not distributed, and let nothing, not even a needle, belong to any one in particular. Let your body and your spirit, to say nothing of your goods, be ever divided in equality of love among all your spiritual children and brethren. Use no authority over the two brothers of yours who are my sons. Do nothing, by way of command or of ordination, beyond the injunctions of the Fathers. Do not join in brotherhood or close relation with secular persons, seeing that you have fled from the world and from marriage. Such relations are not found in the Fathers, or but here and there, and not according to rule. Do not sit at a feast with women, except with your mother according to the flesh, and your sister, or possibly with others in case of necessity, as the Holy Fathers enjoin. Do not go out often, nor range around, leaving your fold without necessity. For even if you remain always there, it is hard to keep safe your human sheep, so apt are they to stray and wander.

By all means keep to the instruction three times a week in the evening, since that is traditional and salutary. Do not give what they call the little habit [of novice or postulant?] and then, some time later, another as the larger. For there is one habit, as there is one baptism, and this is the practice of the Holy Fathers. Depart not from the rules and canons of the Fathers, especially of the Holy Father Basil; but whatever you do or say, be as one who has his witness in the Holy Scriptures, or in the custom of the Fathers, so as not to transgress the commandments of God. Do not leave your fold or remove to another, or ascend to any higher dignity, except by the paternal decision. Do not make friends with any canoness, nor enter any women's monastery, nor have any private conversation with a nun, or with a secular woman, except in case of necessity; and then let it be so that two are present on either side. For one, as they say, is cause of offence. Do not open the door of the sheepfold to any manner of woman, without great necessity; if it is possible to receive such in silence, it is all the better. Do not procure a lodging for yourself, or a secular house for your spiritual children, in which there are women, for that were to run great risks; but provide yourself with what is necessary for journeys and other occasions from men of piety. Do not take as pupil into your cell a youth for whom you have a fancy; but use the services of some one above suspicion, and of various brothers.

Do not have any choice or costly garment, except for priestly functions. But follow the Fathers in being shod and clad in humility. Be not delicate in food, in private expenditure, or in hospitality; for this belongs to the portion of those who take their joy in the present life. Do not lay up money in your monastery; but things of all kinds, beyond what is needed, give to the poor at the entrance of your court; for so did the Holy Fathers. Do not keep a safe place, nor have a care for wealth. But let all your care be the guardianship of souls. As to the money, and various necessaries, entrust them to the steward, the cellarer, or to whosesoever charge it falls; but so that you keep for yourself the whole authority, and change offices among persons from time to time as you see fit, receiving account as you may demand, of the tasks entrusted to each. Do nothing, carry out nothing, according to your own judgment, in any matter whatever, in journeying, buying or selling, receiving or rejecting a brother, or in any change of office or in anything material, or in regard to spiritual failings, without the counsel of those who stand first in knowledge and in piety, one, two, three or more, according to circumstances, as the Fathers have directed. These commands, and all others that you have received, keep and maintain, that it may be well with you, and that you may have prosperity in the Lord all the days of your life. But let anything to the contrary be far from you in speech and in thought.

THE ALEXIAD

ANNA COMNENA

The Alexiad is a history of the reign of the Byzantine Emperor Alexius I from 1081 to 1118, written by his daughter, Anna Comnena. If the Princess shows an expected loyalty to her father, she was also independent, intelligent, and insightful. When her father died, he was replaced by Anna's younger brother. She schemed for the throne on behalf of her husband instead but was defeated. She retired to a convent and wrote the history, originally as a long poem.

The section here concerns the attack on Byzantium by the Christian crusaders. Alexius had asked Pope Urban of Rome in 1095 for aid. He was being pressured by the Normans in the South and the Seljuk Turks in the East and asked for mercenaries. This was a significant request since relations between Byzantium and Rome had been ruptured in 1054. Pope Urban saw the request as an opportunity for a general mobilization of Christian forces that might regain the Holy Land from the Saracens as well. The resulting army of pilgrims, priests, families, and the forces of independent princes was not easily controlled. They even included Bohemond of Sicily, the Norman leader who had already attacked Byzantine outposts. Anna Comnena writes of her father's reaction. How did she and her father view these "Frankish" or European armies? Were the Europeans "barbarians," as she says, or were she and her father merely ungrateful?

Before he had enjoyed even a short rest, he heard a report of the approach of innumerable Frankish armies. Now he dreaded their arrival for he knew their irresistible manner of attack, their unstable and mobile character and all the peculiar natural and concomitant characteristics which the Frank retains throughout; and he also knew that they were always agape for money, and seemed to disregard their truces readily for any reason that cropped up. For he had always heard this reported of them, and found it very true. However, he did not lose heart, but prepared himself in every way so that, when the occasion called, he would be ready for battle. And indeed the actual facts were far greater and more terrible than rumour made them. For the whole of the West and all the barbarian tribes which dwell between the further side of the Adriatic and the pillars of Heracles, had all migrated in a body and were

From *The Alexiad of the Princess Anna Comnena*, translated by Elizabeth A. S. Dawes. Copyright 1967. Permission granted by Barnes & Noble Books, Totowa, New Jersey 07512.

marching into Asia through the intervening Europe, and were making the journey with all their household. The reason of this upheaval was more or less the following. A certain Frank, Peter by name, nicknamed Cucupeter, had gone to worship at the Holy Sepulchre and after suffering many things at the hands of the Turks and Saracens who were ravaging Asia, he got back to his own country with difficulty. But he was angry at having failed in his object, and wanted to undertake the same journey again. However, he saw that he ought not to make the journey to the Holy Sepulchre alone again, lest worse things befall him, so he worked out a cunning plan. This was to preach in all the Latin countries that "the voice of God bids me announce to all the Counts in France that they should all leave their homes and set out to worship at the Holy Sepulchre, and to endeavour wholeheartedly with hand and mind to deliver Jerusalem from the hand of the Hagarenes.* And he really succeeded. For after inspiring the souls of all with this quasi-divine command he contrived to assemble the Franks from all sides, one after the other, with arms, horses and all the other paraphernalia of war. And they were all so zealous and eager that every highroad was full of them. And those Frankish soldiers were accompanied by an unarmed host more numerous than the sand or the stars, carrying palms and crosses on their shoulders, women and children, too, came away from their countries and the sight of them was like many rivers streaming from all sides, and they were advancing towards us through Dacia generally with all their hosts. Now the coming of these many peoples was preceded by a locust which did not touch the wheat, but made a terrible attack on the vines. This was really a presage as the diviners of the time interpreted it, and meant that this enormous Frankish army would, when it came, refrain from interference in Christian affairs, but fall very heavily upon the barbarian Ishmaelites who were slaves to drunkenness, wine, and Dionysus.[1] For this race is under the sway of Dionysus and Eros,[2] rushes headlong into all kind of sexual intercourse, and is not circumcised either in the flesh or in their passions. It is nothing but a slave, nay triply enslaved, to the ills wrought by Aphrodite. For this reason they worship and adore Astarte and Ashtaroth[3] too and value above all the image of the moon, and the golden figure of Hobar[4] in their country. Now in these symbols Christianity was taken to be the corn because of its wineless and very nutritive qualities; in this manner the diviners inter-

---

*Saracens, who were considered "children of Hagar" (cf. Genesis 16).—Ed.

1. Anna's account of the beliefs of the Muslims was highly biased. Muhammad forbade his followers to drink intoxicating liquors.

2. Dionysus was the Greek god associated with wine and revelry; Eros was the patron of lovers, and son of Aphrodite, goddess of love.

3. Names of the Semitic goddess of fertility.

4. i.e., Hathor, the Egyptain goddess of love, usually depicted with the head of a cow. (N.B. Idol worship was strictly forbidden by Islamic law.)

preted the vines and the wheat. However let the matter of the prophecy rest.

The incidents of the barbarians' approach followed in the order I have described, and persons of intelligence could feel that they were witnessing a strange occurrence. The arrival of these multitudes did not take place at the same time nor by the same road (for how indeed could such masses starting from different places have crossed the straits of Lombardy all together?) Some first, some next, others after them and thus successively all accomplished the transit, and then marched through the Continent. Each army was preceded, as we said, by an unspeakable number of locusts; and all who saw this more than once recognized them as forerunners of the Frankish armies. When the first of them began crossing the straits of Lombardy sporadically the Emperor summoned certain leaders of the Roman forces, and sent them to the parts of Dyrrachium and Valona[5] with instructions to offer a courteous welcome to the Franks who had crossed, and to collect abundant supplies from all the countries along their route; then to follow and watch them covertly all the time, and if they saw them making any foraging-excursions, they were to come out from under cover and check them by light skirmishing. These captains were accompanied by some men who knew the Latin tongue, so that they might settle any disputes that arose between them.

Let me, however, give an account of this subject more clearly and in due order. According to universal rumour Godfrey,[6] who sold his country, was the first to start on the appointed road; this man was very rich and very proud of his bravery, courage and conspicuous lineage; for every Frank is anxious to outdo the others. And such an upheaval of both men and women took place then as had never occurred within human memory, the simpler-minded were urged on by the real desire of worshipping at our Lord's Sepulchre, and visiting the sacred places; but the more astute, especially men like Bohemund and those of like mind, had another secret reason, namely, the hope that while on their travels they might by some means be able to seize the capital itself, looking upon this as a kind of corollary. And Bohemund disturbed the minds of many nobler men by thus cherishing his old grudge against the Emperor. Meanwhile Peter, after he had delivered his message, crossed the straits of Lombardy before anybody else with eighty thousand men on foot, and one hundred thousand on horseback, and reached the capital by way of Hungary.[7] For the Frankish race, as one may conjecture, is always

5. Ports on the Adriatic, directly opposite the heel of Italy in modern Albania.
6. Godfrey of Bouillon, the duke of Lower Lorraine (c. 1060–1100). To raise money for the Crusade, he sold two of his estates, and pledged his castle at Bouillon to the bishop of Liège.
7. Peter's contingent probably numbered about 20,000 including non-combatants.

very hotheaded and eager, but when once it has espoused a cause, it is uncontrollable.

The Emperor, knowing what Peter had suffered before from the Turks, advised him to wait for the arrival of the other Counts, but Peter would not listen for he trusted to the multitude of his followers, so crossed and pitched his camp near a small town called Helenopolis.[8] After him followed the Normans numbering ten thousand, who separated themselves from the rest of the army and devastated the country round Nicaea, and behaved most cruelly to all. For they dismembered some of the children and fixed others on wooden spits and roasted them at the fire, and on persons advanced in age they inflicted every kind of torture. But when the inhabitants of Nicaea became aware of these doings, they threw open their gates and marched out upon them, and after a violent conflict had taken place they had to dash back inside their citadel as the Normans fought so bravely. And thus the latter recovered all the booty and returned to Helenopolis. Then a dispute arose between them and the others who had not gone out with them, as is usual in such cases, for the minds of those who stayed behind were aflame with envy, and thus caused a skirmish after which the headstrong Normans drew apart again, marched to Xerigordus[9] and took it by assault. When the Sultan[10] heard what had happened, he dispatched Elchanes[11] against them with a substantial force. He came, and recaptured Xerigordus and sacrificed some of the Normans to the sword, and took others captive, at the same time laid plans to catch those who had remained behind with Cucupeter. He placed ambushes in suitable spots so that any coming from the camp in the direction of Niceae would fall into them unexpectedly and be killed. Besides this, as he knew the Franks' love of money, he sent for two active-minded men and ordered them to go to Cucupeter's camp and proclaim there that the Normans had gained possession of Nicaea, and were now dividing everything in it. When this report was circulated among Peter's followers, it upset them terribly. Directly they heard the words "partition" and "money" they started in a disorderly crowd along the road to Nicaea, all but unmindful of their military experience and the discipline which is essential for those starting out to battle. For, as I remarked above, the Latin race is always very fond of money, but more especially when it is bent on raiding a country; it then loses its reason and gets beyond control. As they journeyed neither in ranks nor in squadrons, they fell foul of the Turkish ambuscades near the river Dracon and perished miserably. And such a large number of Franks and Normans were the victims of the

8. I.e., Peter moved his forces across the Bosphorus and into Asia Minor.
9. A castle held by the Turks.
10. Qilij Arslan I, ruled 1092–1106.
11. An important Turkish military commander.

Ishmaelite sword, that when they piled up the corpses of the slaughtered men which were lying on either side they formed, I say, not a very large hill or mound or a peak, but a high mountain as it were, of very considerable depth and breadth—so great was the pyramid of bones. And later men of the same tribe as the slaughtered barbarians built a wall and used the bones of the dead to fill the interstices as if they were pebbles, and thus made the city their tomb in a way. This fortified city is still standing to-day with its walls built of a mixture of stones and bones. When they had all in this way fallen a prey to the sword, Peter alone with a few others escaped and reentered Helenopolis,[12] and the Turks who wanted to capture him, set fresh ambushes for him. But when the Emperor received reliable information of all this, and the terrible massacre, he was very worried lest Peter should have been captured. He therefore summoned Constantine Catacalon Euphorbenus (who has already been mentioned many times in this history), and gave him a large force which was embarked on ships of war and sent him across the straits to Peter's succour. Directly the Turks saw him land they fled. Constantine, without the slightest delay, picked up Peter and his followers, who were but few, and brought them safe and sound to the Emperor. On the Emperor's reminding him of his original thoughtlessness and saying that it was due to his not having obeyed his, the Emperor's, advice that he had incurred such disasters, Peter, being a haughty Latin, would not admit that he himself was the cause of the trouble, but said it was the others who did not listen to him, but followed their own wills, and he denounced them as robbers and plunderers who, for that reason, were not allowed by the Saviour to worship at His Holy Sepulchre. Others of the Latins, such as Bohemund and men of like mind, who had long cherished a desire for the Roman Empire, and wished to win it for themselves, found a pretext in Peter's preaching, as I have said, deceived the more single-minded, caused this great upheaval and were selling their own estates under the pretence that they were marching against the Turks to redeem the Holy Sepulchre.

12. According to other accounts of the battle, Peter was in Constantinople at the time.

13. Western European Civilization

CHARLEMAGNE

JOSEPH STRAYER

This selection is a modern historian's introduction to Charlemagne (742?–814), his family, his world, and his achievements. How was the world of Western Europe in the seventh and eighth centuries different from the Muslim and Byzantine worlds? What were the most important factors that made Western Europe a single unit in this period? Do you think it could have happened without Charlemagne?

The regions of Western Europe resembled each other more closely than any one of them resembled Syria or Asia Minor, but there were sharp differences between Frankish Gaul and Anglo-Saxon England, between Lombard Italy and Bavarian or Saxon Germany. The social and cultural heritage from the Roman Empire was unevenly exploited and was combined with new elements in different proportions by the people of each area. For example, the most active center of classical studies in the seventh century was in the British Isles, whereas Gaul, which had been much more thoroughly Romanized, rather neglected the work of scholarship. The authority of the pope was more respected in England, which had been converted by his agents, than it was in the Lombard kingdom of Italy, which was politically hostile to Rome. The line between Roman and German was sharply drawn in Italy and Gaul, and the distinctions between Frank and Lombard, Saxon and Bavarian were almost as great. Each of these peoples "lived their own law," to use the expressive phrase of that period; they had their own customs, institutions, and beliefs which were not shared with their neighbors. Until some of these sharp differences were erased, Western Europe could not have even the foundation of a common civilization.

Uneven development was equally conspicuous in the political sphere. In the seventh century there was only one state in Western Europe which had any real strength, the kingdom of the Franks. The Anglo-Saxons in England were divided into small, warring principalities; the Visigothic kingdom of Spain was torn by internal feuds and was soon to be wiped out by the Mohammedans; the Lombards in Italy had never conquered the whole peninsula and were weakened by frequent civil wars. But the Franks held most of Gaul and much of the Rhine valley in Germany, as well as an uneasy suzerainty [overlordship] over Aquitaine and Bavaria. Their center of power was in the north, between the Seine and the Rhine, so that they were not greatly hurt either by the conquests of Justinian or the later expansion of the Arabs. They had acquired enough of the Roman idea of the state from their occupation of Gaul to rise somewhat above the limited Germanic concept of the "folk," but they had retained enough contact with Germany to secure first-class fighting men.

The Frankish kingdom was strong, however, only in comparison with its neighbors. It had suffered from the same weaknesses which had ruined other Germanic kingdoms. It was difficult for the ruler to maintain his authority over outlying dependencies, such as Aquitaine. High officials and great landowners were rebellious and disobedient even in the heart of the kingdom. Frankish monarchs had treated their domains as private property and had repeatedly divided them among their sons. There was bad feeling between the Germanic districts of the east and the more Romanized western provinces. Altogether, the seventh-century Frankish kingdom did not offer a very secure foundation on which to build a new European civilization.

Yet from these unpromising materials a Frankish family was able to create an empire in which German, Roman, and Christian elements were fused to form a common way of life. This family, called Carolingian from its greatest representative, Charles the Great or Charlemagne, came originally from the borderlands between Gaul and Germany. It first appears as a group of great landholders, German in blood and outlook, only slightly influenced by Latin and Christian ideas. The earliest Carolingians were as selfish and short-sighted as most of their wealthy neighbors—they struggled for land and power, and did not hesitate to oppose the king or to precipitate civil war if it was to their advantage to do so. As they became more prominent in the affairs of the kingdom they gradually developed more sense of responsibility and more interest in religion and learning. Their rise to power was made easier by the existence of a peculiar Frankish institution—the mayorship of the palace. Originally this office may have been no more than the stewardship of the king's household, but since the mayor was in close personal contact with the king he gradually became a sort of prime minister. All the business of the central government passed through his hands, and a capable mayor often had more power than a weak king. The great men of the realm naturally sought this office, and during the seventh century it became the prize of civil war. The kings of this period were weak both physically and morally; most of them died young and accomplished little during their brief lives. The mayors of the palace controlled the government and the great landowners tried to control the mayors. The mayor was usually the leader of a faction of the oligarchy and held office until some other group gained strength enough to pull him down. In this welter of intrigue and violence the Carolingians had remarkable success. Members of the family held the mayorship repeatedly, and finally Charles Martel, the grandfather of Charlemagne, gained permanent possession of the office in 717. His son, Pippin, succeeded him as mayor, and in 751 felt strong enough to depose the nominal king and take the crown for himself. The dynasty thus established ruled Western Europe until the end of the ninth century and during its two hundred years of power established a common civilization for the peoples of the West.

What were the objectives of this remarkable family? The basic plan seems to have been to unite all the peoples of the West into a single Christian kingdom. Force had to be used to overcome immediate opposition, but the Carolingians were wise enough to realize that force alone would never give them a secure position. They had to gain the loyalty of their subjects by giving them a common set of ideals, and the only ideals which could be accepted by all the inhabitants of the West were those of Christianity. Therefore, the Carolingians consistently and energetically supported missions to the pagans and reform movements among the nominally Christian inhabitants of their empire. They used the Church for their own purposes, but they gave the Church more influence over the peoples of the West than it had ever had before. With the moral authority and the universally accepted ideals of the Church behind them, they found it possible to override many regional and racial differences and to legislate for Europe as a whole.

This policy was foreshadowed by Charles Martel, who encouraged missionary work in Frisia and central Germany. Pippin made the idea clearer by creating what was practically an alliance between his family and the Church. He requested papal approval for his assumption of the kingship and strengthened his position even more by having himself anointed king when the pope visited Gaul a few years later. He was the first Western ruler to receive this unction, and the ceremony greatly increased the prestige of his family. Pippin was now the Lord's anointed, the officially recognized lieutenant of God on earth. He had become a semi-ecclesiastical personage and rebellion against him was not only a crime, but also a sin. In return he protected the pope against the Lombards and fought successfully against them in Italy. In his own dominions he continued his father's policy of protecting missionaries and reformers. Greatest of these was the Anglo-Saxon Boniface, who spent almost forty years in converting the eastern Germans and reorganizing the Frankish Church. The first task was easier than the second, for most of the Germans across the Rhine were either nominal Christians or lukewarm pagans and were quite willing to follow a man who spoke with authority. The real difficulty was to build a centralized system of church government which would ensure co-operation among Christians of the Frankish Empire and subordinate local bishops to the pope. Charles Martel and Pippin gave Boniface steady support in this effort, which smoothed the path for their own policy of centralization, and by the end of his life Boniface had improved the discipline of the clergy and greatly increased papal authority in both Gaul and Germany.

Charlemagne added little that was new to the basic family policy, but he continued it in such an intensive form that it began to yield striking results during his reign. He did not merely support the pope against the Lombards; he annihilated the Lombard kingdom and annexed two-thirds of Italy to the Frankish domains. He was not satisfied with the slow progress of missions among the remaining heathen east of the Rhine; he made relentless war on Saxons, Slavs, and Avars until they accepted the Christian faith and Frankish government. He used all his authority to preserve discipline among the clergy, and he tried to raise a new generation of churchmen who would accept discipline through conviction rather than through coercion. His rough and ready methods did not always bring immediate success, but Charles showed that he deserved his name of the Great by adhering steadfastly to his ends while modifying his means. When penal laws and military force failed to complete the conversion of the Saxons he substituted persuasion and intensified missionary activity. When legislative threats failed to purify the clergy he began a great campaign to improve their education and succeeded in raising both their intellectual and their moral standards. He also encouraged the development of the parish system, which had begun much earlier among the Franks, and made it a really effective agency for spreading and maintaining Christianity among the great masses of the rural population. The parish, centered around a village church, was a logical answer to the weakness of the older system which required a predominantly rural population to attend city churches. But bishops had had little authority over parish priests, and the priests, in turn, had not always been able to secure the obedience of their parishioners. Charlemagne definitely subordinated to the newly established archbishops. At the same time, he gave the parish clergy far greater authority over laymen by establishing a system of compulsory tithes and by encouraging the practice of hearing confessions.

In the light of this policy, carried on without faltering for forty-six years, Charlemagne's assumption of the title of emperor was a logical and necessary step. There had been endless and unprofitable discussion about the ceremony held on Christmas Day in 800, but certain conclusions seem well established. In the first place, Charlemagne received the title from the pope because he wanted it. He was absolute master of the Church; the pope depended on him for protection against dangerous enemies, and it is inconceivable that an act of such importance could have been planned without the king's consent. In the second place, the imperial title added nothing to Charlemagne's *political* authority. He was already ruler of most of Western Europe and he gained no new lands or rights by becoming emperor. Finally, the real advantage of the coronation was increased *spiritual* authority; it emphasized Charlemagne's position as head of Western Christendom.

There were many kings, but there was only one emperor in the West. The old Roman tradition of imperial control over the Church had not been forgotten, and Charlemagne could claim to be heir to this authority. Convinced as he was that he could rule his empire only through an appeal to Christian ideals, his new title gave him an additional right to make such an appeal. It was an official confirmation of his position as defender of the faith, protector of the papacy, and vice-regent of God on earth.

From another point of view, the imperial coronation was a declaration of independence by the West. The shadowy suzerainty of the Byzantine Empire, recognized in papal documents as late as 772, was ended. Western Europe was no longer a spiritual and intellectual dependency of Constantinople; it was now self-sufficient in all things. The Byzantine court understood this clearly; it protested vigorously at the time, and was never quite reconciled to the existence of a line of Western emperors. Neither protests nor temporary compromises made any difference in the essential fact—Byzantium was now almost as foreign to Western Europe as Bagdad.

The Carolingian age saw the establishment of a Western European culture, strong enough to endure terrific strains, independent enough to keep its identity when brought into contact with other traditions, broad enough to include all the peoples of Western Europe, rich enough to develop new forms and ideas from its own resources. By reforming and strengthening the Church, the Carolingians made a nominally Christian Europe really Christian. The great mass of the population was in constant contact with Christian doctrine through the services held in the parish churches, confessions to the parish priest, and visits of bishops and other supervisory authorities. Some clergymen were still immoral, illiterate, and incompetent, but the Carolingian reforms had reduced the number of unworthy priests and prelates. Everywhere in Europe there were churchmen who were well-educated, intelligent, and pious; everywhere in Europe there were laymen who resolutely supported Christian ideals. As a result, a European conscience developed, based on Christian ethics—a conscience which could be easily aroused by spiritual leaders. There was plenty of brutality and stupidity in the centuries after Charlemagne, but it no longer passed without protest as it had in the earlier barbarian kingdoms. Reform movements succeeded each other with hardly a break from the tenth to the thirteenth century, and each wave of reform played a part in shaping medieval civilization.

In the field of education and learning the Carolingian age saw the establishment of a common basis for European scholarship. The works of the Church Fathers and Latin secular writers were copied, studied, and digested. The mere physical effort of copying older manuscripts had important consequences. Many works have survived only because they were copied in the Carolingian period; many others became better known because they were reproduced in different regions by Carolingian scribes. The Carolingian revival almost ended the loss of classical learning; very little disappeared in the post-Carolingian centuries compared to the wastage of the Late Roman Empire and the barbarian kingdoms. Even more important was the diffusion of ancient learning throughout Western Europe. Gallo-Romans, Anglo-Saxons, Franks, Scots from Ireland, and Lombards all studied and worked together at the courts of the Carolingian rulers. Great monasteries in England, France, Italy, and Germany built up collections of manuscripts and trained scholars to use them. These centers of learning were still widely separated, for not every monastery had the teachers or the resources necessary for scholarship, but there were enough of them to arouse interest in learning in every region of Europe. The work of Carolingian scholars was not especially original (with a few striking exceptions), but originality was not what was most needed at the time. The legacy from the past had to be assimilated before new steps could be taken, and Carolingian writers performed this task admirably. In their commentaries they demonstrated the necessity for consulting and correlating many different sources; in their treatises they restated what they had learned in their own words. These were particularly valuable exercises at a time when Latin was ceasing to be a spoken language, when the rise of local dialects was depriving the peoples of Europe of a common tongue. Latin was needed for serious thinking on any subject, since the new dialects had serious deficiencies in vocabulary. It was even more necessary for purposes of inter-European communication, since no other language covered more than a local area. If medieval Europe possessed a common fund of ideas, it was largely due to the work of Carolingian scholars.

Carolingian government was not entirely uniform—each major part of the empire kept its own laws and customs—but it did tend to lessen the sharp distinctions which had prevailed between different peoples. The old division between Roman and German practically disappeared during the Carolingian period and the basis of law tended to be territorial rather than personal. For example, the people of Burgundy now settled their disputes by referring to a single set of customs; they were no longer divided into groups "living" Burgundian, Frankish, or Roman law. Moreover, there were institutions and laws which were common to the whole empire. The county and the count were much the same everywhere, and these basic elements of local government long survived the collapse of the Carolingian monarchy. Coinage and weights and measures also followed the Carolingian pattern for centuries in most European countries. Newly acquired territories such as Italy and Saxony were usually governed by men who came from the older Frankish domains, and this also tended to establish a degree of uniformity. As a result, there came to be a certain similarity in the laws and institutions of most Western countries, and it was not difficult for men of one region to fit into the political systems of other areas.

At the end of the Carolingian period Europe, for the first time, formed a distinct political and cultural unit. It had separated from the worlds of Byzantium and Islam; it had its own traditions and characteristic patterns of behavior. In spite of local differences a European felt at home in any European region, but he was immediately conscious of being in a foreign country when he visited Constantinople or Cordova. This establishment of a specifically European tradition was the great and enduring work of the Carolingian family. The empire fell; the facts of Carolingian history were forgotten, but the impression remained that the reign of Charlemagne marked a turning-point in the development of Western Europe. The wildest legends about the great emperor still contained the essential truth—the belief that he stood at the beginning of Western European civilization. The strange and wonderful structure of European civilization still rests on the foundations laid in the age of Charlemagne.

ERIK THE RED
AND THE VIKINGS

Even after Charlemagne's empire had risen and collapsed, much of Europe was still quite unsophisticated compared to the civilizations of Islam and Byzantium. The Vikings suggest the raw energy of barbarians on the fringes of civilization anywhere. Like the nomads that overran the Roman and Han empires centuries before, they demonstrated a coarseness and brutality that was shocking to civilized contemporaries. Like the Arabs of the seventh century, they also demonstrated an unusual vitality.

The Saga of Erik the Red, *from which this brief excerpt it taken, was written about 1265. It describes the Icelandic traditions of the Greenland and American voyages of the period from 980 to 1020. What kind of people were these? How were their lives similar to, or different from, those of Muslims or Byzantine Christians of the same period?*

From *Erik the Red and Other Icelandic Sagas*, translated by Gwyn Jones. Copyright © 1961 by Oxford University Press. Reprinted by permission of Oxford University Press.

1

There was a warrior-king named Olaf who was known as Olaf the White. Olaf went raiding in the west and conquered Dublin in Ireland along with the territory that went with it, and made himself king there. He married Aud the Deep-minded, the daughter of Ketil Flatnose, son of Bjorn Buna, a man of rank from Norway; and the name of their son was Thorstein the Red. Olaf fell in battle there in Ireland, whereupon Aud and Thorstein made their way to the Hebrides, where Thorstein married Thurid the daughter of Eyvind the Norwegian and sister of Helgi the Lean. They had many children.

Thorstein became a warrior-king and allied himself with Earl Sigurd the Mighty, the son of Eystein Glumra, and they conquered Caithness and Sutherland, Ross and Moray, and more than half Scotland. Thorstein made himself its king, till the Scots betrayed him and he fell there in battle. Aud was in Caithness when she heard tell of Thorstein's fall. She had a merchant ship built secretly in the forest, and once she was ready she hoisted sail for the Orkneys and found a husband there for Thorstein the Red's daughter Gro, the mother of that Grealada whom Earl Thorfinn Skull-splitter married. After that she set off to seek Iceland and had twenty freemen on board her ship. She reached Iceland and spent the first winter in Bjarnarhofn with her brother Bjorn. Later Aud took in settlement all Dalelands between Dogurdara and Skraumuhlaupsa. She made her home at Hvamm and had a chapel at Krossholar, where she had crosses set up, for she had been baptized and held the Christian faith.

Many notable men accompanied her to Iceland who had been taken prisoner on the western raids and were, in a manner of speaking, slaves. One of these was called Vifil. He was a man of good family who had been taken prisoner over the western sea and was, nominally at least, a slave till Aud set him free. When Aud gave homes to her ship's crew, Vifil asked why she did not give him one like the rest of them, but Aud said it hardly mattered, maintaining that he would be held a fine man as he was. However, she gave him Vifilsdal and he made his home there. He married a wife, and their sons were Thorbjorn and Thorgeir. These were promising men and grew up with their father.

2

There was a man by the name of Thorvald who was the son of Asvald Ulfsson. Thorvald's son was called Eirik the Red, and both father and son left Jadri in Norway for Iceland because of some killings. They settled in the Hornstrandir and made a home at Drangar, where Thorvald died. Eirik then married Thjodhild, the daughter of Jorund

Ulfsson and Thorbjorg Ship-bosom, who was by this time married to Thorbjorn the Haukadaler. Eirik now left the north and cleared land in Haukadal and made his home at Eiriksstadir alongside Vatnshorn. In time Eirik's thralls caused a landslide to crash down upon the farm of Valthjof at Valthjofsstadir, whereupon Valthjof's kinsman Eyjolf Saur killed the thralls by Skeidsbrekka above Vatnshorn. For this Eirik killed Eyjolf Saur. He killed Holmgang-Hrafn too at Leikskalar. Gerstein and Odd of Jorvi, both kinsmen of Eyjolf's, took up his case, and Eirik was driven out of Haukadal. He then settled Brokey and Oxney, and lived at Tradi in Sudrey for the first winter. It was now that he lent Thorgest his hallbeams. Later Eirik moved to Oxney and made his home at Eiriksstadir. He asked for his beams but could not get them. Eirik went to Breidabolstad after the beams, but Thorgest gave chase, and they came to blows a short way from the house at Drangar. Two of Thorgest's sons fell there as well as certain other men.

From now on both parties kept a large body of men under arms. Styr and Eyjolf from Sviney, Thorbjorn Vifilsson and the sons of Thorbrand from Alftafjord backed Eirik, but backing Thorgest were the sons of Thord Bellow together with Thorgeir from Hitardal, Aslak from Langadal, and Illugi his son.

Erik and his following were outlawed at the assembly for law at Thorsnes. He put his ship all ready in Eiriksvag, while Eyjolf kept him in hiding in Dimunarvag for as long as Thorgest and his men were combing the islands for him. Thorbjorn, Eyjolf, and Styr escorted Eirik on his way out through the islands, and they parted on warm terms of friendship, Eirik promising that they should receive just such help themselves if it lay in his power to provide it and he knew they had need of him. He told them he meant to look for that land Gunnbjorn Ulf-Lrakuson sighted the time he was storm-driven into the western ocean and discovered Gunnbjorn's Skerries. He would be coming back, he said, to make contact with his friends should he discover that land.

Eirik sailed to the open sea by way of Snaefellsjokul and made a landfall in Greenland at the glacier which is called Blaserk, or Bluesark. From there he headed south, to discover whether the land was habitable there. He spent his first winter at Eiriksey, near the middle of the Eastern Settlement, and the following spring went on to Eiriksfjord where he sited his house. In the summer he made his way into the western wilderness and gave place-names there far and wide. He spent his second winter at Eiriksholm off Hvarfsgnipa, but during the third summer pressed on north the whole way to Snaefell and on into Hrafnsfjord. He now thought he must have got as far as the head of Eiriksfjord, so retraced his steps to spend the third winter at Eiriksey off the mouth of Eiriksfjord.

The following summer he returned to Iceland and reached Breidafjord. He spent the winter with Ingolf at Holmlat. In the spring he came to blows with Thorgest and his men, and Eirik got the worst of it, but later they reached peace terms between them. This same summer Eirik sailed away to colonize the land he had discovered, calling it Greenland, for he maintained that men would be much more eager to go there if the land had an attractive name.

Ari Thorgilsson tells us that twenty-five ships set sail this summer for Greenland from Breidafjord and Borgarfjord, but only fourteen of them arrived there. Some were forced back and some perished. This was fifteen years before the Christian faith became law in Iceland. Eirik afterwards took Eiriksfjord by right of settlement and lived at Brattahlid.

3

Eirik had a wife whose name was Thjodhild, by whom he had two sons, one called Thorstein and the other Leif, both of them promising men. Thorstein was living at home with his father, and no man in Greenland was held as promising as he. Leif, though, had sailed to Norway, where he was staying with king Olaf Tryggvason.

But when Leif sailed from Greenland in the summer, they were driven off course to the Hebrides. They had a long wait for a fair wind thence, and had to remain there for much of the summer. Leif took a fancy to a woman by the name of Thorgunna. She was a woman of good birth, and Leif had an idea that she saw further into things than most. As he made ready to sail away Thorgunna asked to come with him. Leif asked whether her people were likely to approve of this, to which she answered she did not care. Leif replied that he didn't see how he could just carry off so high-born a lady while in foreign parts—"For I am short of men for that."

"It is not certain," said Thorgunna, "that you think you have chosen the wiser course."

"That is a chance I must take," said Leif.

"Then I am telling you," said Thorgunna, "that this is no longer a question of just me alone, for I am with child, and the child, I tell you, is yours. I believe that when this child is born it will be a boy, and though you wash your hands of us now, still I shall raise the boy and send him to you in Greenland once he can travel with other men. I believe, too, that having this son will prove just such a pleasure to you as your desertion of me now merits. And I am thinking I may come to Greenland myself before the game is played out."

Leif gave her a gold ring for her finger, a cloak of Greenland woollen, and an ivory belt. This boy came to Greenland, declaring that his name was Thorgils, and Leif admitted his paternity. It is some men's tale that this same Thorgils came to Iceland before the Froda-marvels in the summer. He was certainly in Greenland thereafter, where it was thought that there was something uncanny about him before the finish.

Leif and his men set sail from the Hebrides and reached Norway in the autumn, where he proceeded into the court of the king Olaf Tryggvason. The king paid him many honours, feeling certain he would be a man of parts.

There came a day when the king found occasion to speak with Leif. "Are you counting on Greenland this summer?" he asked him.

"I am," said Leif, "with your permission."

"I think all will be well," replied the king. "You shall go there with my commission and preach Christianity there."

Leif said it was for the king to command, but added that he thought this mission would be a hard one to carry out in Greenland.

The king said he had not seen a man better fitted for this than he. "You will bring it good luck!"

"That will be so," said Leif, "only if I enjoy luck from you too."

Leif put to sea, and was at sea a long time, and lighted on those lands whose existence he had not so much as dreamt of before. There were wheat-fields growing wild there and grown vines. There were also those trees which are called maple, and they fetched away with them samples of all these things—some trees so big that they were used in housebuilding. Leif found men on a wreck and carried them home with him, showing his magnanimity and gallantry in this as in so much else, since it was he who introduced Christianity into the country; and ever afterwards he was called Leif the Lucky.

Leif reached land in Eiriksfjord and then went home to Brattahlid, where they all welcomed him with open arms. He soon preached Christianity and the universal faith throughout the country, revealing to men the message of king Olaf Tryggvason, and telling how many noble deeds and what great glory accompanied this religion. Eirik was slow to abandon his faith, but Thjodhild accepted at once and had a church built, though not too near their house. This church was called Thjodhild's Church, and it was there that she offered up her prayers, together with those men who adopted Christianity. Thjodhild would not live together with Eirik once she had taken the faith, a circumstance which grieved him very much.

There was now a lot of talk that men should seek out this land which Leif had discovered.

ABELARD AND HÉLOÏSE

Much closer than Iceland to the center of European civilization that was emerging in the twelfth century was Paris, where the philosopher Peter Abelard lived. As a philosopher, Abelard was famous for his Sic et Non (Yes and No), which pointed out the contradictions between certain doctrines of the church fathers. Abelard was challenged for using logic to examine matters of faith. One of his opponents, Bernard of Clairvaux, approached the Sufi idea that the way to know God was through love rather than reason, and he was eventually successful in having Abelard's logical method (or "dialectics") condemned by a church council.

It is ironic then that this founder of modern scientific method should also be remembered for his role in an intense love affair. The famous philosopher fell in love with the young Héloïse, whom he had been assigned to tutor by her uncle. Feeling betrayed by Abelard when his niece became pregnant, the uncle had him castrated and sent Héloïse to a nunnery. Out of grief and shame, Abelard became a monk. From his monastery he wrote the following letter to Héloïse in her convent. If this letter were all you knew of Christianity, what conclusions would you draw about Christian ideas of God, love, sex, and sin? In what ways are Abelard's ideas similar to those of the Sufis? What do you make of the letter that Héloïse sent in response?

Write no more to me, Héloïse, write no more to me; it is time to end a commerce which makes our mortifications of no advantage to us. We retired from the world to sanctify ourselves; and by a conduct directly contrary to Christian morality, we become odious to Jesus Christ. Let us no more deceive ourselves, by flattering ourselves with the remembrance of our past pleasures; we shall make our lives troublesome, and we shall be incapable of relishing the sweets of solitude. Let us make a good use of our austerities, and no longer preserve the ideas of our crimes amongst the severities of penitence. Let a mortification of body and mind, a strict fasting, continual solitude, profound and holy meditations, and a sincere love of God, succeed our former irregularities.

Let us try to carry religious perfection to a very difficult point. It is beautiful to find in Christianity minds so disengaged from the earth, from the creatures and themselves, that they seem to act independently of those bodies they are joined to, and to use them as their slaves. We can never raise ourselves to too great heights, when God is the object. Be our endeavors never so great, they will always come short of reaching that exalted Divinity which even our apprehensions cannot reach. Let us act for God's glory, independent of the creatures or ourselves, without any regard to our own desires, or the sentiments of others. Were we in this temper of mind, Héloïse, I would willingly make my abode at the Paraclete. My earnest care for a house I have founded would draw a thousand blessings on it. I would instruct it by my words, and animate it by my example. I would watch over the lives of my sisters, and would command nothing but what I myself would perform. I would direct you to pray, meditate, labor, and keep vows of silence; and I would myself pray, meditate, labor, and be silent.

However, when I spoke, it should be to lift you up when you should fall, to strengthen you in your weaknesses, to enlighten you in that darkness and obscurity which might at any time surprise you. I would comfort you under those severities used by persons of great virtue. I would moderate the vivacity of your zeal and piety, and give your virtue an even temperment. I would point out those duties which you ought to know, and satisfy you in those doubts which the weakness of your reason might occasion. I would be your master and father; and by a marvellous talent I would become lively, slow, soft, or severe, according to the different characters of those I should guide in the painful path of Christian perfection.

But whither does my vain imagination carry me? Ah, Héloïse, how far are we from such a happy temper! Your heart still burns with that fatal fire which you cannot extinguish, and mine is full of trouble and uneasiness. Think not, Héloïse, that I enjoy here a perfect peace; I will, for the last time, open my heart to you; I am not yet disengaged from you; I fight against my excessive tenderness for you; yet, in spite of all my endeavors, the remaining frailty makes me but too sensible of your sorrows, and gives me a share in them. Your letters have indeed moved me; I could not read with indifference characters wrote by that dear hand. I sigh, I weep, and all my reason is scarce sufficient to conceal my weakness from my pupils. This, unhappy Héloïse! is the miserable condition of Abelard. The world, which generally errs in its notions, thinks I am easy and, as if I had loved only in you the gratification of sense, imagines I have now forgot you. But what a mistake is this! People indeed did not mistake in thinking, when we separated, that shame and grief for having been so cruelly used made me abandon the world. It was not, as you know, a sincere repentance for having offended God which inspired me with a design of retiring; however, I considered the accident which happened to us as a secret design of Providence, to punish our crimes; and only looked upon Fulbert as the instrument of Divine vengeance. Grace drew me into an asylum, where I might yet have remained if the rage of my enemies would have permitted; I have endured all their persecutions, not doubting but God himself raised them up in order to purify me.

When he saw me perfectly obedient to His holy will, He permitted that I should justify my doctrine; I made its purity public, and showed in the end that my faith was not only orthodox, but also perfectly clear from even the suspicion of novelty.

I should be happy if I had none to fear but my enemies, and no other hinderance to my salvation but their calumny; but, Héloïse, you make me trouble; your letters declare to me that you are enslaved to a fatal passion; and yet if you cannot conquer it you cannot be saved; and what part would you have me take in this case? Would you have me stifle the inspirations of the Holy Ghost? Shall I, to sooth you, dry up those tears which the evil spirit makes you shed? Shall this be the fruit of my meditations? No: let us be more firm in our resolutions; we have not retired but in order to lament our sins, and to gain Heaven; let us then resign ourselves to God with all our hearts.

I know every thing in the beginning is difficult; but it is glorious to undertake the beginning of a great action; and that glory increases proportionably as the difficulties are more considerable. We ought, upon this account, to surmount bravely all obstacles which might hinder us in the practice of Christian virtue. In a monastery men are proved as gold in the furnace. No one can continue long there, unless he bear worthily the yoke of our Lord.

Attempt to break those shameful chains which bind you to the flesh; and if by the assistance of grace you are so happy as to accomplish this, I entreat you to think of me in your prayers. Endeavor with all your strength to be the pattern of a perfect Christian. It is difficult, I confess, but not impossible; and I expect this beautiful triumph from your teachable disposition. If your first endeavors prove weak, give not yourself up to despair; that would be cowardice. Besides, I would have you informed, that you must necessarily take great pains, because you strive to conquer a terrible enemy, to extinguish raging fire; and to reduce to subjection your dearest affections, you must fight against your own desires; be not therefore pressed down with the weight of your corrupt nature. You have to do with a cunning adversary, who will use all means to seduce you. Be always upon your guard. While we live, we are exposed to temptations. This made a great saint say, that "the whole life of man was a temptation." The Devil, who never sleeps, walks continually around us, in order to surprise us on some unguarded side, and enters into our soul to destroy it.

However perfect any one may be, yet he may fall into temptations, and perhaps into such as may be useful. Nor is it wonderful that man should never be exempt from them, because he hath always in himself their source, concupiscence; scarce are we delivered from one temptation, but another attacks us. Such is the lot of the posterity of Adam, that they should always have something to suffer, because they have forfeited their primitive happiness. We vainly flatter ourselves that we shall conquer temptations by flying; if we join not patience and humility, we shall torment ourselves to no purpose. We shall more certainly compass our end by imploring God's assistance, than by using any means drawn from ourselves.

Be constant, Héloïse; trust in God, and you will fall into few temptations. Whenever they shall come, stifle them in their birth! Let them not take root in your heart. Apply remedies to a disease, said an ancient, in its beginning, for when it has gained strength, medicines will be unavailable. Temptations have their degrees: they are at first mere thoughts, and do not appear dangerous; the imagination receives them without any fears; a pleasure is formed out of them; we pause upon it, and at last we yield to it.

Do you now, Héloïse, applaud my design of making you walk in the steps of the saints? Do my words give you any relish for penitence? Have you not remorse for your wanderings, and do you not wish you could, like Magdalen, wash our Saviour's feet with tears? If you have not yet these ardent emotions, pray that He would inspire them. I shall never cease to recommend you in my prayers, and always beseech Him to assist you in your desire of dying holily. You have quitted the world; and what object was worthy to detain you there? Lift up your eyes always to Him to whom you have consecrated the rest of your days. Life upon this earth is misery. The very necessities to which your body is subject here are matter of affliction to a saint. "Lord," said the Royal Prophet, "deliver me from my necessities!" They are wretched who do not know themselves for such, and yet they are more wretched who know their misery, and do not hate the corruption of the age. What fools are men to engage themselves to earthly things! They will be undeceived one day, and will know but too late how much they have been to blame in loving such false good. Persons truly pious do not thus mistake; they are disengaged from all sensual pleasures, and raise their desires to heaven. Begin, Héloïse; put your design in execution without delay; you have yet time enough to work out your salvation. Love Christ, and despise yourself for His sake. He would possess your heart, and be the sole object of your sighs and tears; seek for no comfort but in Him. If you do not free yourself from me, you will fall with me; but if you quit me and give up yourself to Him, you will be steadfast and immovable. If you force the Lord to forsake you, you will fall into distress; but if you be ever faithful to Him, you will be always in joy. Magdalen wept, as thinking the Lord had forsaken her. But Martha said, "See, the Lord calls you." Be diligent in your duty, and obey faithfully the motions of His grace, and Jesus will remain always with you. . . .

I hope, Héloïse, that after having deplored the irregularities of your past life, you will die, as the prophet prayed, the "death of the righteous." Ah, how few are there who make their end after this manner! And why? It is because there are so few who love the cross of Christ. Every one would be saved, but few will use those means which religion prescribes. And yet as we can be saved by nothing but the cross, why then do we refuse to bear it? Hath not our Saviour borne it before us, and died for us, to the end that we might also bear it, and desire to die also? All the saints have been afflicted, and our Saviour Himself did not pass one hour of His life without some sorrow. Hope not therefore to be exempted from sufferings. The cross, Héloïse, is always at hand, but take care that you do not bear it with regret, for by so doing you will make it more heavy, and you will be oppressed by it unprofitably. On the contrary, if you bear it with affection and courage, all your sufferings will create in you a holy confidence, whereby you will find comfort in God. Hear our Saviour, who says, "My child, renounce yourself, take up your cross, and follow me." Oh, Héloïse! do you doubt! Is not your soul ravished at so saving a command? Are you deaf to His voice? are you insensible to words so full of kindness? Beware, Héloïse, of refusing a husband who demands you, and is more to be feared, if you slight his affection, than any profane lover. Provoked at your contempt and ingratitude he will turn his love into anger, and make you feel his vengeance. How will you sustain His presence, when you shall stand before His tribunal! He will reproach you for having despised His grace; He will represent to you His sufferings for you. What answer can you make? He will say to you, "Go, you proud creature, dwell in everlasting flames. I separated you from the world to purify you in solitude, and you did not second my design. I endeavored to save you, and you took pains to destroy yourself; go, wretch, and take the portion of the reprobates."

Oh, Héloïse, prevent these terrible words, and avoid by a holy course the punishment prepared for sinners. I dare not give you a description of those dreadful torments which are the consequences of a life of guilt. I am filled with horror, when they offer themselves to my imagination; and yet, Héloïse, I can conceive nothing which can reach the tortures of the damned. The fire which we see upon earth is but the shadow of that which burns them; and without enumerating their endless pains, the loss of God which they feel increases all their torments. Can anyone sin who is persuaded of this? My God! Can we dare to offend Thee? Though the riches of Thy mercy could not engage us to love Thee, the dread of being thrown into such an abyss of misery should restrain us from doing any thing which might displease Thee!

I question not, Héloïse, but you will hereafter apply yourself in good earnest to the business of your salvation; this ought to be your whole concern. Banish me therefore for ever from your heart; it is the best advice I can give you; for the remembrance of a person we have loved criminally cannot but be hurtful, whatever advances we have made in the ways of virtue. When you have extirpated your unhappy inclination toward me, the practice of every virtue will become easy; and when at last your life is comfortable to that of Christ, death will be desirable to you. Your soul will joyfully leave this body, and direct its flight to heaven. Then you will appear with confidence before your Saviour; you will not read characters of your reprobation written in the Book of Life; but you will hear your Saviour say, "Come, partake of my glory, and enjoy the eternal reward I have appointed for those virtues you have practiced."

Farewell, Héloïse! This is the last advice of your dear Abelard! This last time, let me persuade you to follow the holy rules of the gospel. Heaven grant that your heart, once so sensible of my love, may now yield to be directed by my zeal! May the idea of your loving Abelard, always present to your mind, be now changed into the image of Abelard truly penitent; and may you shed as many tears for your salvation, as you have done during the course of our misfortunes!

HÉLOÏSE TO ABELARD

A consolatory letter of yours to a friend happened some days since to fall into my hands; my knowledge of the writing and my love of the hand gave me the curiosity to open it. In justification of the liberty I took, I flattered myself I might claim a sovereign privilege over everything which came from you. Nor was I scrupulous to break through the rules of good breeding when I was to hear news of Abelard. But how dear did my curiosity cost me! What disturbance did it occasion, and how surprised I was to find the whole letter filled with a particular and melancholy account of our misfortunes! I met with my name a hundred times; I never saw it without fear, some heavy calamity always followed it. I saw yours too, equally unhappy. These mournful but dear remembrances put my heart into such violent motion that I thought it was too much to offer comfort to a friend for a few slight disgraces, by such extraordinary means as the representation of our sufferings and revolutions. What reflections did I not make! I began to consider the whole afresh, and perceived myself pressed with the same weight of grief as when we first began to be miserable. Though length of time ought to have closed up my wounds, yet the seeing them described by your hand was sufficient to make them all open and bleed afresh. Nothing can ever blot from my memory what you have suffered in defense of your writings. I cannot help thinking of the rancorous malice of Alberce and Lotulf. A cruel uncle and an injured lover will always be present to my aching sight. I shall never forget what enemies your learning, and what envy your glory raised against you. I shall never forget your reputation, so justly acquired, torn to pieces and blasted by the inexorable cruelty of pseudo pretenders to science. Was not your treatise of Divinity condemned to be burnt? Were you not threatened with perpetual imprisonment? In vain you urged in your defense that your enemies imposed upon you opinions quite different from your meanings.

O think of me—do not forget me—remember my love and fidelity and constancy: love me as your mistress, cherish me as your child, your sister, your wife! Remember I still love you, and yet strive to avoid loving you. What a terrible saying is this! I shake with horror, and my heart revolts against what I say. I shall blot all my paper with tears. I end my long letter wishing you, if you desire it (would to Heaven I could!) forever adieu!

MAGNA CARTA

The Magna Carta was a contract between King John of England and his nobles (or "liegemen") in which the King agreed to recognize certain rights and liberties of the nobility. In return the nobles accepted certain obligations to the king. What were some of these rights and obligations? Can you tell from these provisions what some of the noble's complaints had been? Did the signing of this agreement in 1215 improve the position of the common people, women, or foreigners? What does the document tell you about English society in the early thirteenth century?

John, by the grace of God, King of England, Lord of Ireland, Duke of Normandy and Aquitaine, and Count of Anjou: To the Archbishops, Bishops, Abbots, Earls, Barons, Justiciaries, Foresters, Sheriffs, Reeves, Ministers, and all Bailiffs and others, his faithful subjects, Greeting. Know ye that in the presence of God, and for the health of Our soul, and the souls of Our ancestors and heirs, to the honor of God, and the exaltation of Holy Church, and amendment of Our Kingdom, by the advice of Our reverend Fathers, Stephen, Archbishop of Canterbury, Primate of all England, and Cardinal of the Holy Roman Church; Henry, Archbishop of Dublin; William of London, Peter of Winchester, Jocelin of Bath and Glastonbury, Hugh of Lincoln, Walter of Worcester, William of Coventry, and Benedict of Rochester, Bishops; Master Pandulph, the Pope's subdeacon and familiar; Brother Aymeric, Master of the Knights of the Temple in England; and the noble persons, William Marshal, Earl of Pembroke; William, Earl of Salisbury; William, Earl of Warren; William, Earl of Arundel; Alan de Galloway, Constable of Scotland; Warin Fitz-Gerald, Peter Fitz-Herbert, Hubert de Burgh, Seneschal of Poitou, Hugh de Neville, Matthew Fitz-Herbert, Thomas

From *Magna Carta*, translated by A. E. Dick Howard. Copyright © 1964 by The University Press of Virginia. Reprinted by permission.

Basset, Alan Basset, Philip Daubeny, Robert de Roppelay, John Marshal, John Fitz-Hugh, and others, Our liegemen:

1. We have, in the first place, granted to God, and by this Our present Charter confirmed for Us and Our heirs forever—That the English Church shall be free and enjoy her rights in their integrity and her liberties untouched. And that We will this so to be observed appears from the fact that We of Our own free will, before the outbreak of the dissensions between Us and Our barons, granted, confirmed, and procured to be confirmed by Pope Innocent III the freedom of elections, which is considered most important and necessary to the English Church, which Charter We will both keep Ourself and will it to be kept with good faith by Our heirs forever. We have also granted to all the free men of Our kingdom, for Us and Our heirs forever, all the liberties underwritten, to have and to hold to them and their heirs of Us and Our heirs.

2. If any of Our earls, barons, or others who hold of Us in chief by knight's service shall die, and at the time of his death his heir shall be of full age and owe a relief [a form of tax], he shall have his inheritance by ancient relief; to wit, the heir or heirs of an earl of an entire earl's barony, £100; the heir or heirs of a baron of an entire barony, £100; the heir or heirs of a knight of an entire knight's fee, 100s. at the most; and he that owes less shall give less, according to the ancient custom of fees.

3. If, however, any such heir shall be under age and in ward, he shall, when he comes of age, have his inheritance without relief or fine.

4. The guardian of the land of any heir thus under age shall take therefrom only reasonable issues, customs, and services, without destruction or waste of men or property; and if We shall have committed the wardship of any such land to the sheriff or any other person answerable to Us for the issues thereof, and he commit destruction or waste, We will take an amends from him, and the land shall be committed to two lawful and discreet men of that fee, who shall be answerable for the issues to Us or to whomsoever We shall have assigned them. And if We shall give or sell the wardship of any such land to anyone, and he commit destruction or waste upon it, he shall lose the wardship, which shall be committed to two lawful and discreet men of that fee, who shall, in like manner, be answerable unto Us as has been aforesaid.

5. The guardian, so long as he shall have the custody of the land, shall keep up and maintain the houses, parks, fishponds, pools, mills, and other things pertaining thereto, out of the issues of the same, and shall restore the whole to the heir when he comes of age, stocked with ploughs and tillage, according as the season may require and the issues of the land can reasonably bear.

6. Heirs shall be married without loss of station, and the marriage shall be made known to the heir's nearest of kin before it be contracted.

7. A widow, after the death of her husband, shall immediately and without difficulty have her marriage portion and inheritance. She shall not give anything for her marriage portion, dower, or inheritance which she and her husband held on the day of his death, and she may remain in her husband's house for forty days after his death, within which time her dower shall be assigned to her.

8. No widow shall be compelled to marry so long as she has a mind to live without a husband, provided, however, that she give security that she will not marry without Our assent, if she holds of Us, or that of the lord of whom she holds, if she holds of another.

9. Neither We nor Our bailiffs shall seize any land or rent for any debt so long as the debtor's chattels are sufficient to discharge the same; nor shall the debtor's sureties be distrained so long as the debtor is able to pay the debt. If the debtor fails to pay, not having the means to pay, then the sureties shall answer the debt, and, if they desire, they shall hold the debtor's lands and rents until they have received satisfaction of the debt which they have paid for him, unless the debtor can show that he has discharged his obligation to them.

10. If anyone who has borrowed from the Jews any sum of money, great or small, dies before the debt has been paid, the heir shall pay no interest on the debt so long as he remains under age, of whomsoever he may hold. If the debt shall fall into Our hands, We will take only the principal sum named in the bond.

12. No scutage [a payment in place of a personal service] or aid shall be imposed in Our kingdom unless by common counsel thereof, except to ransom Our person, make Our eldest son a knight, and once to marry Our eldest daughter, and for these only a reasonable aid shall be levied. So shall it be with regard to aids from the City of London.

13. The City of London shall have all her ancient liberties and free customs, both by land and water. Moreover, We will and grant that all other cities, boroughs, towns, and ports shall have their liberties and free customs.

14. For obtaining the common counsel of the kingdom concerning the assessment of aids (other than in the three cases aforesaid) or of scutage, We will cause to be summoned, severally by Our letters, the archbishops, bishops, abbots, earls, and great barons; We will also cause to be summoned, generally, by Our sheriffs and bailiffs, all those who hold lands directly of Us, to meet on a fixed day, but with at least forty days' notice, and at a fixed place. In all letters of such summons We will explain the cause thereof. The summons being thus made, the business shall proceed on the day appointed, according to the advice of those who shall be present, even though not all the persons summoned have come.

15. We will not in the future grant permission to any man to levy an aid upon his free men, except to ransom his person, make his eldest son

a knight, and once to marry his eldest daughter, and on each of these occasions only a reasonable aid shall be levied.

16. No man shall be compelled to perform more service for a knight's fee or other free tenement than is due therefrom.

17. Common Pleas shall not follow Our Court, but shall be held in some certain place.

20. A free man shall be amerced [fined] for a small fault only according to the measure thereof, and for a great crime according to its magnitude, saving his position; and in like manner a merchant saving his trade, and a villein [serf] saving his tillage, if they should fall under Our mercy. None of these amercements shall be imposed except by the oath of honest men of the neighborhood.

21. Earls and barons shall be amerced only by their peers, and only in proportion to the measure of the offense.

22. No amercement shall be imposed upon a clerk's [clergyman's] lay property, except after the manner of the other persons aforesaid, and without regard to the value of his ecclesiastical benefice.

23. No village or person shall be compelled to build bridges over rivers except those bound by ancient custom and law to do so.

28. No constable or other of Our bailiffs shall take corn or other chattels of any man without immediate payment, unless the seller voluntarily consents to postponement of payment.

29. No constable shall compel any knight to give money in lieu of castle-guard when the knight is willing to perform it in person or (if reasonable cause prevents him from performing it himself) by some other fit man. Further, if We lead or send him into military service, he shall be quit of castle-guard for the time he shall remain in service by Our command.

30. No sheriff or other of Our bailiffs, or any other man, shall take the horses or carts of any free man for carriage without the owner's consent.

31. Neither We nor Our bailiffs will take another man's wood for Our castles or for any other purpose without the owner's consent.

35. There shall be one measure of wine throughout Our kingdom, and one of ale, and one measure of corn, to wit, the London quarter, and one breadth of dyed cloth, russets, and haberjets [types of cloth—Ed.] to wit, two cells within the selvages. As with measures so shall it also be with weights.

38. In the future no bailiff shall upon his own unsupported accusation put any man to trial without producing credible witnesses to the truth of the accusation.

39. No free man shall be taken, imprisoned, disseised [dispossessed], outlawed, banished, or in any way destroyed, nor will We proceed against or prosecute him, except by the lawful judgment of his peers and by the law of the land.

40. To no one will We sell, to none will We deny or delay, right or justice.

41. All merchants shall have safe conduct to go and come out of and into England, and to stay in and travel through England by land and water for purposes of buying and selling, free of illegal tolls, in accordance with ancient and just customs, except, in time of war, such merchants as are of a country at war with Us. If any such be found in Our dominion at the outbreak of war, they shall be attached, without injury to their persons or goods, until it be known to Us or Our Chief Justiciary how Our merchants are being treated in the country at war with Us, and if Our merchants be safe there, then theirs shall be safe with Us.

42. In the future it shall be lawful (except for a short period in time of war, for the common benefit of the realm) for anyone to leave and return to Our kingdom safely and securely by land and water, saving his fealty to Us. Excepted are those who have been imprisoned or outlawed according to the law of the land, people of the country at war with Us, and merchants, who shall be dealt with as aforesaid.

52. If anyone has been disseised or deprived by Us, without the legal judgment of his peers, of lands, castles, liberties, or rights, We will immediately restore the same, and if any dispute shall arise thereupon, the matter shall be decided by judgment of the twenty-five barons mentioned below in the clause for securing the peace. With regard to all those things, however, of which any man was disseised or deprived, without the legal judgment of his peers, by King Henry Our Father or Our Brother King Richard, and which remain in Our warranty, We shall have respite during the term commonly allowed to the Crusaders, except as to those matters on which a plea had arisen, or an inquisition had been taken by Our command, prior to Our taking the Cross. Immediately after Our return from Our pilgrimage, or if by chance We should remain behind from it, We will at once do full justice.

14. Mongol Eurasia

THE IMPACT OF TURKISH AND MONGOL CONQUESTS 1000–1500

WILLIAM H. McNEILL

The explosion of the Mongol and Turkish nomads from the grasslands of Eurasia after A.D. 1000 had a decisive effect on the Christian, Islamic, Indian, and Chinese civilizations of the continent. In this selection, the modern historian William H. McNeill looks at some of the ways these invasions changed the balance of Eurasia.

What were the Mongol and Turkish invasions? What changes did they bring about across Eurasia? What effects did they have on Orthodox Christendom and traditional Chinese civilization?

Close ties between steppe nomads and the civilized world had been a prominent feature of the centuries before A.D. 1000. During the ensuing five hundred years, this led to a series of infiltrations and conquests that brought Turkish and Mongol rulers to China, the Middle East, India, and eastern Europe. Civilized victims and subjects reacted in different ways.

The Moslems altered the emphasis and internal balance of their society and civilization in a far-reaching and strikingly successful fashion. In effect, the Moslems captured the military energy of the steppe peoples for themselves. Turkish and (much less important) Mongol recruits gave Islam a new cutting edge that established it as the ruling faith in all of India and in eastern Europe. Simultaneously, merchants and wandering holy men carried the religion of Mohammed to southeast Asia and through east and west Africa as well, and even penetrated some of China's western provinces.

The Chinese found nothing to admire in the novelties brought to their attention by Mongol conquerors, and at the first propitious moment they rallied to cast off what was always felt to be an alien and barbarian yoke. Hence the episode of Mongol rule (the Yuan dynasty, 1260–1368) left remarkably few traces behind, unless the Ming dynasty's (1368–1644) enhanced determination to value old and authentically Chinese culture can be attributed to their reaction against Mongol rule.

The great majority of Indians and orthodox Christians who found themselves under the government of Islamized Turks remained faithful to their respective religious traditions. Nevertheless, prolonged geographical intermingling provoked a good deal of interchange between the rival religious communities, despite official efforts by guardians of the faith on each side to maintain the purity of their respective versions of theological truth.

THE TURKISH INFILTRATION

Before examining civilized reactions in more detail it will be well to recapitulate the course of world events. In A.D. 1000 Turkish-speaking tribes lived throughout the middle reaches of the steppe, from the Altai mountains as far west as southern Russia. In eastern Iran, extensive interpenetration between Moslem towns and cultivators and Turkish nomads had already occurred, and many Turkish tribes had accepted Islam, usually in a somewhat casual and superficial fashion. The Iranian barons who for so many centuries had held the steppe nomads at bay ceased to be effective after about A.D. 850 or 900. The reasons are obscure, but it seems possible that many moved into towns, acquired a far richer culture than their forefathers had known, and in the process lost their taste for war and hard knocks, leaving that role to Turkish mercenaries, who presently found themselves in a position to hold the Moslem heartlands of Iran, Iraq, and Syria up for ransom.

When, therefore, Turkish mercenaries and tribesmen started everywhere to dominate the political life of Islam (after about A.D. 900) the newcomers already knew a good deal about both Persian and Arab versions of Moslem culture. Yet the Turks maintained their own languages and a certain sense of military camaraderie against the rest of Islamic society. Their rule was disorderly. Detribalized military adventures competed with the unstable power of clan leaders, whose followers regularly deserted tribal discipline after a few years in a civilized environment. Rivalries and alliances among such precariously situated rulers were unusually fragile and created an endless political kaleidoscope throughout the heartland of Islam.

Nevertheless, the newcomers extended Moslem frontiers very substantially. Penetration deep into India began with massive raids launched by Mohammed of Ghazni in the year 1000. Within three centuries only the southern part of that sub-continent had escaped Moslem conquest; and in 1565 the south capitulated also when the empire of Vijayanager fell before a coalition of Moslem princes. Turkish successes against Christendom were also very great. After the battle of

Manzikert (1071) the Byzantines lost control of the interior of Asia Minor to Seljuk Turks. Simultaneously other Turkish tribes (Kipchaks) pressed across what is now the Ukraine, where they cut off easy communication between Byzantium and freshly Christianized Russia. These heavy blows helped to precipitate the First Crusade (1096–99); but despite its dramatic success, this and later crusades failed to check the Turkish advance. On the contrary, when the Fourth Crusade actually attacked Constantinople and captured and sacked the city (1204), the weakness of the Byzantine state was advertised to all the world. Partial recovery—there was a Greek emperor again in Constantinople after 1261—was not sufficient to check the force of Italian commercial exploitation on the one hand and Turkish military assault on the other. The Ottoman Turks reaped the ultimate victory. They won their first foothold in Europe in 1354 by crossing the Dardanelles and seizing the peninsula of Gallipoli. After 1389, when they defeated the Serbians at the battle of Kossovo, the Turks won military supremacy in the Balkans. Not until 1453, however, when they conquered Constantinople and made it the capital of their empire, was the last trace of Byzantine power erased from the face of the earth.

THE MONGOL CONQUEST

This vast tide of Turkish advance into India and Europe was punctuated in the thirteenth century by a sudden storm emanating from Mongolia. The founder of Mongol greatness was Genghis Khan (ruled 1206–27). In his youth an all but helpless refugee from local enemies, Genghis succeeded in welding together a vast military confederacy among the peoples of the steppe. He then raided successfully in every direction— southward into China, westward against the Moslems of Iran and Iraq, and against the Christians of Russia as well. On his death the empire was divided among his four sons. They transformed the massive raiding of Genghis' time into a somewhat more stable form of political rule. For some time, there continued to be effective co-operation among the separate parts of the vast empire. Leadership rested, according to Mongol custom, with Genghis' youngest son and that son's heirs. They ruled Mongolia and China and commanded nearly the whole of the Mongol army.

In Genghis' time the Mongol tribesmen were pagan shamanists. They treated their human victims much as they treated their animals— tending or slaughtering them as convenience might dictate. But once encamped amid more cultivated peoples, the Mongols did what every other nomadic conqueror had done: they quickly took on the color of their subjects' civilization. In the Middle East and Russia this meant the acceptance of Islam. In China, matters were different, for the Mongol emperors could not afford to see the armed forces upon which their power depended dissolve into the Chinese mass. The effort to hold themselves aloof from the Chinese led the Mongols to accept Tibetan Lamaism as the preferred religion of state, although a grand mixture of faiths—Christian, Moslem, shamanist, and others—continued to be represented at court. Yet the penalty of remaining distinct from the Chinese was vulnerability to native reaction, which brought the Ming dynasty to power only a century and a half after Genghis had launched his raids.

Mongol rule therefore constituted no more than an episode in China's long history. In the Middle East and Russia almost the same was true, for after an initial anti-Moslem policy the Mongols not only accepted Islam (Russia, 1257; Persia, 1295) but rapidly assimilated themselves to the Turkish community, which was already dominant everywhere on the central and western steppe. There were too few Mongols and their culture was too crude to permit any other result. Hence in the fourteenth and fifteenth centuries Islamized Turkish warriors, often led by captains who claimed descent from Genghis Khan, again pressed forward against Christendom and Hindustan. The Moslem world had by then largely recovered from the set-back wrought by the pagan Mongol conquest of the thirteenth century. Baghdad, however, and the irrigation system that made Iraq fertile, were not restored. Mongol destruction had been too great. As a result, the former seat of the caliphate remained in ruins until the twentieth century.

THE OTTOMAN EMPIRE

By far the most durable and important of the new states that arose in the course of this renewed Turkish offensive was the Ottoman empire. It originated as a small frontier principality in northwestern Asia Minor. Turkish warriors flocked to the service of the Ottoman sultan from all over the Moslem world, because his raids against Christian territory made religious merit and heroic exercise of violence coincide, as was true nowhere else in the Moslem world. Under these circumstances territorial advance became rapid, especially after 1354, when the Turks made their first permanent lodgment across the straits in Europe. Presently, the Sultan faced difficulty in commanding the loyalty and obedience of his followers, who had been assigned conquered lands on the usual feudal pattern. The Ottoman rulers met this difficulty by expanding their personal household into a standing army. This became the famous janissary (i.e. "new troops") corps. Its members, together with the officers who commanded them, were legally classed as slaves. So were the specially trained and selected men who went out into the provinces as agents of the Sultan and took command of local Moslem landowners and warriors when they were called up for active service with the Sultan in war. Since these special slave commanders were backed up by the janissary corps and by the Sultan himself, their commands were usually obeyed. The Ottoman state therefore had at its disposal both an effective standing army, the janissaries, and an obedient feudal army of Turkish warriors.

Personnel for the Sultan's slave family numbered several thousand. At first, war captives provided most of the needed manpower, supplemented by purchases from commercial slave dealers. But soon this method of recruitment proved inadequate. The Turkish Sultan therefore fell back upon rough-and-ready conscription among the Christian villages of the remote Balkans. Thus it happened that young men born as Serb, Greek, or Albanian peasants in the western mountain zone of the Balkan peninsula provided a strategically decisive element in the military and administrative cadres of the Ottoman empire.

No other Moslem state achieved such a remarkable and effective internal organization; and none played anything like the role in world affairs that the Ottoman empire was to do.

•   •   •

ORTHODOX CHRISTENDOM

The separation between Latin (Roman Catholic) and Greek (Orthodox) Christendom achieved formal and lasting definition in 1054, when the pope and the patriarch of Constantinople anathematized each other, thus creating a schism which has endured until the present. The occasion of the quarrel was a difference of opinion about the proper phrasing of the Apostles' Creed; but the distinction between the two halves of Christendom ran very deep, and the gap widened when a new and vigorous civilization began to arise in western Europe, in which the Greek Orthodox had no real share. Instead, as the Latin west increased in wealth, power, culture, and self-confidence, eastern Christendom became one of the victims of Latin expansive energy.

The Orthodox world's loss of Asia Minor and of southern Russia to Turkish invaders coincided with a similar double thrust from the west. Italian merchant traders came by sea; Norman knights seized southern Italy (by 1071) and Sicily (by 1091) from the Byzantines, and then crossed the Adriatic to march overland against Constantinople. Byzantine diplomacy was able to parry this first thrust from the west by diverting the formidable "Franks" to the Holy Land, where they could expend their ferocity on Byzantium's other dangerous enemy, the Turks. The result was the First Crusade, 1096–99. Later, however, the Greeks were less fortunate. The climax came in 1204 when the Fourth

Crusade actually captured the city of Constantine, and left behind a short-lived Latin empire of the Levant.

From the point of view of Orthodox Christians, Moslem Turks were definitely preferable to Latin Christians. The Latins insisted on trying to force the Orthodox Christians to accept their version of Christian doctrine at the expense of the immutable truths of Orthodoxy. The Moslems, on the contrary, were prepared to allow Christians of whatever persuasion to continue to follow their accustomed rites. Moreover, the theologians of the church officially classified Islam as Christian heresy: hence Moslem error was really no worse theologically than Latin schism. In addition, the Ottoman Turks, when they first appeared in the Balkans, were much less oppressive tax gatherers than their Christian predecessors had been. The Turks, indeed, in accordance with the Sacred Law gave their Christian subjects far wider local autonomy than they were likely to enjoy under any Christian ruler. Every consideration, therefore, predisposed the Orthodox Christians to opt for Turkish Moslems against Latin Christians if and when choice between the two became necessary. The option expired in 1453 when Constantinople fell to the Turks. Nearly the same factors applied further north in the Russian forests, where such a ruler as Alexander Nevsky (d. 1263) resisted Latin conquest heroically and then tamely submitted to the Mongols.

· · ·

The northern offshoot of Orthodox Christendom, Holy Russia, underwent a slow but very significant development during the period of Mongol rule (1240–1480). Agriculture crept deep into the forest, back from the river banks where the population had first congregated. Little by little great areas of ground were cleared for farming. This allowed a comparatively numerous, though extremely poor, peasantry to establish itself despite the inhospitable soil and severe climate.

Politically, the Mongols were content to farm out taxes, first to corporations of central Asian merchants and then to native Russian princes, of whom the Grand Duke of Moscow became the chief. As agent for a harsh though distant taskmaster, the Grand Duke of Moscow created an administrative bureaucracy of tax gatherers. The result was that in 1480, when Ivan III repudiated Mongol suzerainty, he had a ready-made administrative machine at his command. Moscow thus became the only great and independent Orthodox state. Russian churchmen soon developed the idea that Moscow was the Third Rome, succeeding to Constantinople as Constantinople had succeeded the first Rome on the Tiber, because only in Russia had Orthodoxy remained pure and undefiled. Ever since then the notion that Russia was uniquely chosen for the special mission of guarding the true faith on earth has never ceased to play a part in Russian public life, not least since the Communist revolution of 1917.

CHINA—THE TRIUMPH OF TRADITION

As already explained, the outward appearance of Chinese civilization was remarkably little affected by the episode of Mongol domination. Neo-Confucianism attained its full development under the later Sung, when the greatest philosopher of this school, Chu Hsi (1130–1200), flourished. But the whole effort of Chu Hsi and his fellow literati was to remain faithful to the ancients, as Confucius himself had tried to be. Hence innovation was never consciously admitted, whether in thought or in art, in manners or in government.

Nevertheless, during the Mongol period important socio-economic changes put considerable strain upon the traditional frame of Chinese civilization. In the end, the old Confucian forms triumphed decisively, but this should not blind us to the importance of the forces which nearly transformed Chinese society. The late Sung and Mongol periods saw a great development in trade and commerce, based upon regional specialization within China and upon far-ranging export and import up and down the coast. Fukien and adjacent parts of the south China coast were among the most active centers of this development.

Early in the Ming period (1368–1644) official organization was brought to the maritime enterprise of south China. Results were spectacular. Between 1405 and 1433 a court eunuch named Cheng-ho launched a series of expeditions into the Indian Ocean, in the course of which truly imperial fleets of several hundred vessels visited all the strategic gateways to the southern seas—Malacca, Ceylon, Calicut, and even Hormuz at the mouth of the Persian Gulf—and temporarily established Chinese control over most of these places. Then the Ming emperor ordered the expeditions stopped, and forbade Chinese subjects from building sea-going vessels or leaving the country. Court intrigues between rival cliques may have had something to do with this decision, so pregnant for the future commercial and imperial balance of power in Asia. But basically the Ming rulers, from their capital at Peking near the ever-dangerous Mongol border, felt that imperial resources should not be squandered on such distant enterprises when the need for protection against the nomads required all the strength the government could muster.

This deliberate abdication from an active role in the southern seas condemned Chinese overseas colonies to speedy decay. Mastery of the seas passed to Japanese and Malay pirates, who soon made the coasts of China unsafe for peaceable shipping. From time to time they even succeeded in interrupting transport on the Grand Canal by penetrating inland along China's numerous waterways.

Merchants had always, of course, ranked as social parasites in Confucian estimation, whereas Mongols and other steppe peoples accorded them a much more dignified place in society. The trading community, which had prospered under barbarian protection, was therefore particularly disadvantaged by the Ming restoration of Neo-Confucian orthodoxy. Yet the failure of the mercantile interest to hold its own after the really great advances made in Sung and Mongol times seems, at least to a Westerner, to require further explanation. The fact that Chinese agriculture also underwent a very great development may help to explain why the conservative Confucian ideal prevailed. About A.D. 1000 new varieties of rice were introduced that could ripen quickly enough to permit double cropping on well-watered land. Even more important, this early ripening rice could mature successfully on hilly ground where water was available for the paddy fields only during a short period of the spring run-off. The total agricultural productivity of China was thereby greatly enlarged, especially in the far south, where hilly ground, previously unsuited to rice growing, prevailed. Hence, as trade and commerce prospered, so did the landowning gentry. Their numbers and weight in society presumably increased more or less equally with the increase in the importance of merchants and artisans. Then, with the overthrow of the Mongol rulers who had been special patrons and protectors of merchants (witness Marco Polo), the stage was set for the native Ming dynasty first to organize and then officially to throttle China's overseas trade.

The social dominance of the gentry class meant that even such potentially disturbing inventions as gunpowder (reported in Chinese sources from about 1100), printing (invented 756), and the magnetic compass (first mentioned early twelfth century) were kept under control and used simply to strengthen the existing social order. Printing, for example, widened the circle of Confucian literati; it was not employed to bring unorthodox novelties to public attention, as happened so dramatically in Reformation Europe. Gunpowder, similarly, made suppression of local warlords easier than before and allowed the imperial government to maintain a more or less effective central control over all of China (with only a few brief periods of breakdown) from the time the Ming dynasty completed the expulsion of the Mongols until 1911. Nothing could be more traditional. The equally traditional, high-handed yet effective, fashion with which the Ming court warded off the distraction of sea-borne enterprise, which use of the compass and other navigational improvements permitted, has already been mentioned.

Chinese culture and institutions had, in short, attained such inner perfection and balance that nothing short of wholesale social breakdown, of a sort that did not occur in China until the twentieth century, sufficed to make more than superficial, transitory impression upon the bearers of the Chinese learned tradition. The myth of immutability, so eagerly accepted by nineteenth-century Europeans, fed upon this fact, overlooking earlier times and aspects of Chinese society which continued to alter, even when the government and official culture remained frozen to the ideal of Confucian propriety.

A CHINESE TAOIST TRAVELS TO GENGHIS KHAN

Ch'ang Ch'un, a learned Taoist priest, was invited by Genghis Khan to visit the court of the Mongols "10,000 li" (about 3300 miles) to the west. In 1219 he set out with an escort of twenty Mongol warriors and nineteen of his own followers, including his pupil, Li Chih-Ch'ang, who wrote the following account of the trip to Mongolia, Tashkent, Samarkand and Perwan (just north of Kabul) in Afganistan.

What does the travel account tell you about the world of the Mongols? Why do you think Ch'ang Ch'un was invited? You might try to trace the trip on a map. What would it have been like to make such a trip?

On the first day of the fourth month (April 24) we reached Prince Tämügä's encampment. By now the ice was beginning to melt and there was a faint touch of colour in the grass. When we arrived a marriage was being celebrated in the camp. From five hundred *li* round the headmen of the tribes had come, with presents of mares' milk, to join in the feast. The black wagons and felt tents stood in rows; there must have been several thousand of them.

On the seventh day the Master interviewed the Great Prince, who questioned him concerning the possibility of extending one's span of life. The Master said that only those who had fasted and observed certain rules could be told of these things. It was agreed that he should receive instruction on the day of the full moon. But by then heavy snow was falling and the matter was overlooked. Or rather, His Highness seemed to have changed his mind, for he now said that it would be improper for him to anticipate his father in receiving instruction from one whom the Great Khan had been at pains to summon from so great

From *The Travels of an Alchemist* by Li Chih-Ch'ang. Translated with an introduction by Arthur Waley. London: Routledge & Klegan Paul, Broadway Travel Series, 1931.

a distance. But he ordered A-li-hsien to bring the Master back to him after the interview with the Emperor was over.

In this country it is cold in the morning and hot in the evening; there are many plants with yellow flowers. The river flows to the north-east. On both banks grow many tall willows. The Mongols use them to make the framework of their tents. After sixteen days' traveling we came to a point where the Kerulen makes a loop to the northwest, skirting some mountains. We therefore could not follow it to its source, but turned south-west, into the Yüĕrh-li postroad. Here the Mongols we met were delighted to see the Master, saying they had been expecting him since the year before. . . .

The peaks of the great mountains were now gradually becoming visible. From this point onwards, as we traveled west, the country remained hilly and well-inhabited. The people live in black wagons and white tents; they are all herdsmen and hunters. Their clothes are made of hides and fur; they live on meat and curdled milk. The men wear their hair in two plaits that hang behind the ears. The married women wear a head-dress of birch-bark, some two feet high. This they generally cover with a black woollen stuff; but some of the richer women use red silk. The end (of this head-dress) is like a duck; they call it *ku-ku*. They are in constant fear of people knocking against it, and are obliged to go backwards and crouching through the doorways of their tents.

On the 27th day of the eighth month (September 15th) we reached the foot of the Yin Shan. Here some Uighurs came out to meet us, and presently we reached a small town. The ruler of the place brought us grape-wine, choice fruits, large cakes, huge onions, and strips of Persian linen, a foot for each person. . . .

Further west is the large town of Beshbalig. The king's officers, with many of the nobles and people, and some hundred Buddhist and Taoist (? Manichean) priests came in great state a long way out of the town to meet us. The Buddhist priests were all dressed in brown. The head-dresses and robes of the Taoists were quite different from those worn in China.

On the eighteenth day of the eleventh month (December 3rd, 1221) after crossing a great river, we reached the northern outskirts of the mighty city of Samarkand. The Civil Governor his Highness I-la, together with the Mongol and local authorities, came to meet us outside the town. They brought wine and set up a great number of tents. Here we brought our wagons to a stop. . . .

The town is built along canals. As no rain falls during the summer and autumn, two rivers have been diverted so as to run along every street, thus giving a supply of water to all the inhabitants. Before the defeat of the Khwārizm Shah there was a fixed population here of more than

100,000 households; but now there is only about a quarter this number, of whom a very large proportion are native Hui-ho. But these people are quite unable to manage their fields and orchards for themselves, and are obliged to call in Chinese, Kitai and Tanguts. The administration of the town is also conducted by people of very various nationality. Chinese craftsmen are found everywhere. Within the city is a mound about a hundred feet high on which stands the Khwārizm Shah's new palace. . . .

The Governor gave a banquet in his honour, and sent ten pieces of gold brocade, but the Master would not receive them. After that he sent a monthly allowance of rice, corn-flour, salt, oil, fruits, vegetables and so on; he became every day more attentive and respectful. Noticing that the Master drank very little he begged to be allowed to press a hundred pounds of grapes and make him some new wine. But the Master answered: "I do need wine. But let me have the hundred pounds of grapes; they will enable me to entertain my visitors."

These grapes keep for a whole winter. We also saw peacocks and large elephants which come from India, several thousand *li* to the south-east.

At the end of the intercalary month (February 12th, 1222) the envoy and his horsemen returned from their reconnoitring. Liu Wēn reported to the Master that the Khan's second son (Chagatai) had advanced with his troops and repaired the damaged boats and bridges. The local bandits were dispersed. Ho-la, Pa-hai and others had been to the Prince's camp and informed him that the Master desired an audience with the Emperor. The prince replied that his father had proceeded to the south-east of the Great Snow Mountains (Hindukush), but that the snow in the mountain pass at present lay very deep for more than a hundred *li*, and it would be impossible to get through. The prince, however, pointed out that his own encampment lay directly on the route to the Emperor's, and invited the Master to stay with him, till a journey across the mountains was practicable.

Hence we traveled south-east, and towards evening halted near an ancient canal. On its banks grew reeds of a peculiar kind not found in China. The larger ones keep green all through the winter. Some of these we took and made into walking-sticks. Some we used that night to hold up the wagonshafts, and so strong were they that they did not break. On the small reeds the leaves fall off in winter and grow afresh in the spring. A little to the south, in the hills, there is a large bamboo with pith inside. This is used by the soldiers to make lances and spears. We also saw lizards about three feet long, blue-black in colour.

It was now the twenty-ninth of the third month (May 11th) and the Master made a poem. After four more days of traveling we reached the Khan's camp. He sent his high officer, Ho-la-po-tē to meet us. . . . When arrangements had been made for the Master's lodging, he at once presented himself to the Emperor, who expressed his gratitude, saying "Other rulers summoned you, but you would not go to them. And now you have come ten thousand *li* to see me. I take this as a high compliment."

The Master replied: "That I, a hermit of the mountains, should come at your Majesty's bidding was the will of Heaven." Genghis was delighted, begged him to be seated and ordered food to be served. Then he asked him: "Adept, what Medicine of Long Life have you brought me from afar?" The Master replied: "I have means of protecting life, but no elixir that will prolong it." The Emperor was pleased with his candour, and had two tents for the Master and his disciples set up to the east of his own. . . .

The weather was becoming very hot and the Emperor now moved to a high point on the Snow Mountains to escape the heat, and the Master accompanied him. The Emperor appointed the fourteenth of the fourth month (June 24th) as the day on which he would question the Master about the Way. This engagement was recorded by his state officers, Chinkai, Liu Wēn and A-li-hsien, as well as by three of his personal attendants. But just as the time was arriving, news came that the native mountain bandits were in insurrection. The Emperor was determined to deal with them himself, and put off the meeting till the first of the tenth month (November 5th). The Master begged that he might be allowed to return to his former quarters in the city. "Then," said the Khan, "you will have the fatigue of traveling all the way back here again." The Master said it was only a matter of twenty days' journey, and when the Khan objected that he had no one whom he could give him as an escort the Master suggested the envoy Yang A-kou. . . .

We crossed a great mountain where there is a "stone gate," the pillars of which look like tapering candles. Lying across them at the top is a huge slab of rock, which forms a sort of bridge. The stream below is very swift, and our horsemen in goading the pack-asses across lost many of them by drowning. On the banks of the stream were the carcases of other animals that had perished in the same way. The place is a frontier pass, which the troops had quite recently stormed. When we got out of the defile, the Master wrote two poems.

Now when he reached the Khan's camp, at the end of the third month the grass was green and trees everywhere in bloom, and the sheep and horses were well grown. But when with the Khan's permission he left, at the end of the fourth month, there was no longer a blade of grass or any vegetation. On this subject the Master wrote a set of verses.

MARCO POLO TRAVELS
TO KUBILAI KHAN

Marco Polo was born into a Venetian trading family around 1254. The family had already developed trading contacts with the Mongol Khans when Marco joined his father and uncle on a visit to China in 1271. Kubilai [Kublai] Khan, whom they visited at his capital Khan-balik (Beijing), was much more sophisticated than his ancestors, such as Genghis, who had conquered northern China. Kubilai combined the vigor and simplicity of his fathers with the humanitarian spirit of Buddhism and a unique vision in administering the Chinese bureaucracy. It was equally characteristic of him to sow the wild grasses of Mongolia in his palace gardens to remind him of the freedom of his youth and to discuss the finer points of theology with invited missionaries from all over the world.

Notice how different the world of Kubilai is from that of Genghis Khan. Judging from Marco Polo's description and comments, is the world of Kubilai Khan more, or less, developed than the Venice he knew? In what ways was it different?

Emperors and kings, dukes and marquises, counts, knights, and townsfolk, and all people who wish to know the various races of men and the peculiarities of the various regions of the world, take this book and have it read to you. Here you will find all the great wonders and curiosities of Greater Armenia and Persia, of the Tartars and of India, and of many other territories. Our book will relate them to you plainly in due order, as they were related by Messer Marco Polo, a wise and noble citizen of Venice, who has seen them with his own eyes. There is also much here that he has not seen but has heard from men of credit and veracity. We will set down things seen as seen, things heard as heard, so that our book may be an accurate record, free from any sort of fabrication. And all who read the book or hear it may do so with full confidence, because it contains nothing but the truth. . . .

Let me tell you next of the personal appearance of the Great Lord of Lords whose name is Kubilai Khan. He is a man of good stature, neither short nor tall but of moderate height. His limbs are well fleshed out and modelled in due proportion. His complexion is fair and ruddy like a rose, the eyes black and handsome, the nose shapely and set squarely in place.

He has four consorts who are all accounted his lawful wives; and his eldest son by any of these four has a rightful claim to be emperor on the death of the present Khan. They are called empresses, each by her own name. Each of these ladies holds her own court. None of them has less than 300 ladies in waiting, all of great beauty and charm. They have many eunuchs and many other men and women in attendance, so that each one of these ladies has in her court 10,000 persons. When he wishes to lie with one of his four wives, he invites her to his chamber; or sometimes he goes to his wife's chamber.

He also has many concubines, about whom I will tell you. There is a province inhabited by Tartars who are called Kungurat, which is also the name of their city. They are a very good-looking race with fair complexions. Every two years or so, according to his pleasure, the Great Khan sends emissaries to this province to select for him out of the most beautiful maidens, according to the standard of beauty which he lays down for them, some four or five hundred, more or less as he may decide. This is how the selection is made. When the emissaries arrive, they summon to their presence all the maidens of the province. And there valuers are deputed for the task. After inspecting and surveying every girl feature by feature, her hair, her face, her eyebrows, her mouth, her lips, and every other feature, to see whether they are well-formed and in harmony with her person, the valuers award to some a score of sixteen marks, to others seventeen, eighteen, or twenty, or more or less according to the degree of their beauty. And, if the Great Khan has ordered them to bring him all who score twenty marks, or perhaps twenty-one, according to the number ordered, these are duly brought. When they have come to his presence, he has them assessed a second time by other valuers, and then the thirty or forty with the highest score are selected for his chamber. These are first allotted, one by one, to the barons' wives, who are instructed to observe them carefully at night in their chambers, to make sure that they are virgins and not blemished or defective in any member, that they sleep sweetly without snoring, and that their breath is sweet and they give out no unpleasant odour. Then those who are approved are divided into groups of six, who serve the Khan for three days and three nights at a time in his chamber and his bed, ministering to all his needs. And he uses them according to his pleasure. After three days and nights, in come the next six damsels. And so they continue in rotation throughout the year. While some of the group are in attendance in their lord's chamber, the others are waiting in an ante-chamber hard by. If he is in need of anything from outside, such as food or drink, the damsels inside the chamber pass word to those outside, who immediately get it ready. In this way the Khan is served by no one except these damsels. As for the other damsels, who are rated at a lower score, they remain with the Khan's other women in the palace, where they are instructed in needle-work, glove-making, and other elegant accomplishments. When some nobleman is looking for a wife, the Great Khan gives him one of these damsels with a great dowry. And in this way he marries them all off honourably.

You must know that for three months in the year, December, January, and February, the Great Khan lives in the capital city of Cathay, whose name is Khan-balik. In this city he has his great palace, which I will now describe to you.

The palace is completely surrounded by a square wall, each side being a mile in length so that the whole circuit is four miles. It is a very thick wall and fully ten paces in height. It is all white-washed and battlemented. At each corner of this wall stands a large palace of great beauty and splendour, in which the Great Khan keeps his military stores. In the middle of each side is another palace resembling the corner palaces, so that round the whole circuit of the walls there are eight palaces, all serving as arsenals. Each is reserved for a particular type of munition. Thus, one contains saddles, bridles, stirrups, and other items of a horse's harness. In another are bows, bowstrings, quivers, arrows, and other requisites of archery. In a third are cuirasses, corselets, and other armour of boiled leather. And so with the rest.

In the southern front of this wall there are five gates. There is one great gate in the middle, which is never opened except when the Great Khan is leaving or entering. Next to this, one on either side, are two small gates, by which everyone else enters. There are also two more large gates, one near each corner, which are likewise used by other people.

Within this outer wall is another wall, somewhat greater in length than in breadth. In this also there are eight palaces, just like the others, and used in the same way to house military stores. It also has five gates in its southern front, corresponding to those in the outer wall. In each of the other sides it has one gate only; and so has the outer wall.

Within this wall is the Great Khan's palace, which I will now describe to you. It is the largest that was ever seen. It has no upper floor, but the basement on which it stands is raised ten palms above the level of the surrounding earth; and all round it there runs a marble wall level with the basement, two paces in thickness. The foundation of the palace lies within this wall, so that as much of the wall as projects beyond it forms a sort of terrace, on which men can walk right round and inspect the outside of the palace. At the outer edge of this wall is a fine gallery with columns, where men can meet and talk. At each face of the palace is a great marble staircase, ascending from ground level to the top of this marble wall, which affords an entry into the palace.

The palace itself has a very high roof. Inside, the walls of the halls and chambers are all covered with gold and silver and decorated with pictures of dragons and birds and horsemen and various breeds of beasts and scenes of battle. The ceiling is similarly adorned, so that there is nothing to be seen anywhere but gold and pictures. The hall is so vast and so wide that a meal might well be served there for more than 6,000 men. The number of chambers is quite bewildering. The whole building is at once so immense and so well constructed that no man in the world, granted that he had the power to effect it, could imagine any improvement in design or execution. The roof is all ablaze with scarlet and green and blue and yellow and all the colours that are, so brilliantly varnished that it glitters like crystal and the sparkle of it can be seen from far away. And this roof is so strong and so stoutly built as to last for many a long year.

In the rear part of the palace are extensive apartments, both chambers and halls, in which are kept the private possessions of the Khan. Here is stored his treasure: gold, and silver, precious stones and pearls, and his gold and silver vessels. And here too are his ladies and his concubines. In these apartments everything is arranged for his comfort and convenience, and outsiders are not admitted.

Between the inner and the outer walls, of which I have told you, are stretches of park-land with stately trees. The grass grows here in abundance, because all the paths are paved and built up fully two cubits above the level of the ground, so that no mud forms on them and no rain-water collects in puddles, but the moisture trickles over the lawns, enriching the soil and promoting a lush growth of herbage. In these parks there is a great variety of game, such as white harts, musk-deer, roebuck, stags, squirrels, and many other beautiful animals. All the area within the walls is full of these graceful creatures. except the paths that people walk on.

I assure you that the streets are so broad and straight that from the top of the wall above one gate you can see along the whole length of the road to the gate opposite. The city is full of fine mansions, inns, and dwelling-houses. All the way down the sides of every main street there are booths and shops of every sort. All the building sites throughout the city are square and measured by the rule; and on every site stand large and spacious mansions with ample courtyards and gardens. These sites are allotted to heads of households, so that one belongs to such-and-such a person, representing such-and-such a family, the next to a representative of another family, and so all the way along. Every site or block is surrounded by good public roads; and in this way the whole interior of the city is laid out in squares like a chess-board with such masterly precision that no description can do justice to it.

In this city there is such a multitude of houses and of people, both within the walls and without, that no one could count their number. Actually there are more people outside the walls in the suburbs than in the city itself. There is a suburb outside every gate, such that each one touches the neighbouring suburbs on either side. They extend in length for three or four miles. And in every suburb or ward, at about a mile's distance from the city, there are many fine hostels which provide lodging for merchants coming from different parts: a particular hostel is assigned to every nation, as we might say one for the Lombards, another for the Germans, another for the French. Merchants and others come here on business in great numbers, both because it is the Khan's residence and because it affords a profitable market. And the suburbs have as fine houses and mansions as the city, except of course for the Khan's palace.

You must know that no one who dies is buried in the city. If an idolater dies there, his body is taken to the place of cremation, which lies outside all the suburbs. And so with the others also; when they die they are taken right outside the suburbs for burial. Similarly, no act of violence is performed inside the city, but only outside the suburbs.

Let me tell you also that no sinful woman dares live within the city, unless it be in secret—no woman of the world, that is, who prostitutes her body for money. But they all live in the suburbs, and there are so many of them that no one could believe it. For I assure you that there are fully 20,000 of them, all serving the needs of men for money. They have a captain general, and there are chiefs of hundreds and of thousands responsible to the captain. This is because, whenever ambassadors come to the Great Khan on his business and are maintained at his expense, which is done on a lavish scale, the captain is called upon to provide one of these women every night for the ambassador and one for each of his attendants. They are changed every night and receive no payment; for this is the tax they pay to the Great Khan. From the number of these prostitutes you may infer the number of traders and other visitors who are daily coming and going here about their business.

You may take it for a fact that more precious and costly wares are imported into Khan-balik than into any other city in the world. Let me give you particulars. All the treasures that come from India—precious stones, pearls, and other rarities—are brought here. So too are the choicest and costliest products of Cathay itself and every other province. This is on account of the Great Khan himself, who lives here, and of the lords and ladies and the enormous multitude of hotel-keepers and other residents and of visitors who attend the courts held here by the Khan. That is why the volume and value of the imports and of the internal trade exceed those of any other city in the world. It is a fact that every day more than 1,000 cart-loads of silk enter the city; for much cloth of gold and silk is woven here. Furthermore, Khan-balik is surrounded by more than 200 other cities, near and far, from which traders come to it to sell and to buy. So it is not surprising that it is the centre of such a traffic as I have described.

In the centre of the city stands a huge palace in which is a great bell; in the evening this peals three times as a signal that no one may go about the town. Once this bell has sounded the due number of peals, no one ventures abroad in the city except in case of childbirth or illness; and those who are called out by such emergencies are obliged to carry lights.

Every night there are guards riding about the city in troops of thirty or forty, to discover whether anyone is going about at an abnormal hour, that is after the third peal of the bell. If anyone is found, he is promptly arrested and clapped into prison. Next morning he is examined by the officials appointed for the purpose, and if he is found guilty of any offence, he is punished according to its gravity with a proportionate number of strokes of a rod, which sometimes cause death. They employ this mode of punishment in order to avoid bloodshed, because their *Bakhshi*, that is, the adepts in astrology, declare that it is wrong to shed human blood.

It is ordered that every gateway must be guarded by 1,000 men. You must not suppose that this guard is maintained out of mistrust of the inhabitants. It is there, in fact, partly as a mark of respect to the Great Khan who lives in the city, partly as a check upon evil-doers—although, because of the prophecy of his astrologers, the Khan does harbour certain suspicions of the people of Cathay.

You must know that most of the inhabitants of the province of Cathay drink a wine such as I will describe to you. They make a drink of rice and an assortment of excellent spices, prepared in such a way that it is better to drink than any other wine. It is beautifully clear and it intoxicates more speedily than other wine, because it is very heating.

Let me tell you next of stones that burn like logs. It is a fact that throughout the province of Cathay there is a sort of black stone, which is dug out of veins in the hillsides and burns like logs. These stones keep a fire going better than wood. I assure you that, if you put them on the fire in the evening and see that they are well alight, they will continue to burn all night, so that you will find them still glowing in the morning. They do not give off flames, except a little when they are first kindled, just as charcoal does, and once they have caught fire they give out great heat. And you must know that these stones are burnt throughout the province of Cathay. It is true that they also have plenty of firewood. But the population is so enormous and there are so many bath-houses and baths continually being heated, that the wood could not possibly suffice, since there is no one who does not go to a bath-house at least three times a week and take a bath, and in winter every day, if he can manage it. And every man of rank or means has his own bathroom in his house, where he takes a bath. So it is clear that there could never be enough wood to maintain such a conflagration. So these stones, being very plentiful and very cheap, effect a great saving of wood.

To return to the provision of grain, you may take it for a fact that the Great Khan, when he sees that the harvests are plentiful and corn is cheap, accumulates vast quantities of it and stores it in huge granaries, where it is so carefully preserved that it remains unspoilt for three or four years. So he builds up a stock of every sort of grain—wheat, barley, millet, rice, panic [a cereal grass], and others—in great abundance.

Then, when it happens that some crops fail and there is a dearth of grain, he draws on these stocks. If the price is running at a bezant for a measure of wheat, for instance, he supplies four measures for the same sum. And he releases enough for all, so that everyone has plenty of corn to meet his needs. In this way he sees to it that none of his subjects need ever go short. And this he does throughout all parts of his empire.

Let me now tell you how the Great Khan bestows charity on the poor people of Khan-balik. When he learns that some family of honest and respectable people have been impoverished by some misfortune or disabled from working by illness, so that they have no means of earning their daily bread, he sees to it that such families (which may consist of six to ten persons or more) are given enough to cover their expenses for the whole year. These families, at the time appointed, go to the officials whose task it is to superintend the Great Khan's expenditure and who live in a palatial building assigned to their office. And each one produces a certificate of the sum paid to him for his subsistence the year before, and provision is made for them at the same rate this year. This provision includes clothing inasmuch as the Great Khan receives a tithe of all the wool, silk, and hemp used for cloth-making. He has these materials woven into cloth in a specially appointed building in which they are stored. Since all the crafts are under obligation to devote one day a week to working on his behalf, he has this cloth made up into garments, which he gives to the poor families in accordance with their needs for winter and for summer wear. He also provides clothing for his armies by having woollen cloth woven in every city as a contribution towards the payment of its tithe.

You must understand that the Tartars according to their ancient customs, before they became familiar with the doctrines of the idolaters, never used to give any alms. Indeed, when a poor man came to them, they would drive him off with maledictions, saying: "Go with God's curse upon you! If he had loved you as he loves me, he would have blessed you with prosperity!" But since the sages of the idolaters, in particular the *Bakhshi* of whom I have spoken above, preached to the Great Khan that it was a good work to provide for the poor and that their idols would be greatly pleased by it, he was induced to make such provision as I have described. No one who cares to go to his court in quest of bread is ever turned away empty-handed. Everyone receives a portion. And not a day passes but twenty or thirty thousand bowls of rice, millet, and panic are doled out and given away by the officials appointed. And this goes on all the year round. For this amazing and stupendous munificence which the Great Khan exercises towards the poor, all the people hold him in such esteem that they revere him as a god.

15.   Mature Islamic Civilization

THE CIVILIZATION OF MEDIEVAL ISLAM
J. J. SAUNDERS

In this selection the author, a modern historian, suggests answers to three important questions. First he asks why the Arab invasions of the seventh century brought about a cultural flowering while the German invasions of Western Europe in the fifth century had the opposite effect. What, in other words, were the causes of this rise of Arabic civilization? Next he asks about the nature of that civilization. What were its notable features? Finally, he asks about its decline after the thirteenth century. How was such a vigorous civilization overcome by the previously backward West?

What are the author's answers to these questions? Which answers do you find most convincing? Why?

For some four centuries (roughly between A.D. 800 and 1200) the lands conquered by the Arabs were the soil from which grew and blossomed one of the most brilliant civilizations in the history of humanity. To give it a suitable name is a matter of some difficulty. It has been variously styled Arab, Muslim, Islamic and Arabic. The first is clearly a misnomer, implying as it does that this culture was created or dominated by men of Arab race, which was by no means the case; the second and third define it too narrowly in religious terms, whereas many of its most distinguished figures were Christians, Jews or pagans, and not Muslims at all. "Arabic" seems open to the least objection, since it draws attention to the fact that the literature of this particular civilization was written almost wholly in the Arabic language and acquired its characteristic unity largely from this circumstance.

The causes of the rise and fall of civilizations are often hidden from us, and the questions which start to mind are more easily framed than answered. Why were the German invasions of Western Europe in the fifth century followed by a long "dark age" of barbarism and ignorance, while the Arab invasions of the seventh century were followed by a

From *A History of Medieval Islam* by J. J. Saunders. Copyright © 1978. Routledge & Kegan Paul. Reprinted by permission.

general rise in the cultural level of the countries affected by them? So startling a contrast demands explanation, which must take the form of showing that certain conditions favourable to the growth of the arts and sciences were present in one case and absent in the other.

1. The Arab conquests politically unified a huge segment of the globe from Spain to India, a unity which remained unbroken until the fall of the Omayyads in 750. The disappearance of so many dividing frontiers, above all the one which had so long separated Rome and Persia, was a useful preliminary to the building of a new civilization.

2. As the Arabs overran one country after another, they carried their language with them. But that language possessed a unique status: to every Muslim it was not just one form of human speech among others, but the vehicle through which God had chosen to deliver his final revelation to men. Arabic was "God's tongue," and as such enjoyed a prestige which Latin and Greek and Hebrew had never known. The Koran could not, must not be translated: the believer must hear and understand and if possible read the divine book in the original, even though Arabic were not his mother tongue. To study, illustrate and elucidate the text became a pious duty: the earliest branch of science developed by Muslims was Arabic philology, traditionally founded at Basra in the late Omayyad age. The further Islam spread among non-Arabs, the further a knowledge of Arabic spread with it. A century or so after the conquests even Christians, Jews and Zoroastrians within the Caliphate found it convenient to speak and write Arabic. Thus to political unity was added the widespread use of a common language, which immensely facilitated the exchange of ideas.

3. The first conquests of the Arabs were made in lands which had been the home of settled, urban civilizations for thousands of years, that is, the river valleys of the Nile and the Tigris-Euphrates. The fighting here was relatively brief (Syria was conquered in six or seven years, Egypt and Iraq in two or three), and the physical destruction was light. The native population was akin to the Arabs in race and speech, and stood aside from a struggle which was essentially between the invaders and the Byzantine or Sassanid [Persian dynasty ruling just before the Arab invasion] ruling class. The local officials often stayed at their posts, and administrative continuity, at least at the lower levels, remained unbroken. From motives of policy, the Caliphs cultivated friendly relations with the Jacobite and Nestorian Christians, who constituted the bulk of the people, and who during the long period of Roman rule had learnt a good deal of the science and philosophy of the Greeks. This learning, translated into Syriac, a Semitic tongue closely related to Arabic, was at the disposal of the newcomers, who were impressed by the rich and ancient culture of the region, and it was this region, and not Arabia proper, which was the birthplace of the Arabic civilization.

4. Once invasion and re-settlement were over, the lands brought

under the sovereignty of the Caliphs enjoyed immunity from serious external attack for three or four centuries. There was plenty of fighting on the frontiers and many internal revolts and disturbances, but no prolonged and ruinous barbarian assaults such as the Latin Christian West had to endure from the Vikings and Magyars. Under the shield of the *Pax Islamica,* which may be compared with the Augustan and Antonine Peace of the early Roman Empire, the arts and sciences rose to a new and flourishing life. Not until about 1050 did this peace begin to break down: Islam was then exposed to a series of attacks from the nomads of the steppes and deserts, culminating in the dreadful Mongol explosion of the thirteenth century.

5. The creation of the vast Arab Empire, besides levelling barriers and abolishing frontiers, brought into existence a great free trade area, promoted safe and rapid travel, and gave a tremendous stimulus to commerce. During these four centuries (800–1200) international trade was more vigorous than at any time since the heyday of imperial Rome. Merchants from the Caliphate were found in places as far apart as Senegal and Canton. The hoards of Arabic coins dug up in Scandinavia reveal the brisk exchange of goods between Northern Europe and the cities of Iraq and Persia via the great rivers of Russia. The negro lands south of the Sahara were drawn into the stream of world commerce. The ancient Silk Road through the oases of Central Asia which carried the products of China to the West had never been so frequented. Cities expanded, fortunes were made, a wealthy middle-class of traders, shippers, bankers, manufacturers and professional men came into being, and a rich and sophisticated society gave increasing employment and patronage to scholars, artists, teachers, physicians and craftsmen.

6. The pursuit of knowledge was quickened by the use of paper and the so-called "Arabic" numerals. Neither originated in the Islamic world, but both were widely employed there by the ninth century. The manufacture of paper from hemp, rags and tree-bark seems to have been invented in China about A.D. 100, but it remained unknown outside that country until some Chinese prisoners of war skilled in the art were brought to Samarkand in 751. In 793 a paper manufactory was set up in Baghdad; by 900 the commodity was being produced in Egypt, and by 950 in Spain. The Arabic numerals, despite their name, are probably Hindu, and may have reached Islam through the translation of the *Siddhanta,* a Sanskrit astronomical treatise, made by order of the Caliph Mansur in 773. The oldest Muslim documents employing these signs date from 870–890: the zero is represented by a dot, as has always been the case in Arabic. These innovations multiplied books and facilitated calculation, and the rich scientific literature of the next few centuries undoubtedly owes much to them.

Such are some of the possible causes of the rise of the Arabic civilization. To attempt a detailed description and analysis of that civilization would be impossible, but certain notable features or peculiarities of it may be considered:—

1. It was not specifically Muslim. Islam provided it with a framework and a universal language, but its only creations which possess a definitely Muslim character are Arabic grammar, law and theology. All else came from non-Muslim sources, even Arabic poetry and belles-lettres, which were based on a literary tradition going back to pre-Islamic times, the "days of ignorance" of the sixth century.

2. The biggest single influence which helped to shape it was Greek science and philosophy, but this reached it indirectly, chiefly through the medium of Syriac. Of course, the great days of Hellenism were long over by the time of the Arab conquests: Greek science went out with Ptolemy in the second century, and the noble line of Greek thinkers ended when Justinian closed the schools of Athens in 529. But if nothing new was being created or discovered, the work of preserving and transmitting what had already been accomplished went on among the Byzantine Greeks and their Syriac-speaking pupils in Syria, Egypt and Iraq, and when the Arabs broke into these lands most of the leading works of Greek medicine and metaphysics had been translated into Syriac by scholars of the Oriental Christian communities. Established in an educated society, the invaders grew ashamed of their ignorance, and the Caliphs encouraged learned Christians and Jews to turn these books into the dominant language of the Empire. This translating went on for some two centuries (800–1000), at the close of which educated Muslims could read the masters of Hellenic thought in Arabic versions of Syriac translations of the Greek originals.

3. As the Syriac-speaking Christians spread through the Islamic world a knowledge of Greek thought, so the Persians introduced to it much of the lore of Sanskrit India. Hindu influences had travelled west in late Sassanid times: the game of chess and Sanskrit medical writings are said to have reached Ctesiphon in the reign of Khusrau Nushirvan. When the Abbasids moved the metropolis of Islam to Iraq, Persian scholars were given every facility to pursue this quest. At the command of Mansur, Fazari translated the *Siddhanta*; Ibn al-Mukaffa turned into Arabic the famous *Fables of Bidpai,* an Indian collection of animal stories which has gone round the world, and the celebrated mathematician al-Khwarizmi, from whose name the European word "algorism" (the old term for arithmetic) was derived, founded the science of algebra (Arabic *al-jabr,* a restoring, literally, setting a bone) on the basis of Hindu mathematical achievement. Translation from Sanskrit into Arabic went on till the time of the great Persian scientist al-Biruni (973–1048), who among numerous learned works left an admirable sociological description of India. The double and simultaneous impact of Greece and India provided a powerful stimulus to the building of the Arabic civilization.

4. The centre of Arabic intellectual life was long fixed in Iraq, the

ancient home of culture, "a palimpsest (as it has been styled) on which every civilization from the time of the Sumerians had left its trace." A meeting-place of Hellenic and Iranian culture, it had been the heart of the old Persian monarchy and was the seat of the Caliphate from 750 to 1258. Baghdad became a greater Ctesiphon, the capital not simply of a State but of a world civilization. Perhaps in no other region of its size could such an extraordinary variety of belief and speech have been found. Jews and Zoroastrians, Nestorian, Monophysite and Greek Orthodox Christians, Gnostics and Manichaeans, the pagans of Harran and the strange baptist sect of the Mandeans, all mingled in the same province. In the Arab camp settlements of Basra and Kufa the Muslims first found leisure to devote themselves to things of the mind: here was inaugurated the study of Arabic philology and Islamic law. In Baghdad the Caliph Ma'mun, the son of a Persian mother, founded and endowed as a centre of research the Bait al-Hikma, or House of Wisdom, which was at once a library, an observatory and a scientific academy. Men of many races and faiths contributed to the fame of Baghdad as a home of scholarship, and Arabic civilization never recovered from the sack of the city by the Mongols in 1258.

5. The culture of medieval Islam was multi-racial. Arabs, Syrians, Jews, Persians, Turks, Egyptians, Berbers, Spaniards, all contributed to it. One of its leading philosophers, al-Kindi, was an Arab of the tribe of Kinda (as his name implies), al-Farabi, a Neo-Platonist and commentator on Aristotle, a Turk from Transoxiana, Ibn Sina or Avicenna, perhaps the finest scientific thinker of Islam, a Persian from Bukhara, and Ibn Rushd, best known under his Europeanized name Averroes, a Spanish Moor from Cordova. A remarkable feature of Arabic philosophical literature is that much of it was written by Jews. As the Jewish religion, like the Christian, was a tolerated one among Muslims, Jews were found settled in almost all the great cities of Islam, where they learnt to write Arabic and to share in the vigorous intellectual life around them. In Spain they acted as mediators between the Muslim and Christian Spanish cultures, helping Christian scholars to translate Arabic works into Latin and so making them available to the then backward West. Spain was also the birthplace of Maimonides, "the second Moses," perhaps the acutest Jewish thinker before Spinoza, who was born in Cordova in 1135 and died in Cairo in 1204, and whose *Guide for the Perplexed*, a bold attempt to reconcile reason and religious faith, finds readers to this day.

6. By far the biggest share in the construction of the Arabic civilization was taken by the Persians, a people whose recorded history was already more than a thousand years old when the Arabs broke into their land, and who found in their cultural superiority compensation for their political servitude. Persia has been described as "the principal channel irrigating the somewhat arid field of Islam with the rich alluvial flood of

ancient culture": Sufism was virtually a Persian creation, and the Persian al-Ghazali was the greatest of Muslim theologians. In secular learning the Persians were predominant. "If knowledge were attached to the ends of the sky, some amongst the Persians would have reached it," was a traditional saying. Among the famous men of the age sprung from this gifted race were Razi (Rhazes), the great physician who first distinguished smallpox from measles, Tabari (died 923), the Arabic Livy, whose *Annals of Apostles and Kings* provided us with our chief source of information on early Muslim history, Ibn Sina, whose medical writings instructed the world for centuries, Biruni, a many-sided genius whose fame now rests chiefly on his description of medieval India, Omar Khayyam (died 1123), more celebrated in the East for his mathematical achievements than for his poetry, Shahrastani (died 1153), whose *Book of Religion and Sects* is really a pioneering study in comparative religion, Nasir al-Din al Tusi (died 1274), a distinguished astronomer who collected valuable data at his observatory at Maragha in Azerbaijan, and Rashid al-Din Fadl Allah (died 1318) author of the first world history worthy of that name. If to these scholars and scientists we add the poets (Firdawsi, Sa'di, Rumi, etc.), who shone lustre on their country's literature, the picture is even brighter.

7. The core of the scientific studies of medieval Islam was medicine. Socially, the medical profession had always stood high in the East: whereas in the Greco-Roman world doctors were often freed slaves, in Persia and Babylonia they could rise to be the prime ministers of kings. At the time of the Arab conquests the classical medicine of Hippocrates and Galen was being studied by Egyptian Greeks in Alexandria and Nestorian Christians at Jundi-Shapur, in south-west Persia. The Caliphs employed graduates of these schools as their personal physicians: members of one Nestorian family, the Bakht-yashu (a name meaning "happiness of Jesus") served in this capacity at the court of Baghdad for several generations. Nestorian medical professors translated most of Galen and other authorities into Arabic, and by 900 the science of medicine was being assiduously cultivated by Muslims all over Islam. Razi was the first of their faith to acquire world fame through his vast medical encyclopedia, the *Hawi* (best known under its Latin title *Continens*), which was filled with long extracts from Greek and Hindu writers and displayed a knowledge of chemistry most unusual in that age. A similar work by Ibn Sina, the *Canon*, attained even greater celebrity and was treated for centuries as a kind of medical Bible. The branch of medicine most successively investigated was ophthalmology, eye-diseases being sadly common in the East, and the *Optics* of Ibn al-Haitham, court physician to the Fatimids in Cairo where he died in 1039, remained the standard authority on its subject till early modern times, being studied with profit by the astronomer Kepler in the seventeenth century. It was through the medical schools that many of

the natural sciences found their way into Muslim education, the curricula including instruction in physics, chemistry and botany as well as in anatomy and pathology, and it was in this field that the Arabic writers made their greatest contribution to human knowledge. They added substantially to the achievement of the Greeks in the theory and art of healing disease; they founded hospitals and invented new drugs, and they filled libraries of books with detailed and accurate clinical observations. Their long superiority is proved by the fact that most of the Arabic works translated into Latin in the twelfth and thirteenth centuries were medical writings and that these were among the first to be printed at the time of the Renaissance. Razi, Ibn Sina and Ibn al-Haitham in their Latinized form continued to be "set books" in the medical school of Europe till as late as the mid-seventeenth century.

8. Like all civilizations, the Arabic was highly selective in its borrowings from outside. Human societies take over only those elements which seem well suited to fill a conscious gap, and disregard those which conflict with their fundamental values; thus in modern times Russia has appropriated the science rather than the humanism of the West, and China has borrowed Marxism and rejected almost all else of European origin. Islam drew extensively on Hindu mathematics and medicine, but took small notice of Hindu philosophy, which being the reflection of a polytheistic society and of belief in the world as *maya* or illusion, was wholly repugnant to the teachings of the Koran. It helped itself to a good deal of Greek (chiefly Aristotelian) logic and metaphysics, in order to clothe its religious doctrines in a form more acceptable to a sophisticated society and enable it to defend them against philosophically trained opponents, but though it knew Aristotle's *Poetics* and *Rhetoric*, it ignored the Greek poets, dramatists and historians as spokesmen of a pagan past it had no desire to investigate. In architecture it was ready to use Byzantine and Persian models, but painting and sculpture were virtually banned because the Prophet [Mohammad] was alleged to have pronounced representational art a temptation to idolatry. Of classical Latin literature it knew nothing: the only Latin work ever translated into Arabic is said to have been the *History* of Orosius.

That the Arabic culture was merely imitative, that it copied and transmitted what it learnt at second-hand from the Greeks, and lacked the ability to strike out on independent lines of its own, is a judgment no longer accepted. It certainly borrowed freely from the Greeks—so did the West later—but what it built on these foundations was truly original and creative, and one of the great achievements of the human spirit. For more than four hundred years the most fruitful work in mathematics, astronomy, botany, chemistry, medicine, history and geography, was produced in the world of Islam by Muslims and Christians, Jews and Zoroastrians, pagans and Manichaeans. Neither the collapse of the Caliphate nor the Isma'ilian schism checked the process, for the local dynasties which sprang up on the ruins of the old Arab Empire competed with one another to attract scholars and artists to their courts, and the possession of a common language far outweighed the loss of political unity. Yet this brilliant culture, which shone so brightly in contrast to the darkness of the Latin West and the stagnation of Byzantium, began to fade from the thirteenth century onwards. Arabic philosophy was dead by 1200, Arabic science by 1500. The nations of Western Europe, once sunk in barbarism, caught up and overtook the peoples of Islam. How did this come about? The question has hardly yet received a complete and satisfactory answer, but some tentative suggestions may be offered:—

1. The collapse of the *Pax Islamica* after about 1050. The end of the long peace was marked by wave after wave of nomadic invasion, the Banu-Hilal in North Africa, the Turkomans and Seljuks in Western Asia, and the mighty Mongol devastations which inflicted such irreparable damage on so many Muslim lands between 1220 and 1260. Cities were sacked and burnt, wealth dissipated, libraries destroyed and teachers dispersed. The loss to culture in the fall of Baghdad alone is incalculable. The Christian West escaped all this, since after the Northmen and Magyars had been tamed and converted around 1000, it had nothing more to fear from barbarian attack, and the Mongols never got farther west than Hungary and Silesia.

2. The decay of city life and economic prosperity. The Arabic civilization was essentially urban, and its material basis was the vigorous commercial activity which once covered an area extending as far as Scandinavia, China and the Sudan. This activity was much diminished when nomad raids and invasions threatened the security of the caravan routes. From the eleventh century onwards the volume of international trade contracted, urban wealth declined, and social and economic conditions in the Muslim world underwent drastic change. Princes, finding their revenues falling, were obliged to pay their civil and military officers out of the rents and produce of landed estates: hence the growth of the *ikta* system, which has been compared, rather loosely, to Western feudalism. Owing presumably to the prevalence of slavery, which assured a plentiful supply of labour, there was no stimulus to technological progress and invention, which might have provided some compensation for the loss of distant markets. Nor did the cities of Islam ever develop self-governing institutions or combine in defence of their interests like the Lombard League or the Hansa in contemporary Europe: it was not that civic patriotism was wholly lacking (Arabic literature contains many town histories and biographical dictionaries of famous citizens), but that in this society the primary loyalty of a man was to his religious community, and in cities where Muslims, Christians and Jews lived together in separate quarters, it was not easy for the inhabitants to feel and act as a united body. Thus the middle classes

(merchants, traders, shippers, shopkeepers and craftsmen) had little defence when the economic basis of their position weakened, and the decline of the town was almost certainly related to the falling off of intellectual capacity and output.

3. The loss of linguistic and cultural unity. In the days of its widest expansion, Arabic was written and understood wherever Islam prevailed, but its intellectual monopoly was threatened and finally broken by the revival of Persian in the lands east of the Tigris. The fall of the Sassanid Empire reduced the native tongue to the level of Anglo-Saxon in England after the Norman conquest, but under the Abbasids it began to re-emerge in an altered form, its vocabulary swollen with Arabic words and the old Pahlawi script replaced by the Arabic. With the rise of native dynasties after the disintegration of the Caliphate, Persian experienced a literary renaissance; the Samanids and Ghaznavids in particular were generous patrons of poets and scholars, and Firdawsi's great epic, the *Shah-nama*, or Book of Kings, finished in 1010, gave the new Persian a position in world literature it has never since lost. Fewer and fewer Persians wrote in Arabic, though the sacred language of the Koran continued to be used for works of theology, law and devotion. When the Turks entered Islam *en masse* with the Seljuks, it was the Persianized provinces that they first occupied, and it was on Persian officials that they relied for the administration of their Empire. Deeply affected in consequence by Persian culture, the Turks carried it with them westwards into Asia Minor and eastwards into northern India: by contrast, they set little store by Arabic, except for purely religious purposes. The Mongol invasions, the fall of Baghdad and the destruction of the Caliphate dealt a fatal blow to Arabic in eastern Islam, where in the field of secular learning and literature it was steadily overshadowed by Persian and Turkish. Never again was the Muslim world to be dominated by a single language.

4. Probably the biggest factor was the strongly religious character of Islam itself and the absence of a vigorous pre-Islamic secular tradition. Behind Christian Europe lay the science and rationalism of classical Greece: behind Islam lay nothing save the cultural poverty of "the days of ignorance." The Muslims did, as we have seen, borrow a good deal from Greece, but in a limited and indirect fashion: the Greek past never *belonged* to them in the sense in which it did to Christendom, and there was never a joyous acceptance or recovery of it as took place in the West at the time of the Renaissance. The spirit of Islam was not rational in the Greek sense of the term, in that God is beyond reason and his ordering of the universe is to be accepted rather than explained. True knowledge is that of God and his Law, and the Law embraces all human activity: secular learning for its own sake is to be strongly discouraged, and intellectual pursuits are permissible only insofar as they further a deeper piety and understanding of religious truth. Such an attitude was implicit

in Islamic thinking from the onset, but it became explicit only at a later stage, largely in consequence of the reaction against the Isma'ilian heresy and of a fuller realisation of the dangers to orthodoxy lurking in Greek philosophy. The shift in outlook became noticeable in the Seljuk age. The great Ghazali devoted his life to the defence of Koranic truth against what he regarded as the insidious encroachments of unbelief. Islamic dogma was linked with Sufi mysticism. Muslim education was geared to the new orthodoxy by the founding of *madrasas,* where the religious sciences alone received intensive study. The Shari'a came to dominate Muslim life as the Torah had dominated post-exilic Judaism. The door was closed against further borrowings from outside: philosophy was repudiated as a danger to the Faith, because it was alleged to deny a personal God, creation *ex nihilo,* and the resurrection of the body. The attempt of Ibn Rushd (Averroes) in Spain to answer Ghazali and defend the pursuit of secular science fell on deaf ears and exposed him to the charge of teaching atheism. How far the reaction went can be seen from the attitude of Ibn Khaldun (1337–1406), often regarded as Islam's profoundest thinker, who dismissed all knowledge unconnected with religion as useless. Plato (he says) admitted that no certainty about God could be attained by the reason: why then waste our time on such futile inquiries? Truth is to be sought only in divine revelation. The profane sciences, which had always operated on the fringe and had never been free from the suspicion of impiety, were largely and quietly dropped as "un-Muslim."

THE GREAT ISLAMIC EMPIRES

C. E. BOSWORTH

The Mongol invasions of the thirteenth and fourteenth centuries not only reunified Asia, they also dramatically changed the character of the Muslim world, the previous unifier. After the defeat of the Abbasid Caliphate in 1258, there was no longer a single Muslim state. But as the

From *Introduction to Islamic Civilization,* edited by R. M. Savory. Copyright © 1976 Cambridge University Press. Reprinted by permission of Cambridge University Press.

West Asian Mongol Khans adopted Islam, a new Muslim cultural unity spread from North Africa to India. By 1500 three Muslim states (Ottoman Turk, Persian, and Indian) dominated southern Asia. What were the strengths and weaknesses of these Islamic empires, according to this modern historian?

The Mongol invasions of the thirteenth and fourteenth centuries constituted a "time of troubles" for all the Islamic lands east of Egypt, out of which various powerful and comparatively long-lived empires emerged. The Mongols expanded from their homeland around Lake Baikal in eastern Siberia in one of those eras of expansion which population pressures and the emergence of forceful leaders seem regularly to have generated. Under an outstanding leader, Chingiz [Genghis] Khan, the Mongols irrupted both into China and into western Asia, the Islamic world. Within a few years of Chingiz's appearance on the Oxus River in 1219, the Muslim powers in Central Asia and eastern Persia had been overturned, and a trail of desolation left by the Mongol or Mongol-Turkish cavalrymen. Later, Mongol forces rode through the Siberian steppes into Russia, and defeated German-Polish and Hungarian armies in Central Europe. The impetus here was not maintained, but the Mongols remained in South Russia, and the Golden Horde, as this part of the Mongol empire was known, held the Russian princes tributary for one-and-a-half centuries. Within the Islamic world proper, Baghdad fell to Chingiz's grandson Hülegü in 1258. A line of *fainéant* Abbasid Caliphs was set up soon after this in Cairo under Mamlūk protection, but the medieval Caliphate, the symbol of orthodox, Sunnī Muslim unity, had gone for ever. The Mongols had originally been shamanists, i.e. pagan animists, but with some sympathies for other faiths of Inner Asia like Buddhism and Nestorian Christianity. The various branches of the Western Mongols gradually adopted Islam: the Khanate which was set up in Iraq and Persia, that of the Il-Khanids ("Subordinate Khans," i.e. subordinate to the Greak Khan in Mongolia), became Muslim in 1295.

Despite the fact that the name of the Mongols ranks in the popular mind with those of the Goths, Huns, and Vandals as perpetrators of mass destruction, this initial violence subsided and the age of the Mongols had its favourable aspect. Domination over such a great expanse of the Old World, from the Ukraine to Korea, opened up the possibility of East-West cultural exchanges on an unprecedented scale. Chinese artistic techniques and motifs began perceptibly to affect Islamic Persian art. People could move freely across Inner Asia as never before or since, unhampered by political boundaries. Impelled by the search for Prester John, the legendary Christian monarch who was tentatively identified with the Mongol Great Khan, many Europeans travelled to Mongolia and have left us fascinating accounts of life there.

That an alliance between the western Europe Papacy and the pagan Mongols against the Muslims of the Near East never really materialised in the thirteenth century was largely due to the vigour of a great imperial power in Egypt and Syria, that of the Mamlūks [Mamelukes]. As their name implies ("owned"), these were of slave status, gaining independent power in 1250 and retaining it till the Ottoman conquest of 1516–17. The earlier Mamlūk Sultans were predominantly Qipchāq Turks from the South Russian steppes, and so for about a century after 1250 the Mamlūks pursued a policy of friendly relations with Byzantium, the surviving Seljuk line in Anatolia, and the Golden Horde, in order to ensure replenishments of slaves. The Mamlūks won prestige in orthodox eyes by their defeats of the Mongols in Palestine and Syria, their ejection of the last Crusaders from the Levant coast, and the reduction of the Christian kingdom of Little Armenia. Their diplomatic and commercial policies embraced Christian Mediterranean powers like Aragon, Naples and Venice on the one hand, and the princes of the Indian Ocean coastlands on the other. They cultivated the support of the Sunnī 'ulamā or religious scholars, maintaining the line of puppet Caliphs but ignoring them for practical purposes. The Arabic scholarship of the Mamlūk period was outstanding in quantity and not infrequently in quality; the sheer volume of material extant makes it possible to reconstruct Mamlūk history in remarkable detail as compared with many other Islamic states.

The impressive achievement of the Mamlūks was founded upon a hierarchy of military slavery, from the Sultans downwards; free soldiers had only a subordinate, socially depressed position in the state. Thus we have the paradoxical situation, duplicated, as we shall see, in Ottoman Turkey, of slaves ruling over free men and being able to rise to the highest positions in the state without social stigma. This phenomenon seems to have been peculiar to the Islamic world; it is strange that Christian powers like the Byzantines, who must have been perfectly familiar with the military slavery system, never attempted to emulate it. The later Mamlūks were recruited from the Circassians of the Caucasus, and in the fifteenth century the state grew perceptibly poorer in resources and fighting manpower. The successive conquest of Syria and Egypt by the Ottomans in 1516–17 therefore occasioned no surprise. One factor in the Mamlūks' failure to withstand the Ottomans was their reluctance to use hand-guns, for wholesale adoption of these new weapons would have relegated the Mamlūk mounted archer to a position inferior to the infantryman and thus destroyed the whole basis of the state.

More than any other Muslim power of the late classical period, the Ottoman Turks struck terror into the hearts of Christian Europe, so that the Elizabethan historian of the Turks, Richard Knollys, described them as "the present Terror of the World." Backed by the Turkish military qualities of self-discipline and endurance, the Turkish invasions of Europe were indeed a potent threat, reaching on two occasions to Vienna itself. The Ottomans began as a group of *ghāzīs* (i.e., corps of mystically inspired warriors) in northwestern Anatolia, confronting the truncated Byzantine empire there, and eventually eclipsing other Turkish principalities by their superior *élan* and experience in war. In 1354 they crossed the Dardanelles into Europe, cutting off Constantinople in its rear, and expanded relentlessly into the Balkans. States like Serbia and Bulgaria were humbled, and for 500 years to come were to be nations without history. The Ottoman victory at Mohács in 1526 brought most of Hungary under Turkish rule for a century-and-a-half, providing a base from which to threaten Austria and the very heart of Christian Europe. The Balkan provinces came to form Rumelia, the European "twin" of Anatolia. Turks were settled there, and there were also converts from the indigenous peoples, giving a strongly Islamic impress to much of the Balkans down to the nineteenth century and after; in 1939 one-third of the Yugoslavian province of Bosnia was still Muslim and about half of Albania. Ottoman authority in Anatolia received a setback from the invasion of the Tatar military conqueror Timur (or Tamerlane) at the opening of the fifteenth century. Half a century later, it revived under a series of outstanding Sultans: Mehmed the Conqueror, who attained the glittering prize of Constantinople in 1453; Selīm the Grim, conqueror of Syria and Egypt and humbler of the Ottomans' rivals to the east, the Safavids of Persia; and Sulaymān the Magnificent (called by the Turks "the Lawgiver"), conqueror of Hungary and Iraq. Ottoman fleets and their allies, the corsairs of Barbary (i.e., North Africa), operated in the Mediterranean and beyond, terrorising the Christians and carrying off captives from as far afield as Ireland and Iceland; and in the late seventeenth century, the Ottomans enjoyed their last major success by capturing Crete from the Venetians.

Much of this Ottoman vigour sprang from the use of a system of military slavery analogous to that of the Mamlūks. The Janissaries or "New Troops," a crack corps of highly trained soldiers and officials, were recruited from the Christian populations of the Balkans and later, from those of Anatolia, from the late fourteenth down to the early eighteenth centuries. Like the Arabs in the first stages of their expansion, the Turks themselves were a military class comparatively thinly spread over what had grown to be a vast empire. Utilisation of the subject population was a brilliant device for tapping the manpower of the Balkans. Moreover, the lengthy and arduous training of a Janissary in a thoroughly Islamic atmosphere conduced to his adopting a soldierly type of Islam. It was the discipline and fire-power of these troops (the Ottoman army made use of artillery and hand-guns from the mid-fifteenth century onwards) which did much to create in Europe the image of Ottoman ferocity and invincibility.

Yet in its heyday, the Ottoman empire was the most powerful and lasting state known to the Islamic world since the early Arab Caliphate. It gave autocratic, but often good government to lands which had previously suffered internal chaos and dislocation, and only towards the end, when the political and economic pressure of the West contributed to administrative breakdown and internal economic decline, did the quality of Ottoman rule deteriorate.

The Safavids of Persia established the one late medieval empire which was Shī'ī* in faith. Somewhat remarkably, it arose from a local Azerbaijan Sūfī or dervish order which gradually became transformed into a militant Shī'ī propagandist movement. The Safavids came to power in an area where the ground had been prepared for Shī'ī heterodoxy, and consciously adopted Shī'ism as an affirmation of the Persian national identity against the pressures of adjoining, hostile Sunnī powers like the Ottomans on the west and the Özbeg states of central Asia on the northeast. In the opening years of the sixteenth century, Shāh Ismā'īl Safavī brought the whole of Persia under his control; later, the capital was moved first to Qazvīn and then to Isfahān, which was transformed into one of the finest cities of the Islamic world. The Safavids maintained their power for over two centuries, till in the early eighteenth century they were overthrown by the Afghans. Shāh 'Abbās I (1588–1629) cultivated relations with European powers such as England and Holland in an effort to obtain allies against his enemies, the Ottomans and the Portuguese; and we owe many valuable accounts of seventeenth-century Persia to the western diplomats, travellers, missionaries and traders who visited "the Grand Sophy." The title "Sophy" for the Shāhs almost certainly stems, of course, from Sūfī, and the Safavid state began as a theocracy, with the Shāhs claiming semi-divine status as emanations of the Godhead, with infallibility as representatives on earth of the Hidden Imām; thus the Shāhs demanded spiritual as well as political allegiance from their Turkish troops, the Qïzïl-bāsh or "Redheads" (from the red caps which they wore). In addition to these last, the Safavids followed prevailing military fashion by forming regiments of slave troops (ghulāms), comparable with the Ottoman Janissaries. The ghulāms were mainly of Christian origin, from such peoples of the Caucasus region as the Georgians and Armenians; by contrast with the Ottoman system, they were not levied on a regular basis.

* Shī'ī refers to the Shī'ah ('party of 'Alī') which is that group of Muslims who believed that leadership of the Muslim community ought to be held by descendants of Ali, the cousin and son-in-law of Muhammad, whether recognized by the majority or not. They are opposed to the Sunnīs, the majority of Muslims who accept the authority of the whole first generation of Muslims and the custom of the historical Muslim community.—Ed.

The remaining great Muslim empire arose in northern India, where the ubiquitous Turks and the Afghans founded military dynasties from the eleventh century onwards. Many of these stemmed from Turkish slave commanders, as the name of one dynasty of Delhi Sultans, the "Slave Kings" (1206–90) shows. Muslim rule was extended as far as Bengal (early thirteenth century), Lashmir (fourteenth century) and into the Deccan or South India, where several local dynasties of considerable cultural splendour arose. All through its existence, the dominant feature of Indian Islam has been its minority position, numerically speaking, within a non-Islamic, predominantly Hindu environment; hence Muslim princes often ruled over extensive non-Muslim populations and relied on them as officials or soldiers. The comparative isolation of Islam in India meant a perpetual struggle to preserve the faith from syncretism and from the characteristic absorptive influence of Hindu religion; thus Indian Muslim rulers and the 'ulamā usually identified themselves strongly with Sunnī Islam and the maintenance of orthodoxy.

The empire of the Mughals (this name being a form of "Mongols") arose out of the successful efforts of Bābur, a Turkish prince from Central Asia, to carve out a principality for himself in northern India in the early sixteenth century. Under a series of remarkable Sultans in the sixteenth and seventeenth centuries the Mughal empire expanded over the greater part of the subcontinent. Akbar the Great, a contemporary of Elizabeth I of England, in a dramatic divergence from traditional Indian Islamic thought, attempted a rapprochement with his Hindu subjects, toying with a new, monotheistic creed of his own, "the Divine Faith," which would transcend existing religions and bring about religious harmony in his dominions; such policies were, however, reversed by his successors, and Aurangzīb (d. 1707), the last great Mughal Emperor, reverted to strict enforcement of Muslim orthodoxy. A feature of these two centuries—one hardly noticed by the Muslim rulers of India, but portentous for the future—was the establishment of coastal trading stations or "factories" by European merchants, such as the Portuguese, English and French. The English settlements formed the bases for subsequent territorial expansion in the eighteenth and nineteenth centuries, and it was the British who, in the aftermath of the Indian Mutiny, in 1858 deposed the last feeble representative of the Mughal line in Delhi.

THE GULISTAN

SA'DI

Muslihuddin Sa'di (1193–1292) is said to have travelled from North Africa to India, but settled in Shiraz (Persia) where he wrote the Gulistan around 1257. Sa'di wrote in Persian and expressed lessons of Sufism in the form of poetic stories. The great historian of Islam, Marshall Hodgson, has written:

> *"The lessons Sa'di taught and the wisdom he preached made no pretense to originality. Indeed, wisdom is seldom original. What Sa'di aimed to do was to put the old truths well. He phrases in unforgettable images the truths that people always know and yet spend a lifetime learning."*

What were these old truths? What do these stories tell us about Persian or Muslim society? What do they tell us about ourselves?

An unjust king asked a devotee what kind of worship is best? He replied: "For thee the best is to sleep one half of the day so as not to injure the people for a while."

A schoolboy was so perfectly beautiful and sweet-voiced that the teacher, in accordance with human nature, conceived such an affection towards him that he often recited the following verses:

> I am not so little occupied with thee, O heavenly face,
> That remembrance of myself occurs to my mind.
> From thy sight I am unable to withdraw my eyes
> Although when I am opposite I may see that an arrow comes.

Once the boy said to him: "As thou strivest to direct my studies, direct also my behavior. If thou perceivest anything reprovable in my conduct, although it may seem approvable to me, inform me therefore that I may endeavour to change it." He replied: "O boy, make that request to someone else because the eyes with which I look upon thee behold nothing but virtues."

> The ill-wishing eye, be it torn out
> Sees only defects in his virtue.

From *The Gulistan of Sa'di,* translated by Edward Rehatsek. New York: Capricorn Books, 1966. Reprinted by permission of George Allen & Unwin.

> But if thou possessest one virtue and seventy faults
> A friend sees nothing except that virtue.

A vezier who had a stupid son gave him in charge of a scholar to instruct him and if possible to make him intelligent. Having been some time under instruction but ineffectually, the learned man sent a note to his father with the words: "The boy is not becoming intelligent and has made a fool of me."

> When a nature is originally receptive
> Instruction will take effect thereon.
> No kind of polishing will improve iron
> Whose essence is originally bad.

> Wash a dog in the seven oceans,
> He will be only dirtier when he gets wet.
> If the ass of Jesus be taken to
> Mekkah [Mecca] He will on his return still be an ass.

A sage, instructing boys, said to them: "O darlings of your fathers, learn a trade because property and riches of the world are not to be relied upon; also silver and gold are an occasion of danger because either a thief may steal them at once or the owner spend them gradually; but a profession is a living fountain and permanent wealth; and although a professional man may lose riches, it does not matter because a profession is itself wealth and wherever he goes he will enjoy respect and sit in high places, whereas he who has no trade will glean crumbs and see hardships:

> Once confusion arose in Damascus.
> Everyone left his snug corner.
> Learned sons of peasants
> Became the veziers of padshahs.
> Imbecile sons of the veziers
> Went as mendicants to peasants.

> If you wanted thy father's inheritance, acquire his knowledge
> Because this property of his may be spent in ten days."

An illustrious scholar, who was the tutor of a royal prince, had the habit of striking him unceremoniously and treating him severely. The boy, who could no longer bear this violence, went to his father to complain and when he had taken off his coat, the father's heart was moved with pity. Accordingly he called for the tutor and said: "Thou dost not permit thyself to indulge in so much cruelty towards the children of my subjects as thou inflictest upon my son. What is the reason?" He replied: "It is incumbent upon all persons in general to converse in a sedate manner and to behave in a laudable way but more especially upon padshahs because whatever they say or do is commented on by everybody, the utterances or acts of common people being of no such consequence.

> If a hundred unworthy things are committed by a dervish
> His companions do not know one in a hundred.
> But if a padshah utters only one jest
> It is borne from country to country.

"It is the duty of a royal prince's tutor to train up the sons of his lord in refinement of morals—*and Allah caused her to grow up as a beautiful plant*—more diligently than the sons of common people."

POEMS OF KABIR AND NANAK

The Muslim conquest of India, beginning in the late twelfth century, created conflicts between Hindus and Muslims which have continued until today. Hinduism has tended to accommodate a variety of incarnations (avatars) of God, while Islam vigorously upholds monotheism and discourages artistic representations of God. Hinduism stresses the variety of avenues to the sacred, the importance of caste, ritual, and ceremony, and the divinity in all things. Islam dismisses caste and ceremony in favor of a singular, total commitment to one God.

Despite initial antagonisms, however, Hindu and Muslim thinkers did develop accommodations to each other's religion. Hinduism increasingly centered its faith on the god Vishnu, and Muslims borrowed elements of Vishnu worship. In this way, new sects developed, especially in the fifteenth century, that attempted to combine Hinduism and Islam. One of the earliest representatives of these syncretic sects was the holy man and poet Kabir (1440–1518), a Muslim weaver from the Hindu holy city, Benares. Another was Nanak (1469–1539) the founder of Sikhism. How do their poems call for a union between Hindu and Muslim? Is Kabir still more Muslim, or Nanak more Hindu? Why do you suppose more people did not follow the lead of these two thinkers?

From *One Hundred Poems of Kabir* by Rabindranath Tagore. New York: Macmillan, 1915; and From *The Sacred Writings of the Sikhs,* translated by Trilocaan Singh et al. London: George Allen & Unwin, 1960. Reprinted by permission of the publisher.

FROM THE POEMS OF KABIR

1

O servant, where dost thou seek Me?
Lo! I am beside thee.
I am neither in temple nor in mosque: I am neither in Kaaba nor
in Kailash:
Neither am I in rites and ceremonies, nor in Yoga and
renunciation.
If thou art a true seeker, thou shalt at once see Me: thou shalt meet
Me in a moment of time.
Kabir says, "O Sadhu! God is the breath of all breath."

2

It is needless to ask of a saint the caste to which he belongs;
For the priest, the warrior, the tradesman, and all the thirty-six
castes, alike are seeking for God.
It is but folly to ask what the caste of a saint may be;
The barber has sought God, the washerwoman, and the carpenter—
Even Raidas was a seeker after God.
The Rishi Swapacha was a tanner by caste.
Hindus and Moslems alike have achieved that End, where remains
no mark of distinction.

3

O how may I ever express that secret word?
O how can I say He is not like this, and He is like that?
If I say that He is within me, the universe is ashamed:
If I say that He is without me, it is falsehood.
He makes the inner and the outer worlds to be indivisibly one;
The conscious and the unconscious, both are His footstools.
He is neither manifest nor hidden, he is neither revealed nor
unrevealed:
There are no words to tell that which He is.

FROM THE HYMNS OF NANAK

1

The Vedas proclaim Him,
So do the readers of the Puranas;

The learned speak of Him in many discourses;
Brahma and Indra speak of Him,
Shivas speak of Him, Siddhas speak of Him,
The Buddhas He has created, proclaim Him.

The demons and the gods speak of Him,
Demigods, men, sages and devotees
All try to describe Him;
Many have tried and still try to describe Him;
Many have spoken of Him and departed.

If as many people as lived in all the past
Were now to describe Him each in His own way,
Even then He would not be adequately described.
The Lord becometh as great as He wishes to be.
If anyone dares to claim that he can describe Him,
Write him down as the greatest fool on earth.

2

Going forth a begging,
Let contentment be thine earnings,
Modesty thy begging bowl,
Smear thy body with ashes of meditation,
Let contemplation of death be thy beggar's rags;

Let thy body be chaste, virginal, clean,
Let faith in God be the staff on which thou leanest;
Let brotherhood with every man on earth
Be the highest aspiration of your Yogic Order.
Know that to subdue the mind
Is to subdue the world.

Hail, all hail unto Him,
Let your greetings be to the Primal God;
Pure and without beginning, changeless,
The same from age to age.

16. African Civilizations

MALI IN THE FOURTEENTH CENTURY

AL OMARI

The power and wealth of the states in the African Sudan can be seen in this account by Al Omari, a Muslim visitor to Cairo. He tells of the 1324 visit to Cairo of Mansa Musa of Mali, who was on his way to Mecca. Twelve years later, people were still talking about the huge amounts of gold Mansa Musa distributed in Cairo. What does this account tell you about the political administration of Mali? What does it tell you about the Mali economy?

During my first journey to Cairo and sojourn there I heard talk of the arrival of the Sultan Musa [*Mansa Musa*], emperor of Mali and I found the Cairenes very glad to talk of the large expenditures of those people. I questioned the Emir Abu'l 'Abbas Ahmed ben Abi'l Haki, el Mehmendar, who spoke of the sultan's noble appearance, dignity and trustworthiness. "When I went out to greet him in the name of the glorious Sultan el Malik en Nasir [of Egypt]," he told me, "he gave me the warmest of welcomes and treated me with the most careful politeness. But he would talk to me only through an interpreter [that is, his spokesman or linguist] although he could speak perfect Arabic. He carried his imperial treasure in many pieces of gold, worked or otherwise.

"I suggested that he should go up to the palace and meet the Sultan [of Egypt]. But he refused, saying: 'I came for the pilgrimage, and for nothing else, and I do not wish to mix up my pilgrimage with anything else.' He argued about this. However, I well understood that the meeting was repugnant to him because he was loath to kiss the ground [before the Sultan] or to kiss his hand. I went on insisting and he went on making excuses. But imperial protocol obliged me to present him, and I did not leave him until he had agreed. When he came into the Sultan's presence we asked him to kiss the ground. But he refused and continued to refuse, saying: 'However can this be?' Then a wise man of his suite

From *The African Past,* edited by Basil Davidson. Copyright © 1964 Basil Davidson. Reprinted with permission of Curtis Brown, Ltd., London.

whispered several words to him that I could not understand. 'Very well,' he thereupon declared, 'I will prostrate myself before Allah who created me and brought me into the world.' Having done so he moved towards the Sultan. The latter rose for a moment to welcome him and asked him to sit beside him: then they had a long conversation. After Sultan Musa had left the palace the Sultan of Cairo sent him gifts of clothing for himself, his courtiers and all those who were with him; saddled and bridled horses for himself and his chief officers. . . .

"When the time of pilgrimage arrived, [the Sultan of Egypt] sent him a large quantity of drachmas, baggage camels and choice riding camels with saddles and harness. [The Sultan of Egypt] caused abundant quantities of foodstuffs to be brought for his suite and his followers, established posting-stations for the feeding of the animals, and gave to the emirs of the pilgrimage a written order to look after and respect [the Emperor of Mali]. When the latter returned it was I who went to greet him and settle him into his quarters. . . ."

"This man," el Mehmendar also told me, "spread upon Cairo the flood of his generosity: there was no person, officer of the [Cairo] court or holder of any office of the [Cairo] sultanate who did not receive a sum in gold from him. The people of Cairo earned incalculable sums from him, whether by buying and selling or by gifts. So much gold was current in Cairo that it ruined the value of money." . . .

Let me add [continues Omari] that gold in Egypt had enjoyed a high rate of exchange up to the moment of their arrival. The gold *mitqal* that year had not fallen below twenty-five drachmas. But from that day [of their arrival] onward, its value dwindled; the exchange was ruined, and even now it has not recovered. The *mitqal* scarcely touches twenty-two drachmas. That is how it has been for twelve years from that time, because of the great amounts of gold they brought to Egypt and spent there.

THE EMPIRE OF MALI

The king of this country is known to the people of Egypt as the king of Tekrur [roughly, inland Senegal]; but he himself becomes indignant when he is called thus, since Tekrur is only one of the countries of his empire. The title he prefers is that of lord of Mali, the largest of his states; it is the name by which he is most known. He is the most important of the Muslim Negro kings; his land is the largest, his army the most numerous; he is the king who is the most powerful, the richest, the most fortunate, the most feared by his enemies and the most able to do good to those around him.

His kingdom consists of the lands of Gana, Zagun, Tirakka, Tekrur, Bambugu, Zarquatabana, Darmura, Zaga, Kabora, Baraguri, Gao-gao.

The inhabitants of Gao-gao are of the tribes of Yarten. The region of Mali is that where the residence of the king is situated [in] the town of Niane, and all the other regions are dependent on it; it has the official name of Mali because it is the capital of this kingdom which also includes towns, villages and centers of population to the number of fourteen.

The honorable and truthful Sheikh Abu Sa'id Otman ed Dukkaldi, who has lived in the town of Niane for thirty-five years and traveled throughout the kingdom, has told me that this is square in shape, being four months [of travel] in length and at least as much in breadth. . . .

The sultan of this country has sway over the land of the "desert of native gold," whence they bring him gold every year. The inhabitants of that land are savage pagans whom the sultan would subject to him if he wished. But the sovereigns of this kingdom have learned by experience that whenever one of them has conquered one of these gold towns, established Islam there and sounded the call to prayer, the harvest of gold dwindles and falls to nothing, meanwhile it grows and expands in neighboring pagan countries. When experience had confirmed them in this observation, they left the gold country in the hands of its pagan inhabitants, and contented themselves with assuring their obedience and paying tribute.

RECEPTION AT COURT

The sultan of this kingdom presides in his palace on a great balcony called *bembe* where he has a great seat of ebony that is like a throne fit for a large and tall person: on either side it is flanked by elephant tusks turned towards each other. His arms stand near him, being all of gold, saber, lance, quiver, bow and arrows. He wears wide trousers made of about twenty pieces [of stuff] of a kind which he alone may wear. Behind him there stand about a score of Turkish or other pages which are bought for him in Cairo: one of them, at his left, holds a silk umbrella surmounted by a dome and a bird of gold: the bird has the figure of a falcon. His officers are seated in a circle about him, in two rows, one to the right and one to the left; beyond them sit the chief commanders of his cavalry. In front of him there is a person who never leaves him and who is his executioner; also another who serves as intermediary [that is, official spokesman] between the sovereign and his subjects, and who is named the herald. In front of them again, there are drummers. Others dance before their sovereign, who enjoys this, and make him laugh. Two banners are spread behind him. Before him they keep two saddled and bridled horses in case he should wish to ride.

THE IMPORTANCE OF HORSES

Arab horses are brought for sale to the kings of this country, who spend considerable sums in this way. Their army numbers one hundred thousand men of whom there are about ten thousand horse-mounted cavalry: the others are infantry having neither horses nor any other mounts. They have camels in this country but do not know the art of riding them with a saddle. . . .

The officers of this king, his soldiers and his guard receive gifts of land and presents. Some among the greatest of them receive as much as fifty thousand *mitqals* of gold a year, besides which the king provides them with horses and clothing. He is much concerned with giving them fine garments and making his cities into capitals.

ROYAL BUREAUCRACY

It is one of their customs that whenever someone charged with a certain task of important affair reports to the king, the latter questions him on everything that has happened from the time of his departure to the time of his return, and in great detail. Legal cases and appeals also go up to the sovereign who examines them himself. Generally he writes nothing; but gives his orders, most of the time, orally.

TRAVELS IN MALI

IBN BATTUTA

The gold of Mali held a strong attraction for Muslim traders from North Africa. A grueling trade developed across the Sahara desert in which salt from the desert salt beds was traded for Sudanese gold. The great traveller Ibn Battuta gives us an idea of this trade. He made the trip in 1352. He also gives us an insight into both North African attitudes towards blacks and life in Mali. What kind of things impress him most? In what ways does he add to your understanding of Mali?

At Sijilmasa[1] I bought camels and a four months' supply of forage for them. Thereupon I set out on the 1st Muharram of the year seven

---

1. Principal trading station south of the Atlas, near modern Tafilelt.

From *Travels of Ibn Battuta in Asia and Africa,* written and translated by H. A. R. Gibb. London: Routledge & Kegan Paul, 1927.

hundred and fifty-three (18th February 1352) with a caravan including, amongst others, a number of the merchants of Sijilmasa. After twenty-five days we reached Taghaza,[2] an unattractive village, with the curious feature that its houses and mosques are built of blocks of salt, roofed with camel skins. There are no trees there, nothing but sand. In the sand is a salt mine; they dig for the salt, and find it in thick slabs, lying one on top of the other, as though they had been tool-squared and laid under the surface of the earth. A camel will carry two of these slabs. No one lives at Taghaza except the slaves of the Masufa tribe, who dig for the salt; they subsist on dates imported from Dara[3] and Sijilmasa, camel's flesh, and millet imported from the Negrolands. The Negroes came up from their country and take away the salt from there. At Walata a load of salt brings eight to ten *mithqals*; in the town of Mali it sells for twenty to thirty, and sometimes as much as forty. The Negroes use salt as a medium of exchange, just as gold and silver is used elsewhere; they cut it up into pieces, and buy and sell with it. The business done at Taghaza, for all its meanness, amounts to an enormous figure in terms of hundredweights of gold dust. . . .

Thus we reached the town of Walata after a journey of two months to a day. Walata is the northernmost province of the Negroes, and the sultan's representative there was one Farba Husayn, *farba* meaning deputy (in their language). When we arrived there, the merchants deposited their goods in an open square, where the blacks undertook to guard them, and went to the *farba*. He was sitting on a carpet under an archway, with his guards before him carrying lances and bows in their hands, and the headman of the Masufa behind him. The merchants remained standing in front of him while he spoke to them through an interpreter, although they were close to him, to show his contempt for them.[4] It was then that I repented of having come to their country, because of their lack of manners and their contempt for the whites. . . .

Later on the *mushrif* (inspector) of Walata, whose name was Mansa Ju, invited all those who had come with the caravan to partake of his hospitality. At first I refused to attend, but my companions urged me very strongly, so I went with the rest. The repast was served—some pounded millet mixed with a little honey and milk, put in a half calabash shaped like a large bowl. The guests drank and retired, I said to them, "Was it for this that the black invited us?" They answered, "Yes; and it is in their opinion the highest form of hospitality." This convinced me that there was no good to be hoped for from these people, and I made

2. Important outpost of the Negro empires.
3. The Wadi Dra which drains the southern slopes of the anti-Atlas mountains.
4. It was common practice in West Africa for rulers to communicate only through the medium of an official "interpreter," who relayed the speech backward and forward. There was a similar practice at the Ethiopian court.

up my mind to travel back to Morocco at once with the pilgrim caravan from Walata. Afterwards, however, I thought it best to go to see the capital of their king (at Mali). My stay at Walata lasted about fifty days; and I was shown honor and entertained by its inhabitants. It is an excessively hot place, and boasts a few small date-palms, in the shade of which they sow watermelons. Its water comes from underground water beds at that point, and there is plenty of mutton to be had. The garments of the inhabitants, most of whom belong to the Masufa tribe, are of fine Egyptian fabrics. Their women are of surpassing beauty, and are shown more respect than the men. The state of affairs amongst these people is indeed extraordinary. Their men show no sign of jealousy whatever; no one claims descent from his father, but on the contrary from his mother's brother. A person's heirs are his sister's sons, not his own sons. This is a thing which I have seen nowhere in the world except among the Indians of Malabar. But those are heathens; *these* people are Muslims, punctilious in observing the hours of prayer, studying books of law, and memorizing the Koran. Yet their women show no bashfulness before men and do not veil themselves, though they are assiduous in attending prayers. Any man who wishes to marry one of them may do so, but they do not travel with their husbands, and, even if one desired to do so, her family would not allow her to go.

The women have their "friends" and "companions" amongst the men outside their own families, and the men in the same way have "companions" amongst the women of other families. A man may go into his house and find his wife entertaining her "companion" but he takes no objection to it. One day at Walata I went into the qadi's[5] house, after asking his permission to enter, and found with him a young woman of remarkable beauty. When I saw her I was shocked and turned to go out, but she laughed at me, instead of being overcome by shame, and the qadi said to me, "Why are you going out? She is my companion." I was amazed at their conduct, for he was a theologian and a pilgrim to boot. I was told that he had asked the sultan's permission to make the pilgrimage that year with his "companion" (whether this one or not I cannot say) but the sultan would not grant it.

When I decided to make the journey to Mali, which is reached in twenty-four days from Walata if the traveler pushes on rapidly, I hired a guide from the Masufa (for there is no necessity to travel in company on account of the safety of that road), and set out with three of my companions. On the way there are many trees, and these trees are of great age and girth; a whole caravan may shelter in the shade of one of them. There are trees[6] which have neither branches nor leaves, yet the shade cast by their trunks is sufficient to shelter a man. Some of these

5. Qadi: a Muslim judge.
6. Baobab trees.

trees are rotted in the interior and the rain water collects in them, so that they serve as wells, and the people drink of the water inside them. In others there are bees and honey, which is collected by the people. I was surprised to find inside one tree, by which I passed, a man, a weaver, who had set up his loom in it and was actually weaving.

A traveler in this country carries no provisions, whether plain food or seasonings, and neither gold nor silver. He takes nothing but pieces of salt and glass ornaments, which the people call beads, and some aromatic goods. When he comes to a village the women-folk of the blacks bring out millet, milk, chickens, pulped lotus fruit, rice, *funi* (a grain resembling mustard seed, from which *kuskusu*[7] and gruel are made), and pounded haricot beans. The traveler buys what of these he wants, but their rice causes sickness to whites when it is eaten, and the *funi* is preferable to it. . . .

Ten days after leaving Walata we came to the village of Zaghari, a large village, inhabited by Negro traders called *wanjarati*,[8] along with whom live a community of whites of the Ibadite sect. It is from this village that the millet is carried to Walata. After leaving Zaghari we came to the great river that is the Nile,[9] on which stands the town of Karsakhu. The Nile flows from there down to Kabara, and thence to Zagha. In both Kabara and Zagha there are sultans who owe allegiance to the king of Mali. The inhabitants of Zagha are of old standing in Islam; they show a great devotion and zeal for study. Thence the Nile descends to Timbuktu and Gao, both of which will be described later; then to the town of Muli in the land of the Limis, which is the frontier province of (the kingdom of) Mali; thence to Nupe, one of the largest towns of the Negroes, whose ruler is one of the most considerable of the Negro rulers. It cannot be visited by any white man because they would kill him before he got there. . . .

I saw a crocodile in this part of the Nile, close to the bank; it looked just like a small boat. One day I went down to the river to satisfy a need, and lo, one of the blacks came and stood between me and the river. I was amazed at such lack of manners and decency on his part, and spoke of it to someone or other. He answered, "His purpose in doing that was solely to protect you from the crocodile, by placing himself between you and it."

We set out thereafter from Karsakhu and came to the river of Sansara, which is about ten miles from Mali. It is their custom that no persons except those who have obtained permission are allowed to enter the city. I had already written to the white community (there) requesting them to hire a house for me, so when I arrived at the river, I crossed by the ferry

7. Cereal dish of Northwest Africa made from coarsely ground flour.
8. Wangara traders from Mali.
9. It was, of course, not the Nile but the Niger.

without interference. Thus I reached the city of Mali, the capital of the king of the blacks. . . .

The sultan of Mali is Mansa Sulayman, *mansa* meaning (in Mande) sultan, and Sulayman being his proper name. He is a miserly king, not a man from who one might hope for a rich present. . . .

On certain days the sultan holds audiences in the palace yard, where there is a platform under a tree, with three steps; this they call the *pempi*. It is carpeted with silk, and has cushions placed on it. (Over it) is raised the umbrella, which is a sort of pavilion made of silk, surmounted by a bird of gold, about the size of a falcon. The sultan comes out of a door in a corner of the palace, carrying a bow in his hand and a quiver on his back. On his head he has a golden skullcap, bound with a gold band which has narrow ends shaped like knives, more than a span in length. His usual dress is a velvety red tunic, made of the European fabrics called *mutanfas*. The sultan is preceded by his musicians, who carry gold and silver *gumbris* (two-stringed guitars), and behind him come three hundred armed slaves. He walks in a leisurely fashion, affecting a very slow movement, and even stops from time to time. On reaching the *pempi* he stops and looks round the assembly, then ascends it in the sedate manner of a preacher ascending a mosque pulpit. As he takes his seat the drums, trumpets, and bugles are sounded. Three slaves go out at a run to summon the sovereign's deputy and the military command-ers, who enter and sit down. Two saddled and bridled horses are brought, along with two goats, which they hold to serve as a protection against the evil eye. Dugha stands at the gate, and the rest of the people remain in the street under the trees.

The Negroes are, of all people, the most submissive to their king and the most abject in their behavior before him. They swear by his name, saying, "Mansa Sulayman ki."[10] If he summons any of them while he is holding an audience in the pavilion, the person summoned takes off his clothes and puts on worn garments, removes his turban and dons a dirty skullcap, and enters with his garments and trousers raised knee-high. He goes forward in an attitude of humility and dejection, and knocks the ground hard with his elbows, then stands with bowed head and bent back listening to what he says. If anyone addresses the king and receives a reply from him, he uncovers his back and throws dust over his head and back, for all the world like a bather splashing himself with water. I used to wonder how it was they did not blind themselves. If the sultan delivers any remarks during his audience, those present take off their turbans and put them down, and listen to what he says. Sometimes one of them stands up before him and recalls his deeds in the sultan's service, saying "I did so-and-so on such a day," or, "I killed so-and-so on such a

10. "The Emperor Sulayman has commanded," in Mandingo.

day." Those who have knowledge of this confirm his words, which they do by plucking the cord of the bow and releasing it with a twang, just as an archer does when shooting an arrow. If the sultan says, "Truly spoken," or thanks him, he removes his clothes and "dusts." That is their idea of good manners. . . .

I was at Mali during the two festivals of the sacrifice and the fast-breaking. On these days the sultan takes his seat on the *pempi* after the mid-afternoon prayer. The armor-bearers bring in magnificent arms—quivers of gold and silver, swords ornamented with gold and with golden scabbards, gold and silver lances, and crystal maces. At his head stand four *amirs* driving off the flies, having in their hands silver ornaments resembling saddle stirrups. The commanders, qadi, and preacher sit in their usual places. The interpreter Dugha comes with his four wives and his slave-girls, who are about a hundred in number. They are wearing beautiful robes, and on their heads they have gold and silver fillets, with gold and silver balls attached. A chair is placed for Dugha to sit on. He plays on an instrument made of reeds, with some small calabashes at its lower end, and chants a poem in praise of the sultan, recalling his battles and deeds of valor. The women and girls sing along with him and play with bows. Accompanying them are about thirty youths, wearing red woolen tunics and white skullcaps; each of them has a drum slung from his shoulder and beats it. Afterward come his boy pupils who play and turn wheels in the air, like the natives of Sind. They show a marvelous nimbleness and agility in these exercises, and play most cleverly with swords. Dugha makes a fine play with the sword. Thereupon the sultan orders a gift to be presented to Dugha and he is given a purse containing two hundred *mithqals* of gold dust, and is informed of the contents of the purse before all the people. The commanders rise and twang their bows in thanks to the sultan. The next day each one of them gives Dugha a gift, every man acording to his rank. Every Friday after the 'asr prayer, Dugha carries out a similar ceremony to this that we have described.

On feast-days, after Dugha has finished his display, the poets come in. Each of them is inside a figure resembling a thrush, made of feathers, and provided with a wooden head with a red beak, to look like a thrush's head. They stand in front of the sultan in this ridiculous make-up and recite their poems. I was told that their poetry is a kind of sermonizing in which they say to the sultan: "This *pempi* which you occupy was that whereon sat this king and that king, and such were this one's noble actions and such and such the other's. So do you too do good deeds whose memory will outlive you." After that the chief of the poets mounts the steps of the *pempi* and lays his head on the sultan's lap, then climbs to the top of the *pempi* and lays his head first on the sultan's right shoulder and then on his left, speaking all the while in their tongue, and finally he comes down again. I was told that this practice is a very old custom amongst them, prior to the introduction of Islam, and that they have kept it up.

The Negroes disliked Mansa Sulayman because of his avarice. His predecessor was Mansa Magha, and before him reigned Mansa Musa, a generous and virtuous prince, who loved the whites and made gifts to them. It was he who gave Ibn Ishaq as-Sahili four thousand *mithqals* in the course of a single day. I heard from a truthworthy source that he gave three thousand *mithqals* on one day to Mudrik ibn Faqqus, by whose grandfather his own grandfather, Saraq Jata, had been converted to Islam.

The Negroes possess some admirable qualities. They are seldom unjust, and have a greater abhorrence of injustice than any other people. The sultan shows no mercy to anyone who is guilty of the least act of it. There is complete security in their country. Neither traveler nor inhabitant in it has anything to fear from robbers or men of violence. They do not confiscate the property of any white man who dies in their country, even if it be accounted wealth. On the contrary, they give it into the charge of some trustworthy person among the whites, until the rightful heir takes possession of it. They are careful to observe the hours of prayer, and assiduous in attending them in congregations, and in bringing up their children to them. On Fridays, if a man does not go early to the mosque, he cannot find a corner to pray in, on account of the crowd. It is a custom of theirs to send each man his boy (to the mosque) with his prayer mat; the boy spreads it out for his master in a place befitting him and remains on it (until his master comes to the mosque). The prayer-mats are made of the leaves of a tree resembling a date-palm, but without fruit.

Another of their good qualities is their habit of wearing clean white garments on Fridays. Even if a man has nothing but an old worn shirt, he washes it and cleans it, and wears it at the Friday service. Yet another is their zeal for learning the Koran by heart. They put their children in chains if they show any backwardness in memorizing it, and they are not set free until they have it by heart. I visited the qadi in his house on the day of the festival. His children were chained up, so I said to him, "Will you not let them loose?" He replied, "I shall not do so until they learn the Koran by heart." Among their bad qualities are the following. The women servants, slave-girls, and young girls go about in front of everyone naked, without a stitch of clothing on them. Women go into the sultan's presence naked and without coverings, and his daughters also go about naked. Then there is the custom of their putting dust and ashes on their heads as a mark of respect, and the grotesque ceremonies we have described when the poets recite their verses. Another reprehensible practice among many of them is the eating of carrion, dogs, and asses.

AFRICAN LAW

PAUL BOHANNAN AND
PHILIP CURTIN

Traditional Africa contained wealthy centralized states like Mali, Ghana, and Songhai. It also contained stateless societies in which clans and villages were largely self-governing. In this modern account by Paul Bohannan, an anthropologist, and Philip Curtin, a historian, we get a sense of how traditional African law worked in stateless societies as well as states. How are stateless societies different from states in their law and courts? What are the relative advantages of each?

Although many references to warfare among African societies are found in travel books, in historical source materials, and even in ethnographic accounts, there is no study of warfare in Africa that pretends to tie that information together. With law, that other primary political function, the situation is far different. The written material on African law is extensive; although much of it written by Europeans is uncomprehending restatement of substantive norms as legal rules—the pigeonholes of common law filled with exotic fauna—there is nevertheless a substantial body of knowledge about African law.

Indeed, Africa is one of the homes of advanced legal institutions. Perhaps the most famous of these institutions are the courts still found among the Bantu states of the southern third of the continent. Here the local or provincial chief was one of a number of judges on a large and inclusive bench. The bench included representatives of all the important social groups of the community, whether in any particular case they were seen as territorial segments and communities, as kinship units such as clans, or even as age-sets. The judges formed a regular and pronounced hierarchy, and were seated in a row or an arc. The provincial chief sat in the middle; at his immediate right was the second most senior person (however seniority might be computed locally) and at his left the third most senior. To his right, but farther removed, the fourth most senior, and so on, right and left, until the whole court was deployed more or less in a row.

There were, then, certain areas in which the litigants were to stand or, more often, sit on the ground. There were assigned places for witnesses, for the nobility, for the followers and backers of the litigants, and for the community as an audience. These court sessions were often held out of doors, but there might be a building for them—colonial governments preferred them inside so that regular schedules, based on clock and calendar time, could be maintained even in the face of hostile weather.

There was, in all cases, also a known, and demanded, decorum and order of proceedings. The plantiff (to use an English term with only a 90 percent fit) made his plea—usually without counsel—and was usually allowed to finish his whole complaint, so long as he spoke well and to the point. The defendant (another translation that does not fit precisely) then made a reply and told his version of the story. Witnesses were called—including what we would call expert witnesses and character witnesses. Then, after the principals had each told his side of the dispute, and after witnesses had been heard, the most junior member of the bench, down at the far end, pronounced sentence. His statements probably included moral lectures, statements of the proper kind of behavior that should have been carried out in the situation, and he may have cited precedent. His judgment would be followed by that of the man at the other end of the line, his immediate senior, who might disagree, and who added new views and new opinions. The third most junior man followed, and so on until they arrived at the middle where the head chief pronounced the final sentence. He had heard everything that the representatives of the community had to say. He had a chance to weigh the evidence, the judgments, and the opinions of his junior judges. His word on the decision became final.

In the southern Bantu states, there were also well-known and highly effective means for carrying out the decisions of the court. The community, having been represented in the audience as well as on the bench, brought both sacred and mundane sanctions to bear. The decisions of such courts were obeyed. Indeed, such communities might be reasonably said to have a "body of law" or *corpus juris* in the lawyer's sense—a body of law and adjudged precedent against which to try each succeeding case.

Law in a stateless society was almost as effective but worked differently. Each case became a treaty-making process. The difference between the two is vital, because in the treaty-making process, the role of precedent is far less commanding and the application of sanction far more diffuse. Indeed, the fact that a solution has been used before may be the very thing about it that a case sets out to overcome.

The difference can best be seen from an examination of our own family law. The norms of family living in modern America are fairly well known and fairly circumscribed. The institutionalization of families is such that these norms are fairly well maintained. A very few of these norms are *restated* for legal purposes: the grounds for divorce, the laws against beating children, and perhaps some others. The large range of family activity is not in any wise made part of a body of *law*, in the narrow sense. The mistake of assuming a body of law in an African stateless society is precisely the same mistake as would be the error of reporting all of the norms for living displayed by the American family as if those norms were part of the law of the land.

In order to comprehend African legal systems fully, then, it becomes necessary to have a new theoretical framework: one which is inclusive of both the law of a state system and that of stateless societies. Such a framework is particularly necessary when we investigate the ways in which the stateless societies are changing on the demand first of the colonial governments and now of the independent governments. These people, who are adapting to state forms on demand, often experience severe difficulty because they see law based on precedent as always and necessarily tyrannous.

There is seldom if ever a special body constituted in order to hear and settle disputes in stateless societies. Rather these disputes are settled by meetings that can be profitably compared with the old New England town meetings, except that in the case of the African stateless societies, there are always two factions and the actual size of the unit may change from case to case depending on the closeness of the relationship of the principals to the dispute.

There is, in Old English, a precise and accurate word to describe these "town meetings" or settlement of disputes by the important members of the village. This word is "moot." Well into the twelfth and thirteenth centuries Anglo-Saxon communities settled their disputes by meeting outside, under the shade of a tree, in whole communities, in order to discover correct and just solutions to disputes. Such is, in a sense, the origin of the "common law."

Courts, unlike moots, are special organs and require some sort of state organization from which they derive their power. While moots are a mode of the community, courts are special arms of politically organized states.

Moots and courts can, and in Africa often do, exist side by side within the same society. The jurisdiction of the courts may be limited to certain types of cases or to disputes of people of different villages or something of the sort. Vansina has given an extremely cogent example from the Luba of the Congo. The Luba state has a very complex court system, the personnel of which changes with the nature of the dispute or offense; at the same time, however, many Luba cases are settled by moots rather than by courts.

During the colonial era, and undoubtedly down to the present day, such stateless societies as that of the Tiv had a full-blown system of moots which ran side by side with the system of courts that had been introduced by the colonial government. Among these people it was considered to be totally immoral to call one's close kinsman before a government court. However, disputes obviously did occur between close kinsmen. These disputes were always and necessarily settled in moots. In colonial Nigeria charges of witchcraft could not be brought before courts, since "proof" had to be adduced or else the accused could sue the accuser for slander. Since witchcraft is difficult to "prove" in a court, witchcraft disputes had throughout the country to be settled either in moots or in kangaroo courts.

There were devices other than courts and moots by which Africans sometimes settled disputes. Ordeals and recourse to seers and diviners were both fairly widely spread throughout the continent. An ordeal is a means for settling a dispute in the absence of any kind of evidence which can prove or disprove the charge, either because there are no witnesses or because (as in the case of witchcraft) empirical proof is impossible.

Probably no people claims that oracles and ordeals have anything to do with justice. However, they do settle the dispute. Ordeals ran all the way from taking oaths on shrines through the deliberate administration of poisonous substances either to animals or to human beings themselves. These substances were not necessarily lethal, and if the animals or the person did not die, the party was usually considered innocent. Some tribes such as the Azande of the Sudan checked and counterchecked their oracular mechanisms by requiring corroboration by a second oracle before they would act on them. Ordeals have all but disappeared from modern Euro-American courts. However, the divine sanctions in which ordeals deal are still a part of such courts because it is still necessary for both witnesses and the principals to take oaths on entering the witness stand.

Africans sometimes resorted to contests to settle disputes. This "game" solution to a dispute is one in which the disputants are either forced to or agree to reduce the field of relevance, and determine a winner; they reopen the field and declare the winner in the game to be the winner of the real-life situation. In the early history of Roman law and others, gladiatorial contests to settle disputes were not unknown.

Perhaps the most important of the sanctions, particularly in the stateless societies, was the institutionalized use of self-help (an example of which is the man who takes a goat from another man who legitimately owes him one). Some degree of self-help is either condoned or required in all legal systems. It becomes even more important in non-state organizations than it is in states because the major sanction, and the power behind it, is to be found in the right and ability of the groups concerned to carry out the decisions made by the elders.

If self-help gets out of hand it becomes, of course, akin to lawlessness—in any sort of society. The boundaries have to be fixed and the use of self-help contained if it is to be an adequate judicial mechanism. In states, such limitations can be defined by legislation or by precedent. In non-states, self-help is controlled, but controlled some-what differently. In our example of the man taking the goat, his own group will come to his defense if the others try to retaliate. However, if he takes the goat irrationally, and in a way that they believe the moot would not approve of—if he has a "bad case," or if he is a criminal—his kinfolk will not risk their hides and their reputation for him. Limitation is achieved by balance of power and of organizational principles.

Africans in every part of the continent have proved themselves capable of running complex modern governments. The basic ideas behind the political thinking of many of their citizens, however, are still to be found in the type of situation that has been described here.

On the surface, African institutions are changing very rapidly, but the quickening ideas, molded by experience and language, have deep roots in African tradition and history. Because the deep roots of both African and European tradition tap the same prehistoric reserves, and because Africans have passed through most of the cultural revolutions which have, perhaps in other terms, also been the experience of the West, their adaptation has been fast and successful. For all that, however, the distinct idiom in many instances remains. Whatever trouble Africans and Europeans may have in discussing matters with one another in the postcolonial world, much at least is attributable to the fact that they make different political assumptions.

AFRICAN ART

PAUL BOHANNAN AND
PHILIP CURTIN

African art, especially music, dance, and sculpture, is widely admired and imitated. Does art play a different role in African society from that which it does in American society? Is art in modern society (African or American) less immediate, less necessary?

THE FORMS AND TECHNIQUES OF AFRICAN ART

The main forms of African art that have become widely known outside of Africa are limited to sculpture and music. African music is coming into its own as one of the world's great musics that has several specific contributions to make. Undoubtedly the most dramatic of the special attributes is its polyrhythmic structure. Polyrhythms are complex combinations of fairly simple but different rhythms, all played concurrently. Western music has the "classic" situation of "two against three"—the triplet played against two "full-value" notes during the same time span. Rarely, in Western music, a third rhythm may be added. In African music, on the other hand, five such rhythms are common, and as many as a dozen at a time have been recorded.

Although African dancing has been for a long time one of the two favorite sights of tourists in Africa, few outsiders have been able to realize its full quality and artistic achievement. The point of African dancing in many parts of the continent, at least, is for various parts of the body each to accompany one of the rhythms in the orchestra so that the polyrhythms in the orchestra are reproduced by the dancer's body. The head moves in one rhythm, the shoulders in another; the arms in still a third, the trunk in another, and the feet in still another. Once the viewer has learned to see and feel the polyrhythms in the dance as it reflects the music, he can appreciate that African dancing both demands great precision and allows great freedom of expression to the dancers. African dancing is still a folk art; there have been a few attempts to produce it for the stage—notably the Ballets Africaines of Guinea—but too often the European and American audiences have not been sufficiently sophisticated and the individual dances cut too short to give the dancers sufficient play for their imagination and the variations that each dance requires if the rhythms are to be fully explored.

In African literature the great form is the dramatic tale. African tales have affected the literatures of many lands, particularly of the southern United States and the Caribbean area, where the so-called Brer Rabbit stories have become standard. Collections of African folk tales are also quite common, even though they are usually studied only by specialists. In all of these manifestations, however, the true quality of the original has been left behind in Africa. The mere tale on a page will produce little more than would the retelling of the plot of *As You Like It* in two paragraphs, with a moral tacked on at the end, fable-fashion. These dramatic tales in Africa have a theatrical quality. They are told and acted out before audiences who participate in musical choruses and in spoken responses. The individual tale-tellers may be assisted by a dozen or more people who are costumed and "cast" as in any other theater art. The tale-teller also makes up songs, centering around the situation of the tale; he teaches the choruses of the songs to the audience and assures himself audience response whenever he needs it. The stories of the tales are well known. The achievement of the individual artist is to be found in the music and in the version of the tale and the way he manipulates the dramatic elements in it to enlarge or point his moral. The result is living theater. It cannot be overemphasized that African folk-tales, written on half a sheet of paper in a Western language, lose all but the so-called "plot" of the original. The art is gone. Again, it should be noted that the dramatic tale demands of its performers compliance with a certain set of activities, and then encourages individualization and free expression.

Nevertheless, the best known of the African arts, outside of Africa, is sculpture. It is to sculpture that most attention is to be given here. With a few notable exceptions, such as the soapstone carvings of Sierra Leone, the iron sculpture to be found in a few isolated places, and the ivories of Benin and the Congo, African sculptors work either in green wood or in various alloys of copper, tin, and zinc that hover around bronze and brass.

African carvers work almost exclusively in green wood. The carver must know a great deal about the qualities of different woods, so that they will not crack too much when dry, although cracks appear in most pieces of African art—even in Africa, let alone when they are subjected to the high and dry temperatures of American and European homes and museums.

Woodworking is done with an adze and is finished with a double-edged knife. In some parts of the continent, some sculptors use rough leaves as sandpaper. The carvings may be painted with all sorts of mineral and vegetable colors (and today with imported colors), the most common being lampblack set by the sap of any of several trees.

Indigenous African sculpture falls into three sorts: one is the figurine, which may vary from small and simple figures only a few inches high, to elaborate carved house posts, stools, or other functional forms. The figurines are fundamentally adaptations from the tree trunk, with the heaviest weight at the bottom, proceeding in columnar form. The next form is the mask. African masks are among the best known in the world and artistically are among the most satisfying. They come in three main shapes: those that are worn over the face, those worn on top of the head, and the "helmet"-type masks which fit down over the head. The third form is decoration of various useful objects, ranging from doors to spoons to bobbins.

African bronzes are all cast by the lost-wax method. Each piece is therefore unique. In this method, the technique is fundamentally additive, rather than subtractive as it is in carving. Over a core of some sort—usually dried mud in the traditional forms—the sculptor models in wax whatever he wants to reproduce in metal. When the core is thoroughly dry and the waxen model completely set, it is covered by several coats of the finest pottery slip clay available. The whole is then covered with coarser pottery clay, leaving spaces or passageways for the wax to run out. The trick in casting, then, comes from pouring the molten metal into the cast in such a way that the wax is melted and runs out, to be replaced by the metal in the desired form, avoiding air bubbles.

THE PLACE OF ART IN AFRICAN SOCIETY

Westerners have often, in the past, confused the examination of the place of art in society with the historical development of art. They have been wont to seek for the "origins" of art rather than to perceive its uses. Origins and histories of individual art styles and forms can, of course, be usefully made; but "the origin of art" is too amorphous a question. Sometimes religion is the assigned "cause," sometimes something else. Art can no more have a cause or a single origin than can language. Just as apes did not suddenly one morning awake to find themselves men, so art did not, one day, suddenly spring into being from the fertile mind of some prehistoric genius. Art is a form of communication, and therefore it grows with culture and develops with the beast—and it has always been so.

The forms in African art are by and large associated with religion. So is much of Western art and every other art. This fact has led some art critics and some anthropologists to exaggerate the claims of religion for art. It is quite true that many pieces of art have religious associations. Of course African art has a religious connotation—but the very same claim can be made for its having a political connotation or an economic one or a domestic one.

African masks are one of the most common art forms and are worn as part of a costume. In the court or the ritual, the symbolized forces of politics and religion can be made carnate, so that the drama of justice or of myth can be re-enacted. The myth is not assumed in most societies, as it is in our own, to be pseudo-historical and about the past. The myth is rather used to explain—indeed, to communicate—the here and now. Much African masked drama is a reincarnation of the basic myths of creation, the power structure of the society, the myths of creation, the myths of history and religion, and even the myths of settlement patterns. One of the best ways to assure the efficacy of the myth is to sanctify the objects which Westerners call art. Then it is possible for the priests, or the kings, or simply the public to loan their human vitality to the mythical principles that are symbolized.

Figurines are not "worshipped." They may be used as symbols of forces, ideas, historical events, myths, which are very real in society and held sacred. That is a grave difference. The "heathen" do not "bow down to wood and stone." Neither are saints' symbols in our own society worshipped. Rather they stand for something important and holy. Figurines can be consecrated in that same sense, and for the same purpose.

Giving living reality to the myth through drama and art is the most vivid way of making people recognize their dependence upon the myth and upon the society whose members live more or less by it.

Sometimes, too, African art is for fun. I would even say that some "art" may be no more than playful decoration added to the basic ideas for producing something that is "needed." Art supplies a "need" that is felt or expressed. It is art, in one sense, if it is decorated and goes beyond the mere need. Omitting taste (criticism within a culture cannot omit taste but comprehension across cultures probably must), art is decorated, needed objects. The communication in it is greater if it is great art; so is the mystery. But art for fun both supplies needs and is decorated. As with the Jefferson Memorial, the image draws attention to the principle.

Art permeates African culture, which in turn permeates African art. Art is not set aside from "real life"—it cannot be among a people who do not make such distinctions.

17. American Civilizations

THE SECRETS OF THE MAYA DECODED

ERIK ECKHOLM

The elaborate picture writing of the Maya is finally being translated, and it reveals a darker side to Maya culture than had previously been imagined. This is the subject of the following recent newspaper article.

What is the "darker side" of Maya culture revealed in the translation of the writings? Why was the decoding of Maya script so difficult? What were some of the achievements of Maya culture? What were some of its less attractive features? What questions about the Maya still remain?

Cascading advances in the interpretation of ancient Maya hieroglyphs have extended the written history of the New World back more than 2,000 years, creating the Americas' first written record from the age before the European invasions.

With the Maya script deciphered, the bare, often faulty sketch of their culture drawn from the study of pyramids and temples can finally be fleshed out with real people and real events. Long placed on a mist-shrouded pedestal as austere, peaceful stargazers, the Maya elites are now known to have been the rulers of populous, aggressive city-states. They had a penchant for self-mutilation, warfare and protracted torture of captives.

If their new image is less romantic, it is also more human, scholars are quick to assert. The Maya displayed the full range of human propensities, brilliant and dark.

"The written history of the Americas began in 50 B.C., and from that moment on it resounds with the names and lives of individuals: Pacal of Palenque, Bird Jaguar of Yaxchilán, Yax-Pac of Copán, among many others," according to Linda Schele of the University of Texas and Mary Ellen Miller of Yale University.

The Maya, whose civilization arose in steamy jungles of Mexico and Central America after 300 B.C. and then flowered from the second to the ninth centuries, are now joining the Egyptians and Assyrians as ancient civilizations who speak to modern society through written text as well as mute artifacts.

"I look forward to the day when third-graders will learn Pacal's name along with that of Tutankamen or Alexander the Great," Dr. Schele, an art historian and hieroglyphic expert, added in an interview.

The otherworldly stone monuments, the intricate script and drawings and the astonishing astronomical feats of the Maya have mesmerized generations of scholars and amateur Maya buffs alike. But in the absence of historical accounts, the pictures drawn of Maya culture mirrored the souls of the observers as much as those of the ancients.

Today, Maya studies are in the throes of a revolutionary change in perspective. The messages left by Maya rulers in the form of elegant symbols and images on stone slabs and temple walls have been decoded at an escalating pace in recent years.

"Before, it was a one-sided conversation with rocks and dirt," said David Freidel, an anthropologist at Southern Methodist University in Dallas. "While sweating and swatting at mosquitoes we glared at rocks, trying to give them some humanity."

"Now," Dr. Freidel went on, "the Maya can talk back, telling us about their families, their politics, their wars. Human beings are there."

The new history has debunked many myths. Until recently, many scholars thought the great clusters of pyramids and temples housed peaceful students of the stars and the calendar, who served as aloof priests to scattered populations of primitive farmers. Now it is clear that the temples were built to the glory of kings and sometimes queens who ruled bustling cities of tens of thousands.

Warfare with rival cities was frequent, in large part to capture aristocrats for torture and sacrifice. If the Maya sacrificed humans in lesser numbers than the Aztecs, against whom they have often been held up as superior, they tortured their victims more viciously. Ancient ball games, like Roman gladiatorial contests, pitted captives against one another for their lives; the heads of losers were sometimes used for balls.

"Blood was the mortar of ancient Maya ritual life," Dr. Schele and Dr. Miller wrote in "The Blood of Kings." On important occasions, Maya aristocrats drew their own blood in rituals, designed to nourish the gods or to inspire hallucinations of serpents through which they contacted the gods and the dead. Before going to war, for example, the king would puncture his penis with a stingray spine, while his wife drew a thornbarbed rope through her tongue. The Maya believed such activities were vital for sustaining the universe.

Evidence of these darker practices has been available for decades in the Maya's stone reliefs and paintings, observed Dr. Miller, an art historian, but scholars "seemed to blind themselves to it." A picture of a man squirming under the foot of another may have been interpreted as religious symbolism rather than the suffering of a war captive, for example.

"It's almost as if people were trying to protect Maya history from itself," Dr. Miller said.

Although the earliest known written document from the Maya, of a king's accession, was carved onto stone in 50 B.C., the culture's golden era dates from around A.D. 200, just as the Barbarian invasions of the Roman Empire in Europe were beginning. In an extraordinary, unexplained efflorescence, the Maya built graceful stone pyramids and temples in at least 40 cities of more than 20,000 people each. They practiced advanced irrigation methods, honed their astronomy and mathematics and elaborated their script. Then, just as mysteriously, the civilization collapsed around A.D. 900.

Estimates of the peak Maya population range from one million to three million. In the 16th century, the Spaniards conquered a smaller, less advanced populace. Today, about two million descendants speak assorted Mayan languages in Mexico and Guatemala. Although some still practice ancient rites, essential details of the classical society lay buried in jungle ruins for a thousand years.

With the uncoding of hieroglyphs, "Maya civilization has crossed the threshold from prehistory to history," said Robert J. Sharer, an archeologist at the University of Pennsylvania. "The study of the ancient Maya is undergoing the same profound change that occurred in Egyptian and Mesopotamian studies with the decipherments of hieroglyphic and cuneiform scripts in the 19th century."

The Maya script is one of only five basic writing systems ever developed. The others are Chinese, Harappan, Egyptian and Sumerian, from which the script now used for Western languages was derived.

SYMBOLS FOR SOUNDS AND IDEAS

The Maya hieroglyphs are a mixed system of phonetic symbols, standing for units of sound, and ideographs, standing for words. Some of the ideographs, such as the ones for bat, fish, hand and certain birds, are recognizable renderings, according to Christopher Jones, a hieroglyphic specialist at the University of Pennsylvania. Most are more stylized and baffling.

The same word could be written phonetically or with an ideograph. Hence the name of Pacal, a great 7th-century king of Palenque, was sometimes written with the ideograph for shield, pronounced "pacal" in Mayan, and sometimes with a combination of the three syllables "pa," "ca" and "la." (The last vowel of the last syllable is dropped.)

Interpreters of Maya hieroglyphs have not enjoyed the benefit of a Rosetta Stone. While the sketchy notes of a 16th-century Spanish friar gave scholars a start, the notes also had incorrect information. Three surviving astrological texts written on bark paper, called codices, aided decipherment of numbers and dates.

But progress was slow. Through the 1950's, according to Dr. Jones, scholars debated such basic questions as whether any symbols were phonetic and whether they described actual events or were observations about religion and astronomy.

The breakthrough came in a 1960 paper by Tatiana Proskouriakoff of the Carnegie Institution. She demonstrated that the hieroglyphs documented, in predictable sequences, the life histories of Maya rulers.

This opened the floodgates. The existence of phonetic symbols, for example, was proved when a name such as Pacal was written phonetically at points where it was clear his name should appear. More and more ideographs could be deciphered through their context.

By now, perhaps 80 percent of the hundreds of hieroglyphs have been interpreted, but more important, observed Dr. Freidel, "we have a methodology for translation."

'EXPONENTIAL' PROGRESS

"We have the syntax," he said. "We know where the verbs, the objects, the subjects are, and we know the punctuation."

"Every day now we're making new translations," Dr. Freidel added. "The progress is exponential."

The discovery that real people were depicted in the artwork meant that biographical information could also be derived from the poses, costuming and events. Image and text could be connected and historians could "read" the art.

Together with archeological data, the writings and art provide enough details to evoke with some richness the yearnings, triumphs and tragedies of individuals, Dr. Freidel said. Inscriptions show that in the eighth century Kan-Xul (Precious Animal) assumed the kingship of Palenque after the death of his brother Chan-Bahlum (Snake Jaguar), who had succeeded their father, Pacal. Kan-Xul built a temple for his brother, committing his soul to heaven and also sealing off his monuments.

Kan-Xul began constructing a palace extolling his own achievements but when he was in his 70's, before it was finished, he was captured by the rival polity of Toniná. The narrative on his own monument ends with the coronation of another brother. And inscriptions in Toniná show a bent, broken Kan-Xul being sacrificed.

Palace intrigue, too, is evident in some records. A tablet from a house in Palenque shows a Kan-Xul descendant being ordained in a subordinate role while his younger brother took the kingship. "How did this younger brother maneuver his older brother out of his rightful position?" Dr. Freidel asked.

KINGSHIP AND SACRIFICE

The lessons from inscriptions have been bolstered through a new archeological approach that examines the periphery as well as the core of sites, and small as well as large sites. With these broader studies, Dr. Sharer said that "for the first time, a great deal of information about the nonelite portions of society has become available," showing dense settlements and sophisticated agricultural methods.

Although the stone writings discuss only royalty, evidence indicates a cooperative, sacred relationship between the elite and the commoners, according to Dr. Freidel. "To be king was to be the living sacrifice for young people," he said. The elites were expected to bleed and mutilate themselves for the gods and to capture and sacrifice royalty from other cities while constantly risking the same fate themselves.

If the new history has robbed Maya gazers of some cherished myths and mysteries, the scholars point out that plenty of tantalizing enigmas remain: What spurred the transition from scattered villages to magnificent city-states? What relations did the Maya have with other civilizations? And what political, economic or ecological crises knocked this powerful culture into a tailspin?

Although their writing has been decoded, the Maya still give a long leash to the modern imagination.

THE AZTEC CIVILIZATION OF MEXICO

Bernal Diaz

Aztec civilization was the last of a long line of native American civilizations that had sprung up in the central highlands of Mexico. In this selection it is described by Bernal Diaz, a conquistador who accompanied Cortes to Mexico in 1519. In what ways was the Aztec civilization like that of Spain? In what ways was it different?

From *The Memoirs of the Conquistador Bernal Diaz de Castillo,* translated by I. I. Lockhart. London: J. Hatchard, 1844.

When it was announced to Cortes that Motecusuma [Montezuma] himself was approaching, he alighted from his horse and advanced to meet him. Many compliments were now passed on both sides. Motecusuma bid Cortes welcome, who, through Marina, said, in return, he hoped his majesty was in good health. If I still remember rightly, Cortes, who had Marina next to him, wished to concede the place of honor to the monarch, who, however, would not accept of it, but conceded it to Cortes, who now brought forth a necklace of precious stones, of the most beautiful colours and shapes, strung upon gold wire, and perfumed with musk, which he hung about the neck of Motecusuma. Our commander was then going to embrace him, but the grandees by whom he was surrounded held back his arms, as they considered it improper. Our general then desired Marina to tell the monarch how exceedingly he congratulated himself upon his good fortune of having seen such a powerful monarch face to face, and of the honour he had done us by coming out to meet us himself. To all this Motecusuma answered in very appropriate terms, and ordered his two nephews, the princes of Tetzuco and Cohohuacan, to conduct us to our quarters. He himself returned to the city, accompanied by his two other relatives, the princes of Cuitlahuac and Tlacupa, with the other grandees of his numerous suite. As they passed by, we perceived how all those who composed his majesty's retinue held their heads bent forward, no one daring to lift up his eyes in his presence; and altogether what deep veneration was paid him.

The road before us now became less crowded, and yet who would have been able to count the vast numbers of men, women, and children who filled the streets, crowded the balconies, and the canoes in the canals, merely to gaze upon us? . . .

We were quartered in a large building where there was room enough for us all, and which had been occupied by Axayacatl, father of Motecusuma, during his life-time. Here the latter had likewise a secret room full of treasures, and where the gold he had inherited from his father was hid, which he had never touched up to this moment. The apartments and halls were very spacious, and those set apart for our general were furnished with carpets. There were separate beds for each of us, which could not have been better fitted up for a gentleman of the first rank! Every place was swept clean, and the walls had been newly plastered and decorated.

When we had arrived in the great court-yard adjoining this palace, Motecusuma came up to Cortes, and taking him by the hand, conducted him himself into the apartments where he was to lodge, which had been beautifully decorated after the fashion of the country. He then hung about his neck a chaste necklace of gold, most curiously worked with figures all representing crabs. The Mexican grandees were greatly astonished at all these uncommon favours which their monarch bestowed upon our general.

Cortes returned the monarch many thanks for so much kindness, and the latter took leave of him with these words: "Malinche, you and your brothers must now do as if you were at home, and take some rest after the fatigues of the journey," then returned to his own palace, which was close at hand.

We allotted the apartments according to the several companies, placed our cannon in an advantageous position, and made such arrangements that our cavalry, as well as the infantry, might be ready at a moment's notice. We then sat down to a plentiful repast, which had been previously spread out for us, and made a sumptous meal.

This our bold and memorable entry into the large city of Temixtitlan, Mexico took place on the 8th of November, 1519. Praise be to the Lord Jesus Christ for all this. . . .

The mighty Motecusuma may have been about this time in the fortieth year of his age. He was tall of stature, of slender make, and rather thin, but the symmetry of his body was beautiful. His complexion was not very brown, merely approaching to that of the inhabitants in general. The hair of his head was not very long, excepting where it hung thickly down over his ears, which were quite hidden by it. His black beard, though thin, looked handsome. His countenance was rather of an elongated form, but cheerful; and his fine eyes had the expression of love or severity, at the proper moments. He was particularly clean in his person, and took a bath every evening. Besides a number of concubines, who were all daughters of persons of rank and quality, he had two lawful wives of royal extraction, whom, however, he visited secretly without any one daring to observe it, save his most confidential servants. He was perfectly innocent of any unnatural crimes. The dress he had on one day was not worn again until four days had elapsed. In the halls adjoining his own private apartments there was always a guard of 2000 men of quality, in waiting: with whom, however, he never held any conversation unless to give them orders or to receive some intelligence from them. Whenever for this purpose they entered his apartment, they had first to take off their rich costumes and put on meaner garments, though these were always neat and clean; and were only allowed to enter into his presence barefooted, with eyes cast down. No person durst look at him full in the face, and during the three prostrations which they were obliged to make before they could approach him, they pronounced these words: "Lord! my Lord! sublime Lord!" Everything that was communicated to him was to be said in few words, the eyes of the speaker being constantly cast down, and on leaving the monarch's presence he walked backwards out of the room. I also remarked that even princes and other great personages who come to Mexico respecting law-suits, or on other business from the interior of the country, always took off their shoes and changed their whole dress for one of a meaner appearance when they entered his palace. Neither were they allowed to enter the palace straightway, but had to show themselves for a considerable time outside the doors; as it would have been considered want of respect to the monarch if this had been omitted.

Above 300 kinds of dishes were served up for Motecusuma's dinner from his kitchen, underneath which were placed pans of porcelain filled with fire, to keep them warm. Three hundred dishes of various kinds were served up for him alone, and above 1000 for the persons in waiting. He sometimes, but very seldom, accompanied by the chief officers of his household, ordered the dinner himself, and desired that the best dishes and various kinds of birds should be called over to him. We were told that the flesh of young children as a very dainty bit, were also set before him sometimes by way of a relish. Whether there was any truth in this we could not possibly discover; on account of the great variety of dishes, consisting in fowls, turkeys, pheasants, partridges, quails, tame and wild geese, venison, musk swine, pigeons, hares, rabbits, and of numerous other birds and beasts; besides which there were various other kinds of provisions, indeed it would have been no easy task to call them all over by name.

I had almost forgotten to mention, that during dinner-time, two other young women of great beauty brought the monarch small cakes, as white as snow, made of eggs and other very nourishing ingredients, on plates covered with clean napkins, also a kind of long-shaped bread, likewise made of very substantial things, and some pachol, which is a kind of wafer-cake. They then presented him with three beautifully painted and gilt tubes, which were filled with liquid amber, and a herb called by the Indians tabaco. After the dinner had been cleared away and the singing and dancing done, one of these tubes was lighted, and the monarch took the smoke into his mouth, and after he had done this a short time, he fell asleep.

About this time a celebrated cazique [or cacique, a native Indian chief], whom we called Tapia, was Motecusuma's chief steward: he kept an account of the whole of Motecusuma's revenue, in large books of paper which the Mexicans call *Amatl*. A whole house was filled with such large books of accounts.

Motecusuma had also two arsenals filled with arms of every description, of which many were ornamented with gold and precious stones. These arms consisted in shields of different sizes, sabres, and a species of broadsword, which is wielded with both hands, the edge furnished with flint stones, so extremely sharp that they cut much better than our Spanish swords: further, lances of greater length than ours, with spikes at their end, full one fathom in length, likewise furnished with several sharp flint stones. The pikes are so very sharp and hard that they will pierce the strongest shield, and cut like a razor; so that the Mexicans even shave themselves with these stones. Then there were excellent bows and arrows, pikes with single and double points, and the proper thongs to throw them with; slings with round stones purposely made for them; also a species of large shield, so ingeniously constructed that it could be rolled up when not wanted: they are only unrolled on the field of battle, and completely cover the whole body from the head to the feet. Further, we saw here a great variety of cuirasses made of quilted cotton, which were outwardly adorned with soft feathers of different colours, and looked like uniforms. . . .

I will now, however, turn to another subject, and rather acquaint my readers with the skilful arts practised among the Mexicans: among which I will first mention the sculptors, and the gold and silversmiths, who were clever in working and smelting gold, and would have astonished the most celebrated of our Spanish goldsmiths: the number of these was very great, and the most skilful lived at a place called Ezcapuzalco, about four miles from Mexico. After these came the very skilful masters in cutting and polishing precious stones, and the calchihuis, which resemble the emerald. Then follow the great masters in painting, and decorators in feathers, and the wonderful sculptors. Even at this day there are living in Mexico three Indian artists, named Marcos de Aguino, Juan de la Cruz, and El Crespello, who have severally reached to such great proficiency in the art of painting and sculpture, that they may be compared to an Apelles, or our contemporaries Michael Angelo and Berruguete. . . .

The powerful Motecusuma had also a number of dancers and clowns: some danced in stilts, tumbled, and performed a variety of other antics for the monarch's entertainment: a whole quarter of the city was inhabited by these performers, and their only occupation consisted in such like performances. Last, Motecusuma had in his service great numbers of stone-cutters, masons, and carpenters who were solely employed in the royal palaces. Above all, I must not forget to mention here his gardens for the culture of flowers, trees, and vegetables, of which there were various kinds. In these gardens were also numerous baths, wells, basins, and ponds full of limpid water, which regularly ebbed and flowed. All this was enlivened by endless varieties of small birds, which sang among the trees. Also, the plantations of medical plants and vegetables are well worthy of our notice: these were kept in proper order by a large body of gardeners. All the baths, wells, ponds, and buildings were substantially constructed of stonework, as also the theaters where the singers and dancers performed. There were upon the whole so many remarkable things for my observation in these gardens and throughout the whole town, that I scarcely find words to express the astonishment I felt at the pomp and splendour of the Mexican monarch. . . .

We had already been four days in the city of Mexico, and neither our commander nor any of us had, during that time, left our quarters, excepting to visit the gardens and buildings adjoining the palace. Cortes now, therefore, determined to view the city, and visit the great market, and the chief temple of Huitzilopochtli. . . . The moment we arrived in this immense market, we were perfectly astonished at the vast numbers of people, the profusion of merchandise, which was there exposed for sale, and at the good police and order that reigned throughout. The grandees who accompanied us drew our attention to the smallest circumstance, and gave us full explanation of all we saw. Every species of merchandise had a separate spot for its sale. We first of all visited those divisions of the market appropriated for the sale of gold and silver wares, of jewels, of cloths interwoven with feathers, and of other manufactured goods; besides slaves of both sexes. This slave market was upon as great a scale as the Portuguese market for negro slaves at Guinea. To prevent these from running away, they were fastened with halters about their neck, though some were allowed to walk at large. Next to these came the dealers in coarser wares—cotton, twisted, thread, and cacao. In short, every species of goods which New Spain produces were here to be found and everything put me in mind of my native town Medino del Campo during fair time, where every merchandise had a separate street assigned for its sale. In one place were sold the stuffs manufactured of nequen; ropes, and sandals; in another place, the sweet maguey root, ready cooked, and various other things made from this plant. In another division of the market were exposed the skins of tigers, lions, jackals, otters, red deer, wild cats, and of other beasts of prey, some of which were tanned. In another place were sold beans and sage, with other herbs and vegetables. A particular market was assigned for the merchants in fowls, turkeys, ducks, rabbits, hares, deer, and dogs; also for fruit-sellers, pastry-cooks, and tripe-sellers. Not far from these were exposed all manner of earthenware, from the large earthen cauldron to the smallest pitchers. Then came the dealers in honey and honey-cakes, and other sweetmeats. Next to these, the timber-merchants, furniture-dealers, with their stores of tables, benches, cradles, and all sorts of wooden implements, all separately arranged. What can I further add? If I am to note everything down, I must also mention human excrements, which are exposed for sale in canoes lying in the canals near this square, and is used for the tanning of leather; for, according to the assurances of the Mexicans, it is impossible to tan well without it. I can easily imagine that many of my readers will laugh at this; however, what I have stated is a fact, and, as further proof of this, I must acquaint the reader that along every road accommodations were built of reeds, straw, or grass, by which those who made use of them were hidden from the view of the passers-by, so that great care was taken that none of the last mentioned treasures should be lost. But why should I so minutely detail every article exposed for sale in this great market? If I had to enumerate everything singly, I should not so easily get to the end. And yet I have not mentioned the paper, which in this country is called amatl; the tubes filled with liquid amber and tobacco; the various sweet-scented salves, and similar things; nor the various seeds which were exposed for sale in the porticoes of this market, nor the medicinal herbs.

In this market-place there were also courts of justice, to which three judges and several constables were appointed, who inspected the goods exposed for sale. I had almost forgotten to mention the salt, and those who made the flint knives; also the fish, and a species of bread made of a kind of mud or slime collected from the surface of this lake, and eaten in that form, and has a similar taste to our cheese. Further, instruments of brass, copper, and tin; cups, and painted pitchers of wood; indeed, I wish I had completed the enumeration of all this profusion of merchandize. The variety was so great that it would occupy more space than I can well spare to note them down in; besides which, the market was so crowded with people, and the thronging so excessive in the porticoes, that it was quite impossible to see all in one day. . . .

On quitting the market, we entered the spacious yards which surrounded the chief temple. These appeared to encompass more ground than the market-place at Salamanca, and were surrounded by a double wall, constructed of stone and lime: these yards were paved with large white flag-stones, extremely smooth, and where these were wanting, a kind of brown plaster had been used instead, and all was kept so very clean that there was not the smallest particle of dust or straw to be seen anywhere.

Before we mounted the steps of the great temple, Motecusuma, who was sacrificing on the top to his idols, sent six papas and two of his principal officers to conduct Cortes up the steps. There were 114 steps to the summit. . . . Indeed, this infernal temple, from its great height, commanded a view of the whole surrounding neighbourhood. From this place we could likewise see the three causeways which led into Mexico— that from Iztapalapan, by which we had entered the city four days ago; that from Tlacupa, along which we took our flight eight months after, when we were beaten out of the city by the new monarch Cuitlahuatzin; the third was that of Tepeaquilla. We also observed the aqueduct which ran from Chapultepec, and provided the whole town with sweet water. We could also distinctly see the bridges across the openings, by which these causeways were intersected, and through which the waters of the lake ebbed and, flowed. The lake itself was crowded with canoes, which were bringing provisions, manufacturers, and other merchandize to the city. From here we also discovered that the only communication of the houses in this city, and of all the other towns built in the lake, was by means of drawbridges or canoes. In all these towns the beautiful white plastered temples rose above the smaller ones, like so many towers and castles in our Spanish towns, and this, it may be imagined, was a splendid sight.

After we had sufficiently gazed upon this magnificent picture, we again turned our eyes toward the great market, and beheld the vast numbers of buyers and sellers who thronged there. The bustle and noise occasioned by this multitude of human beings was so great that it could be heard at a distance of more than four miles. Some of our men, who had been at Constantinople and Rome, and travelled through the whole of Italy, said that they never had seen a marketplace of such large dimensions, or which was so well regulated, or so crowded with people as this one at Mexico.

On this occasion Cortes said to father Olmedo, who had accompanied us: "I have just been thinking that we should take this opportunity, and apply to Motecusuma for permission to build a church here."

To which father Olmedo replied, that it would, no doubt, be an excellent thing if the monarch would grant this; but that it would be acting overhasty to make a proposition of that nature to him now, whose consent would not easily be gained at any time.

Cortes then turned to Motecusuma, and said to him, by means of our interpretress, Doña Marina: "Your majesty is, indeed, a great monarch, and you merit to be still greater! It has been a real delight to us to view all your cities. I have now one favour to beg of you, that you would allow us to see your gods and teules."

To which Motecusuma answered, that he must first consult the chief papas, to whom he then addressed a few words. Upon this, we were led into a kind of small tower, with one room, in which we saw two basements resembling altars, decked with coverings of extreme beauty. On each of these basements stood a gigantic, fat-looking figure, of which the one on the right hand represented the god of war Huitzilopochtli. This idol had a very broad face, with distorted and furious-looking eyes, and was covered all over with jewels, gold, and pearls, which were stuck to it by means of a species of paste, which, in this country, is prepared from a certain root. Large serpents, likewise, covered with gold and precious stones, wound round the body of this monster, which held in one hand a bow, and in the other a bunch of arrows. Another small idol which stood by its side, representing its page, carried this monster's short spear, and its golden shield studded with precious stones. Around Huitzilopochtli's neck were figures representing human faces and hearts made of gold and silver, and decorated with blue stones. In front of him stood several perfuming pans with copal, the incense of the country; also the hearts of three Indians, who had that day been slaughtered, were now consuming before him as a burnt-offering. Every wall of this chapel and the whole floor had become almost black with human blood, and the stench was abominable.

Respecting the abominable human sacrifices of these people, the following was communicated to us: The breast of the unhappy victim destined to be sacrificed was ripped open with a knife made of sharp flint; the throbbing heart was then torn out, and immediately offered to the idol-god in whose honour the sacrifice had been instituted. After this, the head, arms and legs were cut off and eaten at their banquets, with the exception of the head, which was saved, and hung to a beam appropriated for that purpose. No other part of the body was eaten, but the remainder was thrown to the beasts which were kept in those abominable dens, in which there were also vipers and other poisonous serpents, and, among the latter in particular, a species at the end of whose tail there was a kind of rattle. This last mentioned serpent, which is the most dangerous, was kept in a cabin of a diversified form, in which a quantity of feathers had been strewed: here it laid its eggs, and it was fed with the flesh of dogs and of human beings who had been sacrificed. We were positively told that, after we had been beaten out of the city of Mexico, and had lost 850 of our men, these horrible beasts were fed for many successive days with the bodies of our unfortunate countrymen. Indeed, when all the tigers and lions roared together, with the howlings of the jackals and foxes, and hissing of the serpents, it was quite fearful, and you could not suppose otherwise than that you were in hell.

Our commander here said smilingly, to Motecusuma: "I cannot imagine that such a powerful and wise monarch as you are, should not have yourself discovered by this time that these idols are not divinities, but evil spirits, called devils. In order that you may be convinced of this, and that your papas may satisfy themselves of this truth, allow me to erect a cross on the summit of this temple; and, in the chapel, where stand your Huitzilopochtli and Tetzcatlipuca, give us a small space that I may place there the image of the holy Virgin; then you will see that terror will seize these idols by which you have been so long deluded."

Motecusuma knew what the image of the Virgin Mary was, yet he was very much displeased with Cortes' offer, and replied, in presence of two papas, whose anger was not less conspicuous, "Malinche, could I have conjectured that you would have used such reviling language as you have just done, I would certainly not have shown you my gods. In our eyes these are good divinities: they preserve our lives, give us nourishment, water, and good harvests, healthy and growing weather, and victory whenever we pray to them for it. Therefore we offer up our prayers to them, and make them sacrifices, I earnestly beg of you not to say another word to insult the profound veneration in which we hold these gods."

As soon as Cortes heard these words and perceived the great excitement under which they were pronounced, he said nothing in return, but merely remarked to the monarch with a cheerful smile: "It is time for us both to depart hence." To which Motecusuma answered, that he would not detain him any longer, but he himself was now obliged to stay some time to atone to his gods by prayer and sacrifice for having committed *gratlatlacol*, by allowing us to ascend the great temple, and thereby occasioning the affronts which we had offered them.

THE INCA EMPIRE

WILLIAM H. PRESCOTT

William H. Prescott's The History of the Conquest of Peru *(published in 1847) is still one of the best introductions to the subject. In this brief selection we see the striking physical setting of the Inca empire and its capital at Cuzco, and we learn how the empire was governed.*

How did the geography of Peru affect the development of the Inca empire? How was the empire governed? What was it like to be a ruling Inca or a member of the nobility? If you could have been born a Maya or Inca ruler, which would you choose?

Of the numerous nations which occupied the great American continent at the time of its discovery by the Europeans, the two most advanced in power and refinement were undoubtedly those of Mexico and Peru. . . .

The empire of Peru, at the period of the Spanish invasion, stretched along the Pacific from about the second degree north to the thirty-seventh degree of south latitude; a line, also, which describes the western boundaries of the modern republics of Ecuador, Peru, Bolivia, and Chile. . . .

The topographical aspect of the country is very remarkable. A strip of land, rarely exceeding twenty leagues in width, runs along the coast, and is hemmed in through its whole extent by a colossal range of mountains, which, advancing from the Straits of Magellan, reaches its highest elevation—indeed, the highest on the American continent—about the seventeenth degree south, and, after crossing the line, gradually subsides into hills of inconsiderable magnitude, as it enters the Isthmus of Panamá. This is the famous Cordillera of the Andes, or "copper mountains," as termed by the natives, though they might with more reason have been called "mountains of gold." Arranged sometimes in a

From William H. Prescott, *The History of the Conquest of Peru.* New York: Harper, 1847.

single line, though more frequently in two or three lines running parallel or obliquely to each other, they seem to the voyager on the ocean but one continuous chain; while the huge volcanoes, which to the inhabitants of the tableland look like solitary and independent masses, appear to him only like so many peaks of the same vast and magnificent range. So immense is the scale on which nature works in these regions that it is only when viewed from a great distance that the spectator can in any degree comprehend the relation of the several parts to the stupendous whole. Few of the works of nature, indeed, are calculated to produce impressions of higher sublimity than the aspect of this coast as it is gradually unfolded to the eye of the mariner sailing on the distant waters of the Pacific, where mountain is seen to rise above mountain, and Chimborazo, with its glorious canopy of snow, glittering far above the clouds, crowns the whole as with a celestial diadem.

The face of the country would appear to be peculiarly unfavorable to the purposes both of agriculture and of internal communication. The sandy strip along the coast, where rain rarely falls, is fed only by a few scanty streams, that furnish a remarkable contrast to the vast volumes of water which roll down the eastern sides of the Cordilleras into the Atlantic. The precipitous steeps of the sierra, with its splintered sides of porphyry and granite, and its higher regions wrapped in snows that never melt under the fierce sun of the equator, unless it be from the desolating action of its own volcanic fires, might seem equally unpropitious to the labors of the husbandman. And all communication between the parts of the long-extended territory might be thought to be precluded by the savage character of the region, broken up by precipices, furious torrents, and impassable *quebradas*—those hideous rents in the mountain chain, whose depths the eye of the terrified traveler, as he winds along his aerial pathway, vainly endeavors to fathom. Yet the industry, we might almost say the genius, of the Indian was sufficient to overcome all these impediments of nature.

By a judicious system of canals and subterraneous aqueducts, the waste places on the coast were refreshed by copious streams that clothed them in fertility and beauty. Terraces were raised upon the steep sides of the Cordillera; and as the different elevations had the effect of difference of latitude, they exhibited in regular gradation every variety of vegetable form, from the stimulated growth of the tropics to the temperate products of a northern clime, whle flocks of *llamas*—the Peruvian sheep—wandered with their shepherds over the broad, snow-covered wastes on the crests of the sierra, which rose beyond the limits of cultivation. An industrious population settled along the lofty regions of the plateaus, and towns and hamlets, clustering amidst orchards and wide-spreading gardens, seemed suspended in the air far above the ordinary elevation of the clouds. Intercourse was maintained between these numerous settlements by means of the great roads which traversed the mountain-passes and opened an easy communication between the capital and the remotest extremities of the empire.

· · ·

The ancient city of Cuzco . . . stood in a beautiful valley on an elevated region of the plateau, which among the Alps would have been buried in eternal snows, but which within the tropics enjoyed a genial and salubrious temperature. Towards the north it was defended by a lofty eminence, a spur of the great Cordillera; and the city was traversed by a river, or rather a small stream, over which bridges of timber, covered with heavy slabs of stone, furnished an easy means of communication with the opposite banks. The streets were long and narrow, the houses low, and those of the poorer sort built of clay and reeds. But Cuzco was the royal residence, and was adorned with the ample dwellings of the great nobility; and the massy fragments still incorporated in many of the modern edifices bear testimony to the size and solidity of the ancient.

The health of the city was promoted by spacious openings and squares, in which a numerous population from the capital and the distant country assembled to celebrate the high festivals of their religion. For Cuzco was the "Holy City"; and the great temple of the Sun, to which pilgrims resorted from the farthest borders of the empire, was the most magnificent structure in the New World, and unsurpassed, probably, in the costliness of its decorations by any building in the Old.

· · ·

The government of Peru was a despotism, mild in its character, but in its form a pure and unmitigated despotism. The sovereign was placed at an immeasurable distance above his subjects. Even the proudest of the Inca nobility, claiming a descent from the same divine original as himself, could not venture into the royal presence unless barefoot, and bearing a light burden on his shoulders in token of homage. As the representative of the Sun, he stood at the head of the priesthood, and presided at the most important of the religious festivals. He raised armies, and usually commanded them in person. He imposed taxes, made laws, and provided for their execution by the appointment of judges, whom he removed at pleasure. He was the source from which everything flowed—all dignity, all power, all emolument. He was, in short, in the well-known phrase of the European despot, "himself the state."

The Inca asserted his claims as a superior being by assuming a pomp in his manner of living well calculated to impose on his people. His dress was of the finest wool of the vicuña [South America sheep], richly dyed, and ornamented with a profusion of gold and precious stones. Round his head was wreathed a turban of many-colored folds, called the *llautu*, with a tasseled fringe, like that worn by the prince, but of a scarlet color, while two feathers of a rare and curious bird, called the *corequenque*, placed upright in it, were the distinguishing insignia of royalty. The birds from which these feathers were obtained were found in a desert country among the mountains and it was death to destroy or to take them, as they were reserved for the exclusive purpose of supplying the royal headgear. Every succeeding monarch was provided with a new pair of these plumes, and his credulous subjects fondly believed that only two individuals of the species had ever existed to furnish the simple ornament for the diadem of the Incas.

Although the Peruvian monarch was raised so far above the highest of his subjects, he condescended to mingle occasionally with them, and took great pains personally to inspect the condition of the humbler classes. He presided at some of the religious celebrations, and on these occasions entertained the great nobles at his table, when he complimented them, after the fashion of more civilized nations, by drinking the health of those whom he most delighted to honor.

But the most effectual means taken by the Incas for communicating with their people were their progresses through the empire. These were conducted, at intervals of several years, with great state, and magnificence. The sedan, or litter, in which they traveled, richly emblazoned with gold and emeralds, was guarded by a numerous escort. The men who bore it on their shoulders were provided by two cities, specially appointed for the purpose. It was a post to be coveted by no one if, as is asserted, a fall was punished with death. They traveled with ease and expedition, halting at the tambos, or inns, erected by government along the route, and occasionally at the royal palaces, which in the great towns afforded ample accommodations to the whole of the monarch's retinue. The noble roads which traversed the tableland were lined with people, who swept away the stones and stubble from their surface, strewing them with sweet-scented flowers, and vying with each other in carrying forward the baggage from one village to another. The monarch halted from time to time to listen to the grievances of his subjects or to settle some points which had been referred to his decision by the regular tribunals. As the princely train wound its way along the mountain passes, every place was thronged with spectators eager to catch a glimpse of their sovereign; and when he raised the curtains of his litter and showed himself to their eyes, the air was rent with acclamations as they invoked blessings on his head. Tradition long commemorated the spots at which he halted, and the simple people of the country held them in reverence as places consecrated by the presence of an Inca.

The royal palaces were on a magnificent scale and, far from being confined to the capital or a few principal towns, were scattered over all the provinces of their vast empire. The buildings were low, but covered a wide extent of ground. Some of the apartments were spacious, but they were generally small, and had no communication with one another except that they opened into a common square or court. The walls were made of blocks of stone of various sizes, like those described in the fortress of Cuzco, rough-hewn but carefully wrought near the line of junction, which was scarcely visible to the eye. The roofs were of wood or rushes, which have perished under the rude touch of time, that has shown more respect for the walls of the edifices. The whole seems to have been characterized by solidity and strength, rather than by any attempt at architectural elegance.

But whatever want of elegance there may have been in the exterior of the imperial dwellings, it was amply compensated by the interior, in which all the opulence of the Peruvian princes was ostentatiously displayed. The sides of the apartments were thickly studded with gold and silver ornaments. Niches prepared in the walls were filled with images of animals and plants curiously wrought of the same costly materials; and even much of the domestic furniture, including the utensils devoted to the most ordinary menial services, displayed the like wanton magnificence! With these gorgeous decorations were mingled richly colored stuffs of the delicate manufacture of the Peruvian wool, which were of so beautiful a texture that the Spanish sovereigns, with all the luxuries of Europe and Asia at their command, did not disdain to use them. The royal household consisted of a throng of menials, supplied by the neighboring towns and villages, which, as in Mexico, were bound to furnish the monarch with fuel and other necessaries for the consumption of the palace.

But the favorite residence of the Incas was at Yucay, about four leagues distant from the capital. In this delicious valley, locked up within the friendly arms of the sierra, which sheltered it from the rude breezes of the east, and refreshed by gushing fountains and streams of running water, they built the most beautiful of their palaces. Here, when wearied with the dust and toil of the city, they loved to retreat and solace themselves with the society of their favorite concubines, wandering amidst groves and airy gardens that shed around their soft, intoxicating odors and lulled the senses to voluptuous repose. Here, too, they loved to indulge in the luxury of their baths, replenished by streams of crystal water which were conducted through subterraneous silver channels into basins of gold. The spacious gardens were stocked with numerous varieties of plants and flowers that grew without effort in this *temperate* region of the tropics, while parterres [ornamental gardens with paths between the beds] of a more extraordinary kind were planted by their side, glowing with the various forms of vegetable life skillfully imitated in gold and silver! Among them the Indian corn, the most beautiful of American grains, is particularly commemorated, and the curious workmanship is noticed with which the golden ear was half disclosed amidst the broad leaves of silver, and the light tassel of the same material that floated gracefully from its top.

If this dazzling picture staggers the faith of the reader, he may reflect that the Peruvian mountains teemed with gold; that the natives understood the art of working the mines, to a considerable extent; that none of the ore, as we shall see hereafter, was converted into coin, and that the whole of it passed into the hands of the sovereign for his own exclusive benefit, whether for purposes of utility or ornament. Certain it is that no fact is better attested by the conquerors themselves, who had ample means of information, and no motive for misstatement. . . .

Our surprise, however, may reasonably be excited when we consider that the wealth displayed by the Peruvian princes was only that which each had amassed individually for himself. He owed nothing to inheritance from his predecessors. On the decease of an Inca, his palaces were abandoned; all his treasures, except what were employed in his obsequies, his furniture and apparel, were suffered to remain as he left them, and his mansions, save one, were closed up forever. The new sovereign was to provide himself with everything new for his royal state. The reason for this was the popular belief that the soul of the departed monarch would return after a time to reanimate his body on earth; and they wished that he should find everything to which he had been used in life prepared for his reception.

When an Inca died, or, to use his own language, "was called home to the mansions of his father, the Sun," his obsequies were celebrated with great pomp and solemnity. The bowels were taken from the body and deposited in the temple of Tampu, about five leagues from the capital. A quantity of his plate and jewels was buried with them, and a number of his attendants and favorite concubines, amounting sometimes, it is said, to a thousand, were immolated on this tomb. Some of them showed the natural repugnance to the sacrifice occasionally manifested by the victims of a similar superstition in India. But these were probably the menials and more humble attendants; since the women have been known, in more than one instance, to lay violent hands on themselves, when restrained from testifying their fidelity by this act of conjugal martyrdom. This melancholy ceremony was followed by a general mourning throughout the empire. At stated intervals, for a year, the people assembled to renew the expressions of their sorrow; processions were made, displaying the banner of the departed monarch; bards and minstrels were appointed to chronicle his achievements, and their songs continued to be rehearsed at high festivals in the presence of the reigning monarch—thus stimulating the living by the glorious example of the dead.

The body of the deceased Inca was skillfully embalmed and removed to the great temple of the Sun at Cuzco. There the Peruvian sovereign, on entering the awful sanctuary, might behold the effigies of his royal ancestors, ranged in opposite files—the men on the right, and their queens on the left, of the great luminary which blazed in refulgent gold on the walls of the temple. The bodies, clothed in the princely attire which they had been accustomed to wear, were placed on chairs of gold, and sat with their heads inclined downward, their hands placidly crossed over their bosoms, their countenances exhibiting their natural dusky hue—less liable to change than the fresher coloring of a European complexion—and their hair of raven black, or silvered over with age, according to the period at which they died! It seemed like a company of solemn worshipers fixed in devotion, so true were the forms and lineaments to life. The Peruvians were as successful as the Egyptians in the miserable attempt to perpetuate the existence of the body beyond the limits assigned to it by nature.

They cherished a still stranger illusion in the attentions which they continued to pay to these insensible remains, as if they were instinct with life. One of the houses belonging to a deceased Inca was kept open and occupied by his guard and attendants, with all the state appropriate to royalty. On certain festivals, the revered bodies of the sovereigns were brought out with great ceremony into the public square of the capital. Invitations were sent by the captains of the guard of the respective Incas to the different nobles and officers of the court; and entertainments were provided in the names of their masters, which displayed all the profuse magnificence of their treasures—and "such a display," says an ancient chronicler, "was there in the great square of Cuzco, on this occasion, of gold and silver plate and jewels, as no other city in the world ever witnessed." The banquet was served by the menials of the respective households, and the guests partook of the melancholy cheer in the presence of the royal phantom with the same attention to the forms of courtly etiquette as if the living monarch had presided!

The nobility of Peru consisted of two orders, the first and by far the most important of which was that of the Incas, who, boasting a common descent with their sovereign, lived, as it were, in the reflected light of his glory. As the Peruvian monarchs availed themselves of the right of polygamy to a very liberal extent, leaving behind them families of one or even two hundred children, the nobles of the blood royal, though comprehending only their descendants in the male line, came in the course of years to be very numerous. They were divided into different lineages, each of which traced its pedigree to a different member of the royal dynasty, though all terminated in the divine founder of the empire.

They were distinguished by many exclusive and very important privileges; they wore a peculiar dress, spoke a dialect, if we may believe the chronicler, peculiar to themselves, and had the choicest portion of the public domain assigned for their support. They lived, most of them, at court, near the person of the prince, sharing in his counsels, dining at his board, or supplied from his table. They alone were admissible to the great offices in the priesthood. They were invested with the command of armies and of distant garrisons, were placed over the provinces, and, in short, filled every station of high trust and emolument. Even the laws, severe in their general tenor, seem not to have been framed with reference to them; and the people, investing the whole order with a portion of the sacred character which belonged to the sovereign, held that an Inca noble was incapable of crime.

The other order of nobility was the *Curacas*, the caciques [chiefs] of the conquered nations, or their descendants. They were usually continued by the government in their places, though they were required to visit the capital occasionally, and to allow their sons to be educated there as the pledges of their loyalty. It is not easy to define the nature or extent of their privileges. They were possessed of more or less power, according to the extent of their patrimony and the number of their vassals. Their authority was usually transmitted from father to son, though sometimes the successor was chosen by the people. The did not occupy the highest posts of state, or those nearest the person of the sovereign, like the nobles of the blood. Their authority seems to have been usually local, and always in subordination to the territorial jurisdiction of the great provincial governors, who were taken from the Incas.

It was the Inca nobility, indeed, who constituted the real strength of the Peruvian monarchy. Attached to their prince by ties of consanguinity, they had common sympathies and, to a considerable extent, common interests with him. Distinguished by a peculiar dress and insignia, as well as by language and blood, from the rest of the community, they were never confounded with the other tribes and nations who were incorporated into the great Peruvian monarchy. After the lapse of centuries they still retained their individuality as a peculiar people. They were to the conquered races of the country what the Romans were to the barbarous hordes of the Empire, or the Normans to the ancient inhabitants of the British Isles. Clustering around the throne, they formed an invincible phalanx to shield it alike from secret conspiracy and open insurrection. Though living chiefly in the capital, they were also distributed throughout the country in all its high stations and strong military posts, thus establishing lines of communication with the court, which enabled the sovereign to act simultaneously and with effect on the most distant quarters of his empire.